Romain Gary

ALSO BY
David Bellos

Balzac Criticism in France, 1850–1900:
The Making of a Reputation

Georges Perec:
A Life in Words

Jacques Tati:
His Life and Art

David Bellos

Romain Gary

A Tall Story

Harvill *Secker*
LONDON

Published by Harvill Secker 2010

2 4 6 8 10 9 7 5 3 1

First published in Great Britain in 2010 by
Harvill Secker
Random House
20 Vauxhall Bridge Road
London SW1V 2SA

www.rbooks.co.uk

Addresses for companies within The Random House Group Limited can be found at: www.randomhouse.co.uk/office.htm

The Random House Group Limited Reg. No. 954009

A CIP catalogue record for this book is available from the British Library

ISBN 9781843431701

The Random House Group Limited supports The Forest Stewardship Council (FSC), the leading international forest certification organisation. All our titles that are printed on Greenpeace approved FSC certified paper carry the FSC logo. Our paper procurement policy can be found at www.rbooks.co.uk/environment

Mixed Sources
Product group from well-managed forests and other controlled sources
www.fsc.org Cert no. TT-COC-2139
© 1996 Forest Stewardship Council

Typeset in Linotype Didot by Palimpsest Book Production Ltd, Falkirk, Stirlingshire

Printed and bound in Great Britain by Clays Ltd, St Ives plc

Contents

List of Illustrations vii
Abbreviations ix
An Introduction to Romain Gary 1

I Life
1 Self-Determination. Eastern Europe, 1815–1946 15
2 The Child. Wilno and Warsaw, 1914–1928 26
3 The Cosmopolitan. Nice, 1928–1934 36
4 The Cossack and the Cucumber 54
5 The Student. Aix-en-Provence and Paris, 1934–1938 61
6 The Hero. Military Service, 1938–1945 74
7 The Novelist. *A European Education*, 1943–1945 90
8 Gary and Charles de Gaulle 109
9 Gary's Politics 120
10 Sex 134

II Works
11 The Books Gary Wrote 157
12 Games with Names 166
13 The Way Gary Wrote 184
14 What Gary Meant 192

III The Good Fight
15 Gandhi's Ham Sandwich. *Tulipe*, 1945–1970 199
16 Gary the Rat. Sofia, 1947 209
17 Diplomacy. Gary at the UN, 1952–1954 229
18 Masquerade. Gary in London, 1954–1955 247
19 Top Prize. Los Angeles, 1956 254

IV The Big Time

20	Changing Faces. Writing in English, 1958–1974	265
21	A Pen for Hire	276
22	'It's Over . . .'. *Promise at Dawn*, 1958–1960	283
23	Celebrity Spouse. On the Road, 1960–1979	294
24	If at first you don't succeed . . . Gary on Stage and Screen, 1945–1974	312
25	Cultural Legitimacy. *Pour Sganarelle*, 1965	325

V All of the Above

26	'The problem is the human race.' *Genghis Cohn* and *White Dog*, 1966–1970	335
27	'A Mysterious and Astonishing Adventure.' *Gros-Câlin*, 1972–1974	347
28	Belleville Rendezvous. *Life Before Us*, 1975	366
29	'In the Sombre Folds of Life.' *Womanlight* and *The Way Out*, 1975–1977	377
30	*Hocus Bogus*, 1976	384
31	Happy Ends. *King Solomon* and *The Kites*, 1977–1980	397
32	Last Rites	409

Appendices

I	Curriculum vitae	415
II	The Works of Romain Gary	418
III	A Bibliography of Gary in English	428
IV	A Filmography of Gary and Seberg from 1960 to 1972	435

Works Cited	438
References	455
Notes	458
Acknowledgements	493
Index of Names	495
Index of Titles	511

List of Illustrations

Figure 1	The Writer. Paris, 1975	11
Figure 2	*Le Roi des dupes*	42
Figure 3	A Boston bomber of the Lorraine Squadron	81
Figure 4	The Airman. London, 1943	85
Figure 5	The Hero. London, 1945	89
Figure 6	The flag of the Free Polish Air Force, 1943	92
Figure 7	The Consul General. Los Angeles, 1958	143
Figure 8	The Immigrant. Nice, around 1930	146
Figure 9	Jean Seberg and Romain Gary in *Route de Corinthe*	302
Figure 10	The Mogul. Cimarrón, around 1975	309
Figure 11	'Plucking the Jew'. Warsaw, September 1939	342
Figure 12	Father and Son. Rue du Bac, 1979	396

Abbreviations

AEF *Afrique équatoriale française* French Equatorial Africa

AK *Armia Krajowa* Home Army (Poland)

CP Communist Party

FAFL *Forces aériennes de la France Libre* Free French Air Force

FF Fatherland Front (Bulgaria)

GI General infantryman

IUPN International Union for the Protection of Nature

NCO Non-commissioned officer

NKVD *Narodny Komissariat Vnutrennikh Del* People's Commissariat for Internal Affairs (Soviet secret police)

NYT *New York Times*

OAS *Organisation de l'armée secrète* Secret Army Organisation (Algeria)

OPEC Organisation of Petroleum-Exporting Countries

PCF *Parti communiste français* French Communist Party

RPF *Rassemblement du peuple français* (French political party)

SS Schutzstaffel

STD Sexually transmitted disease

UDR *Union de démocrates pour la Ve République* (French political party)

UNR *Union pour la République* (French political party)

UNRRA United Nations Relief and Rehabilitation Administration

An Introduction to Romain Gary

Born Roman Kacew in Vilna (Russia) in 1914, the individual later known as Romain Gary led an extraordinary multiplicity of lives. An immigrant to France at the age of fourteen, he was educated in Nice and studied law at Aix-en-Provence; after two penniless years in Paris, he did his military service in the French Air Force, but fled to Britain when France signed the Armistice in 1940. He served for the duration of the war in the Free French squadron of the RAF and was awarded high military honours for bravery. In 1945 he joined the Diplomatic Corps and rose to become French Consul General in Los Angeles, resigning his post in 1960 to live with and then to marry Jean Seberg, the star of Godard's *Breathless*. In his early fifties, with a handsome flat in the smarter part of the Latin Quarter in Paris, a hideaway in Geneva and a millionaire's retreat in the Balearic Islands, Gary could have considered himself an uncommonly lucky man with a *vita* to die for (a summary is given in Appendix I).

But none of the above even hints at the reason why Gary continues to fascinate us now. From his teens until his last days, Romain Gary was a prolific and talented writer, producing more than twenty novels and volumes of memoirs that have never been out of print in France. Even more fascinating: he wrote some of his books under assumed names (Romain Gary being only the first of the names he adopted over the course of his life) and by inventing a character to go with the name he hoodwinked the entire literary establishment into believing he was someone else. In a manner equally unprecedented and strange, he wrote a good part of his oeuvre not in French but in English, a language he did not acquire until he was thirty years of age, as his sixth mother tongue.

With a life so varied and exciting, Gary could have simply told stories about himself – Litwak, immigrant, airman, diplomat, Don Juan, novelist and globe-trotting celebrity spouse. He did indeed write several memoirs, including a celebrated and infinitely seductive portrait of his early life, *Promise at Dawn*. But as we shall soon see, that charmingly unreliable narrative is best read like a novel or, rather, like a novel by Gary, in which characters and plots are the fruit not of recollection, but invention.

In November 1945, impressed and moved by Gary's first novel, *A European Education*, Jean-Paul Sartre, then at the height of celebrity, arranged to meet the young writer at La Rhumerie, a café on Boulevard Saint-Germain. Gary, still somewhat flummoxed by the literary prize he had just been awarded, and bewildered by current buzz-words like 'existential' and 'absurd', gave Sartre the main features of his life to date – from Russia to Poland, Nice, Britain, West Africa, Syria, then England again, ending with his Legion of Honour and his literary prize. Sartre listened, then turned to Simone de Beauvoir, who was sitting beside him, and said: '*Quelle mine d'expérience!*' (literally: What a goldmine!). Implicitly: 'I wish I had such a story to tell! This young man will be able to turn his life into a heap of novels!' Sartre's admiring exclamation is perfectly comprehensible, but even at that early stage of his career, Gary took great exception to it. Long after, he still felt angry about Sartre's attitude to literature, to life and to him. At an academic dinner party at Yale University, around 1957, he entertained his hosts with a tall story about how Sartre had confided to him that, as a writer, he regretted not having been arrested and tortured by the Gestapo . . .[1]

Gary did not treat his own experience of life as a natural resource to be quarried, crushed and delivered to consumers wrapped up as books. He was especially averse to treating fallen comrades as literary stock, because they had died to save France, not to help a survivor make a bid for the Nobel. For Romain Gary, writing was not about life in the way Sartre imagined. The philosopher's faux pas in that Paris café gave away the basic key of 'existential' or 'committed' literature: *The Age of Reason*, *The Mandarins*, *The Blood of Others* tell the stories of their authors' lives and those of their friends, lightly disguised by borrowed names and cosmetic changes of chronology and event. Gary's work is of a different order. He made up his characters, including his own, where it appears in memoirs as well as novels, just as he made up some of the vocabulary and syntax he used. Gary sought to be a popular novelist and a topical one, but he wasn't a cannibal or a hack. His life was extraordinary, but his career as a writer was exceptional to an even higher degree.

Gary's own account of his magical life puts it all down to his mother. In the novelised account he gives of her in *Promise at Dawn*, but also in response to questions in many radio, press and television interviews, Gary explained that she had had inordinately high expectations of her only child. With uncommon force of fantasy, she saw little Roman not as 'my son the professor', as in a thousand Jewish jokes, but as 'my son the ambassador', and also, simultaneously, as a great writer in French. He absorbed his mother's desperate yearning for a brighter future, internalised her aspiration for success. The main premise of *Promise at Dawn* is that Gary's life followed a script laid down for it long before. For four years, as French Consul General in Los Angeles, he was only an inch away from being Ambassador to Hollywood. How close he came to being the twentieth century's Victor Hugo is the main subject of this book.

To tell the true story of Romain Gary is a decidedly problematic undertaking. The main difficulty in pinning him down and making sense of the relationship between his life and his work is the awkward but unavoidable fact that he was, among many other things, a skilful liar. Lies and art have a long association. In the fifth century BCE Plato proposed to banish poets from the Republic on the grounds they were liars; in the last century the French partisan-poet Louis Aragon counter-attacked with the concept of art as *le mentir-vrai* (truthful lying); but Gary took the issue to a confusing extreme. He did not do so out of maliciousness or for personal gain (on the contrary, in fact). Like many novelists, Gary wrote stories in order to enjoy, if only for the length of composition, the experience of being someone else. The aesthetic pleasure that he drew from a change of mental clothes he also applied to his own existence. What he sought many times over, and sometimes at the cost of a blatant lie, was the intoxicating experience of being born again. Each new birth – as a Frenchman, as an airman, as a diplomat, as a novelist, as Romain Gary, as 'Fosco Sinibaldi' or as 'Émile Ajar' – was also a way of taking leave of a previous and often equally invented self. However, each of Gary's different identities never really died, even when buried beneath lies and deceptions or replaced with a new set of clothes. In his writing, which was after all what he spent most of his time doing, he was a man of successive and concurrent selves. It's largely for this reason that parts of this book are not laid out in straightforwardly chronological fashion. Gary's lives loop back in and out of each other, and half the fun of his incredible story would be lost if it were presented as a one-track *Lebenslauf*. Introducing *The Strange Case of Dr Jekyll and Mr Hyde*, Robert Louis Stevenson speculated that all men might come to be seen not as unitary individuals but as a 'polity of multifarious, incongruous and independent denizens'. It's a pity he lived too soon to have met Romain Gary, perhaps the only significant writer of the twentieth century who never bemoaned the losses he suffered in his several exiles, but looked on new lives as positive gains.

* * *

Gary was born in a Jewish family in a predominantly Jewish city on the western fringe of the Russian Empire a few weeks before the First World War broke out. Over the following fourteen years he was brought up in Russia and Poland, to begin with in places not known or forgotten, then in a city that changed hands a dozen times (between Russia, Germany, Lithuania and Poland), in several languages, by a relatively aged mother, already divorced, and then divorced a second time. You can go back to Wilno nowadays – it's called Vilnius and is the capital of Lithuania – and find a few tiny traces of the city he grew up in. I've been there, I've seen the apartment building that was his boyhood home and met the archivists who unearthed the surviving documents that record his birth. But even by the time Gary was thirty, absolutely nothing remained of the polyglot Wilno he had known. All trace of his early life (including the majority of his close and distant relatives) had been swept away by another war and by ethnic cleansing of the most atrocious kind the world had ever seen. History gave Gary a free hand to reinvent his past; but you could also say that history obliged Gary to cut free of a sunken ship and to remake himself as something else.

Nothing can be recovered of Gary's life as a child save for a few possibly flawed documents, a couple of photographs, and the memories – but are they memories? – that Gary retails in *Promise at Dawn*. Penned at great speed in a second-rate hotel in a Mexican seaside resort, these memories coalesce into a coherent and persuasive story of how a poor Jewish lad from the East was groomed for a career as a great man of the West. The story is a simple one, close to some spectacular real-life models and to a well-known variant of the American dream: hand-reared by a powerful, coarse, ambitious and overwhelmingly loving mother, he had only ever striven to fulfil all her dreams of him. It really wasn't his fault.

It is a story that Gary undoubtedly wished to believe. But how much literal truth is there in the tale of a life forged by a mother's intense love for her son and her dreams of his success? It's no longer possible to know what Mina Kacewa was really like. (Gary calls her 'Nina' in *Promise at Dawn*, substituting a Russian for a typically Litwak name.) Witnesses of her Russian period have all disappeared. Testimonies gathered in the 1990s by Myriam Anissimov from two very aged people who knew Mina in her Polish years are not very informative, nor can they be considered reliable after such a long period of time.[2] Mina lived in Nice from 1928 until her death in 1941 and only a handful of witnesses have ever dared to comment on her portrayal in Gary's legend of his life in pre-war France. The Swiss journalist François Bondy, who was a classmate of Gary's at his secondary school in Nice, certainly concurred that Madame Kacewa was a woman of unusual strength, but he recalls her as a loud-mouthed, imperious, agitated old lady rather than as an inspiring force. But Gary's art of deception undermines even this seeming qualification. Bondy's comments come from a long conversation that he had with Romain Gary, published in 1974 as *La Nuit sera calme* (I refer to the volume henceforth under the English title Gary gave his own still unpublished translation of it, *A Quiet Night*). The idea of this book probably came to Gary from another Polish *enfant terrible*, Witold Gombrowicz, who had recently published a fake interview with Dominique Deroux.[3] In the same manner, all of *A Quiet Night* – including the lengthy questions and comments attributed to Bondy! – was written by Romain Gary. So the slightly negative side of Madame Kacewa that the text allows us to glimpse is not external corroboration at all, just another part of Gary's portrait of the woman he wants us to believe was the scriptwriter of his life.

Gary's loving portrait of his mother in *Promise at Dawn* – pushy and much put upon, a taker of liberties absolved by all the liberties that history had taken with her, intensely, almost oppressively devoted to the ascent of her one treasure, her son – is too familiar to be entirely untrue. It is also too much of a caricature to be completely right. Most of all, it is part of a broader pattern of belief, which makes imagination the prime mover in human affairs. Mother Mina is both an explanation of Gary's successful reinventions of himself and a retrospective example of the power of dreams.

Such was the intensity of Gary's commitment to the shaping of the world by the imagination that his own work occasionally seems to be prophetic of his life, rather than dependent on it. During home leaves on the Riviera when he was serving in the French Embassy in Berne in 1950–51, Gary wrote a novel describing a passionate love affair between a former Free French fighter and an American film star. Ten years later the former Free French fighter called Romain Gary fell in love with the star of Otto Preminger's *Saint Joan*. What Gary experienced then was not exactly predetermined by his prior imagination of it: life is surely too haphazard for such eerie patterns to work out. All the same, the greatest affair of his life fitted into a place he had already imagined in his work. Similarly, *The Talent Scout*, a novel written in English within the first year of Gary's affair with Jean Seberg, portrays a gorgeous young woman from a strait-laced home in Iowa (as Seberg was) whose naive idealism pushes her into becoming the alcoholic, heroin-addicted mistress of a brutal dictator (which Gary might have seemed to others, and to himself). Unhappily, Jean Seberg, whose passion for social and racial justice is the transparent object of this satire of good intentions, became a victim of substance abuse within a few years.

In these instances, experience must have seemed to Gary to vindicate his underlying belief that imagination can pattern events and to make his belief in the power of his mother's dreams to shape his own life seem less strange to him than it does to us. Literature, for Gary, is not the transcription of life, in the manner of Sartre or Beauvoir. Art nourishes life; myths and legends are not explanations of what is, but motivating scripts that can draw us on to higher things. Conversely, the only real life that we live is the one we imagine. 'I have almost always invented everyone I have met in my life and particularly those who are close to me and share my life,' Gary wrote in the less fictionalised part of his American memoir, *White Dog*.[4] Reading his life like a novel is therefore not too wide of the mark. Being sure of what is true and what is not is quite a different kettle of fish.

Obviously, Romain Gary is not a character from a novel of his own invention. He existed and actually did many, if not quite all, the things that are attributed to him (by himself, by others and by his own fictional stand-ins). Most writers who have tackled the bewilderingly multiple lives of Romain Gary have sought to elucidate the true identity of the man behind the many masks. I, too, believe that there is a solid centre to the complex entity called Romain Gary. However, it is not anything as clear as a 'real self'. In any case, who can know truly who someone else really is? Gary had several lives thrust upon him by the history of the twentieth century and, like the great nineteenth-century novelists he admired, he also aspired to lead innumerably many more. I prefer to allow this remarkable hero of modern times to be not one, but many. He was Russian, and also Polish, as well as being completely French. He was Jewish, but also Catholic, in a secular sort of way. He was a man of great charm, and also a boor and an oaf. He clung to high ideals and was also profoundly cynical about the human race. He was a skilled aerial navigator, but prone to getting hopelessly lost on the ground (even in the side streets of Paris). He hid his identity again and again, but gave a great deal of himself away through the recurrent motifs of his work. That is why the true story of Romain Gary has to be sought in a close reading of his fiction. Conversely, Gary's fiction is particularly enriched by being read – with great caution! – through the lens of his actual life. To separate literature from life, the two have to be read in conjunction, side by side.

* * *

As a writer Gary had a wide audience in France and an even larger mass readership in the English-speaking world for most (but not all) of what he wrote (often more than once, in English and in French). He had a gift for narrative that endeared him to ordinary readers, but won him little respect among critics in an era dominated by figures far more intellectual than he could ever be (but that is not to say there were any smarter). From the heyday of committed literature through the years of the 'new novel' to the emergence of postmodernism and the Oulipo, Gary marched to his own drummer along a path unrelated to the main trends of post-war French literature. Yet he was also a formidable innovator of form and language, and far more engaged with the broader history of the European novel than any of his Parisian contemporaries. Gary's varied and entertaining writing career tells a different story about the making of French and European literature from the one we are accustomed to hear.

Nowadays, Gary is little known in the English-speaking world. Yet his first moment of fame came not in France, but in London, in late 1944, when his first novel appeared as *Forest of Anger* with the Cresset Press, and was widely and favourably reviewed. In the USA Gary scored a second major hit in the English-speaking world with *The Company of Men* in 1951, and for the following twenty-five years he was a well-known personality nationwide, as a writer, public figure, journalist and celebrity in his own right, as well as being a celebrity spouse. His personal memoir, *Promise at Dawn*, touched the hearts of a whole generation and became a Broadway play; most of his major novels were made into big-budget Hollywood films. He slipped from the limelight when his own creation, the fictional writer Émile Ajar, displaced 'Romain Gary' from the literary headlines in Paris. When the hoax was made public after the writer's death in 1980, Gary's international reputation crumbled to dust, for America is peculiarly sensitive to literary heists. All but three of his books (*Promise at Dawn*, *Life Before Us*, and *White Dog*) went out of print in English; it seems only folk old enough to remember having fallen in love in their teens with the boy hero of *Promise at Dawn* still remember the name of Romain Gary.

Over the last fifteen years Romain Gary's rich, funny and fascinating work has been rediscovered by critics in France, Israel and America. The principal path to his rediscovery has lain through rereadings of the four novels published under the name of Émile Ajar, which now seem to anticipate contemporary modes of Holocaust memoir and comedy, as well as being overwhelming strikes against modern forms of false piety. Gary's imposture as Émile Ajar has also fascinated students of literary frauds and hoaxes, of which we have seen rather a large number in recent years, and which seem to have something important to tell us about the nature of writing itself. I myself certainly came to Gary *par ajar*,[5] if I may permit myself a French pun at the start of a book that contains a great number of Gary's linguistic games (in English as well as in and between all the other languages he spoke). Georges Perec's love of pastiche and 'passing off' led me to look again at the Ajar hoax (Perec's mentor, Raymond Queneau, was involved in it, and, to his honour, was the only literary figure to smell a rat). This in turn led me to investigate the wider literary universe of the perpetrator of such a skilful impersonation, and it proved a long, absorbing and rewarding pursuit. What I learned is that there is a great deal more to the man and the work than just a good joke. In strange and unexpected ways, rereading Gary's intentionally middlebrow novels, with their rattling yarns and page-turning style, has made it clearer to me what literature can do. Comedy, kitsch, sentimentality and high ideals don't have to be treated as crimes. They can also be the vehicles and the freight of sophisticated verbal art.

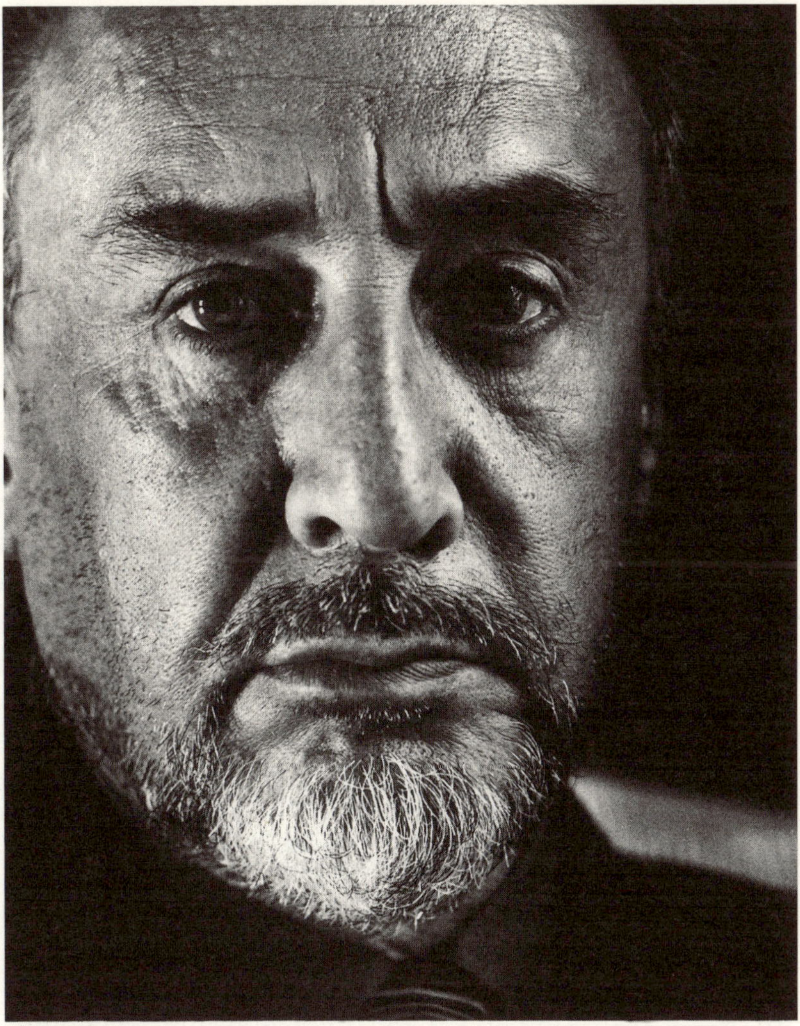

The Writer. Paris, 1975

I

Life

I hazard the guess that man will be ultimately known for a mere polity of multifarious, incongruous and independent denizens.

Robert Louis Stevenson

I

Self-Determination
Eastern Europe, 1815–1946

Gentle ideas are pregnant with mountains of corpses.

WITOLD GOMBROWICZ

The canteen where Princeton professors now take lunch was once the home of Woodrow Wilson, President of the university and thereafter of the United States, which he brought into the war against Germany in 1917. Wilson went to the peace conference at Versailles after the end of the butchery with Fourteen Points to impose on the exhausted, quarrelsome nations of Europe. When he arrived in Paris he was given a welcome such as few men in history have experienced: he was nothing less than a saviour, the man who would create a new and better world, with his eight firm proposals for boundaries that would straighten out the complicated old continent, five general principles to permit the human race to live in lasting peace and – his fourteenth point – a League of Nations to ensure respect of the other thirteen.

Before the long-drawn-out peace conference ended, a little boy found himself stuck with his mother in a quarantine zone at Lida, a small town in the former Pale of Settlement that may be described as being in Lithuania, Poland, the Soviet Union or Belarus, depending on the date involved and the political attitude adopted. At the time Romain Gary was there, walking up and down in the snow with his chamber pot in his hand,[1] it was the border crossing between Russia and the brand-new Republic of Poland, a border that the Versailles negotiations were supposed to be sorting out between still fluid new states that the League of Nations would only admit once it was clear they were in line with the Wilsonian principle of *the right of peoples to national self-determination*.

In Vilna, where Gary was born on 8 May 1914,[2] determining what nation the city belonged to may have been one of the new rights of man, but it was not clear which men would exercise it. Vilna had once been the seat of government of the Grand Duchy of Lithuania, but since the third partition of Poland in 1815 it had been a provincial capital of the Russian Empire. It was located in Lithuania (Lite, in Yiddish) – but that was the name of an ill-defined area, not of a nation or state. The country folk in the surrounding villages spoke an ancient Baltic tongue, Lithuanian, but it was rarely heard in the city save on market days. Russian was the language of the administration, spoken and written by a large part of the educated class. A significant minority of the city's inhabitants spoke Polish and dreamed of being part of a reborn Polish state. Adam Mickiewicz, the great romantic poet of the oppressed Polish nation, had attended Vilna University and published his first book of verse there too. Poles and Russians lived side by side in Vilna with other minorities: German traders who had migrated from East Prussia, barely a hundred miles away; Ukrainians; and Byelorussians. However, none of these communities was particularly large when put beside the Jews, who constituted between one quarter and one half of the population of Vilna in the nineteenth and early twentieth centuries.[3] A place like that could hardly be expected to 'determine' its national status easily. Wilson's principle gave no guidance on how to get rid of the two or three minorities that made local self-determination such a difficult business.

The city was more multilingual than a catalogue of its ethnic composition would suggest. If there had been a big branch of Borders in Vilna on the eve of the Great War, it would have had to stock books in Latin (for the Polish Catholic minority), in French (since educated Russians, or those educated in the Russian style, like Gary's mother, learned French as a matter of course), in German, for the local traders, in Polish, in Lithuanian, in Ukrainian and in Byelorussian. It would have carried a good stock of Yiddish books – alongside a few books in modern Hebrew for those still relatively few Jews who saw that recently revived tongue as a path to the future, and rather more in Esperanto, a language invented in the 1880s by Lejzor Zamenhof in Białystok, a Polish (that is to say, Russian) city 150 miles south and west, as a solution to the Babelian muddle of East European tongues.[4] But nothing like an all-purpose bookshop could have existed in Vilna at that time. Cultural diversity was not a value, but, in the minds of most ambitious politicians of the region, a vicious thorn to be torn out of the local flesh. Wilsonian ideas of self-determination actually made the brooding conflicts worse. The Russians despised the Poles. The Poles hated the Germans. Many Germans scorned the 'primitive' Baltic tribes that the Teutonic knights had beaten in battle and Christianised centuries before. There was little common ground between them – except that none of them liked the Jews.

On the eve of the First World War, the Russian Empire was especially mistrustful of the Jews living on its western fringe, in and around Lithuania. These Litwaks, as they were called, spoke Yiddish, a language closely related to German. They might therefore prefer relatively liberal German rule to the harsher restrictions imposed on them by the Tsarist regime. Strange as it may seem in the light of later history, the imperial authorities evacuated a large part of the Jewish population of Lithuania not to protect it from advancing German armies, but to remove it from the temptation of going over to the other side. To no avail: the Kaiser's army advanced from East Prussia and took Vilna with ease in 1915. Gary's birthplace became Wilna, the capital of the new German province of Litauen.

Wilhelm II made a state visit in 1916 and in Vilnius today you can still buy black-and-white picture postcards of the grand pageant that greeted his presence in the town.

Baby Roman and his mother, whose married name was Mina Kacewa, were two among several hundred thousand Lithuanian Jews who were obliged to move east and south in the summer of 1914. Leiba Kacew, Gary's father, was mobilised and transferred to an unknown location. (The only photograph Gary kept of his father was of a handsome middle-aged man wearing a pre-revolutionary Russian military overcoat.) Where exactly his wife and son went during the war is not known. Most likely, to a city such as Kiev or Odessa, or some other small or large town in the more southerly parts of the Pale of Settlement. Only Jews with special permits were allowed to reside in Moscow or St Petersburg, or anywhere else in Russia proper. But wherever mother and child actually went in the first months and years of Romain Gary's life, they remained in Russia. The first language Gary heard about him, the first language he learned and never forgot, was Russian. He went on speaking Russian with his mother and her relatives in France as long as they lived.

Mina and Roman returned to Vilna as refugees from the Bolshevik Revolution, or else as displaced persons in the disorder of the Civil War that followed. By then – 1919, or maybe a year or so later – the Polish Republic, first established at Lublin in 1917, had its seat of government in Warsaw, and its border with the newly invented State of Lithuania was in process of being established in the peace negotiations at Versailles. One of the first things the new Poland did, even as negotiations continued, was to invade the Ukraine and to gobble up a piece of it from the weak and still poorly defined Bolshevik state in the east. It also had its eye on Vilna, which in Polish is called Wilno. Troops marched in, the population rose, troops withdrew, then marched in again. Wilno changed hands several times between 1918 and 1922, when the difficult issue of Poland's eastern frontier was finally settled in

Lithuania's favour by delegates sitting at the polished table of the Petit Trianon. The ink on the document was hardly dry when the Polish Army marched into Vilnius again, expelled the Lithuanian government, and annexed the city and a small surrounding piece of territory. Yiddish Vilne, Russian Vilna, German Wilna, Lithuanian Vilnius became Polish Wilno in 1922 and settled down as the new frontier.

Previously, the city had been well placed to make its living out of the Russian Empire. It was at the crossroads of east–west rail and road routes leading from the capital, St Petersburg, to Western Europe (via Warsaw and Berlin), and north–south routes from the Baltic coast to Kiev and the Black Sea ports. As a part of Poland, on the other hand, it was ill placed to make any kind of living at all. Its eastern border was hermetically sealed by the USSR. Its northern border was also closed: Lithuania, obliged to use Kaunas (Kovno) as its 'provisional capital', was understandably frightened of its land-hungry neighbour. To the west lay East Prussia, a historic part of Germany cut off from the rest of the country by the Danzig Corridor, which meant that Vilna no longer had easy access to its natural Baltic outlet. In becoming part of Poland, Wilno had turned into a dead end. Economic decline was inevitable, rapid and harsh.

Romain Gary's father, Leiba Kacew, was a businessman in the fur trade and his family seems to have been reasonably prosperous. After he returned from service in the Russian Army during the Great War, he purchased an apartment on one of the main thoroughfares, just opposite the Russian theatre. Number 16 Welko Pohulanka (now 18 Basanavicius) is an imposing block outside the traditional Jewish quarter, but only a short walk from the city's main synagogue, where Leiba worshipped and also served on the management committee. Leiba, Mina and Roman lived together for maybe five years, but Leiba had a second life as well. In or around 1925, he left Mina for another woman, with whom he already had two children, Valentina and Pavel, Romain Gary's half-siblings. Mina, now over forty, was left to fend for herself. When the marriage collapsed, mother and child first retreated to Mina's family's home in Sweciany (Svencionis, in independent Lithuania) but after a few months they returned to Poland. They settled in the capital, Warsaw, where Mina's brother Borukh (who also used the forenames Boris and Boleslaw) now resided with his wife Maria at Poznanska 22. Roman and Mina were refugees once again.

Gary started his schooling in post-war Wilno and picked up Polish straight away. His mother had long before chosen French as her language of culture and she made sure her son acquired it too. In the streets, Yiddish was the language most commonly heard and young Gary absorbed it in Wilno, if he hadn't picked it up earlier on in Russia, where it was a widely spoken tongue. He must have attended synagogue and *heder* at least for a time, since he retained an aural memory of Friday-night prayers in Hebrew decades later.[5] At that stage in his life Gary was far from unique in having a handful of languages under his belt. Multilingualism was the only treasure that Wilno granted all its children.

Moving west was a long-standing local tradition, as ingrained in custom and expectation as sailing to America was for the Irish or the Scots. Several gifted boys from the area had shown the way. The painter Marc Chagall, born in 1887 at Vitebsk, had ended up in Paris in 1923, after sojourns in Moscow and Berlin. Another painter, Chaim Soutine, born in 1894 in a shtetl in the Vilnius region, got to Paris in 1911 and was already famous by the time Romain Gary was at school. Yasha Heifetz, born in 1900 and brought up in the Jewish quarter of Vilna, was a child prodigy on the violin and by 1926 was giving solo concerts at Carnegie Hall. The philosopher Emmanuel Levinas was born in Kaunas, fifty miles from Vilna, in 1906 and moved to France in 1923. Czesław Miłosz was slower to make the move. Born in 1911 in Szetejnie, his family moved to Vilna on the outbreak of the Great War, and that was where he went to school and university, graduating in law in 1934. But Miłosz was a Polish Catholic, not a Jew, and though he first went to Paris in 1935, he returned to Poland on the outbreak of the Second World War. At the end of a conflict that was perhaps more horrific in Poland than anywhere else, Miłosz entered the Diplomatic Service, just like his former neighbour Romain Gary. At one time he served in the Polish Embassy in Washington, DC, but it was during a later posting to Paris that he defected and sought political asylum in the West. He moved to California in 1960, just as Romain Gary was preparing to return to France. Czesław Miłosz won the Nobel Prize for Literature in 1980. Romain Gary committed suicide a few weeks later.

The drift towards the West from the impoverished cities of the old Jewish Pale of Settlement was self-evident. If peoples had the newfound right to determine their own national identities – *de disposer d'eux-mêmes*, (to dispose of themselves), as the official French translation had it – then so did individuals. A few men of genius had made it to Paris and New York. Thousands of others moved down the railway line to Bialystok, to Warsaw, or to Berlin. Where many of them were looking, however, was further west, towards Paris, the city of light, home of revolutions and the Rights of Man.

Romain Gary said his mother suffered from 'galloping Francophilia' all her life.[6] It was a common condition. Some people thought of Argentina, others dreamed of America – but throughout Eastern Europe, especially, but not exclusively, among Jews, France was the predominant destination of the heart. It was the first country in Europe to have given Jews equal rights. It was the land whose writers stood up for the poor and the downtrodden. Hugo's *Les Misérables* was treated almost as a sacred text. Zola had defended the unjustly convicted Captain Dreyfus. And look what then happened! Dreyfus, the Jewish soldier, had had his sentence suspended and ultimately his conviction was quashed. That was something you could not imagine happening in Tsarist Russia, or in the new Republic of Poland. For Mina Kacewa, as for so many, the way to get on was to get out and the place to get to was France. She decided her only child would be French.

The first member of the family to move west was Dinah, Romain Gary's older cousin (the daughter of his mother's brother Eliasz). She left at the age of eighteen, in 1924, for a spell as an au-pair with a family living at 15 Drayton Gardens in South Kensington. But she fell seriously ill with pleurisy and made for the French Riviera, generally thought to be the right place to treat all manner of ailments. It was also near the convalescent resort of Bordighera, on the Italian side, where (at least, according to *Promise at Dawn*) Mina had taken Roman to recover from a bout of scarlet fever in 1925.[7] Reasons of health first brought the tribe to the Côte d'Azur. Mina Kacewa cannot have been destitute to have taken her son on such a long trip. It may have been then that she first learned how to use 'health reasons' to obtain a residence permit in France.

Dinah's mother Bella rushed to Nice to join her ailing daughter in August 1926. Dinah was operated on in December of that year and twelve months later her father, Eliasz Owczynski, also known as Liova, joined the family group. On the pretext of Dinah's poor health, all three managed to wangle residence permits. Eliasz, who had a jewellery business in Wilno, was able to transfer his profession to Nice. Mina and Roman joined them a few months later, in summer 1928. Their departure from Warsaw must have been thought of at the time as part of a general movement towards the West – a typical family resettlement programme, similar to what Georges Perec's parents, aunts and uncles were doing at exactly the same time. But behind Eliasz and Mina, no Kacews or Owczynskis followed. Gary's father, now effectively divorced and remarried,[8] pursued his new life in Wilno and then Kaunas. Mina's own family, most of whom were now middle-class citizens of Warsaw, also stayed behind.

Woodrow Wilson left his name to what is now a very distinguished School for International and Public Affairs. Yet even its most attentive students won't receive as good an education in 'community relations', that is to say, prejudice, hatred and conflict, as the one Gary had in Wilno.

> To say that the French word *minoritaire* simply means 'a member of a minority' nowhere near expresses the history of that term, the millenniums of slavery, massacre, suppression and beastliness . . . I am a born *minoritaire*, and I shall never be anything else, so help me God.[9]

As a 'born minoritarian', Gary had good grounds for claiming victim status: he was a Jew, an immigrant, and a Pole as well. But Gary was also a born contrarian. Instead of exploiting his triply justified membership of the victim class, he became an insistent and brilliant satirist of the delusions and dangers of victimhood. Victims, he argued with an absolutely straight face, are the most dangerous people on earth. There has been no war, no mayhem, no outbreak of human brutality in the twentieth century that has not had a *victim* as its pretext or its cause. Pointing to a sheep, the mythical 'Virginian Pilgrim' in Gary's moral farce, *Tulipe*, declares: 'I've got what they need. The end and the beginning of all great historical movements: a victim.'[10] Gary never cited his home town as a case in point, but the memory of Wilno underlies all his elaborate jokes about the collusion of oppressors and oppressed. Every one of Wilno's many minorities thought itself a victim of one or of all the others. The Poles, for sure, had been victimised by the Russians during the town's long attachment to the Russian Empire. The Russians, once they lost power, were certainly victimised by the Poles. The Lithuanians had been victimised since the seventeenth century and largely excluded from the history of their own land; and the Jews – well, the Jews were victims since for ever. The place where Romain Gary grew up already deserved the name of *Victimgrad*, long before the terrible events of 1941–6, when the entire Jewish population was slaughtered, most of the Poles were displaced and about a hundred thousand Lithuanians deported to Siberia.

Wilson's *right of nations to self-determination* was intended, from afar, to put an end to domination, oppression and the exploitation of one community by another. Closer up, in Eastern Poland, its practical effect in the short and medium term was conflict, war, expulsion and slaughter. It's hardly surprising that Gary became very cynical about history and politics. What's much more noteworthy is that he did not abandon hope. His post-war work made him almost unique among French intellectuals. Throughout the period of ideological subservience in 'committed literature' and the attack on 'humanism' from Robbe-Grillet and others, Gary remained an unapologetic believer in the *possibility* of improvement in human affairs and an outspoken critic of all that limited human freedom. That was not because his background gave him much reason for optimism. It was because the harshness of that world gave him no choice but hope.

Gary's most famous creation, the character of Madame Rosa in *Life Before Us*, is much given to mentioning the right of peoples to self-determination, since she too recalls the muddle and horror of her East European past. Now an obese ex-prostitute running a clandestine orphanage in the poorest part of Paris, Madame Rosa is also concerned with her own right to self-determination, that is to say, in the French formulation of Wilson's famous point, her *right to dispose of herself*. She wants to stay out of hospital however ill she gets, to avoid being kept alive as a vegetable in an intensive-care unit. Momo, the child-narrator, does not even suspect that the question of euthanasia recycles and reinterprets a cliché of European history. He nurses his adoptive mother through senile dementia and, when she dies in the end, he mounts a long vigil beside her corpse in the foul-smelling cupboard-under-the-stairs that Madame Rosa had dubbed her *trou juif* or 'Jew-hole'. Momo's touching, *faux-naïf* account of the old lady's descent into incontinence and debility is a dramatic argument in support of people's right to choose their own end. Gary had reason to smile at the naivety of Wilson's doctrine of national self-determination, but he was a Wilsonian through and through when it came to individuals' rights to dispose of themselves.

2

The Child

Wilno and Warsaw, 1914–1928

Gary's father was called Leiba or Arieh Kacew. In Yiddish and Hebrew respectively, both first names mean 'lion', and are in effect the same name as Lev or Lyova in Russian and Léon in French. Gary was therefore not exactly lying when he used the latter first name for his father on official documents, such as his marriage certificate in 1945.

Leiba was a Wilno furrier and by outward signs a reasonably prosperous man, though it was his brother Borukh who actually ran the family firm. (Confusingly, Gary had two uncles called Borukh – his mother's brother, a Warsaw lawyer, and his father's brother, the furrier, who, just to complicate the family tree, was married to his mother's sister Rivka.) Leiba seems to have been a pious Jew, but in 1912 he took the daring step of marrying a woman several years older than he was and, what is more, a divorcee. Mina Owczynski (the family name probably only means that her forebears came from a small town near Sweciany – now Svencionis[1] – called Owczyn) had been married to a man called Bregsztein, but about that part of her life nothing more is known, save that she had been granted a divorce or *get* under Jewish law.[2] The Kacew couple were separated barely eighteen months after marriage, at the start of the Great War, when Leiba was conscripted into the Russian Army. Roman was just a baby when his father was separated from the family and his travels in Russia with his mother began only a few weeks later (see p. 18). When mother and child returned to Wilno, probably in 1921, Leiba had found a far from squalid apartment at 16 Welko Pohulanka and there the family lived until 1925. Between the ages of seven and eleven, Gary almost certainly knew his father, but in his recollections of the period he erased Leiba from his life. The few words he says about him in *Promise at Dawn* skilfully elide the timescale to make Leiba seem more absent than he probably was:

> My father left us almost immediately after I was born. [. . .] I knew that the man who had given me his name had a wife and children, that he travelled a great deal and had gone to America. I met him several times. He was rather stout, had beautifully kept hands and kind eyes. With me he was always slightly uneasy and a little sad, though very nice, and when he looked at me with his gentle, and, it seemed to me, reproachful eyes, I would lower my own guiltily – he always gave me the impression that I had done him a bad turn.[3]

Gary chooses not to mention that his father 'left' as a conscript in the Russian Army, and that his mother also left (with her baby) in enforced exile and did not return for several years. He had not met his father prior to this moment, and it's not hard to imagine a strained relationship between father and son in the reconstituted family in their new home in Wilno. But as far as records allow us to know, Leiba did not remarry for several more years (Gary's eldest half-sibling was born in 1925, and the official divorce of Leiba and Mina took place in 1929). What he does retain from a fraught family life were the 'home visits' made by the man and he recalls them perhaps more acutely in fictional mode than in the highly decorated memoir that is *Promise at Dawn*. 'I have always greatly respected my poor father,' says Uncle Nat in *Tulipe*. 'He often came to our home and sat me in his lap, and my mother always said, "Come on, come on, say hallo to the gentleman . . ."'[4] Maybe that's how it was at Welko Pohulanka in the early 1920s. On the other hand, there is a reason to believe that Arieh Kacew did live with and help to bring up young Roman until 1925. In a heart-to-heart talk in 1954 with the wife of Henri Hoppenot, Gary's mentor in the Diplomatic Service, the writer once talked about his having been something of a chess prodigy as a child (which is omitted entirely from *Promise at Dawn*). But he never played now.[5] He had given it up entirely at the age of eleven. Why was that? Hélène Hoppenot asked. 'That was when my father left home.'[6]

It was from his mother that Gary learned everything, or so he tells us in *Promise at Dawn*. What he purports to recall from earliest childhood are the folk tales his mother told him about the three evil deities that rule the world: Totoche, Merzavka and Trembloche, respectively the gods of Stupidity, Absolute Truth and Total Righteousness, and Acceptance and Servility. In the English edition only, Gary added a fourth, Filoche, the god of Mediocrity 'full of bilious scorn and rabid prejudice . . . screaming at the top of his voice, "You dirty Jew! Jap! Down with the Yanks! Kill the yellow rats! Wipe out capitalists! Imperialists! Communists!"'[7] Needless to say, no such Russian, Lithuanian or Jewish superstitions exist by these names, and it is hardly likely that Lithuanian folklore in 1920 incorporated proleptic insults about the Japanese. In fact, '*Totoche*' is the transliteration of the name used for the Tin Man in the famous and widely read Russian translation of *The Wizard of Oz*; and the other names probably have similar kinds of origins. Gary's four (or three) deities are obviously charming back-projections of what he learned about the world in his adult life and, like much in his deceptive memoir of childhood, they are not to be taken as literal recollections of the past.

All the same, fetishes and other traces of animistic folklore recur throughout Gary's work. Some critics surmise that this is a hidden inheritance of Lithuanian culture, which thanks to

Prosper Mérimée's eerie short story 'Lokis' has long been seen in France as a repository of pre-Christian beliefs, but that is too ingenious by half. Literary folklore, such as Grimm's tales of animated furniture, S. Ansky's reinvention of the dybbuk legend, or Gorky's play, *The Lower Depths*, are more certain sources for many of the folkloristic topics that crop up in, for example, *The Company of Men*, *The Dance of Genghis Cohn* and the puppet-like character of the Baron (see p. 288). Although many of Gary's child heroes have magical, fetishistic casts of mind (Luc Martin in *The Company of Men*, and Momo in *Life Before Us*, both 'adopt' an umbrella and call it Arthur), that does not mean that Gary indulged in such fantasies himself as a child.

The apartment building in Welko Pohulanka is a large, four-sided and six-storeyed block round an inner courtyard large enough for several trees to grow, and Gary's description of it in *Promise at Dawn* matches its present shape fairly well. It seems ideally suited to spawning a communal life of its own, and much of a small boy's time there must have been taken up with relations with other children on the staircase and the block, in the woodshed and the open fields that led off at the back. Did Gary attend primary school in Wilno? He doesn't mention it in *Promise at Dawn*, yet it seems implausible that he could have been educated exclusively by private tutors. By Gary's own account, his mother did everything she could to elicit dormant talents that would fit him for life as a Polish nobleman: French language and literature, riding, fencing, pistol-shooting, painting, singing, piano, violin and ballroom dancing. Nothing is impossible – especially not in the life of Romain Gary! – but these are quite improbable skills to foist upon a Jewish boy in a Litwak home. In any case, Gary proved quite useless at all these things, save for French. Despite his lingering nostalgia for a career as a painter, he learned nothing but humiliation from these pointless explorations of his potential – and it is perhaps the memory of *humiliation* that is the main point of their later invention.

Gary learned Polish quickly and became a voracious reader.

From his later writings we can be sure he read a wide range of children's classics – almost certainly in Polish, although Russian translations must also have been easy to find in a city that had only recently left the Russian Empire. From the local bookstore, he carried his booty to his 'secret treasure island in the barn . . . and plunged into the fabulous worlds of Walter Scott, Karl May, Mayne Reid and Arsène Lupin'.[8] Other writers Gary must have absorbed in his childhood and youth include Selma Lagerlöf, Dickens, Hugo, Conrad and Dostoevsky – but not Tolstoy, whom he did not really encounter until his years in London. He certainly learned to write the Latin alphabet through the medium of Polish; his (almost illegible) handwriting in later life bears unmistakable traces of the way he was taught to write, in a style now obsolete throughout Europe.

Gary must also have been taught to read if not to write in Hebrew script, but no trace of such skills can be found in his later work. Being Jewish was nothing special in Wilno, even if it was not a way of being liked. But to be ridiculed – that was something else. One day his mother, in a fit of anger and despair, called neighbours on to the landing to declare that they were all dirty little bourgeois bedbugs, and that 'My son will be an Ambassador of France, a Chevalier of the Legion of Honour, a great dramatic author, a second Ibsen, a new Gabriele d'Annunzio . . .'

> The blood still rushes to my cheeks, and I can remember every wounding word they spat at us . . . I believe that nothing has played a more important part in my life than the burst of laughter flung in my face on the staircase of an old block of flats at Number 16, Grand Pohulanka in the town of Vilna. To it I owe everything I am today. For better or worse, that laughter has become me.[9]

The boy's immediate reaction, however, was intense embarrassment: 'I felt that my breast had become a cage from which an animal in the grip of pain and panic was desperately trying to escape.' So he made for the hidey-hole he had carefully constructed in the great woodpile at the back of the building, and there worked out which of the logs he would have to move so as to cause the whole pile to fall and crush him. 'I can still remember . . . the sense of peace that came over me at the idea that I was never again to be humiliated and unhappy. All I had to do was to push the logs simultaneously with my feet and my back.'[10]

It doesn't matter whether this anecdote is actually true or not. It raises themes and forms reworked many times in Gary's fiction and life, and here, in a retrospective and partly legendary narration of his childhood, he gives them a picturesque and sentimental source. What Gary wishes us to understand is that his formative experience in childhood was one of shame – rationalised in this (not necessarily invented) anecdote as shame for being his mother's son, shame for not being already a new Victor Hugo, shame for being an object of ridicule. His escape from humiliation takes the form of self-immolation – just as Janek's escape, in *A European Education*, takes the form of a hole dug in the ground, just as Madame Rosa, in *Life Before Us*, goes to die in her 'Jew-hole' at the bottom of the staircase. Gary and his characters – and they are, often, to be confused – seek safety and peace in a burrow, low down, in the humblest location of all. It all gives Gary's literal and figurative rise – to the skies, as a bomber dropping explosives from on high, and to the heights of fame and fortune as a writer – the hyperbolic form of a trajectory starting at the very bottom of the pile. It is a remarkable unspoken metaphor for the patently real experience of starting out as the single child of a spurned and perhaps already destitute mother in a poverty-stricken city in disputed territory under a regime that was increasingly ungenerous to Jews.

Whether or not Gary really felt suicidal at the age of eight is impossible to know. What we do know is that at the age of forty-five, at the very height of his glory, when he was a consul general, a Goncourt Prizewinner and a secret conqueror of the English-speaking world, Gary conceived of suicide as a personality trait consubstantial with his existence in the world.

In *Promise at Dawn*, shame and embarrassment motivate the child Roman's flight towards a place of safety and death. But it did not turn the boy into a shrinking violet of a man: modesty, humility and awkwardness are certainly not qualities to associate with Romain Gary. What emerged from this originating experience was an unquenchable, lifelong desire to be someone else.

According to her son, Madame Kacewa ran a small business from the apartment. Claiming to be the local representative of a Paris couturier, she made and sold counterfeit schmattes for the fashion-conscious ladies of the town. It's plausible; but it could also be a joke, seeing just how many Jewish immigrants to France (and America) were in the garment trade. At all events, this part of Gary's own story of his childhood might account for his precocious familiarity with women in states of undress, for his early awakening to sex and for his lifelong taste for dressing well, and for dressing up.

Mina and Roman moved to Warsaw in 1926, following the final breakdown of the marriage, and it was there that he entered secondary school, around the age of twelve. Anissimov doubts he could have attended the famous Kreczmar Gymnasium, as it would have been too expensive for a single mother and too exclusive for a Litwak Jew.[11] On the other hand, Gary consistently recalled his time at the Gymnasium and when he visited Warsaw in 1966 he went back to see where it had stood without needing directions from his Orbis 'tour guide' Jolanta Sell.[12] Even more decisive is the inscription of the headmaster of the school (father of the great theatrical producer, Jerzy Kreczmar) in the first version of *A European Education*. In Gary's fiction he appears as the teacher of Adam

Dobranski and thus the intellectual father of the novel's central character. Rather like Luc Jardie in Kessel's *Army of the Shadows*, 'Professor Kreczmar' is also a Resistance leader and the editor of an underground news-sheet, *Nasza Walka* (*Our Fight*).[13] If the Kreczmar Gymnasium is a fantasy, then it is one Gary entertained from very early on.

Gary took German as his foreign language, learning it well enough to read for pleasure. It was in Warsaw, in all likelihood, that he started writing: his first piece of work, by his own account, was a translation of a Russian poem into Polish verse.[14] In Warsaw, Gary's Wilno accent marked him unmistakably as a Jew when he spoke Polish, and we can assume that in those years of rising anti-Semitism, young Roman was humiliated and spat upon more than once.

According to *Promise at Dawn*, mother Nina's business came to a bad end in Wilno and in Warsaw too the family was extremely poor, living by expedients from hand to mouth. Yet nothing was ever too expensive for the golden boy, always well dressed, well groomed and grossly indulged. It is true that in later life Gary behaved in many ways like a spoiled brat. His mother certainly never imparted any practical skills to her son, who didn't know how to boil an egg, sew a button on his own shirt, or manage his accounts. But the poverty of life in Poland as it is described in *Promise at Dawn* makes some of the other anecdotes quite mysterious – for example, Gary's claim that he was taken to the Italian resort of Bordighera to convalesce from scarlet fever in 1925. That was a journey far beyond the means of most people at that time – in today's terms, it's as if a recently bankrupted and unemployed single mother in Clapham could afford to take a convalescent teenager on a long holiday to Antigua. Of course, Gary's father, who seems to have been reasonably prosperous, or one of his many uncles, one of whom at least was a businessman and a gambler, might have made a gift; and it is more than possible that Nina had other, possibly generous, admirers, so frequent are Gary's often inverted references to his mother's status as a cocotte. But let us accept as the truth that young Gary was made aware of the precariousness of life and that the pressure of poverty was never far from the scene. After all, most Poles were poor and the vast majority of Polish Jews even poorer. Gary seems to have been brought up as an over-protected and outrageously favoured child in an environment where destitution was never far away. No wonder he also believed that he just had to make good, to wash away the shame.

In Warsaw, at Poznanska 22, where Gary and his mother lived with Mina's brother Borukh and his wife Maria, the Warsaw telephone directory for 1926 also lists a Rachel Owczynska, a dentist by profession, who was possibly Mina's sister Rivka with her Hebrew forename translated into Polish.[15] These were not poor people, and they were resident not in the ghetto, but in the swankier part of town, a few steps from the Novi świat, not far from where the Hotel Evropeiski now stands and where Gary stayed on his many later returns to the city. These successful and largely assimilated people survived the war. Borukh (who called himself Boleslaw, to be more Polish) died in 1949; Maria lived on until the 1970s and, after the war, Gary supported her financially, sending a monthly allowance of $30 for many years. He also brought her to France more than once for holidays at Roquebrune and Rue du Bac.

When Gary got to Nice in 1928, he was a good-looking, unusually tall youth with five languages under his belt. He promptly decided that one of them – French – would henceforth be his mother tongue. However, even after decades of living and writing in that language, he never lost his accent, and his gravelly voice, with its Russian gutturals and slightly slurred vowels, always bore the trace of his 'exotic' origin. Similarly, even though he abandoned huge domains of his early life in Poland

and Russia (he never set foot in a synagogue again, never once went back to Russia, never sought contact with 'new Russians' of the Soviet era, and never played chess, tried to sing or play the violin), the literary culture he had absorbed as a boy remained with him all his life. *Great Expectations* was Gary's ground floor.

3

The Cosmopolitan

Nice, 1928–1934

Gary's colourful background and his frequent admixture of fiction to the facts of his life have often made people wonder what he really was: Russian, Polish or French? In strictly ethnic terms he was none of these, but a Litwak Jew. In cultural terms, however, the answer is that he clearly was all three. But Gary had very different relationships with the three main languages and cultures that enriched his identity; it is worth trying to pull them apart.

Russian was Gary's first language and Russia the first land of which he had any memory, flimsy though that almost certainly was. However, he never could have had Russian nationality (since he was born Jewish); nor did he ever attend a Russian-language school. He spoke the language well throughout his life, so people say; he learned to read it in the old alphabet, which has six more characters than the simplified version brought in by Soviet reforms, and never liked having to read editions of his favourite books printed after 1917.[1] Did he learn to write Russian? A handful of words in Cyrillic script have been seen in Gary's hand. But if he definitely knew how to write Russian, there's no evidence that he did it very often.

Gary cultivated a kind of Russianness that had nothing to do with Russia as it was in the twentieth century. He felt no bond with Soviet citizens, did not seek their company and never once travelled in the Soviet Union. Given that he visited every other continent save Australia in the course of his exhaustingly far-flung travels – his collected passports must have carried stamps at least for Afghanistan, Algeria, Austria, Belgium, Bolivia, Bulgaria, Brazil, Cambodia, Chad, Colombia, Denmark, Djibouti, Egypt, Germany, Hungary, India, Iran, Israel, Italy, Japan, Mauritius, Mexico, Morocco, Poland, Singapore, South Africa, Spain, Sudan, Sweden, Switzerland, Tahiti, Thailand, Turkey, Vietnam, Yemen, Yugoslavia, the United Kingdom and the USA – the avoidance of Russia has to be counted as a conscious act, especially as he was married for fifteen years to Lesley Blanch, who was passionately keen on travelling on the Trans-Siberian Railway and to the romantic wilds of Chechnya, Daghestan and Azerbaijan. Gary's Russianness was made of literature and folklore, liberally doused with Slavic kitsch such as you find in tea rooms called La Vieille Russie in Paris and New York.

The Enchanters, the only one of Gary's novels to be set in 'Old Russia', is narrated, quite significantly, by a typically Gary-like character (a male adolescent who discovers sex in all its glory in the course of the tale) who is not Russian at all, but the son of travelling Italian illusionists, purveyors of snake oil to the Imperial crown. The Muscovy of yore recreated by Gary is a comical hotchpotch of traditional anecdotes, folk tales and coffee-table kitsch taken from three centuries of Russian history. But however attractive the sleigh bells, grand balls and onion domes of Mother Russia are made to seem, they are part of a world to which the narrator does not quite belong. As the story proceeds, Fosco Zaga finds himself drawn into association with another historical minority within the Old Empire, the Jews. By the end of the novel, which flips into the present time, the Italian illusionist has become a modern charlatan writing books in Rue du Bac and no more distinct from an exiled Jew than from Gary's imagination of himself.

The Enchanters says how Russian Gary really was: linguistically, almost one hundred per cent (the many Russian terms in the novel are genuine and accurately transcribed); emotionally, as full of schmaltzy nostalgia for picture-book Muscovy as any bewhiskered émigré clinging to his last moth-eaten mink hat; but actually, at bottom, not a bit.

Gary's Polishness was of a different order, for an obvious reason: Polish was the language of his primary education and thus the language in which he was first able to write. His mother obtained Polish nationality and it was with Polish identity papers that Gary first arrived in France. In the 1920s, Wilno, having been only recently incorporated into the new Polish state, was subjected to militant and enthusiastic 'repolonisation', and primary education in the town sought to make boys and girls proud to be Polish once again. Gary was a voracious reader as a child and the foundations of his European literary culture, which informs and generates every one of his major works, were built in Wilno and Warsaw, and primarily through Polish-language texts.

In *Promise at Dawn* Gary talks more of the out-of-school curriculum his mother imposed on him through private tutors, and most especially of his learning of French. What this touching and no doubt partly accurate picture leaves out is the great wealth of Polish-language culture that Gary absorbed as a precocious reader in Wilno and Warsaw, and which he continued to develop and enjoy throughout his life.

Unlike many immigrants from the East, Gary did not shut the door on his past when he arrived in France. He quickly acquired a new layer of identity as a Frenchman, of course. His immense energy and natural gifts soon made him able to beat natives at their own game, and he won first prize for French composition at his lycée in Nice within a few years of arrival. But the riches that came to overlay the baggage he had brought with him on the long train ride from the North never smothered the Polish foundations of Gary's identity, which played a larger role in his life and work than most of his commentators suggest.

The reason why Gary was able to maintain his linguistic and cultural multiplicity was that he moved at the age of fourteen not to France but to Nice. Nice in the 1920s was a winter resort and quite empty in summer, but it was also a year-round home to significant communities of wealthy people from all over northern Europe. Nice is not a historic part of France. Its population, part of which spoke Italian and the other part Provençal, had voted to secede from the Kingdom of Piedmont-Savoy and to join the French Empire only in 1861. Britons, who first started moving there at the dawn of the railway age, were the first to give Nice its distinctive international flavour, followed by Swedes (the Swedish royal family, of French descent, maintained a permanent palace in Nice) and by significant numbers of wealthy Russians, who regularly wintered there, travelling in luxurious sleeping cars that ran direct from St Petersburg. The religious establishments in the city centre bear witness to the cosmopolitan make-up of modern Nice: Holy Trinity Anglican Church (built in 1860–2), on Rue de la Buffa, the splendid Russian Orthodox Cathedral (erected in 1912) on Avenue Nicolas II, the Svenska Kyrkan (Lutheran chapel), and the synagogue all served large resident communities in the 1920s.

The most visible foreign community at that time were Russian émigrés who, having fled the Revolution, found their way to what was in many cases a familiar place from holidays in the past and had now become a legendary rallying point for those still faithful to the Tsar. The class Romain joined at the Lycée de Nice in October 1928 was fairly representative of the city's make-up at that time: there was Sigurd Norberg, from Sweden, and François Bondy, a mixture of Czech, Austrian and Swiss, as well as Sacha Kardo-Sissoeff from a White Russian family, Edmond Glicksman, a Polish Jew, and René Ziller, a French Jew. René Agid, the son of a wealthy hotelier who was also a Russian of Jewish ancestry, was in the class above. His slight seniority made him more than a friend: from the start, René became moral tutor to Romain Gary, and remained his support in times of crisis and misery to the end of his life.

Gary was therefore far from being exotic among the boys in his class. Polyglots were ten a penny, Poles were not rare and Jews were all over the place. Nor was he noticeably more talented. René Agid grew up to become a professor of medicine, François Bondy became a distinguished journalist writing with equal elegance in French and German, Glicksman became Edmund Glenn and served in the US State Department, and René Ziller, after fighting in the Resistance inside France, joined the Diplomatic Service, just like Gary. What made Gary different as a teenager in Nice was his being a fatherless only child living with his mother in relative poverty, in a city where insolent wealth was on parade every day on the mimosa-lined Promenade des Anglais.

Mina had a monthly allowance from Leiba Kacew, but it fell far short of what was needed to cover the cost of living in Nice. That does not mean Leiba was tight with his money: the economic situation of Poland meant that many wheelbarrowfuls of złoty would have been needed to pay Mina's rent. She tried touting second-hand silver ('treasures of the last Romanovs', 'to save the life of a ruined Russian aristocrat', 'from one of the noblest tables in all of Holy Russia' and so on) to make a small living, and got her first break when Alexandre Agid, René's father, owner of L'Hermitage, one of the very grand hotels on the Riviera, took pity on the ageing lady and allowed her to solicit for custom in the lobby, and even granted her a showcase of her own. The goods came mostly from Au Rubis, her brother Eliasz's jewellery shop in town. After various other minor and flawed business adventures, Mina became the manageress of a modest boarding house, the Hôtel-Pension Mermonts. The name 'Mermonts' inscribes

Nice's priceless combination of sea – *la mer* – and mountains – *les monts*. Gary-Ajar remembered the formula in *King Solomon*, when he has his eighty-four-year-old hero pack no less than twelve suitcases for his honeymoon on the Riviera, because he had to take 'everything for the sea and the mountains'.[2] Jean Seberg's name was an extraordinary reminder of Gary's first life in Nice. It was as if the actress had been predestined to fill a role in his life, because her name is a perfect translation of his teenage home: *See* and *Berg* are the German words for *mer* and *mont*. He made a huge joke of it, in Russian, with his cousin Dinah, on one of his visits to Nice: 'See-berg! Dinah! *Ponimaesh?* Mer-Mont See-Berg! Dinah, *vidish*?'[3]

Gary would initially have seen the sea (any sea) on his convalescent trip to Bordighera in 1925 or thereabouts, but it was when he got to Nice in 1928 that he had his first dip in the Med. He took to water like a fish and quickly became a strong swimmer. He was never happier than when in or near the sea – at Big Sur, for instance, as in the opening and closing pages of *Promise at Dawn*, or at Cimarrón, his beachside home on Mallorca. Water was Gary's element. 'Here is Might and Reassuring Promise,' he wrote of the ocean in one of his most lyrical and personal essays for *Life* magazine. 'It offers us the promise of something that can never die.'[4] In Paris, New York, Sofia and Los Angeles he would often soak in the bath for hours. In fact, Gary dictated large parts of several novels while reclining in the tub, using a sponge to hide his genitals from a secretary perched on the toilet seat.

Gary lost his home in Nice when his mother died during the war, for she was only the manageress of the Pension Mermonts. After the war, as soon as the opportunity arose, Gary acquired his own pied-à-terre on the Riviera. When he was posted to Berne in 1949 as a junior diplomat, he took a vacation in Nice and his old school friend Sacha Kardo-Sissoeff took him to see a hilltop village a few miles along the road towards Italy. Roquebrune sits on a soaring outcrop of reddish rock rising almost vertically to an altitude of three hundred metres above the Bay of Villefranche. During the war the Germans had evacuated all the inhabitants (Roquebrune's commanding view of the bay made it a strategic site) and many of them never moved back after 1945. The Roquebrune that Gary inspected in 1949 was a half-empty, medieval slum and much of it was on sale for a song. Gary was enchanted with it and committed himself on the spot. With the advance he had from Gallimard for *The Company of Men*,[5] he bought an impractical ruin at the end of a squalid alley. Structured on several levels, like everything else in that *village perché*, the tumble-down property had no running water, electricity or telephone – but it had a wonderful view of the sea. Over the following years his English wife Lesley mended, adapted, expanded and modernised Roquebrune; but it was Gary's beloved writing retreat. What might have clinched the deal he did in 1949 was the local restaurant, worthy of a rosette in the Michelin Guide. It was called Au Grand Inquisiteur, giving Dostoevsky an implausible outpost by the Mediterranean Sea.

Le Roi des dupes

Alongside the sun and the sea, Nice also gave Gary his first sight of a strange and captivating ritual. For the ten days before the start of Lent, Nice abandons itself to the carnival, which turns the world upside down and celebrates the *Roi des dupes* (The King of Fools). The carnival king is materialised in a huge papier-mâché mask that presides over the Promenade des Anglais until the last night, called the *veglione*, when he is destroyed during an all-night masked ball. On each day of carnival a parade of floats, together with comedians on stilts and an army of giant masks, processes through town, throwing flowers at the onlookers, who throw them back, in the tradition known as the

Battle of Flowers. Gary would have seen his first carnival in February 1929, when Jean Vigo was filming it for his cityscape, *A propos de Nice*, a precious visual record of what the teenage immigrant looked upon with bewildered, appreciative eyes.

Only one of Gary's fictions, *The Colours of the Day*, is set against the background of the carnival, but the ritual gave Gary much more than explicit material for his novel. The aesthetics of the outsize carnival masks – grotesque symbolic figures that are simultaneously worshipped and mocked – is kitsch in its pure and original form. The carnival shaped Gary's taste, and his sense of what could be done in art and writing. His comic vein, from *Tulipe* to *Genghis Cohn* and the first two Ajar novels, exploits precisely those features of carnival art that he encountered before he was fifteen.

Deception is the very nature of carnival atmosphere. Every year there is at least one 'false guest' – a make-believe monarch or potentate, played by an actor, but treated with the respect and pomp due to the person thus mocked. In 2006, 'Queen Elizabeth' arrived in a white Rolls-Royce, to be greeted by loud cheers of 'God Save the Queen'. The tradition is an ancient one. Roman, who must have attended at least five and maybe as many as ten carnival periods in his early life, acquired an easy education in the fun that can be had from pretending to be someone else.

It is sometimes much harder to be yourself. In *The Colours of the Day*, anti-clerical stewards refuse entry to the *veglione* ball to a man dressed as a parish priest, on grounds that such a disguise goes beyond the bounds of decency. But I *am* a parish priest! the would-be partygoer insists, to no avail. When everyone is dressed up, as on the last night of the carnival, you simply can't get away with being yourself.

Gary was fourteen when he arrived in Nice. It was a founding moment, and very probably his first and most powerful experience of being reborn as someone else. Throughout his work as Romain Gary and Émile Ajar, he returns with a persistence verging on obsession to the experience of being 'fourteen or thereabouts': Janek, the hero of *A European Education* (1944), is fourteen when his father leaves him for safety in a hole in the forest floor; Luc Martin, the narrator and focus of *The Company of Men* (1949), is fourteen when he is orphaned at the very end of the German Occupation of France; Momo, the charming child-narrator of *Life Before Us* (1975), who half believes that he is still ten years of age, is actually fourteen when his adoptive mother Madame Rosa begins to die; and the great romance of Ludovic Fleury, in Gary's last novel, *The Kites*, also begins when he is aged fourteen. In Gary's fictional universe the awakening of the young male mind – to sex and to love, but also to responsibility, heroism, duty and devotion, always at the age of fourteen – is the means through which the author's most clearly declared aspirations are expressed. It is impossible not to link this literary recurrence with the lived experience of Romain Gary and to deduce that something, on his arrival in Nice or in a relatively short period thereafter, shook him so deeply as to make him always feel that his own real life began there, in the magical environs of the Promenade des Anglais. That is why there is no contradiction between saying that Gary was Polish, Russian, Litwak and Jewish, and a native Frenchman too, born at the age of fourteen or thereabouts.

Alongside the sea, the carnival and the curriculum he followed at his French lycée, Nice gave Gary a cosmopolitan milieu in which he could continue to cultivate his Polish roots without any special difficulty. He had someone in Warsaw send him the weekly issues of the literary journal *Wiadomości Literackie*[6] – he was passionately attached to the *Kroniki* by Antoni Słonimski – as well as books to read. He seems to have had access to writers like Boleslaw Prus, Bruno Winawer and the early Gombrowicz long before they were translated into French ('thirty years before he was discovered by the West', he asserted in 1977),[7] but it's hard to imagine he read them before he was fourteen. As for books in Russian (and in the old script), the second-hand stores in Nice had a more than ample sufficiency. Had Gary landed up anywhere else in France (as more than a quarter of a million Poles did between 1920 and 1932), he would have had a much harder time staying Russian, Polish and French.

There were also continuing links with Poland through travels and visits. In 1929 Mina must have travelled back to Wilno to attend her divorce at the main synagogue. In September 1933 Borukh Kacew, the elder brother of Gary's father Leiba and the main owner of the family's fur business, turned up in Nice. He stayed on for eight months, until May 1934, living with his nephew and sister-in-law at the Pension Mermonts. Borukh had recently divorced from Mina's sister Rivka and his Riviera sabbatical may have been an attempt to get over it; on the other hand, it's more than likely that it was part of an attempt to join the family group in France on a permanent basis. But Borukh went back to Wilno and his brother Leiba moved over the border to Lithuania, taking up residence in Kaunas with his new wife. An incidental result, of course, was to strengthen Romain's ties to Poland. In 1935, when he was a student in Paris, his naturalisation papers came through and entitled him to a French passport. What he did with it was to set off straight away to spend a summer 'back home'.

Few Polish Jews would have wanted or dared to do that at that time, and much mystery and confusion surrounds Gary's first return. Just one photograph has been found to authenticate the trip: it shows Gary and his Swedish school friend Sigurd Norberg, who went with him, standing alongside Leiba Kacew. Anissimov deduces that Gary went back to Warsaw to extract money from his father, so as to be able to continue his studies in Paris.[8] However, in his last novel, *The Kites*, Gary left an involuntary clue as to the truth of his many claims to have gone back to Warsaw in 1935.

The young hero of that novel, Ludovic Fleury, follows his Polish lover Lila back to her homeland on the eve of the Second World War. Ludo starts out on his journey from a fictional village firmly located on the Channel Coast of France, but his eastbound train doesn't cross the border into Belgium or Germany. Contrary to geographical plausibility, Ludo arrives at Ventimiglia, that's to say, at the Italian border next door to Nice. Surprising as it may seem, given his long service as an air force navigator, and despite his vast amount of travel in the Diplomatic Corps and thereafter as a member of the jet set, Gary had no sense of direction at all and frequently got lost even in places he was supposed to know well.[9] Consequently, the geographical blunder in *The Kites* can only be read as the trace of the memory of a journey Gary once made for real. The only way to get to Poland from France via Ventimiglia is if you start from Nice. Short of finding the actual ticket, there could be no better proof that Gary travelled to Poland from his summer base at the Pension Mermonts, at roughly the same age and in almost the same year as Ludovic Fleury does the same thing.

There is plenty of circumstantial evidence that attests to Gary's immersion in Polish culture during his student years. A few days before he died, he gave his last interview, and it is probably no coincidence that he gave it in Polish, to Leszek Kolodziejczyk, a Polish writer based in Paris. He recalls not just reading but going to see Bruno Winawer's surrealist plays at a Warsaw theatre, as well as the savage comic sketches of Lopek Krukowski, the inspiration for the 'hara-kiri humour' of *The Dance of Genghis Cohn*.[10] On another occasion, ten years earlier, he paid homage to his memory of the 'Qui-pro-quo' cabaret in Warsaw, a further source for his personal style of self-lacerating wit.[11] In conversations with a former Polish diplomat who became a real friend in the 1970s, he spoke about his having read Gombrowicz's early stories and plays (*Memoirs of a Time of Immaturity*, 1933; *Princess Ivona*, 1935) and of his liking for Boleslaw Prus.[12] These references reveal the extent and sophistication of Gary's Polish literary culture, which go beyond what could be accounted for by his life there up to the age of fourteen. Anissimov has rightly identified Gary's claim in *Promise at Dawn* to have been taken by his mother to see the premiere of Brecht's *Dreigroschenoper* as a blatant fib, but just as implausible would be visits to Warsaw night-clubs and cabarets in short trousers. Even dressed up to the nines, young Gary would not have been let in. His memories and real knowledge of Polish-Jewish comic theatre and experimental fiction come not just from the books that were sent to him in Nice, but from the summer vacation (or vacations) that he spent in Warsaw in 1935 (and possibly 1936).

Gary stayed with relatives while there, and attended courses on Slavic languages and literature at the university to justify his stay.[13] In *A Quiet Night*, Gary has François Bondy challenge him: 'You were French and Catholic. In Polish universities, Catholic Poles sat together and there were special rows assigned to Polish Jews. You regularly sat with the Polish Jews and got yourself beaten up by the Christians because your papers said you were Catholic and they wanted to stop you sitting with the Jews.'[14] This self-invented reproach must be counted part of Gary's fiction of himself. Gary was still Roman Kacew and the name alone gave away his Jewish identity. He therefore had no option but to sit on the 'Jews' bench' in 1935. If he did get into fights, as he might well have done, given his propensity to engage in punch-ups throughout his life, it was because he was a Jew and a Pole, not because he was French. It's not that Gary was still ashamed to have been a Jew when he penned *A Quiet Night* in 1974. It's more that he wanted to emphasise his self-identification with the oppressed beyond any necessity to do so, and to present himself, in this bizarre and counterfactual way, as an idealist, a Quixote and a gentleman even in his turbulent youth. Those are of course the conventional characteristics of the 'true Pole'.

As Gary had been brought up in Wilno and Warsaw rather preciously by a doting if impoverished mother, he would naturally have been taught the basic gestures of a Polish gentleman, particularly how to bow and to kiss a lady's hand, but it was probably in Warsaw in the 1930s that Gary first exercised those skills. (In laid-back California in the 1950s, Gary found it hard to suppress his habit of kissing a lady's hand, which Americans found offensive, rather than merely quaint. Gary extrapolated from this culture shock a rather tendentious argument against American 'sexual equality' in an article for *Holiday* magazine, where a talent for bullshit is more in evidence than good sense.)[15] It was also not unusual in pre-war Poland for older men to dye their hair and to powder their faces, and the height of elegance could only be achieved with manicured hands. Gary maintained these exotic ideas of style and class throughout his life, often causing misunderstanding and offence. In 1962, for example, he was in London and agreed to do an interview with the left-wing anti-war weekly, *Peace News*. He turned up so well groomed he could have been an entry for Crufts; his suave exterior instantly demolished any confidence that his long-haired interviewer might have had in what the visiting writer would say. 'I think he was even wearing *nail varnish*,' the horrified former journalist recalled.[16] In 1975 he used eyeliner and mascara to accentuate his features – not as a provocation, Paul Pavlowitch says, but simply because of the way he had been brought up.[17]

In interviews, Gary often referred to his having lived in 'Nalewki' (and in *The Dance of Genghis Cohn* and *Hocus Bogus* the address recurs many times). Ul. Nalewki is a street that runs alongside where the Warsaw ghetto once stood, and it debouches on to the square where the monument to the Ghetto Uprising now stands. Gary said that he stayed with relatives of his mother; the telephone directory for those years doesn't list any Owczynskis at that address; Gary seems to have used 'Nalewki' to mean that he was living among Jews.

It may have been in the Poznanska apartment of his maternal uncle Borukh that Gary saw hanging on the wall a German engraving depicting an allegorical scene: 'Humanity was represented in a forest as a fine Lady, and Death stood by her side. A young man kneeling held out his severed head in homage to our demanding and never-satisfied sovereign.'[18] The interpretation his uncle offered him was this: the Lady represents the Ideal, our aspiration towards the good and the perfect; the young man is a figure for all who strive towards an ideal and who must in the end offer up their own lives in its service; Death is the eternal companion of Perfection. The allegorical image is source of the 'mystery plot' of *The Dance of Genghis Cohn* (as made clear in the flap copy of the English first edition), but it is also the probable source for much else in Gary's work. At a trivial level, the severed heads of *Direct Flight to Allah* seem to have rolled out of the same frame. What's more important is the configuration of the unsatisfied Lady and her *cavaliere servente*. Fosco's Teresina in *The Enchanters*, and Ludo's Lila Bronicka in *The Kites*, not to mention the heroines of 'Birds in Peru', *Womanlight* and *The Way Out*, are all similarly *belles dames sans merci* who can never be attained, or satisfied, or had. But the woman in the engraving, even if she recurs as an actual woman in so many of Gary's fictions, is presented in his memory as an allegory not of some particular Ideal, but of the Ideal itself. From *Tulipe* to *The Dance of Genghis Cohn*, from *The Ski Bum* to *A Quiet Night*, Gary denounced the murderous consequences of 'having ideals', as if the price paid by the young man in the picture was scandalously, self-defeatingly high. On the other hand, Gary *was* that young man throughout his life, pursuing, through the mode of fiction as well as in the fight against Nazi Germany, an ideal of humanity and civilisation that his irony, antiphrasis and acid wit never destroyed.

What real image lies behind Gary's memory and his uncle's alleged interpretation of it is hard to say (it might have been a copy of one of the many representations in European art of John the Baptist's severed head offered to Herod's daughter Salome), but Gary's repeated references to it as something he saw and learned from in Poland in childhood or youth cannot be entirely false. Self-defeating idealism, the unattainability of Woman, and the companionship of Death and Perfection belong to the set of ideas Gary attached to his 'Polish roots'.

Gary claimed in *A Quiet Night* that he went back to Poland for summer holidays in the 1930s because his relatives could give him free board and lodging, whereas in Paris or Nice he would have had to work to earn his crust. That's possible, but puzzling too, because long-distance travel (far more expensive in relative terms then than now) was a luxury that a penniless student could ill afford. An even greater potential obstacle to the journey was Nazi Germany, blocking the most obvious route – but since Gary started from Nice, he might well have travelled via Italy and Austria, which was not yet part of the German Reich. All the same, he must have put a lot of trust in his freshly issued French passport to risk travelling in Central Europe in 1935. Was he conning himself that now he was French, he had ceased to be a Jew?

Gary cannot possibly ever have forgotten that he was a Jew, however much he may have suppressed the knowledge. He was a fluent Yiddish speaker, to begin with. In the second place he was circumcised. In Polish, his accent identified his origin without the slightest doubt. As already mentioned, in his first novel, *Forest of Anger*, he transcribed parts of Friday evening prayers in a muddle of half-Polish and half-French phonetics, with inaccurate word breaks suggesting he knew only the sound, not the meaning – like most Jews. In his years of celebrity, in America and in France, Gary never hid the fact that his mother had been Jewish, though he spun many fantastical elaborations about his father's identity, none of which made him a Jew. (He also knew perfectly well that Jewishness is transmitted by the maternal line.) Gary includes Jews as more or less central characters in many of his novels: a child violinist and two of the partisans in *A European Education* are Jews, as are La Marne in *The Colours of the Day*, the American journalist Fields in *The Roots of Heaven*, Genghis Cohn in *The Dance of Genghis Cohn*, Madame Rosa in *Life Before Us* and Countess Esterhazy in *The Kites*. He was happy also to ascribe his particular brand of humour to Jewish tradition and, beneath almost indescribable layers of deception and irony, to play games with his Jewish background in *Hocus Bogus*. On the other hand, Gary stopped going to synagogue the moment he arrived in Nice and never showed the slightest interest in Judaism or in Jewish life. In *A Quiet Night* he asks himself: 'What does it mean to you to be a Jew?' and he replies: *C'est une façon de me faire chier*, that's to say: 'a bloody nuisance'.[19]

The major deception in which Gary engaged with respect to his Jewish roots was to fictionalise the name of his mother. In *Promise at Dawn*, and throughout his other written work, and apparently also in conversation with Lesley Blanch and others, he referred to her as 'Nina', which, as previously stated, is a common Russian name. She was actually called Mina, according to Gary's birth certificate and several other documents that have been tracked down in Lithuanian archives by Galina Baranova and others. 'Mina' is a name typical of Yiddish-speaking Jews of the old Pale of Settlement. Given the history of relations between Russians and Jews, changing 'Mina' into 'Nina' is no slip of the son's pen, but a meaningful fib.

The fib may not have been Gary's own. With the years she spent in Russia and her precarious existence in Nice as a hanger-on in the Russian émigré community, Gary's mother may well have called herself Nina for part – perhaps the major part – of her life. All the same, even if 'Nina' had been a socially or commercially useful *nom de guerre*, Gary did nothing to restore his mother's real identity, even while making her an outsize heroine of Jewish motherhood in *Promise at Dawn*.

In the same memoir Gary asserts that she had him baptised

a Catholic in Nice. No record of such a ceremony has been found. Anissimov dismisses the claim as another one of the writer's fabrications, which it probably is. The fantasy baptism does, however, correspond to a general dejudaisation of Gary's identity during his adolescence and early life in France, of which the most obvious symptom was the young man's attempt to become an air force officer. Although many Jews had served with distinction in the French Army and had occupied high rank in the First World War, the closed, snobbish world of the Air Force was not one in which Jews were very numerous, especially as anti-Semitic prejudice grew ever more acute in 1930s France. A pilot was just about the least likely thing he could become, which may of course have been the secret attraction of the job; on the other hand, it may also have seemed to Gary the best way of casting off his Jewish roots.

The third of Gary's cultures, that of France, was acquired most obviously through the education he received at the lycée in Nice. However, the foundations of Gary's French identity had already been well dug in Wilno and Warsaw, where he learned the language from his mother and from private tutors, and read children's classics, especially La Fontaine and Victor Hugo. In France, Gary turned out to be a disaster at maths and a mediocre student in other subjects except languages. He took German, as Russian and Polish were not on offer as school subjects; and he had joined too late to start Latin or Greek. But in French composition he shone. However, little of the standard literary curriculum seems to have stayed in his mind in later years. There are few reminiscences of Rabelais, Racine, Molière, Corneille, Rousseau, Flaubert, Zola or other *grands auteurs* from the syllabus in Gary's otherwise highly allusive and intertextual work.[20] Most of those who do crop up from time to time – Montaigne, Pascal, Diderot, Balzac, Péguy and especially Victor Hugo – could have been familiar to Gary before he set foot in France. That's not to say that he didn't owe a huge debt to his teachers, among them the captivating philosophy master, Oriol. But what he learned at the lycée in Nice seems to have served to enrich and develop the wider European culture that Gary had already acquired, not to substitute a French cultural identity for a Polish one.

After the war, Gary visited Poland many times. His first planned visit, as early as 1946, was replaced in the end by a written question-and-answer interview, but he was in Warsaw in 1955, then again in a widely publicised visit in 1966. He returned there in 1969, then made several private trips in the 1970s. In his last decade in Paris Gary saw a lot of his new and old Polish friends, notably Stas Gajewski, and he also housed the young actor Wojciek Pszoniak and his young wife at Rue du Bac for several months. As he said to him – in Polish – towards the end of his life: 'It's strange. I was born Russian, I am French, but I only really get on with Poles.'[21]

By then, of course, Gary had gained several more layers of transnational identities – a Swiss residence permit, ex-wives who were respectively British and American, a son who spoke Spanish, a literary agent in New York, a co-conspirator in Brazil, a fake biography under a false name allegedly masking a Palestinian terrorist, a plot of land in Tahiti and theoretical ownership of a house on Crete. What he really *was* hardly mattered any more. In fact, it never did matter very much, because Gary had always treated each of his translations as the enrichment, not the negation, of what he already had in the bag. He never yielded to the facile conventions of post-war culture, which glamorised exile and displacement as trauma, tragedy and loss. All the same, Gary's 'desperate optimism' was principally forged by his experience of the Second World War, in which he fought as a Frenchman – and, as we shall see, wrote as a Pole.

4

The Cossack and the Cucumber

Leiba Kacew's profession is identified on Gary's bilingual birth certificate as *Trokski kupets* in both Russian and Hebrew. The term literally means 'a merchant (*kupets*) from Troki'. That might indicate that his business premises were on Troki Street, one of the main thoroughfares in the old town of Vilnius, or that the professional guild to which he belonged was called 'Troki' for symbolic reasons. But Troki is also the Polish name of a place now called Trakai, about twenty miles west of Vilnius. With its immense moated castle surrounded by souvenir stalls and parking lots for long-distance buses, it is a regular destination for tourists from all over Eastern Europe. But the role of the name, rather than the actual place, is the start of a curious historical-cum-vegetable trail leading to a hidden dimension of Gary's attitude towards his paternal line.[1]

Troki is famous for being the home of a small and ancient Jewish sect called Karaites – they do not celebrate Hannukah and they even mix meat with milk in meals.[2] Karaism existed for a brief period in eleventh-century Spain, but it was in the Crimea, where a Turkic-speaking Tartar tribe converted to Karaism, that the story of Troki begins. Grand Duke Vytautas of Lithuania (1352–1430), a pagan warlord who converted to Christianity twice, went marauding far south of his homeland and one day came across particularly fierce resistance from a group of Crimean Tartars. He was so impressed with their strength and valour that instead of slaughtering them, he offered them jobs. They accepted on condition of being able to bring their families and to keep their faith. Three hundred Karaite families thus trekked nearly two thousand miles north to provide Vytautas with a personal bodyguard. Their descendants are still there, in Trakai – a six-hundred-year-old community of ethnic Tartars living in the shadow of a Lithuanian fortress. These Karaites gave up the practice of arms long ago and have been far better known for centuries as first-rate market gardeners.[3] They grow and pickle by far the best cucumbers in the region, and have given their name to the pick of the crop. In Vilnius, Yiddish speakers called top-quality pickled cucumbers *karaimer*. The word has been adopted into Lithuanian and is used nowadays in the marketplace and grocery stores for crunchy cucumber pickles.

Gary had relatively few food fads, but he was inordinately fond of pickled cucumbers and he sought them out wherever they could be found. Cucumber salads, salted or pickled, with yoghurt or not, are characteristic of Central European cuisine, but they are quite alien to the food culture of France. Few connoisseurs west of the Rhine can distinguish between curcubitae pickled the *malossol*, the *haimische*, and the *karaimer* way. Gary's wolfing down a plate of pickled cucumbers could easily pass as part of his Russian, Polish or Jewish inheritance. (Gary often play-acted the Russian squire by taking friends and acquaintances to dine lavishly in Russian restaurants off the Champs-Élysées. In his Cossack mode he liked to have the balalaikas play his favourite tunes as he ate. Indeed, when it was his turn to be *L'Invité du dimanche* on a television chat show of the same name, where the principal guest gets to specify who else is invited, he insisted on having the balalaika man from a Russian eatery appear on the show with him.)[4]

However, if Gary's father was a *Trokski kupets*, in a child's imagination he could have been a *Karaimer* too.[5] A delight in eating pickled cucumbers in great quantities – and Gary's flamboyant *insistence* on that particular taste, in real life and in written prose – could therefore be interpreted as a homage to his missing father, or else, more probably, as a way of killing him off for good.

Gary liked to believe, or have his readers believe, that he was not the son of a Jew, but a Tartar. Oddly enough, this was a doubly deceptive way of casting his father out yet again, not because it means Leiba was not his father, but because the Tartar Karaites from Troki were not (in the eyes of the Orthodox) real Jews. The question of who was really Jewish arose in Wilno in brutal fashion in the summer of 1941 when Nazi Germany overran the Baltic States. Liquidation of Jews began almost immediately in Wilno, Kaunas, Klaipeda and other smaller towns. In the region called the *Ostbezirk* gas was not used. Jews were herded in groups of five hundred or so – called a 'work detail' – and marched out of town to a secluded spot in the woods. They were made to dig deep pits and shot by the *Einsatzgruppen*. The corpses were incinerated in the pits every few days.

To the Nazis it was important to know that they were killing all the Jews, but also to know they were killing only Jews. They weren't sure what the Karaites were. Lithuanian Karaites read Hebrew, but speak a Turkic language instead of Yiddish. They recognise the star of David, but do not have synagogues. The rabbinical council of Vilna was asked to solve the mystery for the Gestapo. It delivered a long and complicated judgment, which concluded that the Karaites should in point of fact not be considered members of the Jewish faith.[6] It will never be known whether this judgment was made out of sectarian spite, or out of the desire to save at least some part of the Jewish heritage in Lithuania. The result was that the Nazis left the Tartar Jews of Troki alone.

Gary's repeated fabulations about his being only half-Jewish may have their origin in the conflation of his father's official status as *Trokski kupets* with all the stories he heard in Wilno about the odd oriental market gardeners from Troki who sold their vegetables at the markets in town. As a grown man, he conflated Tartar, Mongol, Turk and Cossack into a historically and ethnically impossible 'eastern' entity, but the very vagueness of the allegedly oriental origins of his father fitted effectively into the moral position he adopted after 1945. He was half-victim, through his mother, whose Jewishness was never in question, and half-victimiser – a pogromee and a progromer, a slaughtered babe and a sword-wielding brute. Cruelty is part of what it means to be a member of the human race, Gary tells us in *A European Education*, and at a more metaphorical level in *The Dance of Genghis Cohn*, whose comical name clearly identifies the two strands that Gary wished to identify in his own moral identity – the Mongol warrior and the Jew. From a childhood wound – his father's abandonment of the family home – Gary constructed not just a self-protective fantasy, but a *personal* case for equal identification with opposing extremes.

Gary maintained connections with his maternal family; no continuing relationship with his paternal relatives has been established, save for the long visit that his other uncle Borukh (who was also his mother's brother-in-law) made to Nice in 1933 (see p. 45). In Gary's novels, however, fathers abound. In *The Colours of the Day*, the gorgeous Ann Garantier is chaperoned by her father, a professor of French at a New York university, an aesthete and intellectual of the rarefied kind that Gary detested. Professor Garantier is a moral nihilist who seeks in art and literature that which reminds him least of human life; his sole credited publication is titled 'Fertilization through Death'.[7] Similarly negative, if less caricatural, is the black-marketeer who adopts Luc Martin in *The Company of Men*. But in this novel a real father also exists, and transmits to the teenage hero positive values and a model of human dignity. Luc's father, a Resistance fighter who lost his life on the last day of combat in 1944, has bequeathed the boy little more than his scribblings in the margins of a copy of Pascal's *Pensées*, but these fragmentary reflections on heroism, solidarity and idealism function as a breviary, which leads the adolescent towards redemption. In *A European Education*, too, Dr Twardowski sacrifices himself in a suicidal mission against the German occupiers and thus leaves his orphaned son Janek with a heroic model to live up to. The theme of paternal transmission reappears in 1980 in *The Kites*: young Ludo learns the meaning of his historical memory from his uncle and sole adoptive parent Ambroise Fleury, the kite-maker of Cléry. Fatherhood may have been written out of Gary's largely fabricated life of himself, but in his strongest novels it plays a conventional and central role, as the font of moral values and of the sense of what is right. Maybe all these literary father figures are just instances of a literary trope – a paternalist convention of mass-market 'heroic' fiction. But I find that hard to credit. The occlusion of Leiba Kacew in Gary's ostensible memoirs of his life is heavily outweighed by his resurgence under a dozen disguises in Gary's fiction. The Father plays a huge role in Gary's imagination of the world and of himself.

Gary takes denial of Leiba's existence to a perverse extreme in the last story about his father that he tells in *Promise at Dawn*. In 1957, in the wake of the success of *The Roots of Heaven*, Gary tells us, he received many readers' letters and, among them, one 'that gave me certain details about the death of the man I had known so slightly'.

> He did not die in the gas chamber, as I had been told. He died of fright, on his way to execution, a few yards from the entrance. My correspondent had seen it all with his own eyes: he had been acting as doorman or receptionist – I don't know what to call him, what the official title was that went with this sort of job.
>
> The man wrote me, thinking, no doubt, that it would please me to know that my father had escaped the gas chamber, that

> he had fallen stone dead of a heart attack before he could enter it . . . The man who died of fear on his way to the gas chamber was little more to me than a total stranger, but on that day he truly became my father, and I want him to be known as such.[8]

This is double and treble nonsense. Gary certainly knew what title to give 'the doorman or receptionist' at the gates of hell – if he existed, he was a *Sonderkommando*. He also knew that the Jews of the Baltic States were not sent to the gas chambers of Auschwitz or Treblinka, which had not yet been built at the time of the Nazi onslaught in the summer of 1941. They were shot, just outside town in the case of Wilno, or at the infamous Fort Number 9, outside Kaunas. The whole passage is not so much a fantasy as a blatant fabrication designed to do two things: to erase the real existence of Leiba Kacew even in death;[9] and to allow the personage of Romain Gary, war hero and roustabout, to identify itself all the more with the positive value of weakness, cowardice and flight. (To the question 'What is the military exploit you most admire?' Gary replied: 'Running away.')[10] Thirdly, of course, Gary knew his father much more than he ever wanted to admit. The problem is, he hated him and sought to invent a much more interesting progenitor who would also have made his mother a far more desirable woman than she probably ever was.

The true story of the last years and death of Gary's father, his father's second wife Frida, and his two half-siblings Valentina and Pavel, has been unearthed by the tireless Myriam Anissimov. When Kaunas was absorbed into the Soviet Union in 1940, the family moved back to Wilno and in summer 1941 they found themselves in a Nazi-occupied town. They survived the initial clearing of the ghetto because of Leiba's involvement in the fur trade, but in 1943 almost all remaining Jews were marched out of town to Panerai (Ponary, in Polish) and shot. Arieh-Leiba Kacew was most probably among those shot in the final liquidation on 24 September 1943. Pavel, Valentina and Frida, amazingly enough, were among the few hundred deported further north, to Klooga (Estonia), to work in a slave labour camp for the Todt Organisation. When the Red Army approached the camp in June 1944, the SS proceeded to liquidate all inmates and to remove all traces of what had gone on there. Frida, Pavel and Valentina were among the two thousand five hundred prisoners doused in petrol and burned alive.[11]

Gary had very pale blue eyes, long eyelashes and broad, high cheekbones which, together with a sallow complexion, allowed him to embroider on his allegedly Asiatic roots. The heart-throb of the Russian screen throughout the first half of the twentieth century was similarly endowed with pale eyes and high cheekbones, and it has to be said that there is something of a likeness between Romain Gary and Ivan Moszhukin, who was occasionally resident in Nice in the 1920s and 1930s, when shooting films at the Studios de la Victorine.[12] Gary's fantasy of being a bastard son of a Russian Valentino surely owes more to chance encounters on the Promenade des Anglais than to his mother's adulterous affairs, if she had any at all. (There are no grounds at all to believe that Moszhukin was in Wilno in August 1913, as he would have to have been to father Romain Gary.) But the Moszhukin fantasy, never directly stated but frequently hinted at in all Gary's memoirs, serves above all to make Gary of mixed race, no matter what the admixture is (Cossack, Russian, Tartar, Mongol – who cares!) to his undeniably Jewish other half. It mattered to Gary to be not one thing, but many, and it mattered especially to be a moral mixture too. Alleged ethnicities are in the end just ciphers for historical roles of attack and defence, murder and victim, extermination and survival. He wasn't really a bastard, but he *wanted* to be one, for reasons of principle. Being just a Jew was far too confining for a man like Romain Gary.

5

The Student

Aix-en-Provence and Paris, 1934–1938

By his own account in *Promise at Dawn*, Gary had dreamed of being a writer as a child largely because he seemed no good at anything else: music, painting, tennis, horse-riding, mathematics, juggling and so on were all beyond his grasp. In his teens, while at school in Nice, he allegedly thought up dozens of suitably sonorous pseudonyms with which to launch his literary career. But when he left home to study law at the University of Aix-en-Provence, writing becomes less a case of uncorroborated recollection than something we can begin to pin down.

Only one thing seems certain about Gary's student years: he did not study very hard. It's not just that he said so himself. French law left as little trace in his later literary work as did the French classics he must have studied at his lycée. None of his novels deals with the law, even obliquely; save for the phrase *le mort saisit le vif*, used in *The Dance of Genghis Cohn*,[1] legal language is similarly absent from the huge variety of conventional idioms he plundered and subverted to forge his own rich mix of styles. Gary did, eventually, get a degree in law, but it is clear that studying in general, and the law in particular, were just covers for the pursuit of another life.

Gary's mother, now in failing health, could hardly afford to support him through his years living away from home. The rent of a student room in Aix cost 60 francs a month, and Madame Kacewa's total income was not much more than 500 francs, a good part of which went to purchase the medications that kept her diabetes under control.[2] To help out, Gary did all sorts of odd jobs in the long summer holidays and also through the year. He served in cafés, washed dishes and acted as a tourist guide from his home base in Nice; in Paris, he worked as a hotel receptionist, a washer-up and tricycle delivery man.[3] But what he did most of all, alongside having innumerable adventures with girls, was to write.

Not much of what Gary wrote before 1943 has survived; just two short stories published in newspapers and the manuscript of a novel that was probably written more than once, under two different titles, *Le Vin des morts* and *La Bourgeoisie*, both of which (if they truly exist) remain unpublished and in private hands.

The two published stories, 'L'Orage' (The Storm) and 'Une Petite Femme' (A Brave Little Woman) are set far away from any places Gary knew: the jungles of Annam and an unidentified tropical French island colony. Gary's sources are entirely literary – or, rather, sub-literary, since the colonial dramas narrated are the Maughamish clichés of a vast and now mostly forgotten continent of colonial writing of the earlier part of the twentieth century. Native characters speak in *petit-nègre*, the pseudo-Creole that was then the standard literary representation of the speech of colonial subjects: *Wambo! . . . Toi porter ce casque à la cuisine!* (Pronoun, verb form and noun gender are all wrong, but do not alter the legibility of the sentence.)

'Une Petite Femme' is a spoken story, told to others by Fabiani, a no doubt Corsican NCO in the military detachment protecting the building of a railway line. The 'brave little woman' ventures out in the night and gets captured by Moi tribesmen, and her husband, the railway engineer, shoots himself in despair. The setting is reminiscent of Malraux's earlier tales; the anecdote, involving a courageous woman and a man in despair, is more an exercise in the colonial-romantic genre than a hint of Gary's later themes.

'L'Orage' is more interesting. It tells the story of a desperate love between a woman and a crumpled hero called Pêche, a name Gary reused in later works and which means – in German and in Polish, spelled *Pech* – 'bad luck'.[4] The woman makes love to a man about to condemn himself to death by drowning, and only subsequently does she learn he has leprosy (which makes sense of his name: that's really Bad Luck). At the time leprosy was believed to be contagious, incurable and fatal: so the curtain line of the tale tells us that the adulterous woman has condemned herself to death. In *Promise at Dawn* Gary tells the story of how, when stationed in Bangui during the war, he had an affair – officialised by a 'tribal marriage' – with a native girl, who spoke not a word of French, but whose eyes made speech unnecessary.[5] After a short while a suspicious spot on Louison's upper arm was diagnosed as the first symptom of leprosy and she was flown out of the Ubangi to Brazzaville, to be cared for by French doctors, and Gary never saw her again. This passage in a supposedly autobiographical work is strikingly similar to the basic anecdote of 'L'Orage' (with the gender roles reversed); the *repetition* of the leprosy motif suggests that there could be a common source for the two tales, irrespective of their different statuses as fiction and autobiography. Gary had probably read Mauriac's breakthrough novel, *Le Baiser au lépreux* (1922), but his source for his two 'leper's tales' was more likely to have been one of the legends that cluster around the figures of St Martin, St Anthony and St Francis of Assisi, who are said to have kissed lepers to demonstrate their faith in God.

Standard advice to young writers: stick to what you know. If those words of wisdom were ever told to Gary by a friend, a mentor, or a publisher's rejection letter, he took no notice of them at all, for he persisted in writing about things and places he had never seen. Advice to young mathematicians, from Tom Lehrer's famous song: Plagiarise! Gary did that all the time, borrowing terms, titles, techniques and motifs from his wide reading in European literature. However, the writer he borrowed from most seems to have been himself. But because part of Gary's work purports to be autobiographical, the recurrence of anecdotes like the 'leper's kiss' create major problems for understanding which – of life and literature – comes first.

Of the two surviving tales of the 1930s, 'La Petite Femme' shows Gary's magpie talent most clearly, since, despite its vague reminiscence of Malraux, its manner (oral narration), its setting (the jungle), and its investigation of courage and despair all come from Joseph Conrad. Gary probably first read Conrad's major works in his teens and in Polish translation. When he got to France, Conrad (strongly promoted by Gide, among others) was at the height of his fame, so it's likely Gary read him in French as well in the 1930s. It's not certain that he ever read him in English after he learned the language in the 1940s, but until the end of his days he claimed he had a 'physical need to reread Conrad',[6] and that he turned back to one or another of his novels at least once a year. The fact that they both had Polish backgrounds, wrote in adopted languages and sought to tell gripping yarns while pursuing moral arguments about the nature of man makes Gary's attachment to Conrad not just unsurprising but natural.

The unpublished, long-lost *Vin des morts* ('*The Wine of the Dead*') is the subject of many anecdotes and speculations. In *Promise at Dawn*, Gary says that he penned it furiously at a table on the terrace of the Café des Mauvais Garçons in the Cours Mirabeau, the main and splendid drag of Aix-en-Provence, and therefore in the year 1934–5. He submitted it to the publisher Denoël, who turned it down. In addition, the publisher was so disturbed by the excessive, obsessive sexuality of Gary's youthful work that he asked a psychoanalyst for a report on the author. That report – Gary clearly means us to understand that it was written by Princess Marie Bonaparte, the lady without whose assistance Freud might never have escaped from Nazi-occupied Vienna – was forwarded to Gary, who made twenty typed copies of it and distributed them to all and sundry. He was so proud to have been identified as a *case*! Marie Bonaparte's report, if it ever existed, has disappeared, but some years later Gary abandoned a manuscript entitled *Le Vin des morts* with a former girlfriend in Stockholm. This text was seen and read in the 1990s by a Swedish doctoral student working on Romain Gary, who provides a summary of it in her thesis.[7] The manuscript was eventually sold at auction and purchased by a French sexologist, Philippe Brenot. Somewhat mysteriously, two separate versions of the work were seen by Myriam Anissimov, who quotes extracts from one of them in her biography of Gary.[8] These extracts do not seem particularly related to the story summarised by Östman, which is close to a reprise of a macabre story by Dostoevsky, *Bobok*; nor do they seem to justify the diagnosis of Marie Bonaparte as retailed by Gary in *Promise at Dawn*.

Gary probably wrote a great deal more than the two short stories that were published and the half-submerged novel that may or may not have been worthy of a psychoanalytical study. In *Promise at Dawn* he recalls having sold a story to an American magazine, but that text, if it existed, has never been identified; and there are hints in his fictional work that he may have written and published stories for children, under his own name (Kacew) or any number of pseudonyms. It's unlikely these mysteries will be solved soon, or ever; but if Gary's post-war writing practice is any guide, he must have covered many thousands of sheets with his large, round and illegible hand in his years of student poverty in Paris and Aix.

Gary had no doubt decided to study law in accordance with the very common aspiration among second-generation immigrants, especially Jews, to join the professional classes, the two other canonical routes to assimilation being medicine and business. His move from the provinces to Paris also followed a well-rehearsed script, not just for immigrants, but for ambitious young Frenchmen of all kinds since the days of Balzac. Up to this point, his path resembles that of many thousands of others from his own and other backgrounds. And like any Frenchman – now he was legally French – he would have to submit to the great national bonding experience of military service, which was compulsory for all males over the age of eighteen.

Compulsory military service had been reduced to a twelve-month obligation in 1928 and young men were allowed to defer it until their studies were complete. Gary had only become liable for service at the age of twenty-one, in 1935, since prior to then he was not a French national, and for the following three years his enrolment as a law student kept him free. But once he actually passed his exams in summer 1938, he could defer no longer. He had no choice but to respond to his call-up papers for the 'class of 1939', with induction and initial training to take place in the last weeks of 1938. (Conscription was organised by calendar year.)

In a long conversation about his life and work broadcast on French radio in 1969, Gary explained that he enlisted to avoid being called up. Enlistment would have made sense for a young man in Gary's position.[9] A three-year commitment – against the twelve months required of conscripts – was not an excessive price to pay for the choice of wing, a higher chance of rising in rank, and the better pay and conditions available to enlisted men. Gary doesn't mention enlistment in the story of his life as told in *Promise at Dawn* and nothing in the official record suggests that he really did volunteer. However, he seems to have had a military career in mind even while he was a law student. In his second year at the Sorbonne he joined the French equivalent of the Officer Training Corps and gave two afternoons every week to military preparation classes. The cadet certificate he gained in October 1937 would make him a trainee reserve officer once he got called up and give him a chance of becoming an air force pilot.

As a young man, Gary had innumerable sexual liaisons, but one of them seems to have been a truly fundamental affair of the heart. In June 1938, when Gary returned to his mother's hotel in Nice to fill in the six months before his call-up date, he met a grey-eyed Hungarian beauty, Gesmay Ilona (to put the name in its authentic Magyar form), and he plunged forthwith into a passionate physical relationship with this daughter of a wealthy Jewish family from Budapest. For propriety's sake Ilona moved to another nearby hotel, where Gary and she spent their nights in amorous embrace. But Ilona meant much more than a good lay. Aged twenty-four, Gary was set on marrying his elegant, mysterious Hungarian queen.

Ilona Gesmay had spent all her life since finishing school in idle wanderings around Western Europe: her handsome monthly allowance meant she never even contemplated any kind of work. In 1938, worried by his daughter's dissipation, Ilona's father reduced her allowance, hoping to jolt her into a more focused life. She coped with the cut in funds by staying at the cheaper kind of *pension* that Madame Kacewa ran – but even so, she took a taxi all the way to Cannes when there was a concert to attend.[10]

Her affair with Romain Kacew lasted through the summer and autumn of 1938. In November, the young man left for induction at Salon-de-Provence, then air training at Avord, and a few weeks later Ilona left Nice too. Her destination was a clinic at Locarno, in Switzerland, but she wasn't suffering from a physical ailment. According to her sister, interviewed half a century later by Anissimov, Ilona was a severe hypochondriac and once suffered hysterical appendicitis. Even during her affair with Romain Kacew she would cut herself off for days at a time, doing embroidery or pencilling sketches and doodles in her room, on the grounds of being unwell. Retrospectively, this can be seen as a sign that she was already beginning to go mad, but Gary, in his overwhelming passion, didn't grasp what kind of a person Ilona was at all.

She returned from Switzerland to Budapest just as World War Two broke out and Gary did not hear from her again. He always claimed in later life, on the rare occasions when the matter came up, that he never got over the disappearance of the only woman he had really wanted to stay with for the rest of his life. His first mention of the affair, at the end of chapter 29 of *Promise at Dawn*, is clumsy to a degree that seems to confirm the gravity of the heartbreak he had suffered:

> I must here mention an episode which I have deliberately omitted until now, thus trying to hide from it. Some months before the outbreak of war, I had fallen in love with a young Hungarian girl who was staying at the Hôtel-Pension Mermonts. We planned to get married. Ilona had black hair and large grey eyes, just to say something about her. She went back to Budapest to see her family, the war separated us and I never saw her again; it was another defeat for me and that is all there is to it. I know that I have broken all the rules by skipping such an episode in an autobiography, but it is still too recent, only twenty years have passed, and to write even these few lines I have had to take advantage of an inflammation of the ear which has confined me to bed in a Mexican hotel: this acute but physical pain has acted, in a way, as an anaesthetic, and made it possible for me to touch a much more painful wound.[11]

The 'earache' corresponds to one of Lesley Blanch's more comical recollections in her 1996 memoir of life with the now unbearable Romain Gary. Irritated by the noise of Mexico and fearing he would not be able to sleep, Gary hunted for earplugs, but found none in the village where they were staying. So he soaked bits of bread from his dinner roll in *pulque* and rolled them into self-made aural stoppers. Within a few hours an agonising headache set in – a brain tumour, he was sure, leaving him only hours to live. A long, bumpy taxi ride all the way to Mexico City – between his groans, he dictated a new version of his last will and testament to his wife – brought him to a doctor who, incredulously, tweezered rotting dough out of the diplomat's ear.[12]

Gary assumed that Ilona had disappeared in Eichmann's round-up of half a million Hungarian Jews, or else when Budapest was taken by the Red Army. The muted memorial paragraph of *Promise at Dawn* seems to close the buried chapter of his life that it opens little more than halfway. But life is weirder than fiction. Gary had no idea that Ilona had converted to Catholicism in wartime Hungary, had survived the Holocaust and even the purge of the Hungarian middle class, which followed the liberation of Budapest. In 1945 the Red Cross reunited Ilona with her parents, who had managed to smuggle themselves out of Hungary to Belgium during the war. By then, however, Gary's first love was perceptibly deranged. Her father had her looked after at a private clinic in Switzerland to begin with, then had her interned in a psychiatric hospital run by nuns near Antwerp, where she spent the rest of her long and lonely life. When Gary wrote his brief paragraph in *Promise at Dawn* in Mexico in 1958, it did not occur to him that Ilona might still be alive or that she had long been out of her mind.

In 1963 the American edition of *Promise at Dawn* fell into the hands of Ilona's sister Eva, who had emigrated to the USA. As Gary had used Ilona's name without alteration, she recognised her sister in the paragraph quoted above. She and her other sister Klara, who now lived in Haifa, knew that Ilona had had an affair with a young Frenchman on the Riviera in 1938 and, given the details provided by *Promise at Dawn*, realised that the lover could only have been Romain Gary. Eva and Klara asked a distant relative in Paris to get in touch with the writer, who learned in this roundabout way what had happened to his old flame. Around the same time Klara visited Ilona in Belgium and gave her a copy of *Promise at Dawn*. Gary received a letter from Ilona a few days later. All it said was that she had read the book and would like Gary to write to her; she was living in a convent and had taken her vows. A few days later an identical letter dropped into Gary's mailbox. Then a third, then a fourth . . . Gary was puzzled and asked the French Consul in Antwerp to do some research for him. The colleague reported that the alleged convent was in fact a psychiatric establishment. Ilona Gesmay was considered incurable and the authorities had not allowed her to read Gary's replies. He was kindly asked to stop writing and to stay away.

In *A Quiet Night*, where he retells the story of the affair and of his discovery of Ilona's survival and madness, Gary writes that on learning the truth about the love of his life he flew to Belgium to see Ilona once again, but on arrival in Antwerp, couldn't face it and turned on his heel. In conversations with Anissimov, who was befriended by Romain Gary in 1977–8, he said that on arrival in Antwerp he had gone ahead and seen Ilona in her hospital room. She hadn't recognised him at all. Neither of these stories fit logically with the long later correspondence with Klara from which Anissimov quotes, but even if false, they underscore the importance that Gary attached to his first great love for an incipient schizophrenic. Ilona Gesmay died in 1999.

All that can ever be known about Gary's feelings for Ilona Gesmay comes from the writer's own retrospective accounts, dating from 1958 and 1974. Lesley Blanch's recollection of Gary's undiminished attachment to Ilona in 1945, revealed in a book first published in 1996, was composed long after the revelations of *A Quiet Night*, to which it may well be indebted. However, at the time of the actual events young Kacew seems to have rebounded with characteristic energy and spring. Once Ilona had gone from Nice without leaving so much as a forwarding address, he threw himself into an epistolary re-seduction of his previous mistress, Kristel Söderlund, now happily married to someone else.

Kristel is an essential link in the story of Romain Gary. Gary picked her up at the pool in Nice in July 1937 and, after a few days' torrid lovemaking by the sea, they travelled back to Paris together, where Kristel scraped a living as a freelance journalist. A stunning blonde, Kristel had separated from her husband and left her child in the hands of her own parents in Sweden. Her French wasn't too good, so Gary and she communicated mostly in German. Kristel introduced Gary and his crowd (all friends from the Lycée de Nice, now up in Paris) to her own Scandinavian acquaintances in the capital. The most striking of these was Silvia, an Olympic long-jump silver medallist and a gifted artist and designer. She fell in love with René Agid, gave up her Swedish career, got married and settled down in France. Romain never even tried to seduce Silvia, who remained for the following forty-three years the one woman in whom he could confide his most intimate fears and dreams. She became very fond of her husband's old school chum and viewed him with a mixture of amusement, disbelief and concern, expressed over many years in her own journals and in correspondence with her long-standing Swedish friend, Kristel. These documents provide a precious source of information about Gary's life undistorted by the media, by Gary's affabulations, or by the kind of lingering resentment that makes Blanch's memoir and her later conversation with Anissimov something less than the gospel truth.

Kristel never had the slightest intention of marrying Romain Gary (she already had a husband, anyway), but Gary insisted they were *special* friends. More like comrades than lovers, both of them were devoted to learning how to be a *man*, Gary wrote. He seems to have considered her what an Englishman might call an honorary bloke. In the spring of 1938 Kristel left France to cover the *Anschluss* in Austria. Her reporting there was so well received that she was made a staff reporter and returned to Stockholm. She went back to her husband and child, and settled down to family and professional life. Gary started his affair with Ilona a couple of months after he'd said farewell to Kristel and resumed his correspondence with his Swedish beauty as soon as Ilona had left the scene. Even during his Hungarian affair he'd declared he was determined to travel to Sweden to reclaim Kristel for himself, but he couldn't make it in December 1938 as planned because of his military obligations. However, in summer 1939, with $150 he'd been paid for a story (as yet unidentified) that an American magazine bought from him and two weeks' home leave from the Air Force, he purchased a return ticket and travelled through Nazi Germany to be met in Stockholm by the parents of another one of his classmates from his lycée in Nice, Sigurd Norberg. They warned him that Kristel wanted him to stay away. Undaunted, the swashbuckling hero took the ferry to the island in the archipelago where Kristel was staying for the summer. The girl's mother and sisters met him on the landing stage and politely, but very firmly, told him to go away.

In a superficially self-mocking but fairly biting passage in chapter 25 of *Promise at Dawn*, Gary alleges that Kristel ('Brigitte') is the only woman ever to have deceived him with someone else. The irony hides the hurt, but the comic tone is altogether different from the flat and pained account of his love for Ilona. The fact that Gary set off to reclaim 'Brigitte' *after* Ilona had disappeared, not prior to the whole Hungarian affair, is of course masked by incorrect (and incoherent) dates.

Anissimov's sources suggest that Ilona Gesmay had no more intention of marrying Romain Gary than Kristel did. With the exception of his strange marriage to Lesley Blanch, however, these are the only two really strong attachments Gary is known to have had before he set eyes on Jean Seberg, who was, like Kristel, of Swedish stock and, like Ilona, on her way to going mad.

6

The Hero

Military Service, 1938–1945

Whatever the power of Madame Kacewa's dreams for her son, Gary's life could not have been what it was without two strokes of luck. The first great gift was France. Had Mina not managed to cut her way through the bureaucratic and financial obstacles to immigration, Romain would have remained Kacew and lived as a Pole. Or rather, died as a Jew. There were very few thirty-year-old males of Jewish extraction left anywhere in Poland and none at all in Lithuania in 1945.

The second great gift was the Second World War. *Ma saison a été la France Libre* (My season was Free France), he said to his interviewer, Jacques Chancel, in 1978. Even with the good looks and the boundless energy that nature gave him, even with the languages he mastered easily and the vivid imagination and storytelling gifts that he cultivated, Gary was unlikely to have got very far in life without the Second World War. He might not even have become a published writer and it's hard to see how he could ever have become a diplomat. His uncle Eliasz had allegedly scribbled fifty plays and never seen one performed.[1] Had it not been for his vanity, Gary wrote in a letter to Claude Gallimard after the war, had he not been enslaved by his taste for exploits, 'I would have done none of the things I have done in my life and would now be a *hôtelier* on the Riviera'.[2] It would be just as true to say that what

Gary did manage to do could not have happened without the Second World War. It must have been painful to know and never to forget that you owe the best part of your *vita* to the greatest disaster in world history to date.

Romain Gary, who at that time bore his birth name Roman Kacew – pronounced (and occasionally written) as Kassef[3] – spent seven years in the French Air Force, clocking up a total of 769 hours of flight, sixty-five of which were spent on active duty in twenty-six separate combat missions.[4] While his literary work after 1945 may not be autobiographical in any straightforward way – 'my work is wholly grounded in the imagination,' he insisted[5] – the war, even if it never appears as the explicit subject in any one of his novels, is the matrix from which the man and the writer called Romain Gary emerged.

Flying in those days was a glamorous pursuit. Mermoz and Lindbergh were heroes of the modern age, fêted wherever they went. In France, flying had also acquired literary prestige, with Joseph Kessel's *L'Équipage* (1923) and Saint-Exupéry's two classic narratives of the flier's life, *Courrier Sud* (1929) and *Vol de nuit* (1931). Flying aeroplanes had replaced the lure of the sea of an earlier, Conradian age, and was every boy's dream. Needless to say, most of those who qualified in the end were daring and above all well-born young men.

Gary was daring, but he'd been born on the wrong side of history's tracks. He had no idea what he could do to make a success of his life once he'd finished his law degree. Without connections or money, he had no easy prospects and, looking back on that period, he confessed that he'd gone into the forces out of despair. He'd even thought of joining the Foreign Legion[6] – but once his naturalisation papers came through, he could no longer do that. But how French was he? The mere mention of the Foreign Legion suggests that he hadn't got used to the fact that he'd become French.[7] As he would soon discover, he was not alone in that.

The terrible slaughter of the First World War made France

in the 1930s wary of military adventures. It maintained a large standing army, which was by no means badly equipped. But the nation had no intention of using it in Europe. On the contrary: war with Germany was to be avoided at all costs. Few men of Gary's generation, and even fewer among its aspiring writers and artists, dreamed of going off to fight. Young Kacew was a different kind of man. 'There's only one thing, a single thing that I wish for with all my fervour, rage and civilized heart: to die at long last in a *just war*!'[8]

The phrase is from a patriotic poem by Charles Péguy,[9] but Gary's use of it in this letter was prompted not by literature but by a humiliation in real life, made all the more painful by what it meant about France. Gary joined his regiment at Salon-de-Provence on 4 November 1938 and, after an unusual, perhaps suspicious, delay was transferred on 7 December to the Air Officers' training camp at Avord, near Bourges, in central France. He wasn't selected to train as a pilot, but went through the intensive four-month course as a trainee observer. (In military aircraft of the time, there were three positions: pilot, gunner and observer. There was never more than one pilot in a plane, but some models required two gunners, or two observers. As a result, most of the men in the class that Gary joined at Avord did not become pilots either.) He flew hundreds of hours in now forgotten makes of flying machines and learned to use a parachute. As far as can be told, he was a perfectly decent trainee, got no black marks for misconduct, coped with the physical and technical demands of the job. He expected to pass. Everyone did – for despite the mood of appeasement in the land, the government knew it needed to prepare for war and had asked the Air Force to train up a much larger cohort of flying crew than it currently had. And everyone did pass the test – except Romain Kassef. He was flabbergasted. Cast down. In despair.

Had he done anything wrong? He was not told until a comrade came to see him in his hut to deliver an informal explanation from above. He had been turned down because he was 'too recently naturalised'. In the context, the explanation was a way of saying: because he was a Jew. The story, told by Gary himself in *Promise at Dawn*, is entirely plausible, though not even Anissimov has found any independent corroboration for it. Gary should have known that a man of his background was most unlikely to make it. But he was never attracted to easy options. He wanted to prove his worth by an *unlikely* exploit. This time he failed.

However, the Air Force could not get rid of a conscript and a conscript, however embittered, could not get out of the service until his time was up. Gary thus became a gunnery instructor, with the rank of *sergent*, or NCO, and trained others to do what he had learned how to do.

Gary's first and most serious injury occurred on a training flight. The pilot miscalculated his descent and hit the runway too hard. Gary's nose was badly broken and had to be rebuilt. He wasn't exactly disfigured – he would always retain striking good looks – but his face no longer had the perfect symmetry of his youth.

Throughout the 1930s Germany's aggressive expansion brought the threat of war ever closer even as Britain and France tried to look the other way. In August 1939, to the astonishment and dismay of many sympathisers in the West, Soviet Russia did a deal with Hitler. The Non-Aggression Pact, signed by foreign ministers Molotov and Ribbentrop, allocated the larger part of Poland to Germany and its eastern fringes to the Soviet Union. Under the treaties that had drawn the new map of Europe and set up the League of Nations in 1918–22, Britain and France were guarantors of the territorial integrity of the Polish State. When Hitler's troops marched into Poland on 1 September 1939, knowing that the Red Amy would not respond, Britain and France had no choice but to declare war. Poland did not exactly cause the war against Germany, which in retrospect was almost inevitable: but the legal *casus belli* of the outbreak of the Second World War was Poland's sad fate.

The Polish Army was quickly defeated by the Wehrmacht's aircraft and columns of tanks. Quite large numbers of Polish soldiers and airmen found their way out of the country, some to the Soviet Union, others to the neighbouring and still nominally independent Baltic States, and from there to Britain and France. In addition, substantial contingents of Polish military had been stationed in France in anticipation of the war; and numerous Polish civilians resident in France joined up. All of a sudden Gary turned out to be very useful to the French Air Force. His unit was pulled back to Bordeaux on the declaration of war and one of its tasks was to train Polish crew to fly the types of warplane that France used. *Sergent* Kacew thus spent the months of the 'phoney war', from October 1939 to May 1940, as an interpreter, on the ground and in the air, for French instructors and Polish flying crew.

On the declaration of war, Gary's service, which would normally have ended in late 1939, was automatically extended 'for the duration of the hostilities', as it was for all active servicemen. For eight months, from September 1939 to May 1940, there was no action on the Western front. Then came the débâcle. Germany invaded and overran French defences in a few weeks. Parliament left Paris and ended up in Bordeaux, on its way to Algiers. At the airfield, Mérignac, the chaos was indescribable. Planes, some damaged, some stuffed with officers' families and piles of luggage, landed day and night. All semblance of order disappeared. Like several others, Gary thought it was time to get out. His idea was to go to England, but flying crew were expressly forbidden to leave. Fuel supplies were closely guarded.

News of the armistice to be signed by Pétain, who had been granted full powers to negotiate surrender, reached Bordeaux in mid-June. A few daredevils deserted in what were now stolen planes, but most refused to disobey the order to stay put. Gary was lucky. He found a ride in a plane that was going to risk an illegal dash to England. He was already on the tarmac when an orderly came to tell him his mother was on the telephone and Gary ran back to base to hear Mina's voice. When he'd finished listening to her the plane had already taken off. It was in the air for barely a few seconds before coming down. The plane Gary missed burst into flames and left none of its occupants alive.

The next day – it may have been 15 or 16 June – Gary hitched another lift with a pair of hotheads who had deviously managed to get permission to take off and they set out over the Mediterranean, with not enough fuel to make land on the other side. But the wind was with them and they touched down with empty tanks at Algiers. Then they pushed on to Fez, in Morocco, and finally Casablanca. By this time, however, a new French government had taken over: in Morocco, a French protectorate, Gary became a deserter and a wanted man. He went to a brothel and kept at it all night, so he says, and was protected from the police by an admiring madam.

France had signed an armistice, but Poland had not. Polish troops stationed in Morocco were being allowed to leave and Britain was glad to take them in. What Gary and his comrades needed was Polish cover to effect their escape. Because he could speak Polish, he quickly found what he was looking for in the street – a Polish soldier who agreed to smuggle him and his colleagues Jean Forsans and Maurice Daligot on to a troop ship evacuating Poles to Gibraltar. (Raymond Aron, who had similarly reached North Africa in June 1940, also owed his escape to a borrowed Polish army greatcoat.) At Gibraltar Gary, Forsans and another handful of French rebels switched to the *Oakcrest*, which was evacuating Polish Air Force and Army units to Britain. He landed at Greenock on 22 July. He knew not a word of English and had not yet even heard of Charles de Gaulle. Gary owed it to his Polish inheritance to have found the means of joining Free France.

Gary did not escape in response to de Gaulle's famous broadcast of 18 June 1940. By 18 June 1940, in any case, Gary's mind was made up and his flight to England had already begun. Two things at least had made escape the only possible aim. First, France under German tutelage was not likely to be a good place to be a Jew. Gary had perhaps more foresight than many: he had crossed Nazi Germany by train, on a summer trip to see a girlfriend in Stockholm and had seen, if only briefly, what a Nazi society looked like. (The story Gary tells of hitting an anti-Semite over the head with a beer bottle and spending five days in a Düsseldorf jail on the return trip from Sweden is almost certainly one of the writer's illustrative fabulations.[10]) Secondly, escape to Britain was not just running away from danger to his own person. France, which had been perhaps more powerful as an idea than a reality in steering the course of his life, was in danger of disappearing from the face of the earth. France under Hitler's control could not be France – not just for Jewish immigrants, but in terms of the ideals of liberty, justice and honour that were intrinsic to the meaning of its name. He had no choice but to throw in his lot with those few foolhardy individuals who were prepared to give up their lives so France might survive. Paradoxically, but not incomprehensibly, his patriotism was more visceral and more necessary than it was for any trueborn Frenchman. You could almost say that Gary invented Free France.

Gary's season of war was horrible. He suffered great heat in flyblown camps in the African bush. He was chilled to the bone in miserably damp Nissen huts in the south of England. He caught serious diseases and was badly injured as well, losing muscular control over one side of his lower face. He spent hundreds of hours confined in tiny pods, beset by the thunderous roar of engines and assailed by the pungent odour of kerosene. There was also a lot of waiting around in dismal camps, in mess rooms and barracks dotted all over the place – Chad, Syria, Egypt, Surrey . . . All the while, he was officially a deserter from the nation he most ardently wished to preserve and not even French any more: the Vichy government revoked his naturalisation, as it did for all Jews who had benefited from the laws of 1927. But war was also a boon beyond any that could have been invented. It made things simple. There was no question where duty lay. The path ran unswervingly ahead.

A Boston bomber of the Lorraine Squadron

The Lorraine Squadron, and the broader community of the Free French, gave Gary his first experience of full, unquestioned membership of a clan. There he learned the meaning of comradeship, fraternity and the brotherhood of man.

> Any son-of-a-bitch like myself who has been bombing and killing left and right for many years will tell you that if it's brotherhood you want, you will find it in combat units. There were no French, Arabs, Jews or blacks in the Foreign Legion shock troops or in my 'Lorraine' squadron. There were only brothers who killed and got killed.[11]

It was an experience never to be repeated, and it tied Gary to that long season of his life with bonds of emotion and loyalty that he could never break, not even by antiphrasis or self-hating wit. Because it was the first community that allowed him to belong to it without reservation, misgiving or regret, he went on belonging to that small band and proclaimed his fidelity to the ideals as well as to the man who had guided the Free French, even (or perhaps especially) when it became unfashionable to do so. In 1970 he attended de Gaulle's funeral at Colombey-les-deux-Églises wearing his old air force great-coat, which he could barely button up properly any more. It clashed garishly with the bohemian beard and long hair he wore at the time, and most people who saw him in the procession, walking alongside other *Compagnons de la Libération* in more sober funeral attire, thought he looked like a clown.

Gary had a good war. People used to say that in the 1950s about still quite young men who'd survived weeks, months or (in very rare cases) several years flying for the RAF. But the fact is that most of those who'd been on half as many sorties as Romain Gary ended up dead. He often mentioned in his interviews and books that out of the initial complement of his unit, RAF 324 Squadron, known as 'Lorraine', only five were still alive at the end of the war. It troubled him for the rest of his life. On one of the loose sheets of paper stuffed into the manuscript of an unpublished, unfinished work, probably penned in the 1970s, there's a long list of names, with notes about how and where they died. The nightmare of a 'good war' never ends.

In June 1940 the path ahead may have looked straight, but it could hardly have been expected to be smooth. The handful of air crew who made it to England were an undisciplined bunch by definition – men prepared to take risks and to live by their own lights, motivated not only by a love of France, but by the taste for a fight. Not all of them lost their lives from enemy action. They flew with abandon in rickety craft, pushed them around in the sky as if they were showing off at a circus act, and hedge-hopped the African bush just to scare the elephants. In one outbreak of horseplay, they dropped practice bombs on the governor's residence in Bangui. Romain Kassef was never fully in charge of any of these planes, as he didn't have a pilot's licence, but with his passionate temper and pronounced liking for japes, he might have wrought even worse havoc. Many of these unreliable toys came down in Africa, the Middle East and over the Channel coast as a result of navigational mistakes, risky manoeuvres and stupid bravado. Others were so hastily patched up that their engines stopped in mid-air. Flying for the Free French was a rough game in itself. In addition, the Luftwaffe was trying to shoot it down.

When Gary got to London in late July 1940, he obeyed the call to all French volunteers to assemble at Olympia, then attended the rally at the Albert Hall to launch the armed forces of Free France. The crowd was disappointingly small: there were no more than two hundred men who had any flying skills. Gary did not hesitate. He threw in his lot with the strange new leader of Free France, signed the oath of allegiance and stuck to it for the rest of his days.

French fliers were initially allocated to units of the RAF, and Gary flew two bombing raids over Germany in July and September 1940 with TOE5 Bomber Squadron. Strictly speaking, that was not part of the Battle of Britain, which was fought by fighters (Spitfires and Hurricanes) over the Home Counties and in full view of large crowds.

Initially de Gaulle was in no position to prevent French fliers from serving in RAF units, but he quickly managed to negotiate a separate status for the men who had sworn allegiance to him and thus did the Free French Air Force – *Les Forces Aériennes de la France Libre*, or FAFL for short – come into a very approximate existence. Gary was part of it from inception and was instantly promoted to the officer class, with the rank of *adjudant*, or warrant officer. It was a first step towards burying the humiliation he had suffered at Avord.

Metropolitan France was lost, but the French Empire

included vast swathes of western and central Africa, the whole of Indochina and significant parts of the Middle East. Apart from the straggle of escapees like Gary, de Gaulle's first and most solid support came from the governors of some of the larger colonies, notably Félix Éboué. So the first thing de Gaulle did with his tiny and ill-equipped air force was to ship it out to Africa, to protect the airspace over the huge but mostly empty expanse of Free France. In Africa, FAFL made little real contribution to the war, because the war never got to that part of Africa in any case. Its role was largely symbolic. If the wild pranks of its pilots hadn't destroyed so many aircraft in practice runs, it might have been more useful at a later stage.

It was while he was in Central Africa in the first half of 1941 that Gary learned that his mother had died. There is no record of his reaction to the news. Later on, he would wrap the event, its timing and its significance for him, in a complicated package of fabrications and fantasies that constitute one of most memorable chapters of *Promise at Dawn*.

In Africa, after months of messing around, Gary's unit was assigned to conveying new aircraft arriving by sea to the theatre of operations in Sudan, where Allied forces were pushing Mussolini out of his short-lived Ethiopian empire. It was then transferred to Egypt at the time of the great desert battles between Rommel and Montgomery. Gary caught typhoid and spent many weeks dangerously ill. Next stop was Rayak airbase in Syria, whence he flew missions over the Mediterranean, looking for Italian submarines. He found one, but missed, as he'd forgotten to undo the safety lock before pulling the lever to open the bomb hatch.

Over this period, from late 1940 to the autumn of 1942, the airborne forces of the Free French grew in size and underwent several reorganisations. When the German advance was halted at Stalingrad and the United States finally entered the war, the decision was made to bring more Allied forces back to Britain in preparation for the onslaught on the continent of Europe that would have to come one day. Gary's unit, now formally called 'Lorraine Squadron', was thus repatriated to Britain the long way round, on a ship mostly full of Italian PoWs, through the Suez Canal and round the Cape of Good Hope. By early 1943 they were on airbases in Britain, re-equipped with Boston bombers and under training for new kinds of missions.[12]

The Airman. London, 1943

Thus began the most heroic epoch of Gary's life. For more than twelve months, from Hartford Bridge airfield (near Camberley, in Surrey: it's now Blackbushe Airport), he flew low-altitude sorties over the Channel ports, further inland in France, over Belgium and Holland, dropping high explosive on docks, railways, factories, electricity stations and steelworks. In between missions he wrote, or else went up to London and mingled with a cosmopolitan crowd in bars and clubs associated with the Free French. With his dashing good looks, his stature (Gary was relatively tall, around 1 metre 80 centimetres, just over 5 foot 10 inches), his smart uniform and his *nom de guerre*, he was irresistible. In wartime London, a Free French airman was just about the most romantic thing you could be. Gary had yet another asset: his slight Russian accent, which gave away the fact that underneath his polished French exterior he was really a Slav. After Paulus surrendered to the Red Army at Stalingrad on 9 February 1943, the tide of the war began to turn and a wave of Russophilia swept over the English and the French. London was also awash with Polish soldiers and airmen, known for their almost suicidal courage. In spring 1943 Gary therefore found himself in a most extraordinary position. All of a sudden he had no need to put his allegiance to France before his Russian roots, his Polish education or his Jewish background, because his multiple identities brought together almost the entire alliance against the Axis powers. He was fighting on the right side and the right side just turned out to be everything he was. He was indubitably French. He was Russian too. Part of his heart still lay with Poland. All his many layers had for once come together, all were engaged in the same fight, side by side, and made him absolutely the man of the moment, whole and entire in a way no other historical circumstance would ever provide.

The price of glory in 1943–4 was constant danger and disheartening crime. How many Frenchmen died in the conflagrations he caused? How many children? Gary would never cease to reflect on what he had done, even if he made minor alterations to the record as he did so: 'The bombs I dropped on Germany from 1940 to 1944 may have killed little Rilkes, Goethes and Hölderlins in their cradles! And of course, if it had to be done again, I would do it again.'[13]

And how long could he last? Every day another of the planes leaving Hartford Bridge failed to return. On 1 November 1943 the Gaullist London daily, *France*, published the following news item:

> LORRAINE SQUADRON
>
> The crew of a bomber belonging to the Lorraine Squadron has just given a fine example of the team spirit of our airmen during a recent daylight mission.
>
> Shortly after having crossed the coast of the continent, their aircraft, a Boston, was hit by anti-aircraft fire. The pilot was seriously injured and the aircraft was badly damaged. The pilot was thus obliged to turn back towards England. The radio operator, seeing the pilot slowly pass out, leaned over him so as to handle the controls. The gunner in the compartment below the fuselage had run out of ammunition so he took control of the cockpit armaments. To do that he had to literally sit on the radio operator's back. In that uncomfortable position he managed to fight off a Messerschmitt 109. The radio operator flew the plane for 45 minutes with no visibility, relying solely on instructions from the observer. In that manner he succeeded in bringing the aircraft safely back to a base in southwest England. The crew could have baled out once they reached the English coast but refused to do so as that would have meant abandoning the injured pilot.

A few weeks later something very similar happened to the plane Romain Gary was flying in. The mission of 25 January 1944 was to destroy German V2 launch sites being built near

Saint-Omer. On the point of commencing the bombing run, Gary's aircraft, with Arnaud Langer in the pilot's seat, was hit by anti-aircraft fire. Gary was wounded, but conscious; the pilot's face was a pulp of torn flesh and shattered plexiglass. Fragments of the windscreen had got into his eyes and he could not see. As the plane limped back towards the English coast, Gary kept Langer on course by reading out the altimeter and compass points for him. With the help of the Hartford Bridge control tower, after several approaches that had to be aborted, Langer, relying entirely on Gary's eyes and words, brought the Boston safely down on to the tarmac. Gary had shrapnel in his gut, heavy bruising all over and had lost a lot of blood.

That should have been Gary's last flight on a warplane, but after convalescence he flew two more sorties, including a bombing run on Ijmuiden, in Holland.[14] He was a brave man.

After the war Gary flew as often as he could, and much of his globetrotting, jet-setting life in the 1960s and 1970s came from the fact that an aeroplane ride made him feel safe. He never suffered from insomnia when the hum or the roar of engines was near. Air pockets and turbulence were like a rocking cradle. Taking the next Caravelle to Los Angeles or tripping off on a DC-6 to Tahiti was a relief from the cares of his life. What he found so comforting was that nobody was trying to shoot him down.

The Hero. London, 1945

7

The Novelist

A European Education, 1943–1945

Poland's national epic, *Pan Tadeusz* by Adam Mickiewicz, begins with an invocation that surprised even Czesław Miłosz when he was young: 'O Lithuania!' Almost as curious is the location of Gary's first published novel, which tells the story of Polish resistance to the Nazi Occupation of Wilno. The origins and development of Gary's fable of the Maquis, which launched his career in France and won him his first literary prize, can only be explained by the history of this small part of Eastern Europe to which he remained deeply attached until all hope of return was lost in 1945.

Gary wrote his first full-length novel, a narrative of the partisan struggle in eastern Poland, over a nine-month period in 1943, when he was stationed at Hartford Bridge airbase. Of the many remarkable features of this harrowing book, which formed the first substantial achievement of the literary career to which Gary aspired, the least credible is the fact that he managed to write it. He was on active service in a fighting unit at the height of the war. It is true that flying crew, the elite of the Allies' military force, were treated as the heroes that they truly were and given relatively generous leave. All the same, Gary had to use his night hours to write (the Lorraine Squadron flew Bostons, which were not equipped for night flying). Completing the book, Gary later said, was his greatest wartime exploit. 'I do NOT understand how I managed to do what I did . . . It's quite beyond me.' He forced himself to wake up in the middle of the night, then put on his clothes and got back into his cot, propped himself up with pillows and wrote on his lap. In the small hours he took a bicycle and pedalled over to the quartermaster's hut and typed up, with two gloved fingers, what he had just invented, and was ready for reveille and the day's bombing mission at first light. Gary did not like the cold and he did not like missing his sleep, but for *A European Education* he made every exception to his normal routine, as if in a protracted energised trance.[1]

The first draft in French of what is now called *A European Education* was entitled *La Forêt engloutie* ('The Drowned Forest'), and it was first published in English translation as *Forest of Anger* before being substantially rewritten and brought out in French as *Éducation européenne*. It is a war novel – but as a story of partisans fighting the Germans in a Polish forest, it is not about the war Gary fought in the air, not at all, not even indirectly. Gary seems to have invented every bit of it. At the time, there was precious little information available about how guerrilla operations were proceeding in a part of the world that was completely cut off from the West.[2] The achievement is so bizarre that once the book was out, and applauded, and read around the world, rumours circulated – in Poland especially – that it had not been written by Gary at all, but by a Polish refugee who had died in action in one of the Polish squadrons attached to the RAF. 'Gary' was just the name of a crook who'd stolen the manuscript and passed it off as his own work in French.[3]

Hartford Bridge was the main base for RAF 324 Lorraine Squadron but it also accommodated, for weeks or months, many other Allied air units, which were rotated around the country by Strategic Air Command. Canadian and US units were frequent visitors, and at other times Gary encountered the planes of RAF 322 Squadron, which was entirely Dutch.

But the Allied forces he encountered most often were Poles. RAF 305 Squadron was 'Ziemia Wielkopolska' ('The Land of Greater Poland'), flying Wellingtons and Mitchells; RAF 317 Fighter Squadron was called 'City of Wilno', and it flew the Spitfires that escorted the slow and heavy low-level Boston bombers of units like Lorraine. 'I often saw Polish-crewed fighters escorting my bomber,' Gary recalled in the very last interview that he gave.[4] What Gary did not mention in that warm recollection of his Polish roots is that the friendly fighters flying alongside had the emblem of the Polish Air Force painted on the fuselage. Under the national flag were the words MILOSC ZADA OFIARY (Love demands sacrifice) and above it, the date and place of the incorporation of the force: WILNO 1940.

The flag of the Free Polish Air Force, 1943

Seeing the name of his home town painted with pride on the side of a fighter plane dipping its wings must have shot a strange, strong emotion into the heart of the navigator who'd now been promoted to the rank of *lieutenant* (Flying Officer, in British terms). Wilno was where he'd been born, where he'd grown up and been to school. But by 1943 it had become something else as well. Its name was now the symbol of the Polish nation.

Wilno had been part of Poland only since 1922 and its inscription on Polish-crewed Spitfires and Mitchells arose from an obscure twist in the history of the war. The Non-Aggression Pact of 1939 had allowed the Soviet Union to take a large swathe of eastern Poland under control, but a secret appendix to it acknowledged the interest of Lithuania in Wilno and its surrounding area. Russia moved its troops into eastern Poland in September 1939, but in October it ceded Wilno to the still extant Republic of Lithuania. Units of the Polish Air Force that had escaped destruction thus hopped over the border into neutral Lithuania and in Wilno, in the early days of 1940, reconstituted themselves as the air wing of the Home Army, the underground organisation formed by demobilised Polish soldiers inside the land. The situation of Lithuania itself was of course desperate. President Smetona made his last appeal for help from the West on 15 June 1940. For political reasons he could use neither German nor Russian for his broadcast, and as he wanted to be understood in the West, Lithuanian was out of the question. So he used Latin – almost certainly the very last use of Latin as an international language in European history. But neither France nor Britain could do anything then, and never did do anything to defend the Baltic States. On 3 August 1940 Lithuania was absorbed by the Soviet Union, which was still, at that time, a 'neutral' country. Germany broke the Non-Aggression Pact in June 1941 with Operation Barbarossa, which quickly laid waste the entire Baltic region and took Hitler's army to the gates of Leningrad.

In the meantime a trickle of Polish airmen had made their way to Britain, from Wilno, from the Soviet Union and from occupied France, and had joined the RAF, which allowed them, as it allowed the Free French, to constitute their own national squadrons. Like the Home Army and the Polish government in exile in London, most Free Poles in the United Kingdom sought the resurrection not just of a Polish State, but of 'Greater Poland', incorporating all the historic territories where Polish was spoken. The most easterly of these was Wilno, and its very extremity made it the symbol-city of *Ziemia Wielkopolska* (the land of Greater Poland). Gary's choice of the woods around his home town as the location for his story of resistance to Nazism may have been determined in some measure by the fact that he had good recall of the landscape and of the city into which his characters venture, but it could not avoid having a specific political meaning in 1943. *A European Education*, by the simple fact of its geographical location, asserts that Wilno was part of Poland. That's a territorial claim, not a statement of geographical fact. The irredentist government in exile and the patriotic and mostly very nationalistic Poles fighting on the Allied side had no quarrel with such a view. More or less everybody else in the region did.

The symbolic status of Wilno accounts for what looks like a historical bloomer in Gary's first novel. *A European Education* tells the story of partisan resistance during the 'winter of Stalingrad', from September 1942 to March 1943, and the stages of the great battle in the East are marked in almost every chapter of the book, which ends a little after the lifting of the siege and the surrender of Paulus on 10 February 1943. At the beginning of winter, in Gary's novel, a local innkeeper visits the partisans in their forest hideaway, seeking to put himself on the right side in case the tide turns. He ingratiates himself by teasing and upbraiding the youngsters:

> 'What's all this about, boys?' he exclaimed at last. 'Have you no blood left in your veins? Are you asleep? It's three years since the German occupied our villages and you still do nothing to chase him out?'[5]

Three years? Of course not, if we take the geographical location of the novel in a literal sense. Germany swept through that part of the world in the summer of 1941, little more than a year before Gary's Pan Konieczny ('Mr Necessary') addresses the group of Greens near his village. But this technical error reveals the true meaning of 'Wilno': it stands not for itself but for all of Poland, for the *Ziemia Wielkopolska* which nationalists and patriots still believed could be recovered. The major part of Poland had indeed been occupied by Germans for three years and that is what the innkeeper is referring to in his conversation with the partisans. The separate, contorted history of the Wilno region is set aside and, in *Forest of Anger*, Wilno, Poland's most easterly claim, stands for the whole nation.

A European Education is a loosely knit sequence of stories centred on the painful wartime education of Janek Twardowski, a fourteen-year-old boy from the (invented) village of Sucharki ('dry bread'). His father, a doctor, places him for safety in a dugout hideaway in the woods in September 1942. Soon, the father no longer returns to visit the boy. Janek emerges from his hole and wanders around the forest until he encounters a band of partisans, who adopt him, and for the following months he learns the basic lessons of survival, cruelty, betrayal and loyalty to an ideal. The leader of the band, Adam Dobranski, is a poet and a writer of fables, which he reads aloud to his ragtag army around the campfire at night.[6] What exactly is he fighting for? One of Dobranski's fables, 'Plain Tale of the Hills', adapts *Goldilocks* to express Poland's determination to fight on. After reciting Churchill's famous 'blood, sweat and tears', the 'three hills of Poland' break into the national anthem :

Jescze Polska nie zginęła
Póki my żyjemy . . .

Dobranski's message is that justice, freedom, and *Polish* nationhood must be restored. In its earliest surviving redaction (the English version published in London in 1944), the novel that would come to be called *A European Education* has nothing to do with Europeanist, pan-national ideals. Later revisions of the text have obscured almost entirely what Gary was at the hectic and passionate start of his literary career.

The information that Gary had at his disposal for describing a struggle he had never seen could only have come from two sources: Polish escapees who had made it from the Lithuanian Maquis to London; and Soviet propaganda. Of the former, there were very few indeed, and even fewer who might have crossed Gary's path in the RAF. Of the latter there was an abundance. As soon as German tanks rolled across the Soviet border in June 1941, Stalin appealed to the inhabitants of the conquered territories to establish a guerrilla force to harass the Germans behind the lines. By 1943 Soviet publications widely distributed in Britain were stressing the participation of all the peoples of eastern Europe in this struggle – 'Russians, Ukrainians, Byelorussians, Jews, Poles, Lithuanians, Latvians, Estonians and others'.[7] The same pamphlets describe German tactics of reprisal raids and hostage taking and the heroic role played in the struggle by women, all of which finds a place in Gary's novel. Dobranski's partisan unit includes a Russian, a Ukrainian, a Jew and a Byelorussian; the role of women is represented by Zosia, who winkles important information out of her German clients. The entire group, led as it is by a Pole, also regards the Red Army's struggle for Stalingrad as a battle undertaken on behalf of all humanity. 'On the Volga. At Stalingrad . . . men are fighting for us,' Dr Twardowski tells his son. 'For us, sir?' – 'Yes. For you and me and millions of others.'[8]

While Gary was composing *A European Education* he was also a frequent visitor to London (barely an hour away from his base by train) and in regular contact not only with Free French circles, but with Polish and Russian comrades who were an integral part of expatriate life in the capital. At the offices of the monthly review, *La France Libre*, for example, in Queensberry Place (next door to where the French Institute now stands), he encountered its director, André Labarthe, who had launched the journal in 1940 with funds provided by his companion 'Marthe Lecoutre' who, beneath her French *nom de guerre*, was Polish through and through. The magazine's military correspondent (and Raymond Aron's mentor in strategic thinking, as he acknowledged later on) was a Polish genius called Stanislas Szymonczyk, known as 'Staro', formerly personal assistant to Willi Muenzenberg, the German leader of the Komintern.[9] Gary also met Feliks Topolski, a young Polish artist who would later become a celebrated English cartoonist, and – to his especial pleasure – Antoni Słonimski, the writer-journalist whose column the younger Gary had so much enjoyed. Aron and Labarthe also introduced Gary to Alain Bosquet, at that time a US intelligence officer (his background in Odessa, Sofia and Brussels was as varied as Gary's) and it was probably through Bosquet (who became in later years a poet and novelist in French, as well as an indefectible friend of Ismail Kadare) that first contact was made with the Russian-speaking translator Joseph Barnes, head of the London bureau of the *Herald Tribune*.

Gary also spent time in 'Le Petit Club Français' in St James, run by an eccentric English lady, Olwen Hughes. There he met Joseph Kessel, the famous French reporter and writer of adventure stories, who was as Russian as Romain Gary, and he heard Anna Marly (Anna Betulinskaya) singing her own composition, the 'Ballad of Smolensk', which Kessel and his son-in-law Maurice Druon promptly turned into 'The Song of the Partisans' one evening in May 1943.

Kessel was an important member of the internal resistance in France and had been evacuated to Britain by submarine as a liaison agent. On arrival in London he lost no time in turning his experience into prose. *The Army of the Shadows* was serialised in the daily French-language newspaper in London, *France*, almost as soon as each chapter was written, between March and July 1943.[10] The novel Gary began writing in spring

1943 also deals with the Resistance in occupied Europe, and like Kessel's more famous book (which begins with the execution of a traitor to the cause) it also portrays the cruelty of the partisan struggle. Both novels are episodic in structure and both place the Resistance under the leadership of an intellectual: the philosopher Luc Jardie in *The Army of the Shadows*, the poet Adam Dobranski (with 'Professor Kreczmar' standing behind him) in *Forest of Anger*. Such close parallels can be put down to historical reality, of course; but whereas Kessel's work is an adventure story that barely fictionalises lived experience, Gary's is an *imaginary* account dependent primarily on contemporary and classical literary material. Gary's descriptions of camping out it in a hostile environment owe nothing to experience (Gary never camped out in his life!) and almost everything to the memory of children's classics read in Polish or German, from the Red Indian stories of Karl May (which Janek takes into his hideaway with him), to Mowgli (Kipling is frequently alluded to in the text) and *The Last of the Mohicans*. It is no criticism of Gary to say that he also owed the overall shape of his work to Joseph Kessel – but not the specific meaning it inscribes.

The Franco-Slav community in wartime London was closely watched over by Baroness Moura Budberg. At that time the middle-aged mistress of the much older H. G. Wells (whom she obstinately refused to wed),[11] Budberg was a translator (of sorts), an occasional writer and primarily a spy. Her status in Gary's eyes no doubt rested on the fact that for fifteen years she had been Maksim Gorky's personal assistant; and it may well have been through her that Gary first came across Gorky's essay on 'The Good Life', where he found a damning description of 'humanists and conciliators' playing the part of 'lyrical clowns' in the circus of capitalism.[12] (Gary adopted the accusation as a kind of personal leitmotif and recycled it throughout his work, most notably in the title of *Les Clowns lyriques*, the final revision of his 1952 novel, *The Colours of the Day*. In Gary's use of the expression, needless to say, 'lyrical clown' refers both to the author and to his hero, by antiphrasis.)

The British relied on Moura Budberg for information about the goings-on in the polyglot community swirling around Queensberry Place; in one of the ironies of history, her controller at the Ministry of Information was Sir Robert Bruce Lockhart, with whom she had had a passionate affair a whole lifetime before, in Petrograd, during the Russian Revolution. But she also reported to the NKVD, the Soviet secret police, and her job, insofar as it can be known, was to promote Soviet interests through the manipulation of propaganda and information in British publishing and media.[13] André Labarthe, who had been forced to hand over the editorial direction of *La France Libre* to Raymond Aron, was also a high-ranking Soviet agent. Aron always refused to believe this (rumours about Labarthe being a Soviet spy surfaced soon after the war), but documents have now been released that put the matter beyond doubt.[14] The Franco-Slav milieu in which Gary moved as he took his first steps in literature was thoroughly penetrated by figures who, under plausible covers, were paid to serve the Soviet cause.

Gary finished the first version of his novel, still called *La Forêt engloutie*, towards the end of 1943. All editions of the book, in English and in French, are dated at the end as having been written 'on operations with the Lorraine Squadron, England, Autumn 1943', and there is no reason to doubt the accuracy of the envoi. However, when the book was first published as *Forest of Anger* twelve months later, it contained an epilogue that could not have been penned in autumn 1943. The endpiece (retained without revision in all later editions) is set in a future to which many Poles aspired: Janek returns to the forest, driving a US-made jeep, in the uniform of a second lieutenant in the Polish Free Corps, to bury at the spot where his mentor Dobranski had died the school exercise book in which his unfinished collection of fables had been penned. Zosia is now his wife, the mother of a three-year-old child, and enrolled in the Music Faculty of the (Polish) University of Wilno (Janek had evidently weaned her off the popular trash she had hummed during the war).[15] As he places the manuscript – entitled *Forest of Anger* – on the forest floor, he recalls Dobranski's dying words, uttered as the sound of Soviet cannon grew near. That detail is a giveaway. In autumn 1943 the Soviet Army was still a very long way from Lithuania. Gary could not have taken it for granted at that time that Wilno would be liberated by the Red Army. Wilno was taken back from the Germans on 14 July 1944 and Gary's epilogue was surely not invented before that date. The text Gary completed in autumn 1943 must therefore have ended with what is now chapter 31 of *A European Education* as published in the USA in 1960 and chapter 32 of the 'definitive' edition published in France. It tells the dreadful tale of Sopla, the peasant who betrayed the partisans for a sack of potatoes. Janek's band goes to punish him – to recover the potatoes for themselves. Sopla's wife pleads with the partisans to shoot her husband on the spot and leave her the sack, for without food she and her child will surely die. There is no conclusion to this bleak picture of human desperation and familial inhumanity: Janek and his team simply move off into the forests with the potatoes on their backs. 'And suddenly it seemed to Janek that the world of men was nothing but a vast sack, in which was struggling a shapeless mass of blind and dreaming potatoes: mankind.'[16]

At the behest of Raymond Aron, who read the manuscript and was impressed by it, Gary gave his first work to Moura Budberg, in the hope she might find a publisher for him. Gary returned to action, was seriously wounded, spent several weeks in hospital and convalescence, and moved to London to work in an office job at HQ. Then came D-Day. He was not involved, but his squadron played an important role in laying a smokescreen over German positions on the French coast, from an altitude of fifty feet. Not long after the Normandy landings Gary got a message from a London publisher, Cresset Press, saying that his manuscript had been accepted, would be translated straight away and published before the end of the year.[17]

Publishers often take months to reach a decision, but the half-year delay in Cresset's response to the manuscript submitted by the Queen Bee makes even more sense when viewed in the dramatic, fast-changing military and political context of 1944. Budberg was working for the Soviets. In June 1944, the success of the Anglo-American invasion of northern France suddenly overshadowed the immense sacrifices of the Red Army. The Soviet cause urgently needed whatever propaganda boost it could get. Gary's novel, which portrays Stalingrad as the real turning point in the history of the war and also portrays the unity of the Polish and the Soviet causes, fitted the need of the moment rather well. But its ending – the misanthropic lament of chapter 31 – had no propaganda value at all and casts the struggle of the partisans in a very gloomy light. It is highly likely that as a condition of publication Gary was asked to add a 'more positive' end-piece to boost morale. Thus the epilogue, written in summer 1944, which not only expresses Gary's genuine enthusiasm on learning that Wilno had at last been liberated, but proclaims (among other things) that Poland would recover its eastern lands with the helping hand of both the USA and the USSR.

Gary's stunning exploit of writing a whole novel in a few months while on active service was one thing. Seeing it launched under a new title in a country he had only recently reached was quite another, and it was based on a double-take of which Gary was probably aware. That's why he used the commissioned epilogue to reiterate in a more elaborate metaphorical mode the underlying moral message of his original text. Janek – now effectively revealed as the writer who has completed Dobranski's tale and thus the author of the book – places the original fragment on the ground and ants swarm over it. 'It would certainly take something more than a book to force them to depart from their Way, the Way that millions of other ants pursued before them, and that millions of ants will pursue after.' Industrious ants thus replace potatoes as the image of humankind. 'How many cathedrals will they yet build to adore a God who gave them so frail a back and so heavy a burden?' Not just literature, but all the arts are unable to improve the lot of mankind. 'What use is it to struggle and pray, to hope and to believe? The world in which men suffer and die . . . is a cruel, incomprehensible place.'[18] Gary turns his 'more positive' supplement to *Forest of Anger* towards a conclusion that is less clumsy than the close of chapter 31, but no less bleak, and which almost pointedly refuses to adopt the heroic tone conventional in wartime writing of this kind.

The Cresset Press, run by John Howard, husband of the already famous left-wing journalist Marghanita Laski, hired a distinguished translator for Gary's novel. Viola Garvin, who read Polish as well as French, had for many years edited the books page of the *Observer* (she was also the daughter of its long-running editor, Louis Garvin). In her version, Dobranski's Polish poems[19] are left in the original, with English translations following; but the speech of the characters contains fewer expressions in Polish, Yiddish and German than in subsequent French versions of the text. Even so, the book that appeared in December 1944, and which was a genuine success with British readers, reads like a work translated not from French but from Polish and was treated as such – as a novel about Poland, by a Pole, and expressing Polish aspirations and values – by most reviewers in the London press.[20]

In London, Gary also met the woman who became his first wife. He may initially have met Lesley Blanch quite by chance, at a party for foreign servicemen, as Blanch says in her memoir; or it may have been by arrangement, as his *marraine de guerre*, or 'wartime correspondent' (many London ladies volunteered to act as pen pals for lonely soldiers, met them when on leave, gave them a meal and occasionally what was gracefully called 'a night out').[21] Lesley Blanch was not at all like the girls Gary had been with before, though like Kristel and Ilona, she was not French. She was nearing forty, with a long career as a journalist behind her, and she now occupied a fairly senior position with *Vogue*. She also had a passion for all things Russian. What attracted her to Lieutenant Kacew of the Free French Air Force, she later said, was that she could *see* he was a Slav:

> the singular stranger baffled me until, listening to his boot-deep tones, beneath the wail of the saxophones, I suddenly realised he was Russian. The sombre features were those of an ikon, the voice unmistakably that of a Slav. Free French or no, this man was a Russian.[22]

Why did they marry? Certainly not in order to start a family: Lesley was near if not beyond the limit of childbearing age, and in any case she didn't like children and had no idea how to behave with them.[23] Blanch has said that marriage was a necessary formality if she was to accompany Gary on his first diplomatic posting to Sofia. That cannot be true, because the marriage at Chelsea Register Office, in April 1945, took place not only before the end of the war and the prospect of demobilisation, but many months before Gary even sought entry to the Diplomatic Corps. What is not in any doubt, however, is that towards the end of 1944 *Vogue* commissioned Lesley Blanch to do a feature article on recent fiction, as a result of which she interviewed the author of a new and already well-received novel, *Forest of Anger*. Blanch, whose linguistic talents were the inverse of Gary's (her French accent was so bad that Gary would not let her speak the language within earshot)[24] mingled not only with the other distinguished wartime contributors to *Vogue* – among them Feliks Topolski and Lee Miller – but also with members of high society who featured on her journal's fashion and society pages. She was instrumental in puffing Gary's first book, and her encomia were used by Cresset Press as 'lead quotations' on advertisements placed in the *Observer* and the *Guardian*. She was a catch for the airman-writer – as well as being one of the few women in existence who would put up with his voracious sexual appetite. Their rapid romance was also, at least in part, a literary and business affair.

In the novel Blanch reviewed, Gary's national identity was clearly marked as that of a Pole. But soon history would overtake the dreams of Polish nationhood to which the layered hero-narrators of *Forest of Anger* cling. The Great Powers, meeting at Yalta in February 1945, allocated Poland to the Soviet sphere, leaving the new Russian–Polish frontier exactly where Molotov and Ribbentrop had put it in 1939, that is to say about two hundred kilometres west of where Polish patriots thought it should be. Given the Poles' long experience of Russian control (from 1815 to 1917), in addition to their fears of what a Communist regime would mean, they could all see that Yalta rang the death knell of Poland's aspiration to be free. The Greater Poland to which Dobranski aspired, the Polish Wilno where Gary had already set his epilogue, was not going to be.

The surrender of Poland by Churchill and Roosevelt was a blow for Gary, not just as a man, but as a writer too. His novel had been accepted for publication in French and was scheduled to appear as soon as Calmann-Lévy could get an allocation of paper to print it on. But *La Forêt engloutie* was already a relic of a bygone age. Gary sprang the trap that the changing face of Europe had set him not by retreating into nostalgia or bitterness, but by rewriting the novel before it could be sent to press. In doing so, he invented the 'Romain Gary' of the post-war years.

In the French text that Gary revised in the spring of 1945 he abandoned the irredentist agenda of Polish patriotism for more up-to-date dreams of a Europe free of national divisions.

With deft editing of a manuscript that has not survived, but whose nature is preserved in the English translation, Gary turned a stirring appeal for Polish liberation into a fable about *European* resistance.

The Polish poetry of *Forest of Anger* was replaced by new verse in French. The Polish national anthem was replaced by 'La Marseillaise', now sung not by the 'three hills of Poland', but by *European* hills. To mask the generalisation of what had been a profoundly East European story, Gary added authenticating linguistic touches to the dialogues, having characters speak in bad German, genuine Polish, and fragments of Yiddish and Russian. But the most effective change of all was in the title. The 'forest' disappears, as does its qualification of 'drowned' or 'angry'. The new name of *A European Education* puts the focus on the novel's young hero, Janek, rather than on the partisan group and its plight. By broadening the reference to the whole continent, and by presenting it as a story of something learned, *Éducation européenne* allows much broader allegorical meanings to be attached to the narrative. But the particular formulation of the title in French (devoid of a definite or indefinite article), also alludes directly to Flaubert's novel of disenchantment, *Éducation sentimentale*. At the end of Flaubert's glum masterpiece the central character, Frédéric Moreau, admits in middle age that he had learned nothing of value from the great loves of his early life. The linguistic echo of Flaubert in Gary's title thus seems to imply that Janek also learned nothing from his savage education in warfare, sacrifice and young love. Fighting the good fight had saddened Janek's heart, but not raised him to a new level of understanding (which is of course one of the contradictory messages of the epilogue Gary had added in summer 1944). Gary's book could now be read as a fable of disenchantment, but also as a homage to all the resistance movements throughout Continental Europe during the period of Nazi Occupation. The effect of Gary's rewriting was to make Janek appear less as a Pole than as a representative figure of European youth, an embodiment of its aspirations towards heroism and of its knowledge that no war, however noble, could be innocent. That is how the French read it when it appeared in summer 1945; it was lionised and rewarded with a significant prize not just because it was a strong piece of writing, but because it was also, by implication and analogy, about the *French* Resistance. What escaped all but Polish readers was that the novel's romantic epilogue, set in a future that could not now come to pass, had been transformed from a glorious hope into a sour joke. In formerly eastern Poland, already cleansed entirely of its Jewish population, the Soviets arrested thousands suspected of having helped the Nazis and shipped tens of thousands more to camps in Siberia. Many Polish freedom fighters and officers of the Home Army were slaughtered; some returned to the forests to carry on what was now a hopeless fight.[25] Wilno became the capital of a new Soviet Socialist Republic of Lithuania. Even in London, Poland was humiliated: Churchill refused to allow any uniformed members of the Polish Armed Forces to take part in the Victory Parade.

By switching the focus of his story from Poland to Europe, Gary stepped aside from the disaster that befell his fictional heroes and his actual home town. Far from making him an opportunist with no solid ground of his own, the revision saved the moral lesson of *Éducation européenne* for readers with no stake in Polish history and no knowledge of its unendingly complicated and disastrous turns. What it did to Gary himself was equally important. He didn't abandon the ideals for which he had fought as a warrior and which, thanks to a very particular combination of circumstances, he had somehow managed to allegorise in a fiction of a distant land. But he could see that the only way to treat the obscene betrayals of politics and history was with a loud laugh. Almost before the recomposition of *Éducation européenne* was finished, and weeks before it appeared in France, he drafted a quite new and different work, *Tulipe* – an uproarious satire of good intentions and of the gullibility of man.

Jan Kott, the Polish critic who was later to become a world authority on Shakespeare, read the French version of Gary's novel shortly after it appeared. As a Pole, he was naturally particularly sensitive to the irony of the novel's epilogue, which Gary did not change. 'Let's be blunt: for me, this short book on the Resistance in Poland is first and foremost very funny,' he wrote. In France, of course, the joke was the other way round: Gary found himself enrolled in the autumn of 1945 in the ranks of 'resistentialist' authors by critics as weighty as Sartre, Nadeau and Raymond Queneau. Nadeau, a member of the Communist Party, wrote in Camus's paper *Combat* one of the most enthusiastic notices Gary was ever to receive and virtually gave him an official stamp of socialist approval. Not one of Gary's French readers in 1945 bothered to ask what the epilogue was really about. Gary maintained it in almost identical form in the first and all subsequent rewritings of the text and, as the history of central Europe in the war years faded into footnotes, it became just a sentimental end-piece to a moving portrayal of the harshness and ambiguity of armed struggle of any kind. What it proves, all the same, is that Gary – mercurial, adaptable and quick-witted though he was – never dropped the ideals to which he was really attached, even while the world changed the superficial meaning of his texts. By deduction as well as by personal taste, he thenceforth adopted disguise as his preferred means of being himself.

A European Education went through two more revisions until it reached its 'final' form in the French 'definitive edition' of 1961. Because the Cresset Press edition never appeared in the USA, Gary revised it entirely and rewrote it in English when he was at the peak of his fame and resident in Hollywood (see p. 118). This version, called *Nothing Important Ever Dies* in the

UK and *A European Education* in the USA, is the only version available to American readers, and it is longer, more sentimental and much more pan-European than the original Polish-oriented work. The French definitive edition of 1961 is in most respects a retranslation into French of this American-oriented retelling of the tale, save that the Stalingrad chapter is reinstated, French sensibilities to the Red Army being quite at variance with American ones at that time.[26] But these several 'translations' from one historical and political context to another – from Europe before the fall of Nazi Germany to Liberation Paris, Cold War America and 1960s France – do not in any way cheapen or alter the work's original thrust and intention. They are the means by which a seminal work was kept alive and made fit to engage new readers at new times in new places. Few writers have ever been able to transport their own work so effectively over such wide chasms. Gary's writing strategy clashes entirely with the common critical belief in the 'original' as the true expression of the 'author's intention'. Like Ismail Kadare, but to an even higher degree, Gary was intent on forever improving his own work; he was not going to have it sidelined by anything so trivial as changes in language or in historical context. One predictable but paradoxical result of this admirable persistence in making his work afresh is the accusation that he 'sold his own shadow' in the pursuit of continuing popularity and political correctness.[27] Gary's habit of hiding the fact that changes had been made and his sometimes lamentable tendency to cover his tracks by spreading misleading information about himself has obscured the real meaning of his rewritings of himself. You could say he has only himself to blame. But it is not clear how else he could have got away with his insane but largely successful attempt to deny passing time its hold on the life of books, if not of men.

8

Gary and Charles de Gaulle

Gary's political position throughout the post-war period was commonly thought of as Gaullist, and he certainly described himself many times as a *gaulliste inconditionnel*. However, the tag obscures the nature of Gary's relationship to the man who led Free France, just as it misrepresents Gary's provocative, insubordinate and solitary stand on a wide range of political issues. His allegiance to de Gaulle was personal, moral and historical. It had little to do with party politics in post-war France.

Romain Gary first set eyes on Charles de Gaulle at St Athan's airbase in South Wales, during an early inspection of the seventy-three French airmen being trained there by the RAF, in July or August 1940. He may have encountered him again during the same summer, but Gary's account of the meeting is anything but reliable. Infuriated at being forbidden to fly with the RAF until fully French units had been constituted, Gary and his comrades conspired to assassinate Squadron Leader Chènevier, their commanding officer. In one version of the story it was Gary's job to remove the officer's shoes and socks while he was restrained by his parachute harness on the training flight, but the conspirator was so overcome with the humanity of the man's smelly feet that he gave up the plan on the spot. In another version the hotheads did manage to eject the officer from the aircraft, but his parachute, which they thought they had sabotaged, opened up nonetheless. In both variants of a tall story designed to prove that the pioneers of Free France were a pretty rough bunch, Gary was hauled before a military tribunal (there is no mention of this in his military record, of course). In the most picturesque account of the event, the tribunal sent Gary to see the Commander in Chief in late August 1940[1]. He got a severe dressing down, to which the unrepentant airman replied: 'I came here to fight.'

> De Gaulle's tinny voice then literally rained down on my head.
>
> 'Alright, go ahead. But don't forget to get yourself killed!'
>
> I clicked my heels, said 'Yes, *mon général*', and turned about. I was already at the door when you took a kinder view. Well, almost.
>
> 'But you'll pull through. Only the very best get themselves killed.'[2]

Gary's next (genuine) encounter with de Gaulle was hardly more auspicious. On 27 April 1941 the General passed through Bangui on a tour of inspection, when Gary was stationed there (allegedly living in marital bliss with his native bride Louison). To celebrate the event Gary wrote, directed and acted in an evening's troop entertainment entitled *Hope at Latitude 4°5 N*. It did not go down well. De Gaulle 'did not budge, twitch or show the slightest reaction of any kind from start to finish'.[3]

During his attachment to the Free French HQ from May 1944 to October 1945, Gary had occasion to meet de Gaulle several times. On 20 November 1944, however, Gary returned to Hartford Bridge for a ceremony of immense importance to him. By virtue of an official telegram from Carlton Gardens, the *croix de guerre* was awarded to several members of the Lorraine Squadron. In August 1945 Gary was allowed to make a short trip back to France – his first in five years – to attend the formal ceremony in Nancy where the Lorraine Squadron and its five surviving members from the first cohort of volunteers received the ultimate accolade, the *médaille de la Libération* from the hand of General Vallin.[4] This decoration made Gary a *Compagnon de la Libération*, a member of the elite among the survivors of the Free French. De Gaulle granted the honour to barely more than a thousand men (and a handful of women, towns and regiments too); it made Gary a Frenchman through and through, and a member of what was clearly intended to be a lasting imitation of Napoleon's 'Old Guard'. Throughout the history of post-war France the comradeship of former Free French fighters, and especially of the Companions, constituted a powerful mutual aid network. Gary made use of it from time to time, but unlike many others, he never exploited this high distinction to launch a political or a business career.

After the war, Gary had little contact with the man who became head of the provisional government, then prime minister for a few months, before withdrawing from politics and retiring to Colombey-les-Deux-Églises in 1946. However, in 1956, when Gary won the Goncourt Prize for *The Roots of Heaven*, he sent a signed copy of his book to de Gaulle, who replied with a gracious note. Thereafter Gary sent de Gaulle dedicated copies of all his books and received, on most occasions, more than merely formal thanks. De Gaulle's response to the French edition of *The Dance of Genghis Cohn* is perhaps worth quoting at length:

7 August 1967

My dear Romain Gary,

What talent, most certainly, how many ideas and passions too, and what transcendental irony there is in *The Dance of Genghis Cohn*! You seize us and shake us. Ah! You give no quarter to your readers, whoever they are, not even to the

Jews, scattered and persecuted as they have been for centuries, then shamefully slaughtered, and among whom there is perhaps nowadays an imperialist tendency. But for a book of that sort you won't escape scot free either. I don't think that bothers you.[5]

Gary's relationship to de Gaulle partly explains why he continued to admire and respect André Malraux. Malraux shot to fame in 1933 with *Man's Estate*, which won the Goncourt Prize, and quickly became a world-famous icon of courageous left-wing political commitment for the whole of Gary's generation, especially for the aspiring writers among it. In summer 1938, when Gary was doing odd jobs on the Riviera and still living at the Pension Mermonts in Nice, he heard that the greatest writer of the age, the noble anti-Fascist and organiser of the Spanish Republicans' air brigade, was staying at a hotel in nearby Menton. With the crass enthusiasm of youth, Gary rushed there, forced himself on the novelist and read him aloud his own work (presumably the second version of *Le Vin des morts*) for several hours. Gary reported on this intoxicating night (appropriately punctuated by thunder and lightning) in a letter to his Swedish girlfriend Kristel: unsurprisingly, given Gary's natural prolixity, Malraux urged the young man to cut down his text and, just as predictably, given Malraux's political position, he suggested Gary should make his central figures Communists.[6] Gary was not open to such advice: he was too much part of his mother's Russian émigré milieu. He was much more interested in the idea of France and, as his colonial short stories of the period and his dream of becoming an air force pilot show, he was drawn to forms of assimilation more usually associated with right-wing ideas. But despite this slightly bruising first encounter, Malraux remained for Romain Gary a model of what writing can do in the world.

Gary met de Gaulle long before Malraux did, just as he had met Malraux long before de Gaulle encountered him, and it was only in 1944, after Malraux had emerged as a leader of the internal resistance in France, that the three of them found themselves on the same side. After the war, as Gary devoted himself increasingly to the writing life, Malraux abandoned fiction and threw himself into political action, becoming Minister of Information in de Gaulle's first government, the organiser of the Gaullist party RPF after de Gaulle's resignation, then Minister of Culture when de Gaulle resumed the leadership of France in 1958. But to the end of his days Gary remained as loyal to Malraux as he did to de Gaulle.

In 1940, de Gaulle was a strange, magnificent, almost incomprehensibly courageous figure. France had lost its war: de Gaulle said it would win in the end. What would save France was not so much the military or political manoeuvres to be engaged alongside the Allies, but the *idea* that France represented. A certain idea of France . . . It was almost Polish in its antiquated romantic appeal. Gary was quite sincere in his many post-war declarations about what had bound him to Free France in 1940: ideas of chivalric and honourable behaviour inherited from schoolbook reading in Poland and in France, made flesh in the person of Charles de Gaulle.

When Gary called himself an 'unconditional Gaullist' he did not mean that he supported de Gaulle's actions as a politician in post-war France. Gary never joined a political party and had no political ambitions for himself. What he meant was that his loyalty to his wartime leader could not be altered or broken by anything de Gaulle might subsequently say or do. His fidelity was to de Gaulle as saviour of the honour of the nation. What particularly fascinated Gary was precisely the mythical dimension of de Gaulle. His stature did not derive from any real power in the early days of the defeat, nor did it rest on any wide support. On the contrary, de Gaulle's support grew only as the myth of himself that he projected inspired in others a similar belief in the possibility of defying history and of acting honourably when the nation lay in ruins.

The notion that a single man could incarnate a nation by declaring fidelity to vague ideas of art, civilisation and honour captivated Gary. In effect, de Gaulle had invented a new kind of historical role, one that no one had ever thought of playing: that of the powerless leader with an appeal based on no army, no treasury, no mob, but solely on the grandiloquent expression of an ideal. De Gaulle's genius was not only to invent the role, but to play it to the hilt and to convince the whole world. This analysis is short on detail and leaves aside all the politicking that went on in London and Algiers to give birth to de Gaulle the great leader. What held Gary's complete devotion was de Gaulle's implausible but successful appeal to the higher nature of man. The rest could be left to the footnotes.

Gary's continuing admiration of Malraux was based on much the same moral idea. Malraux had invented himself. His fictions spilled over into life and his eloquence allowed him to reconstruct his past and shape his future. Gary was well aware of the liberties Malraux took with facts, ideas and history, and in *A Quiet Night* he wrote a gently comical portrait of Malraux delivering fluent bullshit at a dinner party in New York.[7] At bottom, however, what he admired without reservation in both Malraux and de Gaulle was something he actually wanted most of all for himself: the ability to determine his own fate and his own identity without reference to origins. The two great men, in their different domains, were for Gary living protests against the arbitrariness of history and life. France was defeated, but in the end won the war because de Gaulle said it would. That's not politics. That's acting on a grand scale and that was what art should be. Gary took some time to discover his own unique means of transferring his aspiration for self-invention to the business of writing books, but his aspiration towards self-creation was exemplified and intensified by the mythical figure of Charles de Gaulle, and by the varied exploits of his henchman and confidant, André Malraux.[8]

Many of the near-tragic misunderstandings between Free

France and the Allies, and the more general *mésentente* between pragmatic Anglo-Saxons and French culture heroes, derive from this point. Roosevelt was exasperated by the tall, aloof Frenchman who 'thought he was Joan of Arc'. Many English readers fail to understand how a mythomaniac like Malraux could ever have been appointed to a position of responsibility. Gary's liberal use of half-truths, subterfuges and outright lies also strikes many British and American admirers as the dark side of his genius. But for Gary the performance was what mattered: only if you try to reach impossible heights can you achieve honour, grandeur or the sublime. In a peculiarly antiquated way, Gary saw the world as a stage – as a *real* stage – and de Gaulle as the greatest performer to have trod its planks.

All the same, Gary kept his feet on firmer ground as far as his French reputation was concerned in decades when French writers were not supposed to be Gaullist supporters. He published nothing in French about the President while he was in power from 1958 to 1969. In America Gary felt less constrained. He published three major essays on de Gaulle in *Life* magazine at three turning points in French history: when de Gaulle was catapulted into the presidency in 1958 ('The Man Who Stayed Lonely to Save France'); on de Gaulle's resignation after a botched referendum on decentralisation in 1969 ('To My General, with Love and Anger'); and on de Gaulle's death in 1970 ('Ode to the Man Who Was France'). What he also did not publish in France were the additions he made to the English-language revision of *The Dance of Genghis Cohn*, which target de Gaulle's remarks about Israel in particular. The passages in *White Dog* and *Trésors de la Mer rouge* on Gary's relationship to de Gaulle did not appear before the General's death; similarly, de Gaulle appears as a named figure only in novels written in English after 1970.

The first of Gary's American essays on de Gaulle defends

the President of the Fifth Republic against American suspicions that he would become a dictator and that the new constitution was designed to allow him to exercise autocratic power. Gary's adept response leads nonetheless to a quaintly medieval image of the politician:

> The fact is that De Gaulle's vision of France imposes on him a code of conduct that is essentially incompatible with political adventurism. To him the distinction between legality and dictatorship is as clear as the distinction between love and rape. And this, perhaps, is the only touch of medieval France upon him. For this code of manners is not too far removed from the rules of chivalry of the medieval knight, with his attitude of infinite courtesy and respect toward the woman he loved. In all his dealings with France, De Gaulle has never deviated from the code of behaviour that is required in the presence of a *grande dame*.[9]

Gary presents de Gaulle as a man who had thought out what would be needed in time of crisis long beforehand. The France that he believed in needed a leader far above it, a leader who would incarnate the spiritual idea of France. When the time came, in 1940, de Gaulle could not therefore allow himself to be seen as an ordinary human being. 'He had to become a legend.' That's why he began to refer to himself in the third person and to behave as if he were already a statue. He used theatrical devices of estrangement to ensure that no one could find out anything about him save what served the 'myth of de Gaulle, the man who was France'.

On de Gaulle's resignation, Gary wrote a piece that is full of Blimpish disdain for the little men now running France. De Gaulle, the incarnation of a higher idea of civilisation and valour, had, Gary suspects, engineered his own defeat in the referendum precisely in order to be able to enter legend as the leader spurned by a 'mini-France' no longer worthy of his leadership. The same attitude is maintained in Gary's 'Ode' on the death of de Gaulle the following year, save that here he returns to his standard theme of de Gaulle as the masterful performer of a theatrical role on the stage of world history:

> For years I have been aware of watching the performance of a very great artist. In that respect what De Gaulle has done is without precedent, and I believe that herein lies the whole secret of the man. *He was a fantastically clever and gifted impersonator of 10 centuries of French history.* With the historical – and histrionic – material known by heart by every Frenchman since school, with debris of the past, with fragments of all the Louis, with the light still feebly reaching us from all the dead stars of past glory, with chips of stone from all our cathedrals and statuary, out of museums and out of legends, with genius, skill, fabulous workmanship, technique and shrewdness, he built a mythological being known as De Gaulle . . .[10]

Here even more than elsewhere, Gary's encomium of de Gaulle sounds very much like an excuse for being Romain Gary, who similarly took bits and pieces from his school curriculum, fragments of books and newspaper clippings, and created a legendary writer known as Romain Gary . . . De Gaulle became Gary's best excuse for his own approach to the relationship between dream and reality, imagination and achievement, truth and showmanship. Gary's Gaullism is neither political nor military. It is a moral conviction which paradoxically puts bullshitting among the supreme devices of art.

Gaullism in this sense – the pursuit of a genuine ideal through showmanship, subterfuge and self-invention – is particularly noticeable in *The Roots of Heaven*, the novel that won Gary his first Goncourt Prize in 1956, and in the rewritten English version of *A European Education*, first published in 1960. *The Roots of Heaven* tells the story of Morel, a member of the French Resistance who, after being released from a German prison camp at the end of the war, travels to central Africa on a self-invented mission to save elephants from pointless slaughter. Throughout Part I of the novel and for all of Part II except for a short passage at the start,[11] we never get to meet Morel, but only hear about him from the evidence given by others to the inquiry into his deeds and misdeeds, as reported some time later by a colonial administrator in conversation with a Jesuit anthropologist. The defender of the honour of humanity is thus an 'absent presence' in the way de Gaulle must have appeared to the French under German occupation. Similarly, Morel's quest encounters massive opposition from every side – from European hunters, from African tribesmen for whom elephants represent the chance of a good meal, and from African nationalist politicians, who see elephants as part of the old Africa they want to replace with modern, efficient economies. What exactly can Morel do? He mounts a few symbolic raids on notorious hunters, to no great effect. He gathers signatures on a petition, hopes for collective action from the international community, agitates and propagandises. Fairly hopeless. And yet, by the mere fact of aspiring to make the world a slightly better place, Morel, an incarnation of a 'certain idea of the human', inspires others to follow in his moral steps, and in his mysterious disappearance leaves a legend that will become part of civilisation. Gary admitted that 'Morel is a pseudonym for Romain Gary' – not because Gary held any special passion for elephants, but because he too considered that fighting for a good cause, winnable or not, was the only honourable thing to do.[12] When the book appeared in Polish translation, Gary told his interviewer Jacques Chancel critics and readers alike found the defence of the rights of elephants highly reminiscent of Polish ideals.[13]

De Gaulle also appears under thin disguise in the new version of *A European Education* that Gary prepared for publication in the USA in 1960. The original British wartime translation, with its poems in Polish, its romanticisation of the Red

Army, and its long and powerful chapter on Stalingrad, was not suitable for straightforward reissue in Cold War America. So Gary rewrote it. He used Viola Garvin's version as the basis, but cut the Stalingrad chapter and added two new ones; he dropped all mention of poetry recitals, expanded the sections dealing with Janek's love affair with Zosia and introduced numerous references to resistance activity throughout the rest of Europe. He also added a new character, or rather, a legend, that of Partisan Nightingale, the leader and co-ordinator of the entire resistance movement, of whom little was known and who, in the end, turns out to be no more than a morale-boosting myth. However, the figure of a leader 'over the water', of an inspiration of a purely moral kind, corresponds quite closely to the 'myth of de Gaulle' as Gary presented it in his later writings explicitly focused on the leader of Free France. The struggles of Morel and of 'Partisan Nightingale' fit the Gaullist model in fundamental ways: physical absence, the appeal to an ideal and a struggle undertaken against all reasonable odds. Poland herself never had a de Gaulle. But the qualities ascribed by Gary to the Gaullist legend, in his journalism as in his fictional transpositions of it, come close to the clichés of Polish valour – a romantic and unrealisable sense of honour in the service of national grandeur.

Neither Polish nationalism nor an admiration for Charles de Gaulle, who fought to save the French colonial empire as well as the honour of his country, fit neatly with most of Gary's other ideas about history and politics. That's because history and politics only ever really served as ways of talking about broader moral and human issues, not because Gary was insincere or muddled about where he stood. The towering figure of Charles de Gaulle dominated Gary's view of what it meant to be a great man, that is to say: a myth.

9

Gary's Politics

Gary's writing covers a wide range of topics in the broad field of political action and ideals: colonialism, race relations, anti-Semitism, Communism, the fight against Nazism, Polish nationalism, European reconstruction, the oil crisis, the youth crisis of the 1960s, Gaullism, women's rights, animal rights, the environment, ecology, John and Robert Kennedy, immigration, the drug problem, the United Nations, the Vietnam War, Islamic extremism, the State of Israel, traffic accidents, Jewish identity and the decline of France.[1] These were far from academic interests: Gary was involved as a human being or else as a professional soldier and diplomat in nearly all the issues he tackled. All his novels are prompted by some topical question – yet none of them could be called a political fiction. Similarly, in his journalism and in his memoirs, he strenuously and sincerely avoids taking up any position that could be identified unambiguously with a political party or programme. That did not endear him to his contemporaries in the politicised literary circles of Paris. Also, his inability to stop expressing himself had less happy results in his journalism than it did in his career as a fiction writer. Gary was just as inclined to invent facts and figures in the realm of political commentary as he was in his novel-writing mode. To be blunt, part of what Gary wrote is bullshit. Even his most ardent admirers have to face up to the fact.

Gary was frequently blunt himself on the positive virtues of stretching a point. The charlatan-hero of his 1973 novel *The Enchanters*, Fosco Zaga, clarified the difference he felt between what might be called his habit of creative adjustment and outright lying: 'Lies have always horrified me, for they are the opposite of art, which creates truth, while lies distort it.'[2] On the other hand, the 'truths' Gary 'created', though they are sometimes no more than schoolboyish pranks, often accompany and, some would say, undermine his most serious political and moral arguments.

Gary's novels are full of leg-pulls that few readers are equipped to enjoy. In *The Ski Bum*, a political romance set among teenage dropouts in Switzerland, he has a group of young skiing fanatics pay homage to one of their cult heroes as he lies dying in hospital by offering him a *grütli*, a wooden fetish symbolising supreme mastery of the Alps. Grütli is actually the name of the meadow near Lucerne where, in the legend of William Tell, the cantons of Schwyz, Uri and Unterwalden signed the treaty which lies at the origin of the Helvetic Confederation. Gary's *grütli*-fetish is a joke accessible only to readers familiar with Swiss national mythology – but for others, that is to say nearly everybody, the *grütli*-ceremony adds a touch of sentimentality to the novel. Some readers love being tricked like this. Most don't even notice.

'I never forgive anything and forget even less,' Gary claimed in *White Dog*. However, it is not hard to catch him remembering things he invented. Hearing the keys jangling on the belt of a zookeeper in California in 1968, he writes in the same memoir, 'I remember thinking of troika bells, with my mother and me driving through the Russian snow, one of the recurring memories of my childhood.'[3] As the child of a Jewish single mother in a time of revolution and civil war, it's unlikely he ever got to ride in the luxurious three-horse sleigh called a troika. Third-class railway carriages and ox-carts were more likely their lot.

These minor examples of plausible balderdash in fiction and memoir – the false *grütli*, the fantasy sleigh ride – are similar to Gary's account of his reaction to the student uprising in Paris in May 1968. Wandering down Rue de Sèvres after dining at the Brasserie Lipp, Gary sees an old chum from his student days staring at the revolutionary graffiti on the walls.

> After a prudent glance right and left, he takes a felt pen out of his pocket and begins to write.
>
> I tiptoe a bit closer, peep over his shoulder:
>
> *Set Thaelmann free!*
>
> *Franco no pasaràn!*
>
> *Hang Chiappe*
>
> *Stuff Daladier!*
>
> *Disband the Fascist leagues!*
>
> A wave of nostalgia overwhelms me. Thaelmann, as I am sure all you kids know, was our Ho Chi Minh, in the early thirties. I am so happy you remember. Chiappe, of course, was the chief of police who gave the order to fire on us during the dissent riots on the 6th of February, 1934. Seventeen dead. Thank you, kids, thank you from the bottom of my heart, for your fraternal knowledge of our own struggles.[4]

Those were indeed the slogans of the left wing of the 1930s and the historical glosses supplied are correct. What's humbug is the implied inclusion of the author in the community of 'us'. We do not know what Gary's political interests or opinions were in the 1930s, since our only access to them are the stories told in *A Quiet Night*, which can hardly be considered a reliable source. However, we can be fairly sure he was not a communist, given his background; it would be less surprising if his ardent wish to assimilate (evident in the short stories of the period) had brought him into contact with the far right, well represented among the students of his law school in Rue d'Assas, but of that we have no evidence either. However, the author of *White Dog* doesn't stop with the adoption by proxy of a generational nostalgia for a 'red' youth.

> I take the pen from him and write:
> *Free Dimitroff!*
> *Vengeance for Matteotti!*
> . . .
> *Avenge Guernica!*
> *Planes for Spain!*
> *All to Teruel!*[5]

In the thirties it was Picasso who painted *Guernica*; Malraux, for all his boasting, really did organise planes for Spain and also made a film about the civil war, *Sierra de Teruel* (adapted from his novel, *L'Espoir*). In 1968 Gary, if he really did add to the writings on the wall in this way, was draping himself in borrowed garb. He did not fight in Spain.[6] He spent the summers of the Spanish civil war period doing odd jobs in Nice, in Warsaw and in Stockholm. Was he therefore *lying* when he scrawled these old slogans as a reminder to rebellious students in May '68 that they owed more respect to their revolutionary elders? Not exactly. Harry Frankfurt makes the point in this way:

> There is nothing in theory, and certainly nothing in experience, to support the extraordinary judgment that it is the truth about himself that it is the easiest for a person to know. Facts about ourselves are not peculiarly solid and resistant to sceptical dissolution. Our natures are, indeed, elusively insubstantial – notoriously less stable and less inherent than the natures of other things. And insofar as this is the case, sincerity is itself bullshit.[7]

Romain Gary certainly knew exactly what Frankfurt is proposing in this paragraph; reciprocally, the philosopher's striking conclusion against sincerity is a sophisticated defence of Gary's life and art. Adopting the voice of his interviewer François Bondy in *A Quiet Night*, Gary points out that 'fraud, imposture and charlatanism play an important role in your work'.[8] This is itself a provocation of his ignorant public, because at the time of publication Gary had already become the non-existent writer Émile Ajar. However, Gary conventionally defended himself against the immorality of bullshitting by claiming that it served a higher purpose:

> I know I am cheating, I am conning myself, but I have only one philosophy left: anything goes, when faith in Man and trust in his future dignity are at stake. When it is a matter of preserving that essential investment, cheating, despair and cynicism have always been a sacred law of the species. Truth can be made.[9]

The peculiar relations between honesty and (in)sincerity in Gary's life and writing cannot be disconnected from his professional life as a diplomat. At the end of the war, Gary was recruited by special procedure to the French Diplomatic Corps. As a war hero and Companion of the Liberation, many doors which would otherwise have been closed to an immigrant and a Jew without relations or financial backing were open to him. Why did he seize on diplomacy as a career? According to *Promise at Dawn,* his future as 'French Ambassador' had been laid down by his mother's extravagant fantasies, and he simply took the opportunity to fulfil her dreams of him. The 'diplomatic fantasy' certainly pre-dates the prospect of Gary joining the service, because when he wed Lesley Blanch in 1945 he entered under 'father's profession' *Diplomat (French).* Gary also explained his decision in more practical terms. He had been in the forces for seven years and had become accustomed to being looked after. He did not know how to cook or shop or care for a home, and he was simply scared of going out into the world. 'My first reaction was to carry on. I almost stayed in the air force.'[10] The Diplomatic Service appealed to him as a cocoon that would maintain most of the basic services (housing, laundry, canteen) that first his mother and then the Air Force had given him up to then.

A second reason was that he hoped he would be able to stay where he was – where his wife Lesley had a house and a job, namely London. He would have liked to have been cultural counsellor at the embassy, just round the corner from the offices of *La France Libre*, and for that plum job he would need to be a member of the Diplomatic Corps. However, Gary's request for the London posting in summer 1945 came to naught. He nonetheless pursued his application to join the Diplomatic Service through a special procedure put in place in 1945 to dilute the conservative mandarinate of the French Foreign Office with people more likely to be loyal to de Gaulle. He got through and was immediately given his first posting abroad – not in London, but in Bulgaria.

Gary spent a few weeks in Paris at the end of 1945 and arrived in Sofia in the early weeks of 1946 with no preparation for his new career. He came armed only with a command of languages, which gave him the means to speak to members of the old elite (in French), the new elite (in Russian) and the Allied Control Commission, which used English. In the twenty-three months he spent in Sofia, Gary wrote a major work about France, *The Company of Men*, and also adapted his second book at least twice for the stage. (*Tulipe*, written in London in 1945, was published in France in 1946 and sank like a proverbial stone.) But he also wrote the 'Annual Report' on Bulgaria for the French Foreign Office at the end of 1946 and again the following year. These two official documents are no ordinary bureaucratic compilations. They tell the awful story of the takeover of a poor, divided country by the unstoppable force of Soviet Communism. Gary's work in Sofia could count as his political education.[11] For many men of his generation, it might also have served as a lesson in disenchantment. But in this respect, as in so many others, Gary was different. His background as an East European in the cosmopolitan, expatriate community of Nice had inoculated him against Bolshevik ideas and not even Malraux could persuade him to move his characters, let alone himself, closer to sympathy with the socialist project. He was therefore more able than most French intellectuals of his generation to describe with clarity what took place in Bulgaria in the aftermath of the Second World War.

Bulgaria had been a wartime ally of the Axis powers and counted as a defeated nation in 1945. It was put under the official authority of the tripartite Allied Control Commission (the USA, the UK and the USSR). Effective power lay with the Soviet Union, which had several hundred thousand troops stationed in the country. Ahead of the final defeat of Hitler in May 1945, power had been seized in Bulgaria by the Fatherland Front, in a particularly bloody coup. Dominated by Communists, the FF nonetheless included the Agrarian Party leader, Nikola Petkov, as well as non-Communist socialists and independents. By 1946 the Front, led by the ageing hero of the Reichstag trial, Georgi Dimitrov,[12] was coming apart at the seams. What divided the factions within it, Gary explained in his report, was a fundamental disagreement about the meaning of the word 'democracy'. The 'Eastern' view was that the only legitimate voice of the people was the Communist Party; the 'Western' view was that pluralism should be the rule. The West lost, and Gary described how, in great detail. First, the CP placed members and loyal activists in all the key posts in the institutions of the state, from national to local levels. Second, it began harassing opposition figures, starting with the lowliest, who were rounded up, imprisoned, deported to labour camps and often executed without trial. Thirdly, it pressured people with 'bad biographies' (for example, members of the pre-war bourgeoisie) into working off their class guilt by serving in the security services.[13] For a time, the regime permitted an opposition press and even encouraged it to express its views clearly. The invitation was exploited to an unreasonable extreme and the crude violence of the political polemics in the press in 1946 astounded even Gary, once he'd learned to read Bulgarian. This gave the regime all the more reason to close down the opposition papers in the spring of 1947 and to imprison journalists for slander and sedition.

What astounded Gary most of all was the belief held by the main opposition figures, and especially by Nikola Petkov, that the United States would not allow a Communist takeover. Gary knew that the US was not going to fight another war so soon – not for Poland and especially not for Bulgaria. It seemed to him that Bulgarians overestimated their own importance in world politics, and his description of the self-centredness of the world seen from Sofia is a masterful portrait of the kind of delusion that has clouded the vision of many Balkan leaders over the years.[14] He saw no less clearly that Petkov, a man of culture and wit, was a dreamer on his way to the scaffold. After a short and shabby trial, Petkov was hanged in autumn 1947 and Bulgaria became one of the People's Republics, not without protest from the Allied Powers, but without action of any kind.

Gary returned indirectly to his Bulgarian past in *The Ski Bum*, a novel he wrote in English in the early 1960s. The father of the novel's American heroine, Jess Donahue, is an alcoholic diplomat who had been American consul in Sofia at the relevant time. He thus stands in for Maynard Barnes, the US official whom Gary met during his posting to Sofia.[15] Barnes was alarmed and despondent about the situation as he saw it unfolding, but Washington thought Barnes was reporting too harshly on the events. An envoy was sent out to check up on his state of mind. He reported: 'I found that far from exaggerating or overstating the case, [Barnes was] understating it. The Russians were just ignoring us . . .'.[16] In Gary's novel, the hanging of Petkov (renamed Stavrov) turns Allan Donahue into an alcoholic.

> His first crack-up could be traced to the hanging of Stavrov, in Bulgaria in 1947: he had personally assured the Agrarian Liberals that the USA, who were at that time members of the Allied Control Commission, would never allow the suppression of the democratic opposition. He had been given no instructions whatsoever to make such a commitment, he was merely acting out of a deep understanding of everything his country stood for. Fatal.[17]

In the later French version of the novel, *Adieu Gary Cooper*, Gary adds:

> He was promptly rebuked and recalled to Washington. But he still had time to put on his tuxedo and go to an official dinner with Stavrov's murderers. Protocol. He never got over it.[18]

Gary returned to his Bulgarian experience in *A Quiet Night*, introducing some variations to the material of his novel:

> I recalled the story twenty years later to draw the portrait of an ambassador crushed by remorse in *The Ski Bum*, but there, the remorse is just part of the fiction . . . Anyway it wasn't the fault of Maynard Barnes: he really believed Gary Cooper was on his way and that the tough, pure and just hero would once again be triumphant. Gary Cooper never came and Petkov was hanged.[19]

The fact is that neither Maynard Barnes nor Romain Gary turned into an alcoholic. In fact, Gary never drank alcohol, which made him almost unique among his generation of French writers, not to mention Russians of all generations. In the 1970s he kept no drink of any kind in his apartment at

Rue du Bac, except when guests were expected.[20] The writer Régine Desforges believes she caught Gary breaking his own rule on one occasion at a dinner with André Pieyre de Mandriargues – but he may just have been in a desperate mood, or under medication.[21] Only Allan Donahue, the fictional character, had his life broken by seeing another man murdered for his beliefs. Donahue represents less how the author *was* and more how he *wished* he had been – that's to say, more sensitive and less stable. A quick reading of these two passages makes the Donahue character sentimental bullshit. But it is not exactly that. Gary appears to be talking about lived experience, when in fact he is pointing us towards an ideal.

The slow renunciation of the methods, ideals and slogans of the Soviet Communist Party is a painful chapter in the history of Gary's generation in France. Because of the centrality of this experience to his readership, Gary felt obliged to broach the subject in *The Colours of the Day*, a romance written mostly in Roquebrune and Berne, after he returned from his posting in Bulgaria. The twin heroes of this rather confusing novel, Jacques Rainier and his formerly Polish comrade La Marne, are not only self-representations of Romain Gary in his roles as war hero and self-destructive wit, but representative figures, standing in for a whole generation of idealists. In the 1930s such men had fought for the Spanish Republicans and either joined or allied themselves to the Communist Party. Jacques Rainier's invented past therefore includes not only the adventure of Free France and a prior spell in Spain, but a lost faith in Communism, to which he is now firmly opposed, to the extent that he volunteers for the French UN battalion fighting Stalin in Korea. In this respect the character of Rainier is an example of how Gary constructs *topical* fictions, stories designed to speak directly to immediate and contemporary concerns, even if they are not his own personal ones. The character of Rainier is an object lesson in the ineluctable development of idealism from a pro-Communist to an anti-Communist stance between the 1930s and the 1950s, and serves to comfort the large numbers of French readers who had already made, or were in process of making, the same adjustment to their political views.

But the trouble with Rainier is this. Because he shares many well-known features of Gary's life (notably, service with the Free French and a house at Roquebrune), it is only too easy to assume that some or all of his other attributes also belong to the author (fighting in the Spanish Civil War, for example). Gary never denied the rumour that arose largely because of this novel that he had fought with Malraux in Spain. He hadn't. But he had no objection at all to acquiring a legendary past.

Gary remained as sceptical of the inheritance of revolutionary thinking as he did of its source. Conventional left-wing intellectuals in 1960s and 1970s France continued trying to distinguish their role and status from that of the bourgeoisie, even though virtually all such figures were either active or former civil servants (as university or school teachers, like Sartre) or persons of independent means, like Philippe Sollers. So when Gary has his stand-in Bondy ask him in *A Quiet Night*, 'What is your position with respect to the bourgeoisie?' he is asking a highly coded question. No other prominent French writer of the day would have dared answer as Gary does: 'Right inside it.'[22]

Gary's antipathy to national boundaries and ethnic discrimination is also entirely sincere, but he took it to logical conclusions that didn't fit easily into conventional political views. Nowhere does the mismatch between political conscience and political sense produce such ambiguity as in his most idealistic parable of all, *The Roots of Heaven*. Written between New York and London in the early 1950s, this African panorama owes a good deal to Gary's experience of third-world politics in the corridors of the United Nations, where he served from 1952 to 1954. Among the Western-educated delegates from countries then seeking independence from the colonial powers Gary recognised the mindset of creeds he had come to regard as abominations: Communism, nationalism, inverted racism and the heedless pursuit of economic development. He wrapped up all his misgivings about the future of Africa in a single charismatic and despicable fictional character whom he named Waïtari, and whose closest probable model (though certainly not his exclusive one) was Kwame Nkrumah, the emerging leader of the British Gold Coast, soon to be renamed Ghana.

Gary's scorn for racial discrimination combined with his bleak view of human behaviour meant that one of the major themes of his African novel echoes and seems to comfort the fears of the right-wing 'Keep Africa French' faction: independence would not be a liberation, but just the dawn of another series of horrors. History has largely proved him right, even if the number of people who now think that the colonial regime was a good idea has shrunk to a tiny fraction of what it was in 1956. All the same, it made Gary's political position in the 1950s seem ambiguous and unclear. He had great sympathy for Blacks, that's clear, but he wasn't optimistic about the future of independent African states. Which side was he on?

In a long interview with Jean Daniel in 1957, Gary was pressed into applying the arguments of *The Roots of Heaven* to the increasingly bitter struggle in Algeria. Gary refused to take sides. He would not admit to backing the maintenance of French Algeria, nor would he declare himself straightforwardly in favour of independence. Instead, he retreated, if that is the right word, into his own ideal of a better, more human way of solving the dispute in a genuine fraternity of different communities. He saw no excuse for the use of terror by the Liberation Front and no justification for the French Army's cruel repression of it.[23] In this he was taking his cue from his friend Albert Camus who, too, hedged about on the issue of Algerian independence, but he was also being quite consistent with the basic import of *The Roots of Heaven*. Nation, system, ideology and politics were altogether secondary matters. The fundamental issue was human decency, and the dogged, obstinate search to achieve it in spite of humanity's eternal slide into exclusion, sectarianism and violence. Of course Gary was right, from a broader, moral perspective, but to the French Left he sounded like a closet colonialist and to the Right like an apologist for independence. (An article he wrote in English for *Holiday* magazine in 1959 on 'The Colonials'[24] defends the moral record of France as a colonial power and would have been considered even more right-wing had it been published in France at that time.) On the Algerian issue Gary succeeded in alienating himself from all constituted political positions inside France and for that reason could be dismissed as a purveyor of waffle.

Tulipe, written in 1945, is more a set of comical sketches than a conventional novel; its aim is to lambast false piety and make fairly cruel fun of political naivety. One of its more striking features is that it appears to recycle a commonplace of Fascist propaganda of the 1930s by treating Blacks and Jews as identical to each other. Of course, Gary intended it to be taken as a mockery of Fascist prejudice, but it is not just a matter of deadpan irony: he really did think Jews and Blacks were identical, as equal (and equally deplorable) members of the human race. Gary's misanthropic sympathy for Blacks also made him a savage critic of the Black Power movement in the 1960s. *White Dog*, written as an almost simultaneous report on the riots following the assassination of Martin Luther King in 1968, portrays Black leaders as crooks and fools. Black separatism, the creation of a Black army, the idea of re-emigration to Africa or the establishment of a separate Black nation in the US, are presented – almost in their own words – as denials of the obvious fact, given the way Black leaders behaved, of the common humanity of Blacks and Whites. In scenes that are as comical as they are tragic, Black Panthers compromise with organised crime, or else set it up; extort money from the liberal-minded stars of Hollywood; exploit the myths of Black sexual potency, while treating their own womenfolk abysmally, and fall into the same racist traps in which their White oppressors have long been imprisoned. *White Dog*, particularly if it is quoted selectively, could thus be used to confirm the fears that many Americans had of the civil rights movement. Indeed, its early popularity in the USA may have been partly based on a misreading of its intentions. What Gary says, however, is unambiguous: Blacks are no better than Whites, and vice versa, because the problem is not of being one or the other, but of being a man. Decency is hard to achieve on either side of the colour line, but that's what the aim has to be. Like Voltaire, who used exaggeration, selective misquotation, antiphrasis and mordant wit to confound superstition in the eighteenth century, Gary conducted his own long campaign against the modern form of *l'infâme*, which is racism, with all the force of bull-shitting raised to the level of art.

10

Sex

Romain Gary was a writer, an airman, a diplomat, a hoaxer – and a prodigious ladies' man. He made no secret of his addiction to straight sex and spoke about it explicitly in his correspondence, his memoirs, on radio and in the press. Myriam Anissimov's biography fills in many of the unavoidably repetitious details, from which it can be deduced, given the stringent French legislation on the protection of private life, that over a hundred women – some of them quite celebrated – are happy to have it known that they had sex with the author of *The Roots of Heaven*. There must be many others who prefer not to have their names printed or who have not yet been identified. Over his life Gary must have come close to equalling Don Giovanni's *mille e tre*, if not Simenon's alleged ten thousand mates.

In his novels Gary writes more about love than about sex, which he almost never describes in any detail except from the point of view of a male adolescent losing his virginity.[1] What's most striking about his large cast of women, however, is that most of them are tarts and many of them very young. Zosia, the teenage heroine of *A European Education*, sleeps with German soldiers to wheedle information out of them; Josette, the tubercular heroine of *The Company of Men*, is a child prostitute; the lovely Teresina, in *The Enchanters*, is not a whore, but she is only sixteen when she appears as Guiseppe Zaga's new wife; Minna, in *The Roots of Heaven*, was gang-raped at the age of fifteen by Soviet troops, and then used sex to survive, regarding it as an act of little importance; 'Lady L.' was a streetwalker called Annette Boudin before marrying into the English aristocracy; Madame Rosa, the central figure of *Life Before Us*, was a whore and then a madam before retiring to look after her co-workers' offspring; and Lila, the unattainable young woman of Ludo's heart in *The Kites*, turns to prostitution to make her way through the Second World War. The most colourful character of all Gary's fiction, who appears in the same last novel, is a Jewish madam who reinvents herself as a Hungarian countess to purvey girls to the Nazis while running a Resistance network at the same time.

This particular feature of Gary's fiction is easily explained and is one of the few dimensions of his work that can be considered autobiographical in a conventional way. He had a taste for very young women and he used prostitutes from his teens until the day before he died. When the deranged narrator of *Hocus Bogus* appeals to 'Ulla, mother to us all',[2] using the name of an ephemerally famous leader of the movement for sex workers' civil rights in France, he is speaking for Romain Gary. Being able to get laid for cash, says Mademoiselle Dreyfus, the part-time tart who drives the narrator of *Gros-Câlin* insane with desire, enhances the value of money no end. 'You know, if you couldn't buy love for money, love would lose much of its value, and so would money.'[3]

Gary was fairly open about wanting to have sex with teenagers. '"My ideal"', he confessed to Lesley Blanch one night before they married, '"would be to have a very pretty young daughter to whom I could . . . make love! Are you shocked?"'[4] In French, *fille* means either daughter or girl, depending on context, and it is possible that the incest fantasy apparently revealed by this anecdote (and which was cut from the French version) is more a matter of mistranslation than scandal. In any case, it is the only mention of it I have ever found. On the other hand, Gary's near-paedophiliac proclivities can be inferred from his very first published novel, as they were by the Polish critic Jan Kott on his first reading of *A European Education*: 'In the otherwise quite touching description of the birth of love between Janek and Zosia,' he wrote in 1946, 'there is for me too much of the dubious charm of Greuze's portraits of fifteen-year-old girls with large, sad, deep blue eyes.'[5] Thirty years later, when Gary went up to kiss goodnight to the daughter of his friend Gabriella van Zuylen during stays at her grand Dutch home, he created much the same impression. The little girl was as terrified of the cigar-chomping old writer with his make-up and manicured hands as she would have been if E. T. A. Hoffmann's 'sandman' had been coming up the stairs.[6] But there was affection as well as lust in the glance Gary cast at some of the Lolitas who crossed his path in life and literature. In the last lines of a harrowing, sentimental late novella, *Clair de femme*, a little girl on the street helps the hero-narrator, Michel Folain, to face life again:

> 'I can't get my shoe on,' she said. 'Can you?'
>
> I knelt on the ground and managed it with ease. A joy of blond hair brushed my cheek and her breath was so sweet and soft that it made me close my eyes.
>
> 'Thanks. You're a nice girl. I live over there.'
>
> She looked at me intently and decided I was still serviceable. She took my hand. 'Come on,' she said. 'I'll help you cross the street.'[7]

Gary did not use prostitutes because he had no other way of getting relief. On the contrary, he was extremely attractive to women and an assiduous and successful seducer. But he did not like to get involved. 'Is she a friend of yours?' someone asks the narrator of one of Gary's last novels, *King Solomon*. 'No, not at all,' he replies. 'We've only slept together.'[8] Social interaction was something that distracted Gary from writing, whereas sex was something that helped him get down to work.[9] Most of the time he found it more effective to use professionals and also safer when indulging his taste for underage sex.[10] In his public pronouncements and through the medium of fiction, too, Gary insisted that morality and sex were entirely different things. The heroine of *The Roots of Heaven* – the only character in Gary's fiction to be named after his mother – puts it this way when challenged about her relationship with Morel, the defender of elephants: 'You can't judge men by what they do when they take off their pants. For their really filthy tricks they dress up – they even put on uniforms, flags and decorations'; and later in the story: 'Sex isn't what really matters.'[11]

It mattered very much to Gary to get his daily dose, which was often more than one shot in the sack. When he was Consul General in Los Angeles, and housed in his official residence with his wife Lesley Blanch, he rented a bachelor pad for assignations with his various girlfriends (he usually had five or six on a string at any one time) and for quickies with call girls hired by telephone. In addition, he usually had sex with his secretary in the late afternoon before beginning dictation of his literary work.

It's not clear what to make of Gary's sex life. It certainly demonstrates admirable energy and persistence, combined with a refreshing lack of cant. From another point of view it seems a desperate search for a comfort that could never be had. In the 1970s, when he had all the money he wanted and a regular supply of prostitutes from Madame Billy and Madame Claude, as well as numerous young women available for free, he could still be seen prowling Rue du Bac after dark, looking for another woman for the night. Gary treated sex more like a drug than a hobby, but the yearning it was meant to satisfy seems to have grown ever worse.

In his writing Gary frequently returns to the origins of his own erotomania, in the sexual awakening of young boys aged around twelve or fourteen. Janek (in *A European Education*), Luc Martin (in *The Company of Men*), Romain Gary (in *Promise at Dawn*), Fosco Zaga (in *The Enchanters*) and Ludovic Fleury (in *The Kites*) all serve as barely fictional vectors for an account of the writer's first experience, and the consistent repetition of the same basic scenario in novels written over a period of thirty-five years is better evidence of what went wrong than anything that documentary evidence or personal testimony could provide. All these self-projections of the teenager that Gary was have sex at around the age of fourteen with a girl of much the same age (Zosia, Josette, Teresina, Lila). We do not know who Gary's first partner was, but the experience, which may have taken place shortly after his arrival in Nice, fixed his tastes for the rest of his life.

Promise at Dawn recounts Gary's sexual awakening as the spectator of an exploit performed by the local baker's boy in a Wilno loft. In *The Enchanters*, Fosco Zaga is first aroused by peeping through a spyhole he makes in the log wall of the bathhouse, and he devises a means to satisfy himself by making another hole in the wall lower down. In both stories, one supposedly autobiographical and the other not, sexual initiation is conducted by a prostitute, hired by the boy's father in the novel and paid for by reselling articles filched from home in the allegedly non-fictional text. In the Zaga version of his early sex life, however, Gary is more explicit about the impersonality of intercourse: 'How many women thought like her that they were loved, whereas all they were for me when our bodies touched was an absence of someone?'[12] For the real Gary, as for his stand-in narrators, women's bodies became interchangeable substitutes for something – a memory, a dream, an aspiration perhaps – that very probably never was. 'The most hilarious aspect of screwing', Gary wrote in *The Guilty Head*, 'is that it gives you a feeling of accomplishment. But then, you do build a better world during orgasm, and it even lasts a few seconds after the act. Sex is a kind of harmless euthanasia, the instant coffee of the absolute.'[13] Which explains why he was jealous of crayfish, whose orgasms, according to some scientific piece he must have read in a newspaper, last twenty-four hours.[14]

Gary married twice and it is not obvious why. His first wife, Lesley Blanch, behaved the same way he did. When she left London to join her husband in Paris in the autumn of 1945 she celebrated her last night in town by sleeping with an Irishman she'd just picked up. On the boat to Istanbul, on her way to join Gary in Sofia in January 1946, she had an affair with a Turkish jewel trader.[15] And so it went on, with husband and wife both sleeping with as many other partners as they could 'conquer' – for a day, a week, or in special cases a month, but never longer than that.

Gary's second wife, Jean Seberg, was the same kind of person, with a pressing, indiscriminate need for sex. Carlos Fuentes had a brief fling with her when she was shooting a movie in Mexico and turned the adventure into one of the least appealing books ever published, but whose merit, from the point of view of understanding Romain Gary, is to provide an indiscreet and quite possibly truthful picture of the sexual nature of a woman he adored.[16]

Whether Gary really performed as much or as well as the legend of him proclaims is not a question that can be answered. Anissimov's own attempt to set the record straight on this point sounds as if it had been written by a committee of lawyers (as it probably had to be):

> He was the discreet lover of many women. They came fleetingly to offer themselves to him, and without their presence, he found dusk unbearable . . . Despite his innumerable conquests, Gary was not a Don Juan, but a hurried, shy, lonely and worried man.[17]

More than one of Gary's male friends thought him less interested in the act itself than in the show of seduction and the appearance of virility. They suspect that the presence of call girls reassured him, but that he did not always take what he paid for. The inner lives of other people are not available for inspection – and their sex lives likewise. In Gary's case it's the legend that counts.

Even in legend, however, his appetite was not universal (he always went after the same type of young-looking woman), and there were limits to his refreshingly broad-minded views on sex. In the 1930s he was a handsome, well-built and sexually attractive youth, and in the circumstances he could easily have become a gigolo. He needed the money; and he found it perfectly acceptable for women to take cash for sex. So why didn't he make ends meet that way? By Gary's own account in *A Quiet Night*, an American called Bradley did offer to introduce him to a male brothel in Rue Miromesnil where women paid for being pleasured. He was tempted, but resisted the idea, provoking a fist fight with 'Bradley', which landed him in a police cell for the night.[18] On release, he went home and cried his eyes out, because he really wanted to go to the brothel and have sex. Had it not been for his mother's 'inner eye', the moral conscience that Mina Kacewa had implanted in the young man, he says, he would have done it. 'But I don't know what would have become of me, because I would never have forgiven myself. I would have seen myself as a piece of shit. And if you think of yourself as a shit-heap, you're bound to become one for real.'[19] It's a message about human nature that Gary attributes to an implausibly Yiddish-speaking 'nice young German' he met on a train in 1937 (though it must have been 1939: see p. 72): '[Jews] have been spit upon and told they were *drek* for thousands of years, and they've become just that, *drek*, through sheer persuasion.'[20]

It is striking and also strange that Gary never imagined that sex work might be just as humiliating for a woman as for a man. He celebrates women who prostitute themselves in almost every one of his novels; but the idea that *he* should offer similar services plunged him into an emotional crisis. He was certain (as a youth, or else as an old man remembering or inventing the episode) that taking cash for sex would have had a lasting negative effect on his life. Something of the same anxiety can be sensed in the portrait of Jeannot, the narrator of Ajar's last book, *King Solomon*, who makes love to a sixty-five-year-old for 'humanitarian' reasons and then becomes very aggressive towards people he suspects of thinking him a gigolo. Gary seems to have been incapable of making a connection between what he felt at the prospect of prostituting himself and what women feel when they do it. It is a stunning failure of empathy in a man who was acutely sensitive to human suffering in every other sphere.

Gary was not completely even-handed about sexual orientation. In an apparently autobiographical digression in *The Enchanters*, the narrator-character Fosco Zaga undergoes a medical inspection (presumably for prostate trouble) that involves an anal probe and the discomfort makes him yell out loud: 'I shall never understand how some people can allow themselves to be . . . !' In the same novel an act of sodomy is described as a humiliation and elsewhere homosexuals mostly figure either as pathetic washouts (like the traitor Arnoldt, in *The Kites*), or, more typically, as thoroughly nasty pieces of work, like the gunrunner Bersch, in *Direct Flight to Allah*, or the perfidious Habib, in *The Roots of Heaven*, whose gunrunning is a cover for the even more lucrative business of exporting Black boys to the harems of the Arab world. There are few homosexual heroes in Gary's world, save in one fine and touching tale which got the diplomat-writer into the devil of a mess.

'The Lute' is set in an imaginary Istanbul, where Gary had never been (though Lesley had visited the city more than once). A French diplomat takes lessons on the oud from a Turkish boy player. As the story proceeds it becomes obvious that the diplomat is in love with the boy. The Frenchman's wife finally realises what is going on behind the closed door of the music room. That is all that happens in a story which is formally quite unique in Gary's work, as it narrates a love affair indirectly, through suggestion and implication, as a conclusion to be drawn less from the sound of music than from its interruption.

Gary wrote 'The Lute' during his posting to Sofia and published it some years later, in 1954, when his tour of duty at the United Nations was nearing its end. He was lucky enough to be appointed Second Secretary in the London embassy, but when he was all packed up and ready to board the liner, the Ambassador, Jean Chauvel, refused point blank to have Gary on his staff. Apparently this sudden veto followed on Chauvel's reading of 'The Lute'. He thought, quite erroneously, that it was about him, as he'd been arrested for sodomy and public indecency in a park in Washington, DC in 1951.[21] The episode doesn't explain Gary's aversion to homosexual men, but it can't have done much to help him overcome it. According to Anissimov, who doesn't give her sources on this point, he even tried to keep Jean Seberg's gay brother David away from three-year-old Diego in 1965, in case he had a bad influence on his son![22]

Male transvestites, on the other hand, fascinated Gary, and he treats them with respect and admiration. In *The Company of Men*, the youngsters who work as runners for the black-marketeer Gustave Vanderputte are attracted by the bizarre personage of Sasha Darlington, a failed actor and drug addict who lives in a brothel. Sasha wears make-up and a kimono, and never leaves his room, decorated with kitsch drapes and plush upholstery. He declaims the Shakespearean roles he has never quite managed to perform on stage and lives in a fantasy world of his own invention, under the thumb of a Russian madam, who is also, as it happens, Madame Darlington. Similarly, in *Life Before Us*, written thirty years later, one of the most engaging characters is a former boxing champion from Senegal who now plies his trade as 'Madame Lola' in the Bois de Boulogne. What makes transvestites important for Gary is not their sexual orientation, but their bid to overcome the laws of nature by insisting on their 'right to determine themselves'. They're among the pioneering heroes of what Gary came to call 'the new frontier', in a short story first published in *Hissing Tales*: a boundary separating humans from their real potential, far beyond the cruel limitations of history, biology and human nature.

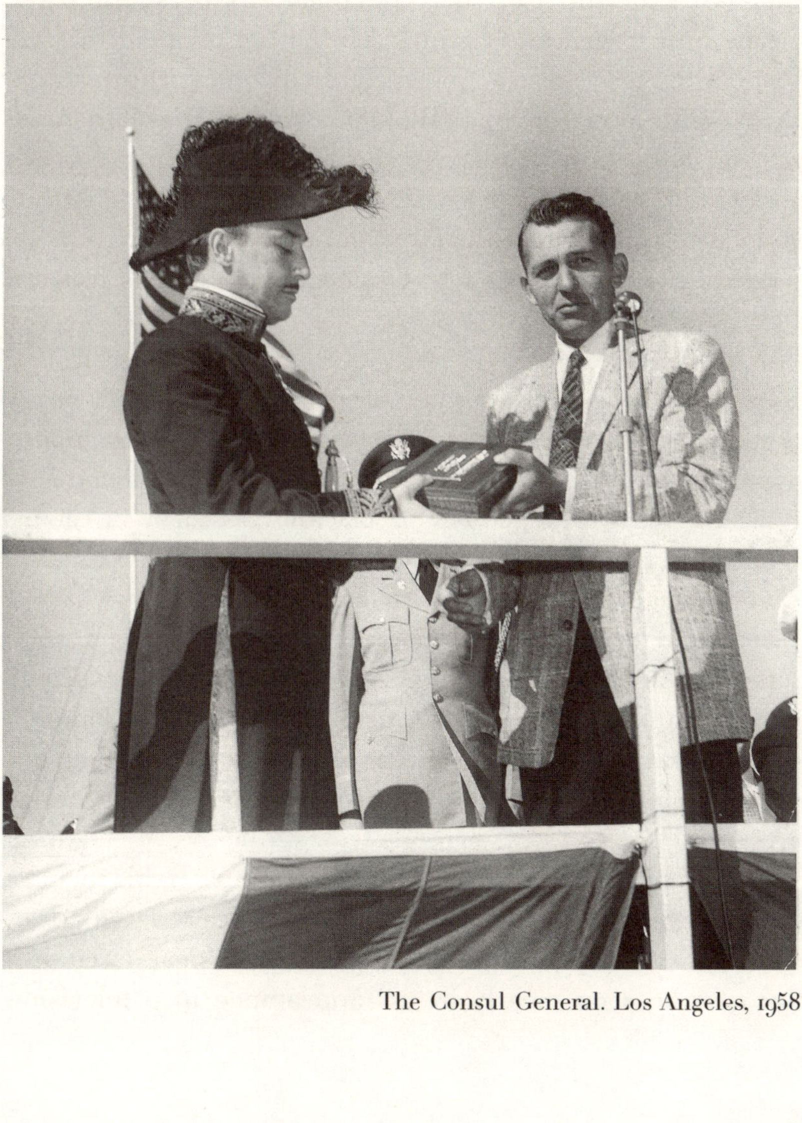

The Consul General. Los Angeles, 1958

Gary's love of dressing up and dressing down provides one of the most searching pages of his travel book, *Trésors de la Mer rouge* (Treasures of the Red Sea, the 'treasures' being the people he met there, not tourist sites). Commissioned by *France-Soir*, the trip took Gary first to Djibouti, the last outpost of the French Empire in Africa, then to Yemen. There he hired a motorcycle in order to travel through the Arabian desert on his own. On leaving Sana'a he was successively relieved of his watch, his pens, his camera, his leather jacket and, lastly, of the bag that contained his passport, plane tickets and travellers' cheques. They were all held 'in safe keeping' by units of the Yemeni armed forces who manned checkpoints along the road. When Gary got to the main guard post on his return to the city, the sergeant in charge of his possessions had left for a visit to his family. Gary was thus obliged to camp out with the other soldiers, waiting for the sergeant's return. After a few days he abandoned his Western clothes and put on native attire.

> Never before had I felt to such a degree the sensation of being nobody, that's to say of at last being *someone* . . . Squatting from dawn to dusk by the roadside, I was a Yemeni tramp in the curious eyes of the few people who passed by in cars, providing them with the reassuring feeling of having escaped from such barbarity and poverty by being born 'well'. That's how from the depths of my indigence I earned a glance from the US Ambassador as he whizzed past, and I am also very happy to have enriched the Yemeni experience of a Chinese civil servant who stopped to take a picture of me, which gave me a wonderful sensation of authenticity.[23]

Gary's enjoyment of disguise may have roots in his teenage wonderment at the fancy-dress capers of carnival-goers in Nice, but it is also part of a more general physical narcissism that can be seen clearly in his appearance in a television documentary about Charles de Gaulle that he made in 1975. *De Gaulle 'Première'* is a fifty-minute homage to the statesman as performer – as the performer of a role that he invented and scripted for himself, that of Charles de Gaulle. The programme shows the fake stateroom in the basement of the Élysée Palace that was constructed from painted flats for the sole purpose of de Gaulle's television broadcasts to the nation, since the real *grand salon* was too cluttered to be suitable for television shows. There are interviews with the deceased leader's cameraman, his producer and his make-up artiste; the powder-puff man is asked to demonstrate precisely what he did to make the General look better on screen, so we get to see Gary being made up by the General's former *maquilleur*. The old roué squirms with pleasure as he is groomed and pampered like the late President of France.

Narcissism cuts both ways, of course, and Anissimov has tried to document all of Gary's many moments of self-disgust. As a teenager in Nice he tried to adopt facial tics to make himself more interesting because, as he said to Silvia Agid, 'Don't you see how ugly I am?'[24] As an old man posing for a lady reporter in 1978, he declared that if he had the means, he would have arranged his appearance – by his own definition a blend of Rudolf Valentino, Gary Cooper, John Barrymore and Leslie Howard! – quite differently.[25] Suffice to say that Gary's preoccupation with what he looked like and with how it could be improved, just like his use of hair dye and make-up and his recourse to manicurists and theatrical costumiers, is of a piece with the self-indulgent dandy we can see being preened in *De Gaulle 'Première'*.

A passage in the remarkably revealing, half-experimental novel *The Enchanters* may give a clue about the origins of Gary's cast of character. 'I then had a "little prince" side that seems hateful to me now,' Fosco Zaga says of his childhood self, around the age of ten. 'With my long curls, silken garments

The Immigrant. Nice, around 1930

and good manners, I was very much the lapdog, always ready to do my tricks for a tidbit. Today we speak of snobbery; then, in Russia, they used to say, "he stinks of perfume".'[26] *Promise at Dawn* also makes it clear that in Wilno, Warsaw and Nice, Gary's mother spared no expense to have her son dress like a Little Lord Fauntleroy. Even in his wildest exercises in dressing down, as in the Arabian desert, Gary was in a sense keeping faith with his mother's attention to appearances. Gary certainly wasn't born with a silver spoon in his mouth but he seems to have been brought up to always have a dab of cologne behind his ears.

Gary's modes of escape into otherness stopped short of drag. The uniforms he wore as a French airman and the spectacular plumed outfit he donned for official occasions when he was French Consul General came with his professional obligations, but his civil attire was often no less exotic. In a beige Burberry, brown homburg and with a fat cigar in his mouth he looked like a caricature of a British spiv; with a pigtail and a Hawaiian shirt he slouched around Paris like an exiled Californian hippy; in a moth-eaten flak jacket and Cossack boots he could easily have been taken for a tramp. At other times he put on his Russian Bear outfit – a black fur coat and an astrakhan hat – or else his Mexican bandit disguise: sombrero, poncho and dark glasses.[27] Alain Bosquet admitted that he sometimes didn't recognise his old friend Gary when he met him in the street: 'He can be dressed like Zorro, then appear as a cowboy in jeans, then in diplomatic attire; he may be bearded or clean-shaven, wear a hat or not, be with or without his cigar.'[28] Nancy Huston has written an entire book about Romain Gary based on his variable clothing, which she counts as a lifelong struggle to find an appearance that would satisfy the impossibly high demands made on him by his mother.[29]

According to *Promise at Dawn,* Mother 'Nina' also instilled in the boy a terrible fear of venereal disease. As a young man in Paris in the 1930s, Gary was certainly worried about catching the clap. On one occasion he rushed in to see his friend René Agid, who was then training to be a doctor, undid his flies on the spot and offered his organ for immediate medical examination, as he'd just had a girl he wasn't too sure was clean. With or without a mother's warning, however, anybody who had as much sex as Gary with so many women he did not know from Eve should have been concerned about the risk to his health. Frequent examination was an elementary precaution. Gary may have been a hypochondriac, but his concern about STDs was just plain common sense. At Cimarrón, in the 1970s, his bathroom was stocked with a huge range of prophylactic creams and remedies against all kinds of venereal infections.[30] Wisely so.

The fear of impotence was a less rational but much deeper anxiety in Romain Gary. On the flap copy of the first French edition of *The Dance of Genghis Cohn* (a text not reproduced in later paperback editions, or in the English translation of the work) Gary says that the idea for the book came to him from reading 'twenty or so years ago, two clinical studies by Steckel, *Frigidity in Women* and *Impotence in the Male*'. These classic psychoanalytic texts (which Gary also places on a bookshelf in the novel,[31] alongside Montaigne, Pascal, Shakespeare, Malraux and Chester Himes[32]) may have crossed Gary's path in wartime London, but it is more likely he read them in New York when they were republished by Vision Press in 1953.[33] Why was a young married diplomat reading such works at that time? In all likelihood because he suspected, or had been told, that his own donjuanism expressed a fear of impotence; or else because he did not know how to satisfy Lesley Blanch, who likewise sought additional partners even while enjoying married life with Romain Gary.

Lesley seems to have been as indulgent towards prostitution and sexual slavery as Gary himself. Her introduction to the memoirs of Harriette Wilson, a celebrated English courtesan of the Georgian period, is a panegyric to the commerce of sex and a bizarre defence of Harriette's right to blackmail her clients.[34] In conversations with her friend Olga Csáky, overheard by the grandchildren who often summered at Roquebrune, she said she had spent a long time in the harem of the Topkapi Palace in Istanbul 'when Romain was Ambassador to Turkey' (which is, of course, nonsense) researching the daily lives of the inmates of the seraglio (which no longer existed, in any case). Lesley's idea of oriental décor, however, probably owed less to the Alhambra in Granada than to the one in Camden Town.[35]

Gary broaches the subject of female frigidity in several stories. In 'Birds in Peru', written not long after the start of his liaison with Jean Seberg, a ravishingly beautiful young woman turns up on a beach one morning with four men in fancy dress. They have come from a carnival ball and it is clear she has had sex with more than one of the men. Rainier, here a rugged hero living in semi-retirement in a beachside café, saves the girl from drowning herself, takes her in and is surprised to see a high-class motor car turn up in pursuit of the girl. It is her husband. We are given to understand that the woman's desperate efforts to find satisfaction are no secret to the man, who regrets only that he has to fish her out of such bizarre situations. The story ends with the departure of husband and wife. Some years later, Gary had Seberg act the role in a film he produced and directed himself. Jean was probably one of the very few women Gary really would have liked to satisfy and in the story, as in the film, he expresses his own despair at the inaccessibility of that part of a woman he could not conquer.

In *The Enchanters*, too, the ineffable object of a boy's desire – his stepmother Teresina – turns out to be physically accessible, but incapable of really participating in sex. She drives Fosco's poor father to distraction, before fading away like an old photograph.

The motif of frigidity is used as a metaphor for the human condition in *The Dance of Genghis Cohn*, or rather, in its secondary plot, which occupies far too much of the text. Lily, the wife of the count of Licht, has disappeared; and at the same time male corpses, all knifed in the back with their trousers round their ankles, are found with astonishing regularity in the nearby forest of Geist. Cut to Lily, with her eternal companion Florian, who is Death, discussing which man she should try next in order to find satisfaction. But Lily can never be satisfied and the price of trying to meet her demands is always death. Her metaphorical significance camouflages a more literal obsession and anxiety on Gary's part. The impulse to 'sacrifice yourself' for a woman may be irresistibly strong, but it is a fruitless pursuit, for woman can never be satisfied. Is that because she is frigid? Or because man is fundamentally impotent?

In his first French-language phase, Gary, for all his flamboyant whoring in real life, did not write very much about sex. The relations between Janek and Zosia in *A European Education*, between Luc and Josette in *The Company of Men*, between Rainier and Ann in *The Colours of the Day*, and between Morel and Minna in *The Roots of Heaven* are handled with elegance and discretion. 'Why is the erotic so absent from your work?' François Bondy asked Gary in 1957. 'I suppose it's because I am still relatively young,' Gary replied evasively (to himself, as Bondy took no part in the interview).[36]

Similarly, in his second incarnation as an English-language novelist, romantic encounters are not described in detail, and the pornographic content of *Lady L.*, *The Talent Scout* and *The Ski Bum* is virtually nil. Gary began to reveal more in *Promise at Dawn* and to give slightly more daring descriptions in *The Dance of Genghis Cohn* and *The Guilty Head*, but the real change occurs in the early 1970s, as Gary approached his sixtieth birthday. In *The Enchanters*, which he published under his own name in 1973, *Gros-Câlin*, the first of the Ajar novels, which came out in 1974, and then in *The Way Out* (1975), in *Hocus Bogus* (1976) and even in the more lyrical *Kites* of 1980, Gary tackles head-on the difficult business of describing acts of sexual intercourse in a variety of different contexts and forms – between teenagers and tarts, between young lovers, between old men and younger women, in brothels and in the woods. Only at this late stage of his career did Gary take advantage of what the British have always thought of as the special freedom of the French to write about sex. It was, of course, a freedom more liberally taken in French writing after 1968 and in that sense Gary's development simply maps on to a more general trend. But it also corresponds to the frenetic programme of Gary's last decade, when his ambition (clearly visible to us only in retrospect) was to say *everything* he had to say.

Gary's sex life seems to contradict a cliché inherited from the vulgarisations of Freud's psychoanalytic approach to creativity, which Gary disliked intensely. Writing can't be counted a substitute for Gary's sexual passions and desires, which he indulged beyond belief. Whatever it was that he might be held to have repressed, it wasn't sexual desire, of any conceivable kind. On the contrary, writing seems to have been more like an extension of Gary's sexual arena, for his books, and most especially his personal memoirs, are clearly designed to seduce. Lesley Blanch, whose valuable but ambiguous testimony of her life with the novelist was not published until the writer had been dead for fifteen years, views Gary's entire literary career as an expression of his need for sex: 'sex was his driving force'.[37]

That may account for the seductiveness of Gary's storytelling manner, but it does not come near to naming what moved him to write. Anger at the world's iniquities, a thirst for justice and an aspiration towards humaneness and common decency among men are what drive Gary's plots, not anything that might be revealed by bedroom secrets, of which he really had none. When he and Lesley went to see the Simenons at their home in Connecticut, the conversation turned exclusively on what the two men found it easiest to talk about – namely, sex.[38] What Gary *wrote* about, on the other hand, was not suitable for a lunchtime chat.

All the same, the army of happy hookers who parade through Gary's fiction is not as straightforward as it might seem. On the surface every one of his lovable whores seems to express the forthright attitude of a man entirely unaware of the suffering and humiliation that is a sex worker's lot. On the other hand, calling someone a whore remains an intolerable insult in the portrait he paints of himself. When he was a schoolboy in Warsaw, he tells us in *Promise at Dawn*, another boy insulted his mother, calling her a 'cocotte', which is a translation of the common Polish oath, *kurwa mac*.[39] When young Roman tells Nina of the insult, she does not comfort her son, but gives him a slap in the face. She commands him never to allow such insults to pass unavenged. The episode provides Romain's first lesson in honour.

Until he began writing as Ajar, Gary created only one character who is literally the son of a whore. Willie Bauché, the anti-hero of *The Colours of the Day*, vaguely based on Orson Welles, is a 'universal genius' of film, but also a scoundrel, a cheat, and a self-abasing crook. He is, too, a man in love, masquerading debauchery to mask his despair. His family name, a false positive of the apparently negative word *débauché*, is there to tell you that. In a convoluted plot line that Gary would reuse in *The Way Out*, Bauché tries to have himself assassinated by a hood. (The mafia assassin, prophetically named Soprano, is not supposed to know whom he is hired to bump off, nor is Bauché supposed to know just who his assassin is.) In the end, however, having seen his wife in the arms of another at Roquebrune – in Gary's own apartment in that picturesque village, in fact – Bauché throws himself off a cliff, dressed as a pantomime clown. The disguise ensures that his death will be seen as an accidental outcome of the drunkenness that is common at carnival time in Nice. All three themes – clowning, suicide and the pursuit of an inaccessible woman or ideal – recur throughout Gary's life and work, but a hidden anecdote ties Bauché to Gary's sense of himself more directly.

Bauché is the son a New Orleans whore. As a child, he had eaten a shoe for love of a girl. This bizarre detail was dropped, together with much other material, when Gary rewrote the book in French twenty-five years later and republished it under the title of *Les Clowns lyriques*.[40] In the meantime, however, Gary had turned the anecdote of the child who eats a shoe for love of a little girl into an explicitly fictional short story in 1956[41], and then introduced it as an episode in the life of *himself*, in an oft-quoted passage of *Promise at Dawn*. Infatuated with a little girl called Valentine, the boy-hero of Gary's self-fabrication was determined to win her from schoolyard rivals.

> 'Janek ate his whole stamp collection for me.'
>
> Such was the beginning of my long martyrdom. In the course of the next few days I ate for Valentine several handfuls of earthworms, her father's rare collection of butterflies, a mouse, a good many decaying leaves and, as a crowning achievement, I can say that at nine years of age – far more precociously than Casanova – I took my place among the greatest lovers of all time and accomplished a deed no man, to the best of my knowledge, has ever equalled. I ate for my lady one of my rubber galoshes.[42]

The fact that Gary attributes fictional episodes to himself does not imply that episodes attributed to fictional characters are close to the literal truth. But what does stand out from the character of Willie Bauché as it is elaborated in the revised and rewritten English text of *The Colours of the Day* is that hopeless love, clowning, suicide and the strange exploit of the eating of shoes form a configuration in which a mother belonging to the oldest profession also has a place, whether asserted (in the case of Bauché) or denied (in the case of the semi-fictional Romain Gary of *Promise at Dawn*). The truth of Mina Kacewa's life does not really matter here. Gary could see himself as a *fils de pute*, the son of a whore. His defence of prostitutes and prostitution in his fictional and journalistic writing seems to express a desperate loyalty to the father-like mother figure he mostly invented to give the strange, unforeseeable turns of his life a semblance of necessity and form.

II
Works

II

The Books Gary Wrote

Gary wrote a lot, under several names, in two languages, and often rewrote his texts when republishing them in the other language, or when putting out new editions within the same tongue; as a result, no library in the world has a complete set of all the books that he wrote.[1]

Not all of his books count as fiction. *Promise at Dawn* (1960) *White Dog* (1970) and *A Quiet Night* (1974) are usually considered memoirs (which does not mean to say that they are to be treated as entirely non-fictional), and *Trésors de la Mer rouge* (1970) is a travelogue; *Pour Sganarelle* (1965) is a long essay on the art of fiction; and *Life and Death of Émile Ajar* is a testament, posthumously published in 1981. There are also major differences between the order in which Gary was able to publish his works in French, and the order in which they appeared in English. Gary's twin careers looked very different to their English and French audiences, who were often intentionally deceived about the nature and authorship of the books they were reading.

Gary's writing life falls into three quite distinct parts. The first, running from the war years to 1956, was devoted to writing novels in French. (The appearance of Gary's first novel in English translation before it could be launched in France was an effect of wartime paper shortages, not a put-up job.) Part III of this book, 'The Good Fight', is devoted to this first major phase of his writing career. In the second phase, which runs from 1957 to 1966, Gary wrote novels *in English*; his only new French works in this decade are short stories, memoirs and essays. Part IV of this book, 'Big Time', deals with this quite different literary adventure. The third phase began with *The Dance of Genghis Cohn* in 1967, when he returned to writing fiction in French.[2] From the time of his divorce from Jean Seberg in 1971 his production accelerated at a prodigious rate. Of the twenty-seven separate projects identified in Gary's thirty-five-year career as a writer, no less than thirteen were invented, written and published in the last nine years of his life. Of these, five were published under a pseudonym. The difference is even more striking if only fiction is included in the count: eight novels between 1944 and 1966 (one under a pseudonym), and thirteen in the shorter period between 1967 and 1980. Part V, 'All of the Above', describes the spectacular achievements of the last phase of Gary's writing career.

From 1971 Gary had heavy commitments and needed to earn a great deal of money to continue living in the style to which he and his dependants had become accustomed. Gary's biographer Anissimov comments: 'That is why for the last ten years of his life, Gary often worked on several novels at a time.'[3] It is true that money had always been a powerful stimulant to Gary's creative energy, but there were perhaps deeper reasons for the stunning burst of creativity under his own name and two others in the later years of his life. In 1845, when publication of the *Human Comedy* was nearing completion and full recognition of his genius seemed to be slipping from his grasp, Balzac wrote to his Russian lover that 'the present time demands that I write two or three major works . . . to show that I am younger, more brilliant and more fertile than ever'.[4] The outcome of that defiant stand against oblivion was two sombre masterpieces, *Cousin Bette* and *Cousin Pons*.

Gary kept his cards closer to his chest, but the extraordinary rhythm of his publications between 1975 and 1980 – with two and sometimes three new, revised or retranslated books appearing each year – suggests something of the same determination to resist and endure, at the onset of what would now be called middle age.

Many of Gary's books were good sellers and reprinted quite often; *Life Before Us* is generally reckoned to have sold more copies than any other French novel in the history of the French book trade. However, reissues of Gary's books were rarely uncorrected reprints of the existing text. Gary took advantage of a reissue to make revisions, ranging from whole new chapters to pages of cuts, and most often these changes were not mentioned on the title or copyright pages. The biggest differences occurred when he moved a text from English to French, or vice versa, since he usually rewrote whatever his translator submitted to him. As a result, Gary's bibliography – presented in summary form in Appendix II at the end of this volume – is devilishly complicated.[5]

By usual reckoning Gary wrote twenty-seven separate works, but if all the different versions of each work in two languages are included, the total comes to no less than fifty-two. If, in addition, abandoned redrafts, adaptations and self-translations among his surviving papers are added to the tally of his writing activity, then it becomes clear that *rewriting* occupied rather more of the author's time than first-run composition in itself.

Gary began the practice of rewriting his own works from the start of his adult career, with the substantial changes he made to his first novel when it was finally able to appear in French as *Éducation européenne*. In his English-language phase, from 1956 to 1967 or thereabouts, most (though not all) of the rewriting he did involved making cuts and additions to French works in process of translation into English. The reverse procedure (making additions to the French translations of works that had been written and already published in English) started with the publication in France of *Lady L.* in 1963. It gathered pace throughout that decade, then turned into a hectic race, in the last five years of Gary's life, to revise all the major books he had written before it was too late.

In the 1960s Gary tried to impose some order on his ramifying work. *The Talent Scout* and *The Ski Bum* were re-presented in French as Parts I and II of a series called *La Comédie américaine*, which has a punning relationship to Balzac's *Comédie humaine*, but the series was discontinued after that. In between those two reverse translations, *Pour Sganarelle* was labelled the first of a cycle named *Frère Océan* (*Brother Ocean*), leading on to *The Dance of Genghis Cohn* (*Frère Océan* II) and *The Guilty Head* (*Frère Océan* III).

One of the more striking features of Gary's habit of rewriting himself is his periodic revisiting of the material of *Tulipe* (1946) in works for the stage, and his reluctance to abandon an early novel that had not sold well in the 1950s, *The Colours of the Day*, by repackaging it in the 1970s as *Les Clowns lyriques*. But the most persistent by far of the material he could not leave alone was his first completed novel, *A European Education*, rewritten several times in two languages over a period of nearly twenty years. But these exploits of self-repetition do not explain what is common and what is different among the twenty-seven basic projects that Gary expanded by his obsessive bilingual self-revisions into such a large number of separate books.

Gary's stories cover an immense number of topics and the range of his characters is similarly wide – from English aristocrats to Ukrainian peasants, from a Buchenwald survivor to a prince of Araby, from a black-marketeer to a captain of industry, from an American film star to an itinerant carpet seller. However, the most clearly defined group of Gary's works deals with resistance to Nazism, which it is entirely appropriate to place at the centre of his real life, at the centre of his work and at the centre of European history in the last hundred years. Gary's 'resistance cycle' includes the several versions of his first novel, *A European Education*, his last work, *The Kites*, as well as a group of short stories written in the 1940s, during and just after the war.

Because Gary was personally involved in the resistance to Nazism as a flyer in the Lorraine Squadron, his several personal memoirs, which constitute a second obvious grouping of his works, cannot be entirely separated from the resistance cycle of novels and stories. *Promise at Dawn* in 1960, *White Dog* and *Trésors de la Mer rouge* in 1970, *A Quiet Night* in 1974 (translated by Gary, but not yet published in English) and, under the disguise of Émile Ajar masquerading at that time as the pen-name of Paul Pavlowitch (the son of Gary's cousin Dinah), *Hocus Bogus*, in 1976, all return in part to the moral implications and personal effects of the great fight.

A third major section of Gary's output constitutes what could be called the pseudo-Christ cycle – stories dealing with a version (often ironical) of a not entirely mortal saviour of human conscience. Among these figure *Tulipe* and the various attempts he made to put it on the stage, as well as his path-breaking Holocaust comedies, *The Dance of Genghis Cohn* and (to a degree) *Life Before Us*, as well as the Tahitian fantasy of *The Guilty Head* and the science-fiction novel *The Gasp*.

Beyond these three thematic groupings, however, Gary's novels are more remarkable for their differences than for their similarities. They are tied together less by common subjects, settings or plots than by repetitions of names and motifs, and a stock of obsessively recurrent proverbs, quotations, set phrases and French idioms. Repeated and subverted clichés are the cement of Gary's work as a writer and reinventor of the language called French. (For all his linguistic gifts, he was not nearly so inventive when writing in English.) Chapter 1 of this book has shown how the official French translation of a key term in European history – 'the right of peoples to national self-determination', expressed as 'the right of people to dispose of themselves' on the other side of the Channel – allowed Gary to construct a meaning that the original phrase never had, and to speak a truth in which he truly believed under the guise of a translinguistic joke. Alongside many similar turns of phrase listed in dictionaries of French idioms, Gary used old film titles (*The Lost Patrol*, *Double Indemnity*, *The Big Sleep*), children's classics, literary allusions, snippets of poems (Yeats, Lovelace, Péguy, La Fontaine . . .) and almost every other kind of linguistic ready-made or, as members of Oulipo now say, 'cooked language', to generate not just comical quips and telling jokes, but anecdotes, characters and storylines. The process is more clearly visible in Gary's comical works and turns into a linguistic riot in the works signed by Émile Ajar, but the device itself is common to all Gary's writing in French. 'Ajarspeak' is the irregular, enriched, unstable, deceptive and bastardised language to which Gary had always aspired.

Gary's literary culture relied most heavily on works he had probably read before he moved to France and his most frequent references are to nineteenth-century European classics that he is most likely to have first read in Russian or in Polish, in the original or in translation: Pushkin, Gogol and Dostoevsky; Fenimore Cooper, Dickens, Robert Louis Stevenson, Conrad and Mayne Reid; Adam Mickiewicz, Selma Lagerlöf and Karl May. To this list must be added the one French classic that had a huge impact in Eastern Europe and is hardly less influential in popular culture worldwide today: Victor Hugo's *Les Misérables*. Sometimes hidden, often mentioned explicitly, Gary's 'familiars' provide him with anecdotes, motifs and characters throughout his career, but most of all with a basic set of ideas about the nature of humankind. Momo, the narrator-protagonist of *Life Before Us*, wants to rewrite *Les Misérables*; Gary, for his part, rewrote books he had read, then rewrote himself, in an intricate conversation between all the languages and cultures he possessed.

There is a sense in which Gary's whole career – in real life as in writing – can be seen as an exercise in translation, carried out with unequalled inventiveness and passion. With only a few exceptions, he only ever translated himself, if by translation we mean shifting meanings from one natural language to another. In another sense his novels, constantly recycling the same range of literary classics, are also *literary* translations, constituting a subtle, half-occluded campaign for intercultural communication. In *The Company of Men* Dostoevsky talks to Dickens in a Paris apartment; in *A European Education* Kipling talks to Karl May in a Polish forest; in *Gros-Câlin* Gogol talks to a character from *White Dog* ('Pete the Strangler') in a language half translated from Yiddish, English and gobbledygook. In life, too, Gary's successive personae can be seen as brilliantly persuasive self-translations – from immigrant to diplomat to international celebrity – that mix and blend much the same disparate cultural elements from which his writing is made. In all these dimensions his translation style is extremely free, but at the same time faithful to the aspirations he clung to. He sought a world where the foreign and the native would be equal and indistinguishable, where *das Eigene* and *das Fremde* ('the own' and 'the other') that Leo Spitzer spoke of amid the ruins of post-war Germany in his memorable defence of language and literature, would be one and the same thing.[6] Bastardy *is* purity in Gary's ideal world.

An interviewer once asked him when it was that he thought one of his books was finished. 'Never, unfortunately,' he replied. Then he added, in his typically misleading way: '*Lady L.* is the only really finished book I've done, where I have nothing to add.'[7] This was because he had already rewritten it *entirely*, adding new chapters, new references and a cod bibliography when he brought it into French for the release of Peter Ustinov's film version in 1963 – and he would revise it yet again for its republication in 1976. Just as Gary's stories do not always end very neatly, so the writing of them was often simply suspended to allow for publication, in the expectation that one day the author would be able to go over it all again.

Gary's publishing career began with short stories, not novels, and in the first phase of his writing, short-form narratives run parallel to the better-known longer works. Gary brought most of his stories together in a collection in 1962, but the earliest individual pieces of *Hissing Tales* date from 1945, and all but a handful were published long before 1962. After that, Gary published only novels; it is not obvious why he abandoned the short form in which he excelled. *A European Education* is structured episodically, as a series of 'scenes', each of which could be taken as a short tale; moreover, the five 'fables' read aloud by the partisan-poet Dobranski to the forest fighters round the campfire at night can stand alone as fine examples of the short-story form.

The short fiction is woven from the same skein of themes, motifs and obsessions as his longer works. Four of them belong to the cycle of works about resistance to Nazism and could be considered offcuts from the tales told by Dobranski in *A European Education*. Several others contain the nugget or conceit from which longer novels were later drawn – 'A Craving for Innocence' adumbrates the 'false Gauguin' anecdote developed in *The Guilty Head* and 'The New Frontier' hints at what Gary did later with the idea of 'human potential' in *The Gasp*. Other tales are woven into later fiction as representations: 'All's Well on the Kilimanjaro' crops up as an actual postcard of the Kilimanjaro on the wall of Vanderputte's apartment in *The Company of Men* and its plot device – messages sent by deception – is strangely similar to the imaginary account he gives in *Promise at Dawn* of the letters his mother had sent to him after her own death. 'A Humanist', one of the strongest pieces Gary ever wrote, has its hero live out the war years, and long after, in a hidey-hole that harks back to Janek's *kryjówka* in *A European Education* and announces Madame Rosa's 'Jew-hole' in *Life Before Us*. What Gary did with short fiction was, in sum, no different from what he wrote in long form, but the brevity of the genre obliged him to fewer self-repetitions and produced some of the finest of all the works that he wrote.

12

Games with Names

Names play an important role even for novelists who stop short of inventing them, like Kafka and his Joseph K. in *The Trial*. It's not just retrospective illusion that makes 'Bovary', 'Karamazov', and 'Bartlebooth' seem *exactly* right for the characters involved: naming is a part of the novelist's art. Gary was a champion in the coining of names, whether you measure his achievement by quantity, by cunning, by the wealth of connotation, or by their impenetrability. An example of sheer quantity is provided by *The Ski Bum*, which contains in its 244 large-printed pages no less than 324 proper names, about half of which are inventions. Allusiveness, on the other hand, abounds in *The Roots of Heaven*, set in Africa, with two characters – Morel and Schoelscher – bearing the names of two great fighters against slavery and exploitation on that continent (the English journalist Edward Dene Morel and the French politician Victor Schölscher). Personal allusions are often cleverly camouflaged: a memory of changing trains at Sliven, in eastern Bulgaria, when Gary was on his way to take up his post in Sofia, is inscribed in the name of a Black deserter from the US army in *The Company of Men*. Gary was very attached to the names he invented, which often seem like the original prompting of the stories in which they appear. He considered Genghis Cohn, for example, who unites the two imaginary sides of Gary's ascendancy, Mongol and Jew, to be a personal property, and even tried to sue Thomas Pynchon for filching it in *The Crying of Lot 49*, from *The Ski Bum*, where the character first appeared.[1]

Gary invented names not just for fictional characters, but for himself as well. His legal birth name was Roman Kacew, written Кацев in Russian, and pronounced 'katsev'. On arrival in France, it changed by force of local custom to 'Kassef', that is to say, with the Polish letters 'c' and 'w' pronounced as if they were written in French. He also made a slight shift in his given name, from Roman to Romain, to make it more familiar in France. In the English-speaking world it is quite common for immigrants to adopt new names. A Mr Fischbein may become Mr Finch overnight, a Cohen may slip into Colquhoun, or a Belastotsky may truncate himself into plain Bellos. Under French traditions, a name is treated as the inalienable property of the person concerned, and changing it requires a long and rarely used legal procedure. As a teenager Gary could not change his name, as he was a Polish immigrant below the age of majority. Once he became naturalised as a French citizen, in 1935, he did not bother to try and remained 'Kassef', written Kacew. But when he got to London in 1940 there were good reasons for adopting a *nom de guerre*. Members of the Free French were all considered deserters by the Vichy regime in France, and were liable to be condemned to death if they returned. Most of them had family members in occupied France, so it was wiser for them to camouflage their names for the duration of the hostilities, like their comrades in the resistance inside France. Gary signed the oath of allegiance to Charles de Gaulle on 8 August 1940 under his adapted birth name, 'Romain Kacew'; a few weeks later, before his unit was shipped to Africa, he was using the form 'Romain de Kacew'. The addition of the 'particle of nobility' can be put down to his desire to fit in with the social group of his closest comrades, as many air force pilots came from the aristocracy. However, by the time he got to Bangui, in February 1941, he was 'Gary de Kacew'. The mysterious bi-syllable 'Gary' was invented and adopted at some point between his first flights in an RAF unit and his long sea journey to West Africa on the *Arundel Castle*. During the war years Gary's *nom de guerre* varied in spelling and formulation: 'Gary de Kacew', 'Gari de Kacew', and 'Romain Gari' appear on various documents. In 1944, however, when his first book appeared in English translation, his pen-name became fixed as 'Romain Gary', and that is what he called himself thereafter – in correspondence, in private and, as far as possible, in his professional life too. Legally, he remained 'Romain Kacew' for a few years more, but he did his very best to hide that fact.

'Gary' is a common English first name and a genuine French family name too. 'Gary' may have commended itself as a code name to a Free French airman based in Britain precisely because it is a real name in both languages. But like Anna Betulinskaya, the Franco-Russian singer of 'The Song of the Partisans', who is much better known as Anna Marly, Gary might simply have got his new name out of the telephone book.[2]

His subsequent career as an almost professional inventor of names and as a pseudonymous writer several times over makes most of his readers unwilling to treat his first adopted name as anything short of a cunning puzzle. The first story Gary published in the UK during the war appeared with the byline 'A. Cary',[3] and 'Cary' could just possibly be a pun on the French word *carie*, meaning dental cavity. Toothache plays a prominent role in the definition of what it means to be human in a text Gary seems to have known almost by heart, Dostoevsky's *Notes from the Underground*. Anything is possible, but this explanation of Gary's name seems far-fetched.

If there is an allusion contained in the name 'Gary' it is most likely to have been a homage to the film actor Gary Cooper, or else an appropriation of the role the actor characteristically represented on screen, notably in *Beau Geste* (1939) – that of a stalwart defender of justice and right, with a knock-out punch.[4] Fifteen years later, when Gary was Consul General in Los Angeles, he met the real Gary Cooper and came to like him a lot; consequently, the choice of *Adieu Gary Cooper* (Gary Cooper died in 1961) as the title of the French revision of *The Ski Bum* (published in 1969) may best be considered a memorial to a lost friend, not a key to Gary's adopted name.[5]

After the war, Gary hung on to his nom de plume and used it in most aspects of his daily life, remaining Romain Kacew only for official purposes in the Diplomatic Corps. His military decorations and his standing as a public figure and a servant of the state now made it possible for him to undertake the procedures leading to a formal change of name, which were completed in 1951. Thereafter, he was Romain Gary for real: Roman Kacew ceased to exist.

For many years Gary did not write or speak about his decision to adopt the name 'Gary'. When he was asked in interviews why he had changed his name, he spoke exclusively about the circumstances of the Free French and gave no clues as to why he had chosen this name rather than that. Many of the code names adopted by Gary's comrades in the Free French were more or less transparent. Raymond Aron called himself René Avord, after the air-training base where Gary (among others) had learned his skills; Marcel Bloch, the aircraft designer, adopted the code name his brother had used in the internal resistance, *char d'assaut* ('attack tank'), thus becoming Marcel Bloch-Dassault. But until the very last days of the leader of the Free French, Charles de Gaulle, Gary's name remained uninterpreted.

It was on a stay in Los Angeles during the Watts riots that Gary was first astounded by the Black Power slogan, 'Burn, baby, burn'. Writing about his experience of that self-deluding mayhem in *White Dog*, which came out in early 1970, Gary drops something that looks like a clue:

> Americans have a way of changing my perfectly Russian name – *gari*, meaning burn, in Russian, as in 'burn, baby, burn' – into a typically American 'Gary' by shifting the accent from the second to the first syllable. My ego thus feels the humiliation of being reduced to the lowest common denominator of American first names.[6]

In the French version of this paragraph there is no mention of 'burn, baby, burn', which may well be what first prompted Gary's reinvention of his 'perfectly Russian name', '*mon nom, bien russe*'.[7] Once reinvented, however, Gary stuck with the back-translation of himself into 'burn!' in interviews and in *A Quiet Night*, published in 1974, almost at the same time as the first of his brilliant literary mystifications under the name of Émile Ajar.

However, 'gari' is not and never can be a 'perfectly Russian name'. Russian has specific rules for name formation, and the second-person imperative of a verb could never fit them. This Gary certainly knew, and his assertions about the meaning of his name must therefore be counted as eyewash.[8]

When the real identity of the author of *Life Before Us* was revealed as Gary had intended by the publication of *Life and Death of Émile Ajar*, Paul Pavlowitch, who had played the role of the fictitious Ajar for the preceding five years, published his own account of the mystification. *L'Homme que l'on croyait* is an invaluable book, full of irreplaceable observations about Gary's personality and literary work. But it is wrong in one respect. Pavlowitch claims that *ajar* (pronounced *azhar* in French: the 'j' has the sound of 's' in 'pleasure') means 'glowing embers' in Russian.[9] In other words the writer who had called himself 'burn!' had wanted to show that he was not entirely burned out yet, that his 'embers' were still glowing. This cannot be right. Ажар (azhar) is not a word of Russian. Жар (zhar) means 'fire', to be sure, and also, in some dialects, 'glowing coals' or 'smouldering log'; but *azhar* does not exist as a word form. *Ajar-azhar* is no more authentic than the troika bells Gary claimed to remember from his Russian infancy. The network of combustible meanings which critics like to assemble around Gary's two best-known pen-names is just hot air.[10]

In an interview after the publication of *L'Homme que l'on croyait*, Pavlowitch speculated that Gary chose 'AJAR' because it was the acronym of an *Association des Juifs Anciens Résistants*, allegedly close to Gary's heart.[11] No such organisation existed, of course; and if it had, Gary would not have joined it. Pavlowitch was just teasing a New York journalist with a game almost worthy of his Uncle Bogey.

Equally implausible as keys to the pen-name adopted for Gary's most successful hoax are all other real-world instances of the word *ajar*. I doubt if Gary wanted his alter ego associated with the Autonomous Republic of Ajaria, a Muslim enclave in Georgia, or with the King of Afghanistan's fabled hunting lodge in the Ajar Valley, or with the famous mosque and university in Cairo known as 'shining bright', El-Azhar in Arabic. A more extensive trawl of the onomastic ocean would probably net many more red herrings with names spelled or sounded out like 'Ajar', a bi-syllable whose virtue is to be phonetically well-formed in all the languages Gary knew without meaning anything at all.

Gary himself bears the main responsibility for setting his readers on a wild goose chase in search of the meaning of his pen-names. Some of the other names that he used for his books and translations are cross-language puns of no great profundity. In 1974 he published a macabre comedy, *Les Têtes de Stéphanie*, under the pen-name of 'Shatan Bogat', which means something like 'rich devil' in Russian; this reading is confirmed by the pseudonym he used for the English translation, *Direct Flight to Allah*: René Deville – 'devil' with a pronounced French accent. (This is quite an achievement – translated pseudonyms are rare indeed!) 'Fosco Sinibaldi', on the other hand, which he used to publish *L'Homme à la colombe* in 1958, is borrowed from a real person, Paul-Louis Sinibaldi, a Free French airman who later worked in civil aviation in Mexico,[12] coupled with Gary's favourite character in nineteenth-century fiction, Count Fosco, the master of disguise in Wilkie Collins's *The Woman in White*. Gary also masqueraded as a 'John Markham Beach', to whom the English translation of *Promise at Dawn*, and the non-translation of *The Talent Scout* (which was written in English) are attributed. This may be an inscription of the Markham Beach Hotel, or simply of Markham Beach in California, where Gary was living when he invented the name. However, the main effect of these pierceable mysteries has been to increase the determination of Gary's exegetes to find a real answer to the questions: Why Gary? Why Ajar?

The invention of names is a field that allows unlimited play to those who have several languages under their command. Gary was well equipped in this respect, as he had Russian, Polish, Yiddish and German to play with alongside and inside French and English. But he had even more. In his youth in Nice he had learned some of the local patois, Nissart, which has some items of vocabulary quite unknown elsewhere, and also a few scraps of Hungarian, from the first great love of his young life. As he grew older, Gary retained the child's magical ability to absorb new languages like a sponge. When he describes himself, as he often does, as still a child aged around eight, or ten, or fourteen, whether through the mode of a fictional character or in apparently autobiographical and confessional texts, he is, in this respect at least, speaking the plain truth. His language-learning abilities in adult life remained more like those of a child than a man.

Gary's acquisition of English in a matter of months in the middle of the war at the age of twenty-nine is the most spectacular instance of his linguistic talent. He learned to speak first of all just by living among English speakers in the RAF; he absorbed more of the language with Lesley Blanch, who gave him children's classics to read aloud; and by the time he left London at the end of 1945, he was as fluent in his sixth language as in all the others. His English was so good, in fact, that it played a key role in his later promotion to a post in New York.

In Bulgaria, in 1946–7, Gary learned the language (Russian and Polish, though entirely different tongues, belong to the same language family as Bulgarian, so gave him a kind of head start) well enough to scan local newspapers and to conduct polite conversation with officials at embassy parties. But that seems to be where Gary's adventures with languages came to a stop. From 1956 until the end of his life he had frequent contact with the Hispanic world – he was chargé d'affaires in La Paz, Bolivia for three months, then lived in California, where Spanish is widely spoken, then had a Spanish housekeeper in Paris. He accompanied his wife, Jean Seberg, to Spain for the birth of their son Diego, who was effectively brought up in Spanish for the first years of his life. In 1965 Gary acquired a villa in Mallorca and thereafter spent about four months there every year. But he never learned more than a smattering of Spanish (a few words are dotted around his later novels). When in residence in Puerto Andraitx, he did not speak Spanish at all and he never uttered a word of the language to his Spanish-born son.[13]

Gary did not need Spanish to play onomastic games, of course, since Russian, Polish, Yiddish and German provided more than enough juggling balls for writing in English or in French. The dim-witted fictional poet laureate of England who acts as a foil to Lady L., in the novel of that name, carries the plausible but non-existent name of Sir Percy Rodiner. It's a transcription of the Russian word *rodina*, meaning 'homeland'. The name of Schatz, an SS assassin turned police officer in the Federal Republic, in *The Dance of Genghis Cohn*, means 'treasure'; we find German soldiers called Kaninchen ('rabbit'), Liebling ('darling') and Jodl ('yodel') in *Forest of Anger*, a Hollywood agent called Belch (in the French version: Beltch) in *The Colours of the Day*, a defender of good causes called Tsoures (Yiddish for 'troubles') in *Gros-Câlin*, and a Russian diplomat called Ivan Ivanovich Aïda-Oukhniem (the refrain of the 'Volga Boatmen's Song') in *L'Homme à la colombe*. In *The Enchanters*, Gary's alter ego and narrator bears the family name Zaga, purportedly Venetian in origin, but more likely to be a truncation of *zagadka*, the Russian word for riddle.

The epigraph of the original French edition of *Hissing Tales* contains a riddle fairly typical of Gary's multilingual wisecracks.[14] It is attributed to a Russian philosopher by the name of Sasha Tsipotchkine, who does not exist. The name comes from the Russian expression *na tsipochkakh*, 'on tiptoes', and the solution is to be found in a proverb allegedly known to all UN diplomats and used in *L'Homme à la colombe*: 'you get further when walking on tiptoe'.[15]

Gary also borrowed names from current affairs. Armand Denis, the divinely handsome anarchist who rescues Lady L. from life on the streets and turns her into a tool of much greater crimes, bears the name of a portly, crumple-faced Belgian television celebrity of the 1950s. Other appropriations of real names may be less arbitrary. Gustave Vanderputte, the repulsive traitor and black-marketeer of *The Company of Men*, borrows his name (bar one letter) from a Belgian popular novelist, Henri Vandeputte (1877–1952), who ran the Ostend casino in the 1920s. The real Vandeputte also used a pseudonym, Pierre de la Marne, for the many children's stories he published – another name that Gary reuses, as the *nom de guerre* of the son of a Jewish tailor from Łodz, in *The Colours of the Day*.[16]

In the first novel Gary published under the false identity of Émile Ajar, his narrator-hero, Michel Cousin, is consumed with longing for a miniskirted, dark-skinned typist who works in the same office. She comes from French Guyana, a French department in South America bordering on Brazil, almost all of whose population is of African descent. Her name is Mademoiselle Dreyfus – which, in that spelling, is characteristic of French Jews from Alsace. She is not the offspring of a mixed marriage, far from it. In Gary-Ajar's ironical fantasy, many Guyanese adopted the name of Dreyfus when the Jewish soldier was unjustly condemned for treason and deported to Devil's Island, a penal colony just off the coast. If only! Gary invents Mademoiselle Dreyfus's name not only to express an ideal of fraternity and solidarity between France's oppressed minorities, but to mock the idea that it might ever come about.

Gary's ease with languages was no doubt connected to another gift and burden that he had to an unusual degree, that of memory. It is no coincidence that his first Goncourt-winning novel, *The Roots of Heaven*, is a defence of elephants, for Gary felt himself to be just such a metaphorical beast. He lends his burden of excessive recall to Ludovic Fleury, the central character of his last novel, *The Kites*. Ludo and his Uncle Ambroise, the maker and flyer of 'memorial' kites, are afflicted with what they call '*mémoire historique*' – a term used by Gary long before, and glossed in the English version of *White Dog* as 'total historic recall'.[17] Gary's memory, like that of Ambroise, is essentially a memory of names.[18]

Gary presents himself quite explicitly as a 'carrier of memory' in his novelised autobiography, *Promise at Dawn*. Recalling his life at 16, Welko Pohulanka in Wilno, around the age of eight or nine, Gary tells a self-congratulatory story about one of his neighbours, a mere mouse of a man called M. Piekelny. Piekelny is so impressed by mother Nina's prediction of greatness for her son that he inveigles the boy into his room with Turkish delight, and then, after beating about the bush for a while, tells Roman that there is something he really wants from the future poet and ambassador.

'Well, when you meet great personages and important men, promise me to tell them . . .' A spark of mad ambition suddenly lit up the mouse's eyes. 'Promise me you'll say to them: at Number 16 Welko Pohulanka Street, in Wilno, there lived a M. Piekelny.'[19]

The narrator accepts Mr Piekelny's request and goes on to fulfil the promise thus made – first when being inspected at Hartford Bridge airbase by Her Majesty the Queen, and then, later on

from the platform of the United Nations to the French Embassy in London, from the Federal Palace in Berne to the Élysée, to Charles de Gaulle and Vyshinsky, to high dignitaries and builders of empires to last a thousand years, I have never failed to mention the existence of the little man, and I even had the joy, more than once, of announcing to tens of millions of viewers of the vast US television networks that at Number 16 of Welko-Pohulanka Street in Wilno there lived a certain Mr Piekelny, may his soul rest in peace.[20]

Many readers have been struck by this passage, which is comic in its implausible excess yet retains an air of sincerity, and marks the charming narrator as a man who keeps even a boyish word. And yet – it is something altogether different. Gary's 'man from hell' (*piekel* is Polish for 'hell') reproduces almost word for word a famous exchange from Act III of Gogol's classic farce, *The Inspector General*. Bobchinsky, one half of a pair of bumbling country landowners, is deeply impressed by the air of authority that the fraudulent inspector Chicherin has managed to create around himself. Bobchinsky hopes to take advantage of such an important personage:

I beg you humbly, when you go to St Petersburg, tell all the bigwigs there – the senators and the admirals – tell them this,

> your Excellency: in such and such a town there lives a certain Pyotr Ivanovich Bobchinsky. That's what you're to tell them: there lives a certain Pyotr Ivanovich Bobchinsky.[21]

Gary's contraband use of a Russian classic seems hard to accept without protest. It's most unlikely the author was responding to the proposal made by the underground avant-garde of the 1950s for the generalised use of 'modified unacknowledged quotation', or anticipating the subtler practices of postmodern masters like Perec, who smuggled artful scraps of other works into their own. A snippet of Gogol masquerading as an episode of a man's own life looks like plain cheating, and its emotional effectiveness makes it all the more objectionable. We should spit it out. Tfui! as Genghis Cohn would have said.

Gary got away with this ambiguous exploit for more than forty years.[22] His well-paced, entertaining narrative style is not conducive to slow or close reading. It's quite *disarming* – and what it disarms in particular are routine critical faculties. It's as easy to miss the Gogol as it is to take Gary's rewriting of Robert Louis Stevenson's *The Wrong Box* in chapter 35 of *Promise at Dawn* for a real-life episode of the Second World War.[23] The grace and ease with which Gary evades capture makes understanding him *as a writer* more demanding than the works of superficially much more difficult authors.

The Piekelny anecdote is not an isolated instance of naming as a memorial in Gary's work, however. Its combination of sentimentality, self-aggrandisement and irony makes it only a particularly memorable performance of an act that recurs throughout Gary's writing of fiction and memoir. Émile Ajar's last incarnation as Solomon Rubinstein, 'the king of the ready-made', probably sums up Gary's point best of all:

> Everyone remembers illustrious men, but no one remembers people who were of no account but who nevertheless loved,

> hoped and suffered . . . The very expression 'people of no account' is odious, true and intolerable. Within all the measure of my modest means, I simply cannot accept it.[24]

In *The Colours of the Day*, Jacques Rainier, a former *résistant*, honours the forgotten in a ritual performance of memory golf, played with his sidekick La Marne, in Pedro's bar, on the Promenade des Anglais:

> 'Bouquillard', Rainier would say, for instance.
>
> 'Who was Bouquillard?' La Marne would ask, on behalf of the period.
>
> 'A Free Frenchman. He flew a Hurricane in the Battle of Britain. Forty years old, five victories. Shot down. Tried to jump but his roof panel jammed. So he sang *La Marseillaise* until the end.'
>
> 'I hate obscene stories', said La Marne . . .
>
> 'Robert Colcanap', Rainier would say.
>
> 'Don't be so rude', La Marne would respond. 'Button up. Be decent. Louis-Ferdinand Céline. Or how about Marcel Aymé.'[25]

Gary uses real names – Bouquillard and Colcanap both died in action in the Lorraine Squadron – to serve as 'tags' for values that are hard to express, but also self-evident: heroism, devotion, self-sacrifice . . . Céline and Aymé, La Marne's ironical antidotes to an excess of ideal, are invoked as examples of moral turpitude because of their real and alleged collaboration with the Germans during the Occupation of France. '*Géographie humaine*', the first story Gary published after his arrival in the UK in 1943, consists almost exclusively of a similar memorial routine: a group of Free French airman sit in the mess of an English base, looking at a map of Africa, where they had previously served. They go over the names that they see: Fort-Lamy, Ounianga-Kébir, Koufra, Mourzouk, Sarah's

Well, Faza . . . The recitation brings back memories of sunnier climes, but the dreadful English weather is not the point. The place names stand for the comrades who had come down nearby in their Blenheims and Lysanders. Listing the names of the places (real personal names could not be printed in wartime: but the 'geography' of the story is explicitly 'human' as its title states) is a ritual for grieving the men who fell.[26]

Other names of Gary's wartime comrades are dotted all round his work: Despiau in *The Colours of the Day* and Fourquet in *White Dog*, and, in *Promise at Dawn*, a veritable litany of the lost: Schlosing, Béguin, Mouchotte, Maridor, Gouby, Max Guedj, de Thuisy, Martell, Colcanap, de Maismont, Mahé . . .[27] Martell comes back again in even more ritual fashion in *A Quiet Night*: 'As no one will ever mention Martell again, I insist on writing his name here. Martell. Done.' The recitation of names is a matter of considerable gravity for Gary, even – or rather, especially – when he wraps it in irony.

Towards the end of the Sabbath service, the Kaddish or traditional prayer for the dead is said, and the names of former members of the synagogue whose anniversary of death, or *yartseit*, falls in the same week are spoken aloud in a ritual list. Readers of Gary who are particularly alert to Jewish themes hear a Kaddish in the name lists that crop up so often in his work. But naming the dead is not an exclusively Jewish tradition. There's not a village in Catholic France that doesn't have its *monument aux morts* bearing the names of its wartime dead; and there can't be a meeting of ex-servicemen anywhere in the world that doesn't also recall fallen comrades by going over their names. What such practices have in common is the superstitious belief that repeating names gives life to the departed. Naming routines of that kind are powerful examples of wishful thinking: if I *say* so, then it *will be* so. Of course Gary did not believe that by writing the name 'Martell' one more time he would bring him back to life. But he did believe it a little bit – as we all do, when it comes to those we loved.

So although the Piekelny anecdote in *Promise at Dawn* was copied out of Gogol, it remains an example of a characteristic use of naming in the writing of Romain Gary. The illusion of sincerity created by the clever borrowing of a literary classic only serves to enhance the magical purpose of *naming names*.

Some of the fictional names Gary created seem to be labels for an idea, because they recur attached to characters who are similar, but not clearly intended to be the same person. Jacques Rainier, for instance, dies in the epilogue of *The Colours of the Day*, but lives again in 'Birds in Peru' and *The Way Out*, in careers that don't dovetail in any practical sense – army volunteer, South American barman and French business magnate. Recurrent identities like Rainier's seem to be close to the narrator, who is not easy to distinguish from Romain Gary. Even harder to separate clearly are all the characters called Tulipe, or Tulip – the protagonist of the sole surviving novel of Gary's youth, *Le Vin des morts*, the pseudo-Christ of the novel entitled *Tulipe* and the signatory of several letters written by Romain Gary.[28]

Just as Gary attributes fictional names to himself (Tulip, Sinibaldi, Bogat, Ajar and so on), he also attributes his own name, or substitutes for it, to some of his fictional characters. The least hidden of these is the lovelorn barber of an early short story called 'All Is Well on the Kilimanjaro'. This pathetic character has sailors who call in to his Marseille parlour take away postcards of exotic places and mail them to his village sweetheart from the depicted locations when their ships put in. The barber thus creates his own legend as an intrepid world traveller, but to no avail. He never gets his girl all his life long, but after his death a bronze statue is put up to honour the explorer he was not. His name? Albert Mézigue – and *mézigue* is Parisian slang for 'me'.

The names Gary claims to have played with as an adolescent when looking for the best pseudonym with which to launch his literary career are all charged with meaning by association: his school reading in French history and literature gave names like Alexandre Natal, Armand de la Torre, Roland de Chantecler, Hubert de Longpré or Lucien Brulard,[29] connoting nobility, imperial adventure, literary eminence and, above all, Frenchness. These names, never actually used, ask to be taken as talismans, or magic charms. They are tools whose task is to fulfil a wish and to project their bearer forward to a new and brighter identity.

Even when Gary is just having fun with verbal smuggling, the names he invents often allude to darker and memorial themes. In *The Talent Scout*, for example, the awful *caudillo* Almayo prays to the gods of his ancestors Talacoate, Ijmujin and Aratuxin. Two of these almost plausibly Mesoamerican deities are contraband topical references: Talacoat is a Californian vineyard, and aratoxin a chemical warfare agent that must have been in the news in 1960. 'Ijmujin', however, stands for Ijmuiden, which has an altogether different kind of charge. It is the name of an industrial city in the Netherlands which RAF 324 Squadron bombed to smithereens more than once. Turning its name into a fake deity makes it an invisible reference to what Gary must have counted as one of his crimes. Like the supposed reiteration of the name of Mr Piekelny, or Rainier's recitation of comrades' names in a bar in Nice, the act of writing out the name of the place under this exotic disguise is a way of honouring the dead.

An equally contorted but no less meaningful game with names is played in the last part of *The Roots of Heaven*, a novel transparently based on Conrad's *Heart of Darkness*. An American journalist named Fields crash-lands near the site where Morel and his small band of followers are trying to protect a thirst-ravaged herd of elephants from slaughter. In Polish, the word for field is *pole*, which, when written as an English word, names the nationality of Joseph Conrad – and of Fields himself, a Polish Jew who had lost all his family at Auschwitz.

The Kites, Gary's last novel, dedicated 'To Memory', ends with an act of naming representative of Gary's work to the highest degree. The action of the novel takes place during the Occupation of France. In the last pages of this beautiful work the war is over and reconciliation begins. Marcellin Duprat reopens his celebrated restaurant, Le Clos Joli, and the narrator's uncle, the kite-maker Ambroise Fleury, resumes his active retirement in the same village by the sea. Then the story breaks off. Without transition, without even a paragraph break, comes a sentence that must be just about the last line of a book that Romain Gary ever wrote:

> *Je termine enfin ce récit en écrivant encore une fois les noms du Pasteur André Trocmé et celui de Le Chambon-sur-Lignon, car on ne saurait mieux dire.*[30]
>
> I now end this tale by writing once more the names of Father André Trocmé and Le Chambon-sur-Lignon, because you can't say better than that.

Le Chambon is a large village in the mountainous and inaccessible heart of the Massif Central and its population belongs to France's historical Protestant minority. Gary had never been there: the invocation of the name of the place and of its former parish priest, André Trocmé, is not a personal reference. Nor does it refer to anything that had happened to Gary's relatives or friends. It's true that Camus, whom Gary had known and admired, spent nearly two years in Le Chambon during the war and used his time there to write the first version of the novel that would become *The Plague*, but Camus, an outsider, knew nothing of what the villagers were doing. Under the guidance of Trocmé, they were giving secret shelter to hundreds of Jewish orphans from the cities and saving them from deportation to the death camps. Their actions were courageous and entirely disinterested. At Yad Vashem, the Holocaust memorial in Jerusalem, Trocmé is honoured alongside Raoul Wallenberg as one of the most prominent of the Righteous Gentiles. What Gary commemorates in this decidedly peculiar way at the end of what he knew was his last work is courage and goodness. The story of Le Chambon, which had been known about for many years, had become topical once again with the publication of Philip Hallie's philosophical essay *Lest Innocent Blood Be Shed*.[31] The adult Gary never denied or hid his Jewish roots, so this last line of his oeuvre should not be taken too firmly as evidence of Romain Gary rediscovering himself as a Jew at the end of his life. The story of Le Chambon is a French one. Most importantly, however, the heroism of Trocmé, unlike Gary's wartime action, did not involve violence, bloodshed or terror. It is the rarest of things: an action that realised the basic human aspiration towards the good, without any of the usual side effects. That is why 'you can't say better than that'.

13

The Way Gary Wrote

Romain Gary had a brilliant, not an organised, mind; nor was he a disciplined man. In his youth he came close to getting into serious trouble, according to *A Quiet Night*;[1] elsewhere in that book he describes himself as a hot-tempered rowdy during his war service and says he was twice hauled before the *conseil de discipline*. Gary had weapons training and knew how to use a gun. He'd handed in his service revolver when he was demobilised in 1945, but fifteen years later the Algerian conflict put French diplomats abroad at risk. Threats were made against Gary's life, among others, and so, at the request of the Foreign Office, the Ministry of the Interior gave the Consul General a permit to carry a weapon for personal protection. In July or August 1960, just after leaving the USA, Gary bought a Smith and Wesson .38, serial number 7099.983, and he hung on to it to the end of his life.[2]

Gary was always ready to use his fists. He's known to have assaulted a hostile critic in a restaurant, to have laid into a young man on the street who he thought was mistreating a woman, to have challenged Clint Eastwood to a knuckle-fight . . . There's even a recording of the start of a punch-up between Gary and Jean-Pierre Elkabach, the radio personality, on a programme that went out live:

JPE: What do you think will become of Émile Ajar?

RG: All I wish for is for him to carry on writing.

JPE: There's been talk of rewriting in connection with Émile Ajar's book . . .

RG: Fuck you! (Sounds of chairs scraping and scuffles.) Rewriting by whom? (Louder:) WHO? I AM NOT . . . (Cut to music.)[3]

Hot-tempered and easily brought to the boil ('like milk soup', as the French saying has it), Gary was not house-trained either. He never put anything away; he hadn't learned how to.[4] He had quite useless hands that 'flapped helplessly like fins attached to his wrists' whenever he was confronted by any practical demand, according to Lesley Blanch.[5] Pavlowitch recalls Gary blundering about with his hands as if he were blind. His finances were often a mess and his apartment likewise. Here is a picture of him happily at work on *The Colours of the Day* in his Riviera retreat at Roquebrune:

> Gary wrote sitting on the bare wood floor, surrounded by wicker baskets into which he threw drafts and pages he would eventually scrap. There was paper everywhere. Some sheets slipped between the floorboards, others flew out of the window on a gust of wind.[6]

Gary's surviving manuscripts are housed in a converted Norman abbey near Caen (Calvados), not far from the three-rosette restaurant where most of *The Kites* is set. With appropriate permission you can have the handwritten drafts of most of his post-1960 work brought in sturdy cardboard boxes to your desk. (Much of his earlier work has been lost, some of it in a fire at Lesley Blanch's home; other vital pieces were lost in airports and railway trains all over the place. The proofs of The *Roots of Heaven* went missing in transit between Bolivia and Paris.)[7] Gary's drafts are a mess. They seem to be just fragments and scraps, with some pages unnumbered, and other series that repeat themselves. The chronological order of the many versions of the same text is impossible to establish. It's not even clear they are in the right folders, but that's not the archivists' fault. Gary's papers are extremely difficult to decipher.

The hand is bold, the pen strokes thick, the letters regular and round, crammed close to each other and running from edge to edge of the page. What do those squiggles actually represent? Are they letters? Or are they crossings-out? Elizabeth Jane Howard saw the manuscript of *The Roots of Heaven* before it was published, but couldn't make head or tail of the sheets Gary handed her: 'The writing was of the kind that, though large, was illegible.'[8] The main reason for this is that Gary learned to write at school in Poland and the style then in use was the old German *Schrift*, which was abandoned in 1945. He carried on using letter shapes based on those obsolete forms all his life, whether writing Polish, English or French. To eyes accustomed to the shapes of English or French handwriting, *Schrift* looks like a series of impenetrable whorls. Gary's lower-case 'a', for example, is shaped like 'oi', and his capital 'T's look like teapot handles. Neatly done it would have been a 𝒯, just as Gary's own name would have begun with 𝒢. But few of Gary's written words could be said to be neat. Even handwriting experts struggle to make out what some of them are.

Gary's punctuation is also bizarre. Quotation marks are given in the old German style („thus"). Accents are sprinkled over the page, as by a salt shaker. Some common or grammatical word endings like *–ment* and *–aient* are scrunched into squiggles, while others, such as the feminine plural agreement on a past participle, *–ées*, are stretched out to fill all the remaining space of the line. Just one glance at a page – any page – tells you that Gary wrote fast. Any dozen sheets will confirm that he almost never corrected himself. There are no crossings-out, interlineal insertions, notes to self in the margin (there is no margin). You can see that the words and the stories simply poured out of the man. Writing was 'an organic necessity to him', wrote Lesley Blanch. '"*Une évacuation quotidienne*", as he said indelicately.'[9] These large, round, overlapping letters flow on and on, page after page, like a river running towards the sea. Sometimes the stream slows down, spreads out, loses its direction. That's when Gary puts a thick diagonal line through a page or two or three and starts over, from the top.

The manuscripts explain a noticeable feature of Gary's published work: his opening pages are almost always very strong, and his conclusions frequently much weaker and sometimes frankly poor. A visit to the archives gives a visible explanation for this. Because he did not correct what he had written, but started over again each time he found the story meandering or running into a dam, Gary wrote his beginnings many times over, improving them a little at each pass. But he wrote his endings far fewer times and sometimes only once.

Gary never learned to type with more than two fingers and nearly everything he wrote was typed by someone else. He was lucky to have a string of devoted secretaries – among them Mireille d'Agostin at Roquebrune, Odette de Bénédictis in Los Angeles and the heroic Martine Carré in Paris – prepared to learn how to decipher his hand. Even so, much of his work was dictated aloud from the sheets of scrawled text of the kind that he left. He was one of the earliest European writers to use a Dictaphone (he nagged his American publisher, Joe Barnes, to get him one as soon as he heard they were available in the US).[10] That helps to explain the illegibility of these manuscripts: they aren't fair copies and, for the most part, weren't intended to be read by anyone else. It also elucidates a central feature of Gary's literary work. The two novels he laboured over most intensely, and which won the Goncourt Prize nearly twenty years apart, are both cast as simulations of direct speech. With the exception of Part III,[11] *The Roots of Heaven* (1956) is a spoken novel, with the same story being told by different characters in overlapping spirals of revelation and mystery; *Life Before Us* (1975) is the spoken narration of a teenager, which appears at first to be addressed to the reader, and then, at the end, reveals itself to be a tape recording, which is exactly what most of Gary's fiction was before being typed up into a book. The art that lies at the root of Gary's literary achievement is close to that of the raconteur. 'I think I have no real talent,' he confided to Joe Barnes in one of his many patches of depression, 'but just a way of telling a story.'[12]

Gary's manuscripts bear no visible trace of the process of invention and no sign of the writer's other preoccupations. What they show – to a spectacular degree – is a mind entirely engaged in the task at hand. These uninterrupted, uncorrected screeds could not but have been produced by a writer who told stories as others breathe and sweat. His outpouring of prose was unstoppable, fluent, compulsive – a biological act.

'Style does not interest me,' Gary declared in a radio interview with Henri Bonnier in 1967. This seems an amazing claim to be made by the author of *Gros-Câlin* and *Life Before Us*, two magnificent exercises in the invention of linguistic style. Yet the manuscripts seem to bear out Gary's claim, in the sense that they betray no hint of the search for the *mot juste*. There's evidence of attention to the rhythm of the tale, but not to the words through which it is told. If it didn't come out quite right, he did it all over again, from some new angle of attack. The voluminous papers stored in the Norman abbey don't contain a single structure plan, chapter plan, outline or book proposal, and it seems safe to say that Gary never bothered with working things out in advance – he found out what the story was by writing it. What he suffered was the exact opposite of writer's block. But for a writer with high ambitions, fluency can be almost as much of a curse.

Gary's improvisational, trapeze-act approach to the composition of long works meant that he often failed to spot elementary mistakes, especially repetitions. In the last novel that he wrote in English, a science-fiction fantasy entitled *The Gasp*, the hero Marc Mathieu quotes Kaiser Wilhelm II's famous self-exculpation after the First World War – '*Ich habe das nicht gewollt*' (I never meant to do that) – on page 46 when talking to his laboratory assistant Chavez, and then, when thinking about the moral conscience of his liberal colleague Valenti on page 61, comes up again with exactly the same phrase. On page 37 of *Lady L.*, anarchists meeting in Paris 'became particularly aggressive about a German called Karl Marx . . .', and on page 100 of the same novel a group of anarchists meeting in Geneva 'hated Bakunin and Kropotkin, but above all they hated Karl Marx . . .' '*Je dois avouer franchement*,' says Fosco Zaga on page 351 of *The Enchanters*, '*qu'à partir de ce moment-là mon père se livra entièrement aux mains des charlatans*' and then says exactly the same thing halfway through the following page. (The English edition omits the repetition.) In *Europa* there is a paragraph on page 73 which repeats the basic premise of *The Talent Scout*, as if Gary had forgotten not only that he'd previously written a novel that gives the 'truth about Faust' but already explained in *Promise at Dawn* that 'the real tragedy is that there is no devil to buy your soul';[13] and in his essay on the art of fiction, *Pour Sganarelle*, self-repetitions are so numerous as to make it hard to follow the thread. These are certainly blemishes, which editors should have picked up before the books were sent to press. But they are not meaningless. At the level of argument and emotion, Gary's work is repetitious from start to finish: repetitions give it its coherence and unitary nature. At the level of linguistic invention, too, Gary's art is to repeat or to recycle fragments of other kinds of text. Repetition is not just the eternal standby of the pedagogue and moralist, it is the basic rhetorical figure of Romain Gary's literary work.

* * *

Gary's practice of writing was instinctive, incessant, obsessive and speedy, and more often tested by ear, in the practice of dictation, than by eye. The obvious disorder of his paperwork mirrors the disordered, intense and hyperactive life that the author led. However, another clue to the unity of the man and his work is found in one recurrent feature of his writing practice, or rather, in the nature of a particular type of recurrence. One of the earliest and least accomplished of Gary's short stories is titled 'Sergent Gnama'. It tells the patriotic tale of an African native who has learned a French colonial identity by rote, without understanding the words of the songs he can sing. His name, however, is authentically African – it means snack food in many dialects and languages of Senegambia.[14] Gary returns to the same word nearly forty years later, in an entirely different and invented sense, as the nickname for the memorial kites constructed by Ambroise Fleury in *The Kites*. To justify this re-appropriation of a word from the past, he gives it an imaginary etymology, making '*gnama*' mean something like 'soul'. In like manner, Gary takes phrases, expressions, names and words from one work and reuses them in a slightly or significantly different sense in works written years, sometimes decades, later – as if the later work had been generated not by a new idea, but by the verbal formula or name invented earlier on. For example, in *The Colours of the Day*, Jacques Rainier, as he enjoys the intense idyll of a love affair with an American film star in the hilltop village of Roquebrune, longs 'to extend his love and the peace of this French village to the entire world . . . because the roots of heaven are planted in man but of heaven he knows nothing but the gripping roots'.[15] Those 'roots of heaven', visually inspired by the soaring outcrop of rock on which Roquebrune is built, gave Gary the title for his 'elephant novel', *The Roots of Heaven*, but in that wonderful romance the title phrase is alleged to come from an Islamic proverb about man's aspiration towards an ideal.[16] Another chapter of *The Colours of the Day* ends with the sentence: 'The world was corroded by ideas, and soon there would remain not one simple love where a man could shelter his guilty head.' Fifteen years later the exact same phrase returns as the title of a novel, *The Guilty Head*.

Other connections of the same kind lead not to whole works, but to themes which weave in and out of many of them: a film title like *The Lost Patrol*, for example, migrates from project to project and is reused many times as an explicit metaphor for the human condition. 'A quality of despair' or 'the quality of despair' is another talismanic expression on planet Gary, serving here for a remark (as on page 112 of *White Dog*), there for the title of a fictional novel written by Jess Donahue in *The Ski Bum*. In the French version of the latter novel the replacement title, *La Tendresse des pierres*, was first used for a stage play written around 1950,[17] but it crops up again in *La Danse de Gengis Cohn*[18] and also served later on as the provisional title for the novel attributed to Ajar and known in English as *Life Before Us*. *The Raft of the Medusa* (after Géricault's painting) also migrates as a phrase (often meaning: man's inhumanity to man) from novel to novel, and provides Gary with the title of one of the dramatised versions of *Tulipe*.

These curious types of repetition suggest not only that Gary chewed the cud and regurgitated stock ideas over and over again, but that words and phrases, including clichés, fixed expressions, titles, quotations and historical allusions, prompted the invention of stories to fit them. The process involved treating such phrases as if they were names – the names of things dormant within the talismanic expression. Recurrent names like Rainier, Genghis Cohn, Harry the Rat and Marc Mathieu, as well as the repeated use of particular quotations from Michaux, Kafka and Maksim Gorky, function in Gary like pieces of verbal magic – sticks to be rubbed together again and again until they make the right illusion appear in plain sight.

14

What Gary Meant

Romain Gary believed quite seriously, as most of us do not, in the Latin adage *nihil humanum a me alienum est* (nothing that is human is foreign to me).[1] This first thesis has two major consequences that explain quite a lot about his life and his work. It accounts for Gary's marginally lunatic aspiration to be everyone, to be all kinds of men, to be many and not one, and thus for his many joyous changes of dress, name, identity and so forth. It also accounts for his self-hatred and misanthropy, for all that is in the human race – notably violence, stupidity, greed and hate – are in him too. That is why he was unable to take sides in politics and even in war, and considered nationalism and racism, which exclude some others from full human rights, to be flat-out contradictions of the human condition. But it doesn't mean to say 'the other' is good. On the contrary. Blacks aren't better than Whites: they're just as prone to the abject inhumanity of mankind as any others.

There is an obvious impossibility in this basic position. If Gary is as evil as any other, what allows him to know that? Something else must exist in human beings – in all of us, necessarily – that permits us to know that some of our impulses are inhuman. Throughout history people have *constructed* the same higher values that are called justice, compassion, love and honour, which alone account for our ability to recognise evil in others and ourselves. What makes us human in the full sense of the word is our ability to imagine better selves.

Playing on the double sense of the French word *humain*, which covers *the human* and *the humane*, or perhaps being creatively confused about a distinction that only English makes, Gary's second thesis is that *we are not yet human*. The human – the humane – is what we aspire to. Our aspirations, not our actions, define our true, unrealized selves. 'Humanity' is a work in progress.

Gary's forward projection of the human ambition is made manifest in his novels and stories through plots and especially those epilogues set beyond the date of the work's appearance. The epilogue of *A European Education* (first published in 1944) happens in an imaginary 1947; the frame story of *Tulipe* is set three thousand years hence; *The Company of Men* is narrated from a perspective that must logically follow the novel's first publication; *The Dance of Genghis Cohn* ends with a vision of the Eternal Jew's future travails; and Gary's most successful novel as Émile Ajar asserts in its very title that life is *before us*, not behind. The later novels repeat this formula, which is also a deep belief: despite the inherently retrospective nature of story-telling, the real story is still to come. *King Solomon* ends with a couple departing on the night train for Nice for their honeymoon, at over eighty years of age; *The Way Out* ends with a bizarre *ménage à trois* setting off for a new life in a chauffeur-driven limousine; and *The Kites* ends with the marriage of its young heroes and the prospect of new life in its most traditional form (Lila is pregnant with Ludo's child). Gary only rarely indulged in explicitly futuristic plots and did not handle them particularly well (*The Gasp* and 'The New Frontier' are the two main examples). Fundamentally, his entire work aspires to the not-yet-here; whereas the genre of science fiction, despite futuristic settings, most often deals with fantasies about the past.

Gary's challenging alternation between cynicism and sentimentality is the necessary, almost mathematically determined product of his twin theses about the human and the humane. But where do his ideals come from? To what philosophical, moral or religious tradition do they belong? Is he a crypto-Catholic, a humanist, or a Jew, in this domain?

Gary did not attribute the existence in man of an aspiration towards a greater humanity (or humaneness) to a transcendental origin. That's to say, he did not ever even hint that he believed in God. It would be flying in the face of his repetitious self-explanations to try to winkle out of his works anything resembling a religious faith. On the other hand, Gary's clear-eyed acknowledgement of the evil inherent in being a man (in being himself) seems quite close to the Catholic concept of original sin: in *A Quiet Night* he went so far as to describe himself as 'a Catholic unbeliever'.[2] My suspicion, however, is that his convictions owe less to any religion than to Dostoevsky's view of the human condition, to his 'Underground Man' especially, and to the three brothers Karamazov – Dmitri the man of passion and debauchery, Ivan the rational thinker, and the studious, good-hearted and faithful Alyosha, taken as a *collective* portrait of the nature of man. Other critics have sought to derive Gary's unique vision of the unfinished life of humanity from the thought of Leon Shestov;[3] in some respects Gary's thinking also led him close to the positions taken up by Emmanuel Levinas; but despite the persuasive parallels that have been made, it is inherently implausible that Gary ever read or studied writers of that kind.

Gary's philosophy of life is a home brew; it was not distilled from philosophical meditation or training. Its principal ingredients seem to me to be three: his own uncontrollable, physical self, which reminded him again and again that he too was a brute (he often *mimicked* the fist-throwing roustabout, but only because, at bottom, that's what he was); his experience of historical events, from the anti-Semitism of pre-war Poland to the sheer inhumanity of the bombing raids he conducted in World War Two; and his deep, passionate reading in his teens of the great sentimental and philosophical novels of the nineteenth century – especially Conrad, Dickens, Hugo and Dostoevsky. Gary is a creation of European literature. Fairly naturally, he saw literature as the only way to create a new man.

Gary often described his own position as 'desperate optimism'. *A European Education*, *The Dance of Genghis Cohn* and *The Kites* show so much inhumanity among men as to justify the despair; but the fact that such men, himself included, are capable of imagining something else is a reason for optimism. With characteristic backward speak, Gary often spoke in favour of the incomprehensible (in talking to people whose language is unknown, in the eyes of animals, in madness, or in the inanimate life of things) because what is not yet known just might contain something really new. The *other* is always the potential receptacle of the *new*, and as nothing can be as bad as the old, it gives grounds for hope.

In a more down-to-earth sense, Gary's ideals were familiar, simple and close to those of Victor Hugo: an end to racism and discrimination of all kinds; an end to war and violence; love between men and women; charity and generosity towards our fellow beings; repudiation of all claims to being absolutely right. It's old hat, to be sure, and it sounded particularly silly and sentimental on the Left Bank in the 1960s. But *Les Misérables* is still the longest-running show on Broadway, and speaks to far more people than Beckett, Robbe-Grillet and Blanchot ever did, or can. Sentimentality may have been branded a literary crime; but there's nothing wrong with having ideals. They are not invalidated by Gary's failure to live up to them, because they are *aspirations* towards a better self.

Gary did not believe that individual works of art and literature could do anything to amend man's inhumanity to man. As he often quipped, war has done far more for literature than *War and Peace* can ever do for peace. The hero of his experimental, chess-based novel *Europa*, Ambassador Danthès (who bears the name of the young man who killed Pushkin in a duel), is a model of the refinement and sensitivity imparted by lifelong immersion in Europe's cultural treasures – but he is also quite useless and goes completely mad. Random icons of European art like the Mona Lisa float around the posthumous mind of Genghis Cohn, but none of them will bring back the Holocaust dead. *The Roots of Heaven* didn't bring elephant-poaching to a halt, and not even *Life Before Us* prompted outbreaks of fraternal hugging among the poor Arabs, Blacks and Jews of Belleville. Gary was repeatedly and often ponderously clear about the zero impact of any individual work of art and this disabused view of his own purpose in the world made him deeply sceptical about 'masterworks'. Things still have much too far to go to give any thought to a creation that would bring man's striving for perfection to a full stop. But the striving itself was far from pointless, it was what gave value (and values) to human life. Each work of art gives nourishment to the imagination; it allows people to perceive their own aspirations towards a higher end; taken together, art and culture are the substance from which a new humanity may one day emerge. Gary's many apparent contradictions in discussions about literature and art are not hard to resolve into a simple, modest and well-worked-out system of thought. Like humanity, literature is a work in progress. It is far too soon to say: the end.

III

The Good Fight

15

Gandhi's Ham Sandwich

Tulipe, 1945–1970

Gary's reaction to the dead end that history made of Polish identity was to write a perplexing and funny book, which was probably only published because of his credentials as the author of a best-selling narrative of the heroic Maquis. *Tulipe*, written in London before Gary joined the Diplomatic Service, is less a single work, however, than the first outburst of an abiding obsession that he never managed to put to rest. In November 1945 Gary described it as 'a philosophical tale, a metaphysical farce in dialogue form, a 140-page humanitarian, anti-racist pamphlet which has nothing in common with *A European Education*',[1] and the same general outline will do for later versions as well.

Called 'Harlem' in first draft, after the New York neighbourhood where the story is set, *Tulipe*'s basic conceit is a deadpan reply to one of the commonest racist slurs of the 1930s – that Jews and Blacks are as bad as each other, and in unholy alliance to bring down the West. Before the war, Sartre had exploited the same ironic vein in the closing café scene of his first novel. Roquentin, the 'existential hero' of *Nausea*, is moved by a jazz record played on the jukebox, which constitutes an 'appeal to freedom' because the music was written by a Jew and played by a Black. That's why Himmler, Céline and *Je suis partout* thought jazz was a degenerate genre. Gary's fantastical imagination of a Harlem in which Jews and Blacks live side by side (some of the latter quipping Yiddish jokes and some of the former wearing bootblack on their faces, out of solidarity) is not about America at all, but about the ideological horrors of the recent European past.

Gary's humour in *Tulipe* is hard to take, even if you grasp from the start that everything said is intended to convey an opposite meaning. It could easily have offended readers unaccustomed to the backward speak of Polish (and Hungarian, Jewish and Russian) jokes; but there were very few readers of this squib, which at the time must have seemed to establish a new pinnacle of bad taste. Gary had high hopes of keeping the English-language audience he had won with *Forest of Anger*, so he translated *Tulipe* into English even before it was published in France.[2] Sartre offered to serialise the French version in the first issues of his new periodical, *Les Temps modernes,* sight unseen.[3] The onslaught on political hypocrisy that *Tulipe* contains caused Sartre to back off as soon as he saw the text. When it appeared as a book in spring 1946, *Tulipe* sank without trace.

'Tulipe', a common nickname among French soldiers in the seventeenth and eighteenth centuries, is now best remembered in the form *Fanfan La Tulipe* (*fanfan* being slang for *enfant*, rather like 'Billy the Kid'), denoting the carefree, swashbuckling soldier of fortune fighting for love and honour. Gary may have picked up the name almost anywhere; even in Poland, he's likely to have encountered Paul Meurice's *Fanfan La Tulipe* (1858), a much-performed vaudeville adapted into operettas and silent movies,[4] and retold in children's readers and comic books in every language. Meurice's Fanfan-la-Tulipe does a deal with a young lady, who promises him the hand of a princess if he joins the Army. But as soon as the jolly swordsman has signed up, he discovers that the young lady is the recruiting sergeant's daughter . . . and so vows to live his life as an impostor and charlatan too. Rollicking adventures turn him by stages into an authentic hero and in gratitude the king offers him the hand of his adopted daughter – who turns out to be none other than the fair Adeline, whose deception had started the whole plot.

Gary often used the name Tulipe for himself – no doubt as a self-identification with a soldier on the side of honour and right (not to mention as a ladies' man); and the signature 'T' and 'T.' on letters to friends is certainly an abbreviation of *Tulip* (Polish spelling) or *Tulipe* (in French). But the hero of the novel *Tulipe* is a Buchenwald survivor and new immigrant to America, starving in a Harlem garret, which he shares with Uncle Nat, a Black bootblack whose skin colour owes all to the blacking he uses as make-up,[5] and Leni, who models brassieres. They have a comical idea about how to solve their need for a square meal: to go on hunger strike. The scam aims to launch a movement, which will surely prompt donations from generous Americans and allow the indigent refugees to live the life of Riley. All this is narrated as from the distant future, from three thousand years after the death of Tulipe, when he has become an obscure figure in the prehistory of a new world. In March 1946, when the legend begins (that is to say, at the envisaged time of the book's publication: as with the epilogue of *A European Education*, Gary imagines *ahead* of the time of writing), a team of Black and Jewish reporters from *La Voix des peuples* (*The Peoples' Voice*) makes news out of the hunger strike, and turns it into a national and international cause. In imitation of Gandhi, Tulipe dresses in a bed sheet, spins wool on a wheel, sprinkles ash on his shaved head and calls on the world to 'pray for the victorious', for unlike all those liberated by the Liberation, only the victorious remain unimproved.

The plot of the story is thin and its main use is to permit Gary a series of moral and political polemics under the guise of screwball comedy. 'What is your view of the Black problem?' a journalist asks the White Mahatma of Harlem. 'I am a sincere friend of Zionism,' Tulipe replies in a complicated quip worthy of the Qui-pro-Quo club in Warsaw:

> It is a great humanitarian movement proclaiming clearly and firmly the right of all Palestinian refugees to return to their European homeland. You may add moreover for the benefit of your readers that as a European I have enormous admiration for the sensitive way in which the Black issue is handled in the United States without ever going to the excesses of Dachau, Belsen, Buchenwald, or Franco.[6]

Gary's pamphlet is also a reflection on collective guilt. Some of its key passages aim directly at undermining the happy consensus among the Allies about who was guilty for the Holocaust. Munching a ham sandwich to gather strength for the rest of his fast, Tulipe-Gandhi muses that Buchenwald and Belsen are not what really lie on his mind.

> What I cannot forgive is not Dachau, that city of thirty thousand people destined for torture, but the village next door, where people lived happily, tilled their fields and breathed in the good smells of hay and fresh bread . . .[7]

This point about the 'village next door', which would form one of Gary's most frequently repeated self-quotations over the following thirty years, is remarkably similar to the voice-over of Billy Wilder's *Death Mills*, a public education movie made at Bergen-Belsen in 1945 for the US Army Signals Corps. It's possible Gary saw it in London in the last months of 1945; equally possible is that Wilder and Gary – both Yiddish-speaking émigrés – had the same reaction of moral outrage to the still emerging news about the Holocaust.

Tulipe also expresses Gary's cynical bewilderment at his own treatment by the French press in the second half of 1945. It's as if he were giving away the secret of his own public image, or rather, seeking to protest that beneath his glorious persona he is, like Tulipe, just a clever fraud. As the pseudo-Gandhian 'movement' launched by Tulipe takes off and financial contributions pour in, he dreams the ordinary American dream:

'Leni.'

'Yes, boss?'

'Soon we'll have a car, a radio and a refrigerator. We'll be happy.'

'Yes, boss.'

'We'll get out of here.'

'Yes, boss.'

'We'll go and live somewhere in Hollywood, far away from civilisation.'

'Yes, boss.' [8]

But the mask Tulipe has made for himself is made to stick fast by the media and by public hysteria, and by stages Tulipe becomes the messiah he had only pretended to be. The masses expect and require miracles, and in the final pantomime scene, Tulipe rises from his bed with wings budding from his shoulders, exits via the window and flies off to the sky. When he gets to heaven and sees Him, he gives a nervous cough, shuffles his feet and says: 'Dr Livingstone, I presume?'

The general outline of *Tulipe* also has a resemblance to the plot of Dostoevsky's *The Idiot*: what would it be like for Jesus to reappear in the modern world? Gary's quirky way of reminding his readers of the mythical stakes takes the form of a quipping conversation between two Black journalists with the unlikely names of 'Flaps' and 'Grinberg' who connive in the scam:

'I'm telling you, Grinberg, that guy reminds me of someone, but I can't remember who.'

'Ta-a-xi!' Grinberg yelled. 'Ta-a-xi! Flaps, you get me down. Make an effort. It's obvious. Think.'

'I am thinking.'

'Taxi, taxi! A fine figure of legend. The only fine spiritual figure in history. Begins with a C. Six letters.'

'Chiang Kai Shek?' said Flaps. 'No. Churchill. No.'

'Ta-a-xi!'

'Cicero,' said Flaps. 'Cagliostro, Charlie Chaplin.'

'I said: a very great human figure. A spiritual light. Six letters. Taxi!'

'Capone,' said Flaps. 'Have you done with yelling?'

'I need to yell. I need to scream so as not to burst. I'm just trying to yell something reasonable. Taxi!'

'Caligula,' said Flaps. 'The world is full of well-intentioned people who spend their lives yelling for taxis that never come. Coolidge. Caesar. Chamberlain.'

'That doesn't stop them trying,' Grinberg said. 'Hasn't stopped people screaming for thousands of years. A great, fine and pure figure of humanity. Begins with C. Six letters. There's not two of them.'

'There's not one,' said Flaps.[9]

In such contorted ways, *Tulipe* tells us that the best hope humanity can have is not for the return of Jesus Christ, but for a pseudo-Christ, an impostor whose performance of Christ-like exploits of self-abasement, generosity and love may raise mortals' hearts to a level more nearly human. In the meantime, hypocrisy, self-delusion, wilful ignorance and self-victimisation are the lot of what is incorrectly identified as civilisation. Wrapped as it is in comic jibes and a fragmentary parable-plot, the message is easily lost. All the same, *Tulipe* lays out the main bases of the moral lesson that Gary's subsequent work would try to teach over the following thirty-five years.

Gary returned to his *Tulipe* material first of all in the immediate wake of his great success, *The Roots of Heaven*, with

L'Homme à la colombe, a transposition of the same topic to the United Nations, published in 1958 under the name Fosco Sinibaldi. Here the pseudo-Christ is figured as a good-hearted Texas cowboy lost in a secret room inside the huge UN building. From this mythical sanctuary, 'Johnny' engages a false hunger strike to remind the world of all the things that Tulipe had guyed: moral responsibility, the absurdity of idealism and its inevitability, political and racial hypocrisy, the power of the media to create myths and the positive virtue of shamming virtuous behaviour. Gary wrote a stage adaptation of this new version of the old *Tulipe* theme as well, but with only marginally better luck. *Johnnie Cœur* was performed at the Théâtre de la Michodière in February 1962, but closed at the end of its first week. Undaunted, or perhaps because he had no choice, given his obsessive nature, Gary returned to the material once again in 1970, when he produced an enlarged edition of the original *Tulipe*, with updated jokes and madcap footnotes. But even that was not the end of the story. In his very last months, Gary took out *L'Homme à la colombe* and marked it up for corrections and additions. The last variation of the *Tulipe* theme did not appear until 1984, four years after Gary's end.

The three main 'Tulipe' episodes in Gary's writing life follow moments of public success: after the Prix des Critiques for *A European Education* in 1945; after the Prix Goncourt for *The Roots of Heaven* in 1956; after the immense, worldwide success of *Promise at Dawn* in 1960–1. This is not because Gary was lost for new material after a major effort. It is because the material of *Tulipe* pre-existed all his popular fictions, and he hoped that a wave of celebrity would allow him to get his fundamental and much harsher message to a wide public. It didn't. The material and form of *Tulipe*, closer to the outrageous insensitivities of Monty Python than to the politer jibes of French farce, would have to be buried far more deeply to gain an audience in France. It is one of the very few works by Romain Gary that has never appeared in any other language.

Jesus Christ crops up in Gary's work most especially when Jewish suffering is at stake. The character who becomes Tulipe is a Jewish survivor of Buchenwald; Genghis Cohn, the Warsaw music-hall comedian who haunts his German assassin as a dybbuk, leaves the stage of *The Dance of Genghis Cohn* with a crown of thorns and a heavy cross on His back. Christological allusions are not rare in French Jewish writing of the 1950s. François Mauriac's preface to Elie Wiesel's narrative of Auschwitz and Buchenwald, *Night* (1958), virtually identifies the young survivor as a newfound Christ; and André Schwartz-Bart's *The Last of the Just* (Prix Goncourt, 1959), has its hero Ernie Lévy adopt a patently Christ-like form of self-sacrifice at the end. Gary is much less obviously a 'Jewish writer' than either of these, but the Christic themes in his work don't make him any less Jewish, or more French.

A disproportionate number of the initial members of the Free French forces were immigrants, and many others, such as Raymond Aron and Pierre Mendès-France, were assimilated Jews. De Gaulle is said to have lamented in 1940: *Je n'ai que les métèques pour moi*, which can be loosely translated as 'The only lot who back me are the bloody foreigners'. During the war, however, Gary played up his Slavic side much more than his Jewish roots, which he kept secret from Lesley until the eve of their marriage.

> 'There's something I have to tell you,' he said gloomily.
>
> I steeled myself for the worst.
>
> 'I think you ought to know – I'm Jewish,' he said.
>
> . . .
>
> Romain had spoken with a curious mixture of defiance and *gêne*, while I was not yet aware of just how heavy a load a Jewish inheritance could seem, how it could close round with

> stifling tentacles of emotion and even shame. I recall him sitting there in one of what I called his 'disaster poses', head in hands.
>
> 'Well, I thought you ought to know,' he repeated lamely. Suddenly, he looked amused.
>
> 'So you'll be my Goy wife,' he said, and with that the matter was closed.[10]

The abandonment of Jewish practice and identity doesn't mean that Gary acquired much familiarity with Christian culture or thought. In fact, his knowledge of the dominant faith seems limited to an approximate awareness of the story of Jesus Christ, alongside a few names of French saints. (For example, in *Gros-Câlin*, the mouse that Cousin cannot bear to feed to his python is called Blondine, punning on Saint Blandine, who was fed to the lions.) The curriculum he had followed at the lycée in Nice was strictly secular, of course (religious instruction has been banned from state schools in France since 1875), and there's no evidence at all that Gary went to catechism classes outside the regular framework of school. But there's no problem finding sources for his knowledge of the figure of Christ. In Polish reading primers or as *articles de culte* in shop windows in Nice, pious images of Jesus were all around him. The sole explicit figuration of Jesus in his work comes in *The Gasp* (1973), where Gary links the image to his years of education:

> He was barefoot and He was walking by their side, bent under the weight of a heavy wooden cross . . . A white sheet covered the body and this whole appearance was so familiar that one had the impression of meeting an old school friend.[11]

The standard authors Gary studied in French literature, history and philosophy in his senior years at the lycée should have given him broad notions of Christian thought, but his later, distinctly idiosyncratic view of Jesus Christ seems to owe little to Montaigne, Descartes, Pascal or Racine.

> Christianity is femininity, pity, softness, forgiveness, tolerance, maternity, respect for the weak, Jesus is weakness. I've already told you I have a dog side to my nature, a determining instinctive side to me, and if I'd met Jesus I'd have wagged my tail straight away, sat up and begged. For me it's got to do with humanity and not transcendence, with the human not the divine . . . He was a man. I've always wanted to shake his hand. Sure, you don't come across him nowadays because demography keeps him hidden in the crowd, but he's still there, dying somewhere or other. There are Jesuses who get lost, I swear it.[12]

However, all the 'lost Jesuses' Gary identified as such in his works (save the divine ghost who materialises at the end of *The Gasp*) are charlatans – Tulipe, Johnny, Genghis Cohn, or the actor performing the Jesus role in the moral Disneyland of *The Guilty Head*. But since the real thing has not yet come into being on the world's stage, the best a man can do is to act up to his aspirations. Gary's Polish-Jewish upside-down idealism means that it is no insult to have Jesus Christ appear as a comedian. In fact, it is his highest form of praise.

16

Gary the Rat

Sofia, 1947

The first of Romain Gary's novels to appear in the United States was entitled *The Company of Men*. Written during the author's posting as a junior diplomat in Sofia, Bulgaria, between 1946 and 1948, it was published in French by Gallimard in the first days of 1949 under the title *Le Grand vestiaire*, literally, The Big Closet. It was the first book Gary published with Gallimard, the most distinguished of all France's literary publishing houses. Gary would stay with Gallimard for the rest of his career, save for works published under the name of Émile Ajar.

Perhaps because of Albert Camus's great enthusiasm for *A European Education*, Gallimard had sought to lure Gary away from his first French publisher, Calmann-Lévy, as early as 1945, but they seemed to have declined *Tulipe*. However, the sale of the English-language translation rights of *Le Grand vestiaire* to Simon & Schuster in New York had nothing to do with Gallimard's foreign rights department – because it did not own them. Gary's original contract with Gallimard contained a most unusual clause excluding all English-language rights in his work, past, present and future. Possibly unique in the annals of French publishing, this clause strongly suggests that the writer had a better idea of what England and America might do for him than Gallimard did. It also proves beyond doubt that the idea of writing in English was not a by-product of Gary's later career as a French diplomat in the USA or of his marriage to Jean Seberg. An English-language career was in his mind almost from the start of his existence as Romain Gary. Despite his total immersion in his identity as a Free Frenchman between 1940 and 1945, his long drift towards the West, which had begun in Wilno twenty years before, was still only half complete.

Joe Barnes, Gary's pal from wartime London, left journalism for an editorial position with Simon & Schuster in 1949, and he was put in charge of a new list of cut-price books called 'Readers' Editions'. Whether Barnes turned to Gary or Gary contacted Barnes at a providential moment is not known, but in the first batch of half a dozen titles in the new collection, alongside reliable earners like *How to Improve Your Tennis*, Barnes brought out his own translation of a new work by his old chum and called it *The Company of Men*.

Le Grand vestiaire is a dense, rich, surprising fable of the moral disarray of Liberation France and must count as one Gary's major achievements. In France, however, despite warm words of approval from Paul Claudel and Roger Martin du Gard (though for quite opposite reasons), *Le Grand vestiaire* sold poorly and was not reissued in Gary's lifetime. In America it did a great deal better and established him as a popular writer two years prior to his first stepping on to American soil. This was not because Gary used the process of translation to prune, expand, or improve the original, as he would do with nearly every one of his subsequent books in French: *The Company of Men* is almost identical to *Le Grand vestiaire*, save for the dropping of a few phrases that seem most likely to be either translator's licence or a slip of his attention, and the correction of film titles that Gary had manifestly got confused.[1] What helped *The Company of Men* find a far wider readership in America than *Le Grand vestiaire* ever had in France is that Gary's story fits straight into a place waiting for it in every English-educated reader's heart – a place dug out by bedtime story readings, by radio or movie adaptations, or by the full text of Charles Dickens's *Oliver Twist*.

Oliver Twist is the story of an orphan boy who comes to London from the country and falls in with a band of pickpockets controlled by a nasty old man, the fence Fagin. *The Company of Men* is the story of Luc Martin, an orphan boy from the fictional Maquis de Véziers in Provence, who comes to Paris and falls in with a band of black-marketeers and thieves controlled by an ugly old man, Gustave Vanderputte. But there is more to the match than the old man and the boy. Just as Fagin's nemesis is his even nastier sidekick Bill Sykes, so Vanderputte's friend and enemy, René Kuhl, undoes him in the end. Dickens's 'flash', Toby Crackit, with his fantastical hair and outlandish costume, has his opposite number in Gary's bizarre transvestite Sasha Darlington, and the role of Nancy, the whore with the heart of gold, who pays for it with her life, is played in Gary's novel by Josette (her death from consumption is, however, borrowed explicitly from *La Dame aux camélias*).

The change of city, of century and of scope cannot mask the model of *The Company of Men*. Once the reader has recognised the reference to *Oliver Twist* – Vanderputte-Fagin's self-justification in Part I, chapter viii, makes it hard to miss – he or she can only suppose that what lies in store is some kind of redemption for the child hero, Luc Martin. For that reason *The Company of Men* is both easier on the English reader and more interesting than *Le Grand vestiaire* is in French. Granted this is a transposition of a classic narrative of crime and rescue, what the Dickens, you might say, is Mr Gary going to do with it?

The answer is obvious to English readers: Fagin is a Jew and Dickens was not, whereas Gary was a Jew and his repulsive rat-man Vanderputte turns out, at the very end, to be an anti-Semite. The final twist in Gary's version of the tale that allows Luc Martin to understand what he needs to do to rejoin the 'company of men' is his and our discovery of Vanderputte's one unpardonable sin. *Le Grand vestiaire* is not an imitation of *Oliver Twist*, but a topical, important, post-Holocaust response to it. Dickens, despite his heart-moving aspiration towards the good and the beautiful, cannot escape the taint of anti-Semitism, however ordinary it was for an Englishman of his age. *Le Grand vestiaire* shows how different the world had become by 1945.

In the existentialist mood of post-war Paris it was fashionable to quote Dostoevsky, as Simone de Beauvoir does in the epigraph of *The Blood of Others*. Gary knew *The Brothers Karamazov* and *Notes from the Underground* very well, and he uses them as barely hidden pillars of his tale. The first-person narrator of the *Notes* presents himself thus: 'I am a sick man . . . I am a wicked man', using a Russian adjective – злой – that encompasses meanings as varied as 'evil', 'sly', 'sour', 'malicious' and 'nasty'. Gustave Vanderputte, the black-market manipulator at the centre of *The Company of Men*, seems to have been designed to fit the entire range of meanings of Dostoevsky's opening shot. What links them even more manifestly is, however, not nastiness (they share that with Fagin in any case), but their self-consciousness of evil, and the conviction that their own cowardice, cruelty, pride and sloth make them more representative of humanity than the shallow hypocrites of civilised society (whom Dostoevsky mocks, in French, as 'l'homme de la nature et de la vérité').[2] When Vanderputte's squad of child-thieves bursts out laughing at the old man's claim that he too once learned to recite La Fontaine by heart, Gary's moral mirror of mankind feels very hurt and shouts out:

> I'm not excluded! I'm a man like other men! I'm like everybody and that's just what's filthy about it! . . . What would La Fontaine have done without the wolf, without the fox, without . . . without me?[3]

What proves Vanderputte to be no more and no less than a member of the human race, despite his mousy cowardice and rat-like greed, is the bout of acute toothache that he suffers as the police finally close in on him at the end. 'He isn't a monster. He's a man,' Luc declares. 'That's what's so rotten about it. The proof is that he has got a toothache.'[4] This too is a reminiscence of the humanity of Dostoevsky's paradoxalist, the Underground Man. 'I had toothache for a whole month,' he declares, introducing a bravura passage on the pleasure that can be got out of pain. 'Your moans express the whole humiliating purposelessness of your pain; your recognition of the whole array of natural laws, which you, of course, don't give a hoot about . . .'[5]

Gary never ceased to rail against the iniquity of the 'laws of nature', notably as Émile Ajar in *Life Before Us*. At the end of his onslaught on the kinds of cheating that can be done by a man with toothache, however, Dostoevksy's Underground Man broaches the main question of *The Company of Men* when he grants that his jokes are 'certainly in bad taste, awkward, stumbling, full of self-distrust. But that is, of course, because I don't respect myself. Can a man of conscious intelligence have any self-respect to speak of?'[6] The same question is put in different language in the title of a lost or unwritten work announced as 'forthcoming' on the half-title page of *Les Couleurs du jour* in 1952: *La Lutte pour l'honneur* (The Struggle for Honour). Can a man of 'conscious intelligence' maintain his honour or self-respect, and if so, how? The answer found by Luc Martin in *The Company of Men* is not the kind of redemption in suffering that Dostoevsky grants Raskolnikov in the epilogue to *Crime and Punishment*, but something more secular, and more painful. It involves accepting that no one can escape the necessity of ratting on his own principles to belong to 'the company of men'. The redemptive turn at the end of Luc's story is explicitly and intentionally paradoxical, for such is the human condition. Unlike Oliver, who can remain loyal to Fagin even up to the moment of his execution, Luc has to execute Vanderputte himself. Dickensian sentimentality is replaced by a harsher mood and a much more complex morality.

Gary's foreign models aren't mentioned by name in the text, which highlights specific symbols of French, not European, culture. Luc Martin's father had been in the resistance and had got himself shot in the eye on the last day of the Occupation. The only object that his orphaned son inherits (as elsewhere in Gary's fiction, no mention is made of a mother) is an annotated pocketbook copy of the *Pensées* of Pascal. Luc doesn't try to read it; instead, he treats the book as a fetish, carrying it around with him and touching it for luck in tricky moments. He puzzles over the pencilled fragments in the margins: vague thoughts about heroism, solidarity and sacrifice, and about how to maintain self-respect in treacherous and violent times. The book-object is a token of Luc's filiation – as a son of his father, and of France – and the notes constitute the transmission of values from the Resistance to the post-war world.

Vanderputte also clings to a French heirloom from the same century in his memory of the *Fables* of La Fontaine. It is his main link to his own childhood, to the innocence and normality that had once been his. The recitation of La Fontaine by this ugly and aged scoundrel parallels the use made by Marcel Aymé, in a novel exactly contemporary with *The Company of Men*, of Racine's *Andromaque*. In *Uranus*, a comedy of political manners in Liberation France, the Gargantuan barkeeper Léopold is touched to the heart when hearing school lessons on Racine, and resolves to become a poet himself, and to rewrite *Andromaque* in more sensible language (but in alexandrines nonetheless). Pascal, La Fontaine, Racine . . . these literary icons are also clearly ideological ones. In Gary as in Aymé, the great names of the French classical period are used to assert the values of France – cultural values, values that constitute culture itself – when almost everything else, such as movies, medicine and even good money, come from somewhere else.

The exception is French cuisine. After the death of Léonce, the ragamuffin who plays the role of Dickens's Artful Dodger in Gary's novel, Luc is robbed, beaten up and left for dead in a ditch. He wakes up in a guest room in a roadside inn. Monsieur and Madame Baju, owners of Les Routiers, had discovered him, rescued him and taken him in. They vow to restore the boy to health the only way they know how – by feeding him. This chapter, a comic interlude after the high drama of a bank robbery gone wrong, fills the slot of Oliver Twist's stay with Mr Brownlow in Pentonville. But it is also an assertion of the enduring value of French civilisation, especially as seen by foreigners. In *The Kites*, Gary returned to the same theme: Le Clos Joli (a three-star restaurant, not a mere roadside inn – but Gary had gone up in the world in the intervening years) stays determinedly open throughout the Occupation in order to say: France will not surrender what she holds most dear.

The role of French cuisine in the salvation of Luc Martin and of France is Gary's homage to a national stereotype, not an indulgence in a personal passion. Afflicted with digestive troubles throughout his post-war life, Gary was picky with his meals, and regularly jealous of his slim wife Lesley, who enjoyed eating any amount of good food. Anissimov speculates that Gary suffered from hiatus hernia as a result of his wartime injuries. He also undertook various forms of dieting, to keep middle-aged spread at bay. Apart from his craving for salted cucumbers and occasional grand gestures at Russian restaurants in Paris, Gary was not a big eater, and was more often content with steamed peas and baby carrots than with a five-course feast of the kind served by the Bajus or by Marcellin Duprat.

During convalescence at the Bajus' hotel-restaurant, Luc Martin begins to see where his future path might lie. Where can he go to escape from evil and solitude? Why, to Africa! 'The grass around me became a jungle; I thought of Lake Chad, and the old elephant that's called a rogue. I had read about them in a travel book . . .' The topic of *The Roots of Heaven* seems here to emerge from the long grass of a French meadow; its title would arise in a lyrical passage in Gary's following novel, *The Colours of the Day* (see p. 190). Just as *The Company of Men* is a dialogue with Dickens mediated by the moral paradoxes of Dostoevsky's Underground Man, so each of Gary's works is part of a broader circulation of themes, words, expressions and symbols in his oeuvre as a whole.

Balzac persuaded himself that he had become a genius when he invented the device of reappearing characters. Gary, who had been taught at lycée to avoid repetition of names and expressions if he wanted a good mark in composition, seems to have invented a subtler but equally obsessive device, that of the reappearing and misapplied cliché. It's something he learned from his mother, or attributed to her in his reinvention of his own early life in *Promise at Dawn*, but put to a use more subversive and comical than she ever did:

> She never balked at using a cliché, less from a lack of vocabulary than from some kind of submission to the society of her day, to its values and gold standards – for the connection between fixed expressions and the reigning social order is one of acceptance and conformism that goes far beyond language itself.[7]

The Company of Men, despite its dense web of literary and philosophical allusion, is a convincing, apparently authentic documentary novel on the dangers confronting vulnerable youngsters in post-Liberation Paris. But Gary had not been in Paris for seven years, except for a few days in August 1945 and less than six weeks at the end of that year. The young crooks and old scoundrels of *The Company of Men* were imagined partly out of extremely rapid observation of the terrain – and for the most part from newspaper stories read at the French Legation in Sofia. The politics of Gary's second novel also owe something to what he could see with his own eyes from the diplomatic balcony where he was perched: the forward march of European Communism.

Communism is the principal topic of political discussion among the major and minor characters of *The Company of Men*. All of them fear it. Sasha Darlington sees the crushing of Germany as a disaster because it brings the Bolsheviks closer to Paris; the pharmacist at the all-night drugstore would rather use the atomic bomb than lose his individuality under Communism; a customer at a second-hand clothes shop dresses up to the nines before jumping into the Seine 'for fear of Communism'; even the urchin Léonce declares that he dislikes Communists because they are 'not French'.[8] Communism has only one defender – the elephantine, manically neat René Kuhl, Vanderputte's only friend. A police inspector whose career seems to have run on seamlessly from the Third Republic to the Fourth without serious disturbance by Vichy, Kuhl votes Communist. He does so not out of sympathy for the labouring masses, even less out of revolutionary fervour, but because he admires a 'good, well-oiled administrative machine', which in the French original is supported by 'rigorous scientific method'.[9] Kuhl presents Communism not as a tool of change but, on the contrary, as the most perfect system of bureaucratic repression that exists. Through Kuhl's encomium of administrative convenience, Gary denounces the Stalinist bureaucracy that most French intellectuals would not begin to criticise for another ten years. The shadow of what Gary saw in Bulgaria – a 'well-oiled machine' swiftly cornering all opposition figures and, by 1948, having most of them hanged – falls over the Paris of *The Company of Men*.

In practice, the Paris of Gary's novel is dominated not by Soviet ideas, but by American things. The drugs Vanderputte has stolen from the UNRRA store are American drugs; when they start thieving in earnest, the youngsters go after dollars, not francs; what they dream of obtaining is a visa for the USA, but, failing that, Luc gives away his dog Roxane to a departing GI, so it can have a better life 'over there'. The major presence of America in France, however, is on the silvered screen. Gary's evocation of the dreamworld induced in a generation of post-war children by Hollywood movies, which fills Part I, chapter ix of *The Company of Men*, bears comparison with the celebrated 'cinema' chapter of Georges Perec's *Things* (1965). But whereas Perec writes about the movies he really had been to see in Paris cinemas, Gary can only imagine the impact made by the sudden release, after the years of German Occupation, of a backlog of thousands of American movies. He could not have seen *The Big Sleep*, *Gone With the Wind*, *Double Indemnity* and so forth in Bulgaria, which was quite closed off to imports from the West; and if he had seen the movies in question, he had seen them in London, where they were shown in their own time, not as part of the joys of Liberation. What seems most authentic in Gary's novel turns out to be imagined.

By imitating the clothes, postures, gestures and language as well as the criminal activities of American movie characters, Luc, Josette and Léonce eventually emancipate themselves from Vanderputte's control, and graduate from being drug couriers and pickpockets on his behalf to robbing tills and banks for themselves. France was afflicted with an epidemic of desperate hold-ups and bank robberies in the post-war years, and in this respect Gary is following the news, not making it. It was also quite common for the crime wave to be blamed on American movies. But in the overall design of *The Company of Men*, the negative impact of American movies balances the Communist threat, leaving a small but all-important space in between for the true values of France.

The Company of Men gives a large place to magical thinking.

Josette, Luc's first love, sings in her room to a black-faced, handless doll;[10] Luc is drawn to a magic charm from the New Hebrides hanging in a bookshop window in Rue Madame and he buys it for Josette;[11] later on, he picks up a broken doll in the Luxembourg Gardens and keeps it in his pocket.[12] Throughout the action of the novel, he hangs on to his father's copy of Pascal and touches it 'like a lucky charm'.[13] Luc also appeals to talismanic figures in dream and in reality: 'Humphrey Bogart, save me!' he cries,[14] or 'Sasha Darlington, protect me!'[15] Children's magic is, however, only small beer alongside Vanderputte's superstitious kleptomania. The old rat collects anything – bits of string, buttons, bottle tops – provided it is imperfect, broken, lost or fragmentary, 'as if he loved and sought humanity down to its humblest traces, to the debris which it strews in its road'.[16]

In memory (or anticipation) of Nina's postcard collection described on page 76 of *Promise at Dawn*, Vanderputte's biggest piece of treasure is an old suitcase stuffed with postcards. But the sole person represented on them is himself – as a baby, as a student, a conscript, and in the many other roles he played as a model for a local postcard printer. Gary returns to the use of old postcards as talismanic objects in *King Solomon*, written thirty years later, but there is one particular postcard in *The Company of Men* that is already a self-quotation in 1949. Under his pillow, Léonce keeps 'a picture of an enormous mountain which split open the sky . . . the sides of the mountain and its summit were all covered with snow. "That's called Kilimanjaro. It's in Africa."'[17]

Léonce has never been there, any more than the barber from Touchagues, in the short story 'All Is Well on the Kilimanjaro', which Gary had written during his London years and first published in *Cadran* in 1945 (see p. 180). The repetition of the motif turns it into a talisman not just for Léonce, but for Romain Gary. The image of a mountain piercing the sky seems to have for the author as well as the character a symbolic and magical meaning. It represents aspiration towards an unattainable height – a doublet and a precursor of 'the roots of heaven'.

Magic from identifiable literary sources colours Luc Martin's view of the sordid life he finds in Liberation-era Paris. His father had read him Grimm's fairy tales, so he sees Vanderputte and Kuhl as two grotesque monsters 'chased by some good fairy out of a particularly sinister story and condemned forever to live in a world without magic in it'.[18] But things get rather more complicated than an absence of magic. Vanderputte adopts a second-hand coat, which he calls by the name of its presumed former owner, Gestard-Feluche (Vanderputte has personal names for all his precious objects). Gestard-Feluche thus becomes the name of 'a coat with no one inside it', the name for the *absence* of Gestard-Feluche. The quality of non-being which its name contains affects the person who does wear it, Gustave Vanderputte, and turns him into the nobody he asserts all men truly are. It's not as bizarre as it sounds. In fact, it is a meditation on a familiar French formulation of a standard philosophical problem.

In a short story later republished as part of the collection entitled *The Wall*, Jean-Paul Sartre pursued the murderous logic of seeing men as marionettes.[19] The narrator of 'Erostratus' looks down from the balcony of a sixth-floor apartment and sees in the street below not men, but coats and hats with limbs sticking out comically, at irregular intervals. Sartre's story, like Gary's novel, is a fictionalisation of a philosophical chestnut from Descartes:

> If I look out of the window and see men crossing the square, as I just happen to have done, I normally say that I see the men themselves . . . Yet do I see any more than hats and coats which could conceal ghosts or simulations of men moved only by mechanical springs?[20]

Descartes argued that 'the faculty of judgment which is in my mind', not the visible world, guarantees the existence of self and other. Sartre's lunatic narrator, on the other hand, believes his eyes only and proceeds to treat other men as they appear to him from on high, as walking wardrobe items, not as fellow men. He ends up firing at random into a crowd and then bungling his own suicide.

Gary had surely read the passage from Descartes at the lycée and he is most likely to have read Sartre's story as well. He picks up the image of men seen from above to build the network of ideas that justifies the title of *Le Grand vestiaire*. The 'big closet' is first of all Vanderputte's collection of cast-off clothes, 'clothes with no-one inside them'. But the bigger closet is the world outside, the hats and coats seen proceeding along Rue Madame from the fifth-floor window of Vanderputte's borrowed flat.

> 'Young man, let me give you one piece of advice: lift yourself above everything. Soar, young man! Soar, open your wings, project all your little problems into the infinite, into the astral world, into metaphysics, and you will immediately see the true proportion of things, which are, young man, infinitesimal. I tell you . . .'
>
> He raised a finger.
>
> '. . . infinitesimal! Treason, heroism, crime, love, all these, young man, with perspective, with horizon, will literally move you with their insignificance. Zero! They don't even exist!'[21]

If other people 'don't even exist', then, as Ivan Karamazov famously exclaimed, 'All is permitted!' Marcel Aymé uses a similar fable to argue along the same lines in *Uranus*. Watrin, the benign teacher in the bombed-out town of Blémont where the novel is set, urges his townsfolk to soar to an even greater height and to look down on the world from the distance of the planet Uranus. What can be seen of the universe from that far perspective is so bleak, he argues, that every tiny bit of life on earth that we can now see, from a blade of grass to an arrant fool or a cowardly hypocrite, is precious and lovable. Gary is not seeking the same kind of consolation, but he too includes the worst of men within the embrace of humanity. Another famous character of 1949 also uses the 'view from on high' as a moral fable – Harry Lime, the arch-criminal in Carol Reed's movie *The Third Man*. A black-marketeer selling drugs past their sell-by date, just like Vanderputte, Harry Lime agrees to a rendezvous with his pursuer in the fairground and there takes him up on the Ferris wheel. In a gripping scene where the viewer is led to fear and expect that someone is going to get thrown out from a great height, Harry Lime only invites us all to look down, and to see how tiny and insignificant men are when viewed from an appropriate height. He claims to have every right to treat them as 'nothings' even when down on the ground.[22]

Graham Greene, who wrote the script for Reed's film, undoubtedly means us to reject Lime's pseudo-philosophical justification of crime, just as Sartre, in 'Erostratus', meant us to see to what destructive ends a failure to acknowledge the humanity of others must lead. Of these four contemporary meditations on Descartes's proof of the existence of the inner eye, Gary's is the most complex and *noir*. Vanderputte glories in his own moral squalor, yet defends it as the characteristic that makes him like other men. He denies others a right to existence ('All zeros!') while asserting that he is like all other men, a worthless scoundrel, a moral zero – and thus a member of the human race. Closer to Dostoevsky's paradoxical Underground Man than to the ciphers of Sartre, Greene and Aymé, Vanderputte is closest of all to Romain Gary. In an important interview with the great Polish figure Konstantin Jelenski that Gary gave shortly after his return from a trip to Warsaw in 1966, he said not only that Vanderputte was his personal favourite among all the fictional characters he had created, but that it was only *after* finishing the novel that he 'realized that the character of the old man represents humanity for me'.[23] The truth that his writing had in a sense been designed to hide is that there is no answer to the paradox of Vanderputte. Just as the novelist could not tidy him up into a merely evil character, so in real life the tangle of conflicting qualities in an individual can never be untied.

La Fontaine, Pascal and French cuisine stand for values that include comradeship, collective action and sacrifice for the sake of others – the mythical morality of the Free French, Joan of Arc and Rudyard Kipling. The meditations of Luc's father, which in their unfinished, posthumous and fragmentary nature mimic the book in whose margins they are scrawled, are more predictable, and thus less interesting as fictional material than the moral contortions of Vanderputte. But that's not to say Gary didn't take them seriously. He just didn't know how to extricate Luc from his loyalty to Vanderputte and his life of crime without a thicker, more historically grounded twist than rereading the moral meditations of an absent progenitor. What allows Luc to begin to return to the company of men is something that no other post-war French writer was yet prepared to touch.

In Part III of the novel, much the shortest and devoted solely to 'the old man', a policeman comes to inform Luc of the crimes Vanderputte had really committed during the Occupation. How does he know? Because Luc had posted the letter given him by Kuhl as the latter lay dying. Kuhl's denunciation relates Vanderputte's involvement in a resistance network, then his betrayal of it. That makes Vanderputte a banal kind of bad man in Liberation France. But what Luc learns when he confronts Vanderputte with the information is something else. The group Vanderputte had betrayed was meeting in Carpentras, which might seem to be just a small town in Provence – but it is not only that. Carpentras is a historic site of Jewish life in France, and it has the oldest synagogue in Europe, in uninterrupted use since 1367.[24] Most of the members of the group were also Jews and that is the excuse that Vanderputte uses to lessen his sin of treason. Even today it is a shock to be confronted by the ordinary, visceral, almost homely anti-Semitism of the 1930s. In 1949 it must have been most unpleasant to read the following attempt at an excuse: 'You know, most of the people I turned in after Carpentras were Jews. It's not that I'm anti-Semitic, thank God! But just the same, it is less serious, isn't it?'[25]

No French fiction of the 1940s and 1950s prior to Schwartz-Bart's *Last of the Just*, which won the Goncourt Prize in 1959, and none of the widely read accounts of deportation and concentration-camp life (such as David Rousset's *Other Kingdom* or Antelme's *The Human Race*) mentions the fate of the Jews. The only writer to dare to tackle anti-Semitism in post-war France was Jean-Paul Sartre, whose *Anti-Semite and Jew* (*Réflexions sur la question juive*) argues that anti-Semitism cannot be accepted as a political opinion like any other, but has to be categorised as a psychological and moral contortion, which puts its holder outside the human community. Sartre's essay transposes into abstract prose the underlying argument of 'Erostratus' and of a more explicit story about pre-war anti-Semitism, '*L'Enfance d'un chef*'. The closing turn in Gary's novel puts Sartre's 'reflection' into practical action. The revelation by Vanderputte that he is not merely a traitor to the Resistance, on top of his now extended career as a fence, but an anti-Semite too (and like all anti-Semites he doesn't believe he is one at all) puts him beyond sympathy and outside the company of men. That is what releases Luc Martin's ability to 'act like a man', in full consciousness of the tragic and paradoxical nature of what he has to do.

Luc shoots Vanderputte in the back of the neck, in an almost ritualised execution scene. In so doing, he betrays his affection for the old scoundrel; he reneges on his loyalty to a man who had taken care of him and given him what affection he could; and he becomes guilty of a capital crime, for he takes a man's life. He will therefore live on as a man, that is to say with a guilty conscience. Rejoining the 'company of men' is not as simple as it sounds in the twentieth century. Luc's final step out of childhood is heavier than Rastignac's and sadder than Oliver Twist's last fond embrace with Fagin just before he is hanged. Can a man of conscious intelligence have any self-respect to speak of? Gary's novel answers Dostoevsky's question quite clearly: yes, and no.

The Company of Men is a first-person narrative, as are many of Gary's later novels. What it shares with the best and worst of his simulations of spoken narrative is a technical feature that it would be easy to count as a flaw. Large parts of the novel are in simultaneous report, as if Luc were telling us, in the present tense and time, what he sees, hears, feels and does, just like Momo in *Life Before Us*. By contrast, Luc's attitude to those events is often wiser and more mature than one that could plausibly be attributed to an ill-educated fourteen-to-sixteen-year-old boy. Now and again, Luc the narrator steps back from his present as an adolescent tearaway and reveals that he is writing retrospectively, from the point of view of the adult he has now become: 'When I try to remember the months which followed . . .', 'Now I remember the weeks which followed . . .'.[26] But these moments of pause in Luc's telling of the tale create an interesting problem. Luc was fourteen when American troops liberated the south of France. As the Toulon landings began on 15 August 1944, Luc could not be more than nineteen when *The Company of Men* was published in January 1949. The adult perspective from which some of the events are recalled is thus located in a future time, not just with respect to the narrative, but with respect to its initial readers too.

In *Life Before Us* the voice speaking to us is at one and the same time that of a ten- or fourteen-year-old Momo, and a later voice of recollection and reflection, speaking into the tape recorder provided by his Mr Brownlow-like rescuers,

Nadine and Ramon. The use of double perspective is one of the hallmarks of Gary's storytelling narrative style. Although it can be easily missed, such is the page-turning quality of the prose, the hypothetical future point from which his stories are seen is the key to understanding his concept of the novel form. Gary himself is both the 'child' and the 'father' looking back on the world from which he comes. 'Luc' and 'Momo', as the grown men who tell their childhood tales, are the children of their own stories and, through a kind of narrative juggling trick, the fathers of themselves.

In *The Enchanters*, written under the name of Gary around the time that he invented Émile Ajar, Gary imagines himself as an eighteenth-century Russian-Italian illusionist and magician . . . still living at 108 Rue du Bac in 1972. It makes explicit the device of paradoxical time that is implicit in the structure of his earliest novels and which is fundamental, in fact, to the kind of novel-writing he admired. Gary's nineteenth-century masters strove to keep it hidden, but in practice the narrative perspective of Hugo in *Les Misérables* and Dostoevsky in *Karamazov* is identical to that of Gary: the third-person narrators of these great monuments of the novel form always *know* in retrospect and yet at the same time *discover* the story as it unfolds. It is this impossible, magical, enchanted time of fiction that allowed Romain Gary to tell a hundred different stories, while never ceasing to tell the same one.

Whose story is Gary telling in *The Company of Men*? Of all the stories told in *The Company of Men*, which one is his? The novelist's privilege is to be Oliver and Fagin, Rastignac and Vautrin, Ivan, Alyosha and Mitya at the same time. In *A European Education* Gary is Janek and Dobranski, and in *The Colours of the Day* he is without any doubt Willie Bauché as well as Jacques Rainier. In *The Company of Men*, however, Gary drops an unusual clue as to where his deepest self-image is to be found among his teenagers and old men.

Part of the action takes place in the fantastical bordello

where the half-English, half-Russian Sasha Darlington resides. The drapes and décor of the place seem to mimic Lesley Blanch's idea of gracious living; and the half-comical, half-serious encomia of prostitution are not very different from Lesley's introduction to the memoirs of Harriet Wilson. But whatever their sources, and however much Gary may have been a patron of such establishments in London and Paris, the Darlington bordello and the failed actor's persona belong to a fantasy world completely at odds with both the realities of post-war Paris or the fantasy world of the Hollywood movies. Equally Baroque are the drifters picked up by the teenage gang at the height of its prosperity – a Hungarian scientist, an Italian baritone and a Polish nobleman, whom the youngsters adopt as a mascot. Gary's gallery of grotesques out-Gogols *Dead Souls*, and means to remind us that the weirdest of people are part of the human race. These Baroque inventions in *The Company of Men* are quite unlike anything else in the French novel of the post-war years: Sartre, Camus and Aymé don't deal in fantasies like Gary's Baron or bordello, whose only possible precedent in French fiction might be Malraux's Clappique, in *Man's Estate*.

Animals, reptiles and insects are a recurrent feature of Gary's writing, both as explicit subjects and as metaphors for human life. In *A European Education*, ants, butterflies and (in later versions) a nightingale have their conventional uses as images of laboriousness, fantasy and the ideal. The elephants and insects of *The Roots of Heaven*, like Ajar's python and its diet of white mice, also tell stories about men, not about our feathered, furred or scaly friends. *The Company of Men* is overrun by rodents, which are not found elsewhere in Gary's work. The band of pickpockets in Vanderputte's sway are called *les ratons* ('little rats'). *Le Raton* is also the nickname of the Algerian boy who joins the gang when it starts thieving cars. It is a now obsolete pejorative racial term for North Africans, of the same level of vulgarity and offensiveness as *bicot* and *métèque* (the latter used for foreigners in general). Vanderputte himself also appears in one of Luc's nightmares as a huge, whiskered rat scurrying around the apartment. Of course, rodents are vermin, they are to be deplored, they are both in reality and in metaphorical terms things to be shunned and put down, and the prevalence of rat terms for the characters of this novel reflects and emphasises their moral squalor. But there is more to it than that.

Thirty years later, when he was writing *Life Before Us*, the first-person story of an Algerian boy, Gary insisted in *A Quiet Night* that when he was a teenager in the 1930s, his position was exactly like that of an Algerian in 1970s Paris. 'I was then, in the south of France, the equivalent of an Algerian today.'[27] The unspoken word seems to be: *raton*. But as he says, he wasn't in Paris then, but in Nice. In the Provençal dialect of the town, which Gary picked up like a magnet in the playground and the street, there is another way of referring to 'little rats'. In Nissart (and also in the street slang of Marseille and other parts of Provence), a 'little rat' is *garrí*.[28] The word can be used as a term of affection for a scamp or a ragamuffin, but it is a pejorative term when applied to a man. There is no reason more convincing, more contorted, multilingual and Gary-like for believing that Luc, Léonce and Josette, the *ratons* or *garrís* of *Le grand Vestiaire*, as well as Big Rat Vanderputte, tell us what it was like to be Roman Kacew, later known as *Gari* de Kacew and finally as Romain *Gary*.

17

Diplomacy

Gary at the UN, 1952–1954

The annual Goncourt Prize, established in 1903 by the will of the Goncourt brothers after the death of Edmond in 1896, aims to acknowledge a new novel of artistic merit appealing to a wide reading public. Most of the winners of the prize in its first thirty years enjoyed only short-lived celebrity, but the Goncourt's prestige grew nonetheless and the prize came to occupy a determining role in the French book trade. Other prizes were established in the following years to challenge the Goncourt: the Fémina, the Renaudot (usually attributed to a first novel) and the Interallié. But the Goncourt remained top prize and every novice writer dreams of winning it. André Malraux won in 1933 for *Man's Estate* when Roman Kacew was scribbling *Le Vin des morts* on the café tables of Aix-en-Provence. By the time he was thirty, Gary had already carried off a string of improbable exploits. After the Order of the Liberation, the Goncourt just had to be his main aim.

He nearly brought it off at the start. In the summer months of 1945, *Éducation européenne* began to create a buzz even before the first reviews appeared. Recommendations of the book from Aron and others who had read it in London, in its earlier version, may have helped. The book fell on the table of Albert Camus, then a senior editor at Gallimard (as well as director of the newspaper, *Combat*), who saw in it the work of a kindred spirit. He wrote a warm letter to Gary, the first piece of fan mail the airman had ever received, and without doubt the most significant too. Gary was overwhelmed. 'Coming from you, this response to my book is something so warm and generous that tears come to my eyes, and I really don't know what to say.'[1]

When the two met later that year, they struck up a real friendship, which remained warm and firm despite the relative infrequency of contact, given Gary's postings abroad. Gaston Gallimard, head of the most prestigious French publishing house, also read *Éducation européenne* early on (perhaps at Camus's suggestion) and he took the most unusual step of approaching Gary directly for rights to his future works. Word of mouth relayed and reinforced these prestigious recommendations, and the book started running off the bookshop shelves. The enthusiastic reviews by Maurice Nadeau (in Camus's *Combat*) and by Raymond Queneau combined with all the other signs of a runaway success to put *Éducation européenne* firmly in line for the Goncourt.

In 1945 the prize was more important than ever. Calmann-Lévy had found enough paper to print 60,000 copies, but all were sold out by October 1945. The publisher had to scrounge around to find enough for 10,000 more – who knows at what black-market price. However, the government, seeking to make life seem as normal as possible in those extraordinarily difficult times, had set aside a special paper allocation for the winner of the Goncourt. No other book would receive such favour. That year, the Goncourt really was top prize.

Yet it was also tainted. Under the German Occupation the Fémina and the Interallié prize committees suspended their activities, but the Goncourt panel carried on as if nothing had changed. Retrospectively, that looked like passive collaboration. The winners it had chosen in 1941 and 1942 were ideologically close to Vichy, and the irremovable president of the Académie Goncourt, René Benjamin, had published a panegyric of Marshal Pétain. Other members of the ten-man panel, such as Roland Dorgelès and Léon Daudet, held right-wing views and had not hidden their pro-German sentiments during the war. The Goncourt needed new clothes and in 1944 it grabbed the first available loincloth by awarding its prize to a not very significant book by Elsa Triolet, the Russian wife of the poet Louis Aragon and a powerful figure in the French Communist Party.

It was in this context that a French publisher, Les Éditions du Pavois, set up an 'anti-Goncourt' prize to be awarded by eleven leading literary critics with much better wartime records: Maurice Blanchot, Jean Paulhan, Marcel Arland, André Billy, Armand Hoog, Roger Kemp, Jean Blanzat, Jean Grenier, Émile Henriot, Frédéric Lefèvre and Gabriel Marcel. Unlike the Goncourt, which granted lots of glory but only a nominal sum of money, the new Prix des Critiques came with a significant cash sum. Gary was reluctant to be short-listed for fear of spoiling his chances of getting the Goncourt, which, with its extra allocation of paper, guaranteed a wide readership. Then a short piece in the press, assumed to be a leak from inside the Académie Goncourt, let out the fact that Gary was Russian and that the panel would not allow itself to reward two Russian authors in a row. The implication that Gary was also sympathetic to Communism, though entirely false, seemed to put an end to his chances, so he relented and let his name to go forward for the first Prix des Critiques – and he won. The Goncourt went to Jean-Louis Bory for *Mon village à l'heure allemande*, also a story of the Resistance, but a much more reassuring one than Gary's. The Prix des Critiques, however, awarded by judges far less entangled with the Vichy regime, offered far greater reassurance about the true worth of Gary's first book.

The near miss of 1945 made Gary covet the Goncourt all the more. But despite his aspiration towards the pinnacle of a novelist's career, his books moved steadily away from the kind of reading that the Goncourt panel normally favours.

Tulipe – more a sequence of sketches than a novel and provocative in the highest degree – was not a runner. *The Company of Men* deals with the black market, collaboration and anti-Semitism in the post-war years, and its uncompromising treatment of these sensitive topics seems designed to alienate at least half of the members of the Goncourt panel. The subject matter of *The Colours of the Day* – idealism and romance – was better suited to the task, but Gary's realisation of it was too prolix and contorted to make it a popular book. From 1945 to 1952 Gary's writing career, which started off so near the top, seemed set on a downward track.

Gary's path through the diplomatic woods was also far from plain. After two years in Bulgaria, he was brought back to Paris and given a subordinate position on the Central Europe desk at the Foreign Office, under Jean Sauvagnargues. Without free accommodation or a foreign living allowance, Gary found it very hard to manage. Diplomatic salaries were based on the assumption that when in France, Foreign Office employees already had a 'family property' to live in, if not a private income to go with it. Gary had neither and was therefore barely able to house himself. He and Lesley moved around the city from third-class hotel to borrowed room, more like tramps than a diplomatic couple. For two years, from April 1948 until February 1950, at a dozen different temporary addresses, Gary strove hard to improve his financially miserable lot. His writing for the theatre, primarily for Louis Jouvet, brought him precisely nothing, but he did manage to negotiate a new contract with Gallimard, which brought him a reasonable advance on his next novel.

But the only real solution would be a new posting abroad. The French ambassador to Greece refused to accept Gary when he was proposed by the Foreign Office – purportedly because he was a 'Slav', which would not go down well in the country, but more probably because he was Jewish.[2] By coincidence, Henri Hoppenot, a distinguished career diplomat with interests in the arts and in literature, got to hear of this discreet blackballing. Hoppenot had served de Gaulle during the war and no doubt felt some duty to promote a *Compagnon de la Libération*; he was also inclined to preserve the long French tradition of writer-diplomats and decided he would take Gary on himself. And that is how Romain Gary arrived in Berne, Switzerland, in February 1950, as Embassy Secretary, with a new and slightly higher rank of *administrateur civil de 2e classe*.

Hoppenot, the French Ambassador to Switzerland, was very indulgent of his new recruit, and left Gary plenty of time to write and to travel. But there was nothing even Hoppenot could do to make the Swiss capital an exciting place. For much of his time in Berne, Gary was bored out of his mind. In later years he invented memories of high jinks intended to break the unbearable Helvetic calm – jumping into the bear pit at the zoo, sending an official telegram reporting snowfall that had not been officially forecast and so on.[3] He was so fed up with his professional life that he thought of resigning from the Diplomatic Service altogether, but changed his mind 'for simple bread reasons'.[4] One thing he most certainly did to while away the time was to seduce the wives of colleagues. He went further, and teased them mercilessly. At one party a potential conquest asked him how the author of *The Company of Men* knew so much about the black market, teenage crime and . . . brothels. Gary chirpily told Madame de Roth that prior to becoming a diplomat he been a prostitute and a pimp himself.[5]

In 1952 Henri Hoppenot was appointed to succeed Jean Chauvel as the leader of the French Delegation to the United Nations Security Council, with the rank of ambassador. Although Gary had hardly distinguished himself as a diligent bureaucrat in Berne, Hoppenot,whose wife Hélène had also taken a great liking to the writer, decided to bring his unconventional and polyglot secretary along with him. It is hard to imagine a luckier break for Romain Gary.

* * *

Ranking number six in the hierarchy and with the post of spokesman for the Delegation, Romain Gary arrived in New York in September 1952 for the opening of the Seventh General Assembly. He found that the trajectory of his American career was quite different from what had befallen his work in France. *The Company of Men* had done very well and would soon be out in paperback. As a result, he promptly sold the English-language rights of *The Colours of the Day* to the same publisher, represented by his old London pal Joe Barnes; and he also sold that novel's film rights to a Hollywood producer in his first months in the US.

Stephen Becker, a Korean War veteran who would later become a distinguished novelist and teacher of creative writing, was commissioned to translate *The Colours of the Day*. On this occasion, inaugurating what would become the hallmark of his deceptive double career in English and French, Gary intervened massively in the process. He focused less on stylistic issues than on the structure of the book as a whole. He cut many of Rainier's lyrical outbursts, reorganised the novel's parts, moved material from here to there and shortened the book by more than twenty per cent. *The Colours of the Day* appeared in its new guise in late 1953 and went into mass-market paperback in 1954. Gary's American career was on the move, which was personally gratifying and also a source of much-needed cash. In those days housing in Manhattan was horribly expensive for a diplomat with a salary paid in French francs.

Gary's duties in New York were to speak for the French permanent delegation to the United Nations Security Council in front of US and world media. It was he who addressed journalists at briefings, spoke into the microphones and stared at the cameras with sincerity in his eyes whenever public statements of the French position were called for. Statements were officially attributed to Henri Hoppenot, the head of mission, but many if not all of them were drafted or at least polished by Gary, who was directly responsible for the English-language versions. It was much more of a full-time job than any that Gary had held to date.

The Security Council, which had previously led a nomadic existence, meeting at Lake Success, Flushing Meadow and the Palais de Chaillot, had only just found its permanent home in the huge new UN building overlooking the East River. Its labyrinthine corridors often confused delegates going from one meeting room to another, and none more than Gary, who had no sense of orientation at all. The list of resolutions passed by the Security Council in 1953 and 1954 is lamentably short; most of them were procedural rather than substantive in nature. However, the official record of its *discussions* runs to several thousand pages. They make for dreary reading. Vishinsky, for the Soviet Union, Gladwyn Jebb for the UK and the irrepressible Mr Malik from Lebanon spent hundreds of hours pouring the treacle of diplomatic prose on to incandescent agenda items – the dispute between India and Pakistan over Jammu and Kashmir, between Israel and its neighbours over water rights, shipping and ceasefire violations, and the membership status of colonial possessions. However, the main business of the French delegation was not to make progress on the Security Council's agenda, but to keep items off it.

The UN Charter makes explicit reference to the aim of making all countries self-governing, and thus entitled to membership of the world body. Although the UN had no direct power to engage in decolonisation on its own account, it strongly favoured the emancipation of what it called 'not yet self-governing territories'. Britain had withdrawn from India in 1947, from Palestine in 1948, and soon the 'wind of change' would blow through its entire African Empire. In 1952–3, however, France had not yet granted independence to any of its colonies or renounced control of protectorates like Morocco and Tunisia, and it was engaged in a bitter military struggle to hang on to Indochina. The governments of the Fourth Republic, under Mollet, Pinay and Mendès-France, though far from Gaullist in their official ideology, nonetheless pursued de Gaulle's wartime ambition of restoring France to its status as a world power through the leadership of an overseas empire, now named 'L'Union Française'. To this end, which seemed quite futile in American eyes, France made a great effort to present its colonial administration as fulfilling 'the civilizing mission of France'. The sixty-five-member delegation (twice the size of the British team) sent from Paris for the opening session of the Eighth General Assembly in September 1953 included the Mayor of Dakar (Senegal) and members of the French parliament returned by Algeria, Morocco and Tunisia. The aim was to persuade the world that the French Union was a worldwide community of peoples willingly accepting the political and moral tutelage of France.

The trickiest issue Hoppenot had to deal with during Gary's New York stint was a bid by a group of Third-World nations to have first Tunisian and then Moroccan complaints about France's conduct discussed by the Security Council. The move had to be nipped in the bud: if allowed to grow, it could have led to who knows what motion in the General Assembly, and possibly terminal embarrassment for French control of North Africa. Hoppenot rallied enough support in the Security Council to have the Tunisian matter thrown out in April 1952, but an alleged slip by a US delegate put it back on the agenda in December. Hoppenot and the rest of the French delegation walked out of the chamber. Then in 1953, another sly move by a group of nations got a Moroccan representative into the UN. An instant protest from the head of mission, relayed by the press attaché:

> The relations of Morocco and France, said Mr Hoppenot, is an issue within the domestic jurisdiction of France and no international organization can interfere.[6]

As a result of these and other manipulations, France ended up losing its empire mostly by force of arms. The battle of Dien Bien Phu in 1954 ended French control of Indochina and the Algerian uprising began at almost the same time. But sub-Saharan Africa remained quiet and it was in those sparsely populated territories that France's 'civilising mission' remained a credible justification for colonial rule.

Much of the UN's important work is done not in the Security Council or the General Assembly but through its specialised agencies. In 1952, one of these, the IUPN (International Union for the Protection of Nature) circulated a long questionnaire to all member states who had been signatories to the 1933 London Convention on the conservation and rational exploitation of African flora and fauna, in preparation for a conference to be held at Bukavu in the Belgian Congo on 26–31 October 1953. The official French responses to these questions would have passed through the offices of the French delegation and Gary must surely have had sight of them then.

Organisation of Hunting

Question: Is legislation on hunting strictly applied? If not, do you think that if it were strictly applied it would suffice in its present form to ensure the survival of the territory's capital assets of wildlife?

Reply (for the AEF):[7] No. Habits of poaching are too entrenched to be affected by means currently at our disposal. It is worth mentioning that in most of the territories commercial poaching has been choked off . . .

Game Management

Question: What measures have been taken to promote and organise hunting tourism?

Reply (for the AEF): The Administration is constructing roads, camp sites and reception centres in areas most suitable for tourism.

Several hundred hunters come on safari each year.

Game Control

AEF: There are no exceptions to the right of self-defence for individuals and property and the repression of predators may be applied anywhere, provided of course that genuine damage has been done.[8]

Near the conclusion of *The Company of Men*, Luc Martin reads in an evening paper about a group of young men who were going to leave for Cameroon to establish a 'communal settlement':

> I lay flat on the grass, chewed on a little twig, and dreamed of Africa. The grass around me became a jungle; I thought of Lake Chad, and the old elephant that's called rogue. I had read about them once, in a travel book . . .[9]

The papers for the Bukavu conference gave a new shape to the dream Gary had loaned his young hero a few years previously. Especially as they reveal that elephants were not Class A protected animals under the London Convention, but only Class B, which made it quite legal to hunt them outside designated nature reserves. But for sheer lack of manpower, even the very loose legislation controlling hunters and the trade in wild animals was not applied. In 1953 the game reserve of Manda, north of Fort-Archambault, was supervised by one part-time European officer and two full-time Africans. At 580 square miles, Manda is the size of the Yorkshire Moors.

The Roots of Heaven was begun in New York within a few weeks of Gary's arrival in 1952. Written in bursts and patches over the period of his appointment at the UN, it was still incomplete when Gary left for London two years later. The final burst of writing happened in France in the summer of 1955; editing and revising was done hastily in the spring of 1956, when Gary was once again in the US, as Consul General in Los Angeles.

The Roots of Heaven is an adventure novel, a moral tract, a political comedy and a meditation on how legends are made. Formally, it exploits the framing device of Conrad's *Heart of Darkness*, a text at that time little known in France, but deeply familiar to Gary, like all Conrad's works. A Jesuit anthropologist, Tassin (Gary's reinvention of the Marlow figure in Conrad's novella), treks into the African bush to find out from an old Africa hand, Saint-Denis, just what he knows about the mysterious man called Morel. Morel seems to have done something even worse than Conrad's Kurtz: he's not just 'gone native', but has transferred his loyalty to another species entirely – to the elephants. The first two parts of the novel[10] consist of Saint-Denis's spoken recollections of what others had told him, including their reports of third-level conversations, which of course themselves allude to information obtained from yet more deeply nested hearsay. As in *Heart of Darkness*, the primary level (Tassin's listening to Saint-Denis around the campfire burning on through a very long storytelling night) re-emerges every now and again, but for much of the duration readers can easily forget just who is speaking sentences embedded in double quotation marks, some of which should rightly be treble. The 'Russian doll' form of the narration creates innumerable opportunities for information to be given a second time over, to be illuminated by a different point of view or style of speech. Repetition is the hallmark of Gary's writing practice, just as redundancy is the key to page-turning narratives, as John Grisham and Frederick Forsyth well know. The 'formula' of *The Roots of Heaven*, though it may be borrowed from Conrad, suits Gary's particular gifts down to the ground: his natural fluency, his tendency to regurgitate and his gift for simulating varieties of speech all found worthwhile roles in these multiple retellings of the mystery of Morel.

In *The Roots of Heaven* Gary does not stray from his professional duties as a UN official and a spokesman for the French government. His central character, Morel, is not opposed to the independence of the territories making up French Equatorial Africa. However, it also portrays middle-rank French administrators as thoroughly worthy folk, carrying out the civilising mission of France with conviction and seriousness. Saint-Denis, the administrator, is deeply drawn to African culture, but retires in the end to become a monk. Tassin, a Jesuit priest, is also a distinguished palaeontologist who treasures Africa as the origin of human life. The head of the Fort-Lamy police, Schoelscher, is a well-meaning and thoroughly professional officer. The earthy missionary, Father Fargue, is a simple-minded man of faith whose devotion to the improvement of Africans' lives is beyond question. Taken together these characters give a heart-warming picture of France's presence in Chad through science, administration and religion.

Negative non-African characters are mostly not French either: Habib, the gunrunner, is Lebanese, Banarjee, the ivory trader, is Indian, de Vries, an obsessive hunter, is Dutch, as is Haas, a trapper and trader of wild animals for zoos. Gary adds complexity to the question of decolonisation through other characters and discussions, but his overall picture of French colonial rule is clear from the thoroughly decent folk who administer it. *The Roots of Heaven* is not an apologia for the French Union, but it is certainly a defence of the integrity of the second rank of colonial administrators. Its position is fully compatible with Gary's position as spokesman for the French delegation to the Security Council of the UN.

The Roots of Heaven is often claimed to be the first 'ecological novel'. Its hero, Morel, fights a campaign to ban the hunting of African elephants. Part of his motivation is what would now be called an awareness of the need for biodiversity. To this end he tries to get the European population of Fort-Lamy to sign a petition he wants to present to the forthcoming Bukavu conference, but the petition is not even put on the agenda. Undaunted, Morel pursues his campaign by carrying out punitive actions on particularly obnoxious hunters and traders, persuaded that through the publicity such raids will get, he will end up changing world opinion. He attracts a small band of supporters, who take to the bush to pursue the practical defence of elephants, in alliance with a minute Chadian independence movement headed by a former member of the French parliament, Waïtari.

Waïtari is a fierce caricature of the ambitious politicians from the emerging Third World who walked the corridors of the UN in the early 1950s, or else issued statements from the jails where the British or the French were holding them. The more sympathetic European administrators in Gary's Fort-Lamy respect the difference of African culture, but Waïtari will have none of that, as he has been too thoroughly civilised by his French education. He wants to lead his nation towards normality, that is to say towards a European style of development, and it is indifferent to him how he reaches that end, as long as he gets to wield power. Tall, handsome, charismatic, Waïtari is a dictatorship waiting to happen. Gary portrays him as a half-pitiful, half-repulsive loner, pinning a general's five stars to his kepi to lead an army not yet born.

The Roots of Heaven argues almost explicitly that the decent colonialists' respect for African difference is based on a misunderstanding. One of the basic points that Gary had made in *Tulipe,* through irony, sarcasm and back-to-front humour, was that Blacks are no different from Whites. He pursues the same argument in *The Roots of Heaven* far more directly. The character of Waïtari is a transparent warning that Africans have a future as bleak and murderous as the European past. This prediction, which flows not from prejudice, but from rigorous even-handedness in Gary's understanding of the human race, nonetheless conforms to the conventional arguments of diehard colonialists in France, who expected independence to be a disaster not just for themselves, but for Africans too. *The Roots of Heaven* is not an example of colonialist literature, but its appeal to a wide readership in France rested at least in part on the way it also confirmed a consensual, middle-class view of the moral worth of the French Union and of the horrors that decolonisation would bring.

The external framework of Gary's second bid for the big prize is grounded in the matters that came across his desk at the UN in 1952 and 1953 – decolonisation and the upcoming Bukavu conference on wildlife protection. But the heart of the novel is not in Africa at all. Morel's campaign to save the elephants expresses a wider moral aspiration that has to do with people, not with animals, and most especially with traditional European ideals. Morel goes around the expats of Chad wearing the Cross of Lorraine on his lapel and carrying a leather briefcase stuffed full of papers. With a strong Parisian accent, he looks and sounds as if he were on his way to a demonstration on the Boulevard Voltaire. In principle, that is exactly what he is: a campaigner for the kind of decency incarnated in the adventure of Free France, transposed to the heart of Africa. What do the elephants represent? In a single interview Gary referred to the elephants being obviously symbolic of himself, of Charles de Gaulle in 1940 and of France as she should be.[11] The term Gary used to name the particular value that Morel's campaign really seeks to defend was *la marge humaine* – literally, 'the human margin', but perhaps more meaningfully translatable as 'room for humanity'. Elephants are the largest vegetarian beasts on earth, they move around in sizable herds, and they strip vast amounts of foliage and crops with great ease. Human life would be much easier without these free-ranging, all-trampling monsters; respecting elephants' rights to a peaceful life in the wild stretches tolerance for otherness to its limit. That is why Morel's assertion of that right is exemplary, and its real point is to inspire the whole world to respect the rights of all 'others', however awkward they may be. Gary chose his symbol well. Readers would have found it harder to accept the moral lesson if the novel's vehicle had been jackals, hyenas, or rats.

The Roots of Heaven is a topical work, but not a fashionable one. The distinction is crucial to understanding Gary's place in literature. The setting and the plot of the novel are imaginative constructions closely based on material Gary had to handle in his professional life, energised by memories of the few months he had spent in Central Africa in 1941. But wildlife had not yet become the book trade's best standby after cooking, fishing and self-help. Joy Adamson's *Born Free* wasn't published until 1960, and even Joseph Kessel needed the prompting of Gary's success to write *The Lion* in 1958, a wildlife novel that hasn't been out of print ever since. In the early 1950s, big-game hunting was still seen as innocent fun, or even (as in Hemingway) as the ultimate expression of masculinity. The idea that wildlife had a basic right to be left alone didn't even occur to the drafters of the Bukavu resolutions, who busied themselves with proposals for the *management* of wildlife in order to maximise the economic viability of impoverished areas of Africa by the development of tourism, that is to say, hunting wild animals. The term, let alone the concept, of ecology was barely known outside specialist circles. Gary told the story of an impromptu survey he did at a dinner party given by the newspaper proprietor Pierre Lazareff after the publication of *The Roots of Heaven*. Of the twenty-two guests, most of whom were journalists or people of considerable education, only two could give even a halfway accurate definition of the word.[12]

Gary often said that everything in his novels was 'invented', and *The Roots of Heaven* suggests how we should understand that assertion. He didn't invent the main location of the novel, the hotel in Fort-Lamy, where he'd been billeted for a while during the war. All he did was to change its name from L'Hôtel de l'Air to Le Tchadien. He didn't invent the scenery either, he recalled it from memory. He didn't invent the crimes of the hunters, trappers and the ivory and wildlife traders – he used facts, figures and anecdotes from the Bukavu minutes and from the few books on African elephants he could find in New York bookstores. He didn't really invent Waïtari, either, he just blended together features of Nkrumah and a few other Third-World agitators he'd come across at the UN. He admitted that one of the more comical aspects of Father Fargue had been borrowed from the chaplain on a boat he'd once taken upriver during his African period, and that his description of Father Tassin's face (but not of his character) was calqued directly on Teilhard de Chardin, whom he'd had occasion to meet in New York. Nor did he invent entirely the character of Forsyth, the US airman who'd been taken captive in Korea and deceived into believing that the US had used biological weapons, because Gary was part of the delegation that took the lead at the UN in proving that the claim had been entirely fabricated by the USSR. What Gary invented was a conflation of a topical matter and a moral argument through two imagined but not entirely unreal characters, Morel and Minna.

Claims have been made that Gary didn't even invent Morel. While he was writing *The Roots of Heaven*, an eccentric French zookeeper called Raphaël Matta was conducting a quixotic campaign to stop native hunting of elephants in the Bouna game reserve, in the ironically named Ivory Coast. Matta was eventually murdered by tribesmen, an event reported in the French press several years after Gary had published *The Roots of Heaven*.[13] Gary's claims that he only learned about Matta after his novel was finished are therefore convincing: Morel was indeed the fruit of the novelist's extraordinarily accurate imagination. As for the name, it may be a reminiscence of the British journalist and campaigner Edmund Dene Morel, whose revelations about atrocities in the Congo gave Conrad some of his information for *Heart of Darkness*; but it's just as likely that it seemed fitting because it is just a vowel away from *moral*.

What Gary truly created in the first two parts of *The Roots of Heaven* is the *legend* of Morel, which arises from the novel's structure in combination with material borrowed from here and there. It's worth recalling that Morel's campaign is entirely ineffective, but has left among the Europeans of Fort-Lamy (whose testimonies as reported by Saint-Denis are the sole substance of the text) a feeling that something or someone of an almost transcendental kind has passed through their isolated and forgotten community. Morel never appears except as recollection; even at one remove, actual sightings of him are rare; and as he is never pinned down or interrogated directly, he becomes an object of interpretation, capable of generating different meanings for different people, like a symbol or myth.

However, Gary's aim was the Goncourt and for that a female lead was required to give his pseudo-gospel an air of romance. Habib, the owner of the town's sole hotel, hires a hostess to make the saloon a more welcoming place. Minna, the only character in all Gary's writing to bear his mother's real name, had had the misfortune to be female and fifteen in Berlin at the time of its fall. Raped by Russian troops, then labelled a prostitute to save the Red Army's face, she quickly became frigid and able to treat sex as a matter of little importance. Gary said that he made his leading lady German because, in the aftermath of the war, 'misfortune was German'.[14] However, the suffering of the women of Berlin was also highly topical when Gary was writing *The Roots of Heaven*. A scandalous anonymous diary of rape and survival by prostitution in post-war Berlin had just been published in New York: Minna's story is a nutshell version of the experiences recorded in that book, now attributed to Marta Hiller.[15] Gary portrayed Minna with the physical features of a well-known German film actress, Hildegarde Neff, and claimed he had been stunned to discover, when Neff published her autobiography many years later, that she had gone through the same kind of suffering in her teens.

Minna also balances Morel, a Frenchman who'd been deported to a German concentration camp during the war. That's to say, the heart of Gary's African novel is in Europe and in the healing of its wounds, as Minna responds instantly to Morel's charisma when he comes into the bar of Le Tchadien. His campaign to save wildlife from slaughter is a calling she cannot refuse. Germany is stereotypically male and France usually represented as a woman, so Gary's pairing of Minna and Morel reverses the convention. Minna's willing sacrifice of herself to Morel's implausible campaign is also a spectacular reversal of the message of the story that serves as the formal model of *The Roots of Heaven*. What Conrad found in the heart of darkness was 'the horror, the horror'. What Gary gives back to the African savannah is the possibility of doing good.

18

Masquerade

Gary in London, 1954–1955

Lesley Blanch gave up her career as a journalist when she married Romain Gary and shortly after became a diplomatic wife. Ten years later, as she approached her fiftieth birthday, she launched on a new life as a writer of books. *The Wilder Shores of Love* – brief lives of four European women fascinated by the allure of the East (Jane Digby, Isabelle Eberhardt, Aimée Dubucq and Isabel Burton) – appeared in 1954 with Simon & Schuster, Gary's own US publisher, and was a runaway success.[1] In America it far outshone Gary's achievements with *The Company of Men* and *The Colors of the Day*. In French translation it took Paris by storm and was serialised in *Elle*.[2] Gary's eventual response to this cruel blow to his pride was a partly self-mocking piece, also for *Elle*, 'Lesley est une sorcière' (Lesley is a Witch).[3] Meanwhile, Lesley had already built on her newfound standing to sign herself up for two easy books intended to make her financially independent. Alongside an edition of the memoirs of an English courtesan mentioned on p. 149,[4] she concocted *Around the World in Eighty Dishes*, a children's cookery book. Apart from her pen-and-ink sketches, most of it seems to have been copied out from pages of *Tante Marie* and Mrs Beeton (veal Marengo, *brandade de morue*, colcannon, kedgeree, toad-in-the-hole . . .). She did slip in a couple of items picked up from life with Romain Gary,

Roqué-brune Tartine and Polish Pickled Cucumbers, though the first tells you more about Lesley's incompetence in French and the second does not tell you how to pickle the cucumbers in the first place.

As Lesley's career took off, Gary's seemed to be running into the ground. With the end of his two-year stint at the UN coming on to the horizon in the summer months of 1954, he had still not finished his 'elephant book'. He'd been kept so busy by his job that all his writing had been done in lunch breaks: '*The Roots of Heaven* was written between twelve and two,' he later told Patrice Galbeau.[5] Evenings were taken up with the receptions and dinner parties that were part of a diplomat's job, as well as with Gary's need for sex. Where would his next posting be? As is apparently customary in the Diplomatic Service, Gary spent a lot of time putting out feelers for a new posting – Venice and Tehran were raised as possibilities – but he set his sights in the end on the job of press attaché at the London Embassy. His appointment came through, he was all set to leave, he was about to board the liner when news arrived that it had been vetoed by Jean Chauvel. Gary caught the boat nonetheless, but sailed to England with no clear prospect ahead.

Gary soon learned why he was being blackballed by Chauvel. The Ambassador, acutely worried about being outed as a gay since his contretemps in Washington in 1951 (see p. 142), had jumped to the erroneous conclusion that 'The Lute', Gary's story of homosexual love in Istanbul, was intended to point the finger at him. Apart from the broad subject and the fact that the main character is a diplomat, however, nothing whatsoever links 'The Lute' to Chauvel. The penalty Gary paid for a paranoid reading of one of his finest short stories was unjustified and it seems to have knocked him for six.

He arrived in London in the last days of 1954 without a proper post, without a new book in the bag or a new publication in train, and also without a wife, as Lesley had resolved to stay in New York. In the rainy, smog-bound city, Gary sank into a depression sufficiently deep to warrant hospitalisation. He had always been prone to mood swings and often gave theatrical performances of despair, with his head in his hands in what Blanch called his 'disaster poses';[6] he was also quite capable of falling in love at lunchtime with a girl he'd forgotten before tea. All the same, Lesley's reaction to Gary's depression seems rather harsh. In Anissimov's account, the consultant psychiatrist at King Edward VII's Hospital for Officers, Roger Saint Aubyn, rang Blanch in New York and said she should come to see her husband straight away. Gary's wife replied that if Romain wasn't actually poised on the window ledge with a leg in the air his depression wasn't worth fussing about.

Gary's need to carry off prizes and to achieve improbable exploits went hand in hand with an equally strong dislike of himself. Conventional Jewish self-hatred doesn't account for the half of it. Gary disliked himself also because of the foul temper he had, which meant he could do others harm, but most of all because he was a man and thus a member of a race collectively and individually guilty of unspeakable crimes. Gary built a moral philosophy that fitted his cyclothymic personality very well, but it's not clear which of his convictions and his feelings was the chicken and which the egg. His work expresses an aspiration towards being a 'real man', by which he meant not at all the muscular virility of a Charlton Heston, but almost the opposite: universal sympathy with humankind and complete solidarity with all that truly belongs to it, including its shabbiness, cruelty and anger. Aspiring towards humaneness while identifying with all that is inhuman in man put Gary in permanent conflict with himself, and also gave his work its underlying unity, alternating in jagged leaps between high satire and deep seriousness.

Gary's self-hatred on behalf of the human race explains, too, the particular role of animals in his life and work. He kept pets whenever he could, and when he was rich and well-housed he lived in a virtual menagerie. But his animal pets didn't serve as stand-ins for the human companions he did not have. He loved them because they were truly different from men. In his writing, dogs, elephants and Cousin's pet python in *Gros-Câlin* are not anthropomorphised. What makes them attractive as subjects for fiction is that they live in a world that humans can never enter. *The Roots of Heaven*, *White Dog* and *Gros-Câlin* are therefore not 'animal stories' in the usual sense, but stories that grant animals the right to be their incomprehensible, alien selves.

In London, in the early weeks of 1955, Gary seems to have recovered sufficiently from his bout of clinical depression to follow the pedals at the non-job allocated to him, in lieu of the embassy press office, at the Brussels Treaty Organisation in Eaton Square. The Brussels Treaty of 1948 was the first step on the path towards the European Union, which would be established by the Treaty of Rome in 1957.[7] One of its provisions was to promote European rapprochement through culture and education, and Gary's vague job related to raising awareness of the cultures of the other member states. He gave a few talks, one of them in Strasbourg, and otherwise pushed paper around on his desk. The elephant novel was at a standstill. What Gary did to get over his breakdown was to imagine he might be someone else.

With New York now behind him, he turned back to his first invention of the city in *Tulipe*, the story he'd wasted so much time trying to adapt for the stage. Transferring its satire of idealism from a Harlem garret to the UN building – that mausoleum of man's aspirations towards the noble and the good – was a piece of cake. Gary dashed off *L'Homme à la colombe* in a few hectic weeks. The intoxicating part of the idea was not to pass off a re-written tract as a new novel, but to make the story of a moral scam a literary mystification in itself. On 25 April he wrote to Joe Barnes that he was sending Jack Goodman, Gary's agent in New York, a farcical story about the

UN 'by a friend of mine, Jack Ribbons. He's an American who can only write in French.' Joe Barnes was kindly requested to translate the typescript. 'But the knot is that nobody must know that the translation has been done from the French. It has to be presented as an American book, and in French it will be labelled *traduit de l'américain*.'[8]

Gary might have been planning to have the English appear first, to create a buzz around the publication of a 'translation' in French, or else he might only have wanted the English to exist as an alibi, to prove the French was a translation. Whatever the real plan, which Gary was also inventing as he went along, Joe Barnes put 'Jack Ribbons's' manuscript into English, and sent the draft back to Gary, who rewrote key parts of it himself, in particular the monologue of a character called Harry-the-Rat. Barnes, who knew Russian as well as he knew French, might have guessed why 'Harry' was so important. Russian has no letter 'H', and replaces the sound in words borrowed from German and English with a 'G'. (My Russian grandmother, for example, disapproved of young women wearing 'Guy Geels'.) A Russian saying 'Harry-the-Rat' can only pronounce it as 'Garry-the-Rat'. Harry-the-Rat is *Gary-garrí*, the author himself under double cover of Russian and Nissart, in a novel to be published under two other covers, as a translation and under a false name.

The hilarious fun of this multiple invention – of a book, a pseudonym, and an author – didn't last very long. As the corrected typescript of *Man with a Dove, or The Last Adventures of Frankie and Johnnie* winged its way back over the Atlantic, Romain Gary collapsed a second time. His antics with Jack Ribbons – which Barnes saw through, but was too kind to say so outright – gave way to another bout of clinical depression and in early May 1955 Gary was back in the psychiatric ward of King Edward's Hospital, where he stayed for several weeks.

The posting to London had brought Gary back into touch with an old friend from Sofia, Petar Christoff Ouvaliev, now known as Pierre Rouve. This remarkable man had made his escape from the nascent People's Republic in 1947, with a little help from Romain Gary (to whom he bore a fairly striking facial resemblance). He was now working for the BBC Bulgarian Service and a hero in his own land as 'the voice of freedom, tolerance and democracy . . . during the darkest days of the Cold War'.[9] He was also active in film production with Anatole and Dmitri Grunwald, the steadfast backers of Jacques Tati, as well as being an art critic of international standing. Pierre Rouve was a polyglot raconteur and bon vivant at the centre of a lively London circle of expatriate intellectuals and wits. Two years later, when Gary came back to his United Nations novel, he enlisted Pierre Rouve to help him perpetrate a mystification to replace the half-cooked plot with Joe Barnes. In 1957, Gary persuaded Rouve to sign a book contract with Gallimard under the false name of Fosco Sinibaldi for the manuscript he'd written about the UN.[10] Gary later claimed that *L'Homme à la colombe* was published under a pseudonym because the *devoir de réserve* does not allow French diplomats to write about anything related to their official duties for three years. Perhaps so, but the aim from the start was to mystify the public and show that Tulipe's impersonation of sainthood could be got away with *in real life*. It didn't quite work out, because although Pierre Rouve agreed to sign the book contract with Gallimard, he refused to commit himself him to acting out the role of Sinibaldi and he wouldn't sign the bizarre 'impersonation deal' that Gary drew up.[11] *L'Homme à la colombe* appeared in 1958 under the name of Fosco Sinibaldi. It was not well received and to revive the book's flagging sales Gary let it be known that it was actually one of his own. That didn't help much either. It went out of print and wasn't reissued until after Gary's death.

The significance of this episode of attempted personation can hardly be exaggerated. It was conceived in the low period after the first draft of the 'big' book had been completed, but before Gary won the Goncourt Prize and started to acquire his almost oppressive celebrity in the media. Gary's desire to create fictions not only in the conventional way, by writing novels, but by inventing the novelist too – like a carnival maestro – accompanied a brief reprieve in a major bout of depression and may be seen as a symptom of the mental imbalance he suffered in 1955. But this kind of madness – plotting to deceive the world into taking a mask for a man – seems to have been an alternative to the other kind, which would have deprived the world of the twenty books Gary still had to write.

The main one waiting for its final shape had already been sent to Joe Barnes, who wrote back on 19 April 1955 with effusive praise for a typescript he refers to as 'Elephants'. A couple of weeks later Gary sent a message to Barnes from his hospital ward to say that he had put the original manuscript of 'Elephants' in a brown suitcase in safe keeping at the London home of Eric Ambler, the celebrated thriller writer, 'in case I cannot pull through'.[12] But he did pull through, left hospital, took sick leave and made his way to Roquebrune to convalesce. He took his brown suitcase with him and set to work on turning 'Elephants' into *The Roots of Heaven*.

19

Top Prize
Los Angeles, 1956

The great depression of London no doubt had many causes, but one among them was Lesley Blanch. Gary had suggested a divorce even during their time in New York.[1] But Lesley's unexpected success with her book prompted a jealousy tantrum and her refusal to accompany her husband to London, now that she had the means to stay in New York, confronted him with his own dependence on her. They had no children to bind them; both partners had treated sex as an out-of-home sport for ten years; yet Gary still had no idea how to cope with ordinary life on his own. He depended on Lesley for sorting out everything from his socks to his invitation diary. She wanted to stop being housemother to a Russian bear and regarded her marriage as at an end. That strengthened her resolve not to return to London, where all her old British friends would see she had made a mess of an adventurous marriage they had probably advised her against at the time. She suspected Gary's hospital stay of being put on to tell her how badly he needed her to come back to him. However, she yielded to his entreaties and returned to London for a time in the winter of 1954–5, staying at a different address. The following summer she and Gary were together at Roquebrune and, in the autumn, Lesley agreed to give her marriage to the French diplomat a second try. The fact that

Gary had just received his nomination to the vacant post of French Consul General in Los Angeles no doubt played some part in helping Lesley make up her mind.

At Roquebrune, in the summer of 1955, Gary wrote Part III of *The Roots of Heaven*, and thereby turned it into a much less challenging book. Part III is an adventure story in traditional third-person style, told in the same order as the events it narrates, and it almost resolves the mystery of what happened to Morel. It's more conventional, routine and middlebrow than anything Gary had penned so far, as if, after the dangerous japes with Sinibaldi and Jack Ribbons in the spring, and the plunge into darkness that followed, he'd now decided to keep his feet on the ground. The literary avant-garde might have taken more notice of the novel in the mid-fifties if it had been published without Part III; but it's a fairly sure bet that without it Gary would not have won the Goncourt.

The summer supplement to the legend of Morel introduces a completely new character, an American photojournalist called Abe Fields, who is made to drop into the plot from the sky, in a chartered aeroplane. In various places Gary claimed that the first idea for a novel about the protection of elephants came from the misbehaviour of his crew in an aeroplane when he was stationed in Africa in 1941: they flew low over a herd to get a better view of the beasts, but the pilot misjudged his altitude, clipped a wing on the back of one of the animals and crashed. As Gary emerged unharmed from the wreck, a game warden came out of nowhere and harangued the young airmen for their irresponsibility – no one, he said, had the right to treat elephants like that.[2] Abe Field's implausible mode of arrival on the fictional scene resembles the alleged personal memory sufficiently well to give the latter an air of authenticity. It's also true that there were a huge number of accidents to the aircraft of the FAFL.

Fields, when he realises that he has come upon the much-sought-after Morel, also sees that the defender of pachyderms is destined to be ditched very soon by his temporary protectors, Waïtari's small band of guerrillas. So he sticks around for the greatest photo-op of his already celebrated career, that of the execution of Morel by Africans who will be seen (depending on the moment it happens and when the photograph gets into the papers) as confirming everyone's views about Communists, or nationalists, or Blacks, or naive idealists, or whatever. What seems certain to him is that the photo itself will be worth his camera's weight in gold. But as the narrative of the slaughter of elephants by Waïtari's mercenaries proceeds, Fields is drawn towards Morel and his campaign. The sight of decency moves him; the charisma of goodness raises him out of the cynicism he had adopted to protect himself from all the horrors a photojournalist has to seek out. Minna and Fields are the last disciples still by Morel's side as the campaign moves ever deeper into the bush to evade capture and to maintain the hero's status as legend. But they cannot go on: Fields's broken ribs have become disabling and Minna is worn out by dysentery. The journalist turns to the German girl and tries to console her as they watch their inspiration depart, alone, to very probable death. '"*Weint nischt*"',[3] he said to her in Yiddish, convinced that he was talking good German.'[4] This is the first appearance of a sentence in Yiddish in any French novel, as far as I know.[5]

Fields, who rapidly takes over as the narrative centre of gravity in Part III, is of course not just American, but Polish and Jewish as well, and his intervention simply underlines what had already been fairly clear in Parts I and II – that Gary's African novel is rooted in European history. In the last leg of Morel's journey into legend, Minna does little more than tag along, as her significance has already been fully explored, leaving Fields as the carrier of new meanings. Why had he decided to stick with Morel? Not just because of that photo-op – and anyway, he'd run out of film. He stuck to the leader of a hopeless campaign in memory of his family, all of whom had been gassed at Auschwitz. This is one of the earliest references to the extermination of European Jews in post-war French fiction. Even Alain Resnais's *Night and Fog*, a short documentary film on Nazi camps almost exactly contemporary with *The Roots of Heaven*, skirts round the fact that nearly all the corpses seen on screen are Jewish ones.

The moral equivalence of saving elephants and saving Jews isn't the only 'key' that Gary gives away in Part III of *The Roots of Heaven*. As the plight of Morel's band grows more desperate, the novelist goes into allegorical overdrive. Morel himself invents a back story to explain his passion for saving peaceable beasts from slaughter. In captivity in a German camp during the war, he and his comrades devised mind games to stay sane. One involved sharing the fictional presence of a lady in the hut, so as to force themselves to keep up appearances and behave with appropriate dignity. Another involved dreaming of the polar opposite of a prison cell – the life of an elephant roaming the vast savannah without constraint. That's why Morel had felt obliged to pay attention to real elephants after his release. Yet another anecdote underlines the moral message of the novel. The German guards treated slave labourers like roaches. Morel and his mates therefore decided to treat insects as if they were human. Weighed down by the sacks of cement they were condemned to hump all day long, they would bend down and put back on their feet any maybeetles they found stranded on their backs. What matters in all of Gary's memorable attempts to provide the key to the meaning of his book is the *gesture* of humanity, not the material effectiveness of the act.

The insertion of Fields into the narrative also gives Gary a sturdy peg on which to hang his ideas about how legends are made – essentially, through the press. It wasn't his job as press officer in New York that had made him particularly aware of the role of the media in moulding minds; in fact, the real story is probably the other way round. The mentor of Adam

Dobranski in *A European Education* is an academic who also runs an underground news-sheet; Tulipe's masquerade is entirely constructed by the black and Jewish journalists of *The Peoples' Voice*; the denouement of *The Company of Men* hangs on the publication of Vanderputte's photograph in the daily press; and in *The Colours of the Day*, Bauché's façade of a happily married man is directed exclusively towards the Hollywood reporters on his wife's tail. The power of the press to inspire, to mislead, to reveal and to oppress is taken for granted in all that Gary wrote *before* he got to New York. In *The Roots of Heaven*, however, 'public relations' occupy an even larger space.

The first journalist who enters the scene is a transparent parody of the obnoxious Robert C. Ruark, a celebrity journalist on the *Washington Post* whose 1954 movie, *Africa Adventure*, follows two 'great white hunters', Harry Selby and John Sutton, as they track water buffalo, a leopard, a rhino and bag 'the biggest bull elephant since time began'.[6] Gary's version of the man is called Ornando and his arrival strikes servility into the entire colonial administration of Chad. Morel puts buckshot into his backside and, in an improbable dramatic reversal, the overweight butcher of African wildlife accepts the campaigner's moral position and files no complaint with the police. The second 'press action' involves hijacking the printing plant of the local newspaper in Sionville and inserting a 'Communiqué of the World Committee for the Defence of Elephants' on its front page, listing the punishments to be meted out against hunters and traders in ivory and in waste-paper baskets, champagne buckets and vases fashioned from the severed feet of elephants and hippos. Thirdly, there is Fields, and the movement from aggression through forcible co-option to the willing enlistment of the press is complete. Morel believes as much as Gary did in the power of the media to shift mentalities and in that sense a novel like *The Roots of Heaven* is campaigning journalism pursued by other means. But it is much more than that as well, because it also represents and demystifies the mechanisms by which modern myths are made.

Gary's summer leave dragged on into the autumn and still he did not know where his next diplomatic posting would be. He spent a few weeks in London to while away time, seeing old friends like Arthur Koestler and trying to seduce Elizabeth Jane Howard, until finally, on 16 November 1955, the French Foreign Minister, Maurice Couve de Murville, appointed Gary to the vacant position of Consul General in Los Angeles. The consulate generalship was not a position of great political importance, but it had glamour and prestige beyond any other posting of equivalent rank. This was because France, which considered itself the true home of cinema (the inventors of the *cinématographe*, the Lumière brothers, were indeed French), felt itself obliged to be represented in Hollywood more grandly than in many capital cities. What had gone on behind the scenes to land Gary such a plum job is not known. Perhaps the post was granted to him in compensation for the shabby way he had been treated in London; at all events, the support of Henri Hoppenot, Gary's mentor and pilot from Berne to New York, must have played a role too. But the appointment was also a good choice for France. Unlike most diplomats of equivalent rank, Gary spoke excellent English and was already well known in the US. He set off from Le Havre on 20 January 1956 – alone, because Lesley was travelling in the Caucasus, researching her next book on the Imam Shamyl.

He took the bulky manuscript of his elephant novel with him, to get it typed up and off to Gallimard. But no Californian typist he could find could make head or tail of his drafts! So Gary copied out the entire novel one more time, in his very best handwriting. It was not until 5 April 1956 that he could dispatch the typescript to Paris. At this point the working title was *Éducation africaine*, playing clumsily on the memory of *Éducation européenne*. Michel Gallimard had it read by two of the firm's senior editors, Albert Camus and Jacques Lemarchand, and both responded with enthusiasm in early May. The book went to the printers straight away. Gary took summer leave from his diplomatic post and spent all of June and July 1956 at Roquebrune, correcting the proofs of a novel that Gallimard had agreed to bring out in September, to allow it a chance of winning a prize, although the firm would have preferred to put it off until the spring, to have time to weed out repetitions and mistakes. In fact, it didn't get into the bookshops until October (Gary had gone back to Los Angeles in August, but managed to wangle a ten-day trip to Paris at the time of the book's release). But it began to sell well and some of the early reviews were highly favourable.

Meanwhile, Gary was obliged to step in as Chargé d'Affaires in La Paz, Bolivia, where France had had no ambassador for several months. He did not spend long in South America – from 8 November until around 10 December 1956. This part of the world seems to have left little trace in his work.

It was while he was in La Paz that he heard (by telegram) first the rumour that he was in the running for the Goncourt and then, on 4 December, that he had won it. The Foreign Office graciously allowed him a few days' leave to return to Paris to receive the prize – but at his own expense![7]

The Roots of Heaven is a rare French example of what in Britain is called middlebrow fiction – a page-turning narrative with a serious point to make. The award of the Goncourt to a novel of that kind seemed to many critics an affront to literary taste. As if it were still possible to be a Conrad or a Dickens or a Victor Hugo in 1956! What Gary's disparagers had forgotten is that the Goncourt was established to reward precisely that kind of nineteenth-century prose and that the choice of *The Roots of Heaven* over Butor's more experimental *L'Emploi du temps* was consonant with the basic aim of the prize. But the more Gary's novel sold, both before and after the award, the louder his enemies cried. Despite the unwavering support of Albert Camus, Émile Henriot and a few others, most of the press around *The Roots of Heaven* was critical and some of it plain hostile – undermining, at least as far as literary criticism is concerned, Morel's belief in the power of the media to change people's minds.

The Roots of Heaven followed hard on the heels of two huge disasters for Europe: the crushing of the Hungarian revolt by Soviet tanks and the embarrassing failure of Franco-British involvement in Israel's raid on the Suez Canal, which was closed for many months thereafter. It was a highly political moment in France and Gary's book seemed to fall outside all camps. The senior critic of the French Communist Party, André Wurmser, denounced Morel's concept of 'the human margin' as 'a marginal question' – as it most certainly was for the devoutly Stalinist PCF. Maurice Nadeau, who had not yet broken with the Party, also derided *The Roots of Heaven* as a 'humanitarian rhapsody, a story designed to impress Tintin'. Attacks from the Right focused on Gary's foreignness and on the poor quality of his French, but it's not obvious that xenophobia and anti-Semitism were the sole factors motivating their campaign against the novel. After all, Morel was explicitly open-minded about self-rule for the African colonies and his main aim was to ban hunting, a proposal which, like gun control in America, can be guaranteed to rally huge opposition from a broad spectrum of the French Right.

Some of the objections raised to *The Roots of Heaven* are justifiable. Gary's novel could certainly have been improved by cuts and a general tightening up of the text – but the same can be said about *Les Misérables*, *Great Expectations*, *The Brothers Karamazov* and *Lord Jim*. Capacious, meandering, fluent and readable fiction was not at all in fashion in Saint-Germain-des-Prés in 1956 and it doesn't seem that many leading critics read any of it very much, as none of them even mentioned *Heart of Darkness* as the archetype of *The Roots of Heaven*.

However, the reading public followed its own taste, far more favourable to Gary than the critical ideas of the day, and it allowed him to laugh all the way to the bank. But the Goncourt Prize and the financial rewards that it brought didn't quite make up for the rough handling he received from Robert Kanters, Kléber Haedens, Maurice Nadeau, André Wurmser and many others. Gary's altogether surprising response to such criticism was not visible to his enemies in France. They said he could not write French – so he stopped. He would prove them all fools by writing his next worldwide success in another tongue.

IV

The Big Time

20

Changing Faces

Writing in English, 1958–1974

In his fake interview with François Bondy, Gary describes his peculiar ability to adapt to changes in circumstance with a parable from Witold Gombrowicz, or else from Jean Cocteau, likening himself to a chameleon, which changes its colour according to the background on which it is set.[1] In *Gros-Câlin*, published under the name of Émile Ajar in the same year as *A Quiet Night*, the narrator Cousin is particularly impressed by his python's ability to shed its skin: 'My long observation and knowledge of pythons has led me to the conclusion that moulting is for them the moment of supreme emotion, when they feel they are about to enter on a new life, certified authentic.'[2] These reptilian images crop up in the early 1970s as substitutes for Gary's original and perhaps more meaningful image of self-transformation, which is rebirth.

In memoir and fiction, Gary characteristically presents the extraordinary turns in his life as moments of coming into the world anew. *Promise at Dawn* is structured overall as a story leading up to the moment when Gary emerged as himself – that is to say, as a writer – on receiving a message from Cresset Press saying that his first book, *A European Education*, had been accepted for publication and would appear within months. 'I took off my flying helmet and gloves and stood for a long time, staring at the telegram. We were born.'[3] Twenty years later, in *Life and Death of Émile Ajar*, Gary used the same language to describe his joy in achieving recognition as someone else: '*It was a new birth. I was renewing myself.*'[4] Gary's fictional heroes, on the other hand, count their 'birth' most often from the date of their sexual awakening. Fosco Zaga, the narrator of *The Enchanters*, reckons he was 'truly born at the age of twelve years and seven months' when he first set eyes on the lovely Teresina.[5] But there is one rebirth that Gary never mentions as such: his entirely successful impersonation of an English-language novelist called Romain Gary.

Two confusions can arise in connection with Gary's many careers and his use of terms like 'born again' to describe and account for them. Many varieties of the Christian faith consider believers to be 'born again' or 'reborn in Christ'. Despite the verbal similarity, Gary's idea of rebirth has nothing to do with religion. Christianity certainly doesn't propose, as Gary did, that you can be someone else in *this* life, not the other one. The second confusion is potentially more awkward. Many individuals who suffer post-traumatic amnesia and the much smaller number who undergo transient global amnesia do have the real-life experience of being 'born again' as they recover part or (more rarely) all of their prior identities. It is never a pleasant experience, as anyone who has visited patients in brain injury rehabilitation clinics can attest. Gary's idea of being reborn as someone else is a literary and moral fantasy, unrelated to the dark suffering of minds that for one reason or another no longer know whose they are.[6]

Gary took up his post in Los Angeles in January 1956 and he made a tremendous impact at the start of his reign as 'French Ambassador to Hollywood'. But as he became the beaming face of France on the West Coast of the United States, he stopped writing in French. Once Gary had made his final revisions to *The Roots of Heaven* in summer 1956 and until his visit to Warsaw ten years later, he wrote all his new fiction in English.

His memoir, *Promise at Dawn*, was first written in French, it is true – but the English version, which Gary wrote himself almost immediately, is fuller and is the basis for the 'definitive edition' he later published in French.[7]

Unlike Conrad, Nabokov, or Eugène Ionesco, who switched from Polish, Russian and Romanian to English and French respectively, Gary was not an émigré when he chose to change his language of writing, but a high dignitary of the French state. He was only a temporary resident of the USA, with a two-year appointment, renewable just once. Within four years at most, he would be posted somewhere else and there was no guarantee it would be to an English-speaking land. The choice of English as the language of a second literary career was not imposed by circumstance, nor was it an obviously rational choice to make. That is certainly why Gary kept it under deep cover for many years. Several of the works that he published in English were alleged to be translations from French, which they were not; and when the works were put back into French, no mention was made that they were translations and the titles were transformed so as to mask their connection to the originals. Perhaps Gary foresaw becoming American, possibly a permanent resident of Hollywood, the far shore on which so many talented Russian, German, Polish, Jewish and other undesirables had finally beached. It's more likely that he hoped to use an American career to return in triumph to Paris and crush mean-minded critics like Kléber Haedens, who had sniped at his 'inability' to write French.

Among the many reasons that lay behind the strange and admirable exploit of Gary's second birth as an Anglophone novelist, the childish desire to teach Lesley a lesson – to prove who the *real* writer among them was – must have been a significant, if not a preponderant, one. The simple fact, quickly learned in LA, that fluent and imaginative writers of English could earn a great deal more money than any Frenchman could dream of must have counted just as much. Thirdly, of course,

Gary had no more prizes to win in France and now needed a higher challenge to provide him with renewed proof of his own genius. But perhaps what attracted him most to the idea of reinventing himself in a sixth language was the gratuitousness of the exploit. He had clearly been pondering the possibility of being an English writer since 1945, when he had tried to translate his ill-starred *Tulipe* by himself. Now he was once again in an English-language environment, with far more resources at his disposal than in London or New York, he was in a position to make a real stab at it.

Until he won the Goncourt Prize, Gary never had much more than his diplomatic salary to live on and he did not manage what money he had very well. He had no property save the quaint ruin at Roquebrune, which was not worth much at all; he had neither savings to invest nor a clue how to do so. The Goncourt Prize carried a nominal purse, but it made high sales almost certain and thus brought Gary the prospect of significant wealth. When he arrived in Paris to collect his award in December 1956, he summoned the businessman father of a friend he'd made in LA, Alain Aptekman, to give him some financial advice. Very soon, however, future royalties from *The Roots of Heaven* were dwarfed by the sale of the novel's film rights. The headline figure of $135,000 – worth more than a million dollars today – must have been partly eaten up by agent's fees and taxes, but even so it was far beyond anything that could be expected from royalty income in France. As Gary owned the rights to his work in English, he could now expect the kind of advances that box-office authors received in America. He set to work to exploit this fabulous opportunity straight away.

Gary's career as a writer in English began in 1957 and took the outward form of a business enterprise. He set up a limited liability company in Geneva, Propintel SA, to handle his overseas income and ascribed the copyright of his next book to it. Like *The Roots of Heaven*, *Lady L.* is a variation on a Conradian theme, but this time his model text is *Under Western Eyes*, a sombre study of the minds of bomb-throwing Russian anarchists and their watchers in late nineteenth-century Geneva. Gary turns political extremism into the subject of a light comedy. On her eightieth birthday, a prominent member of the British aristocracy decides to tell her wimpish long-time suitor the true story of her life. To his utter bewilderment, she explains that she had begun life as a woman of the streets, then fallen in love with a divinely handsome anarchist. He and his nefarious group of idealist-assassins had her properly educated so she could pass as a society lady, then parachuted her into the glittering expatriate community in Geneva in the early years of the twentieth century. Her task was to lead her manipulators to where jewels and money could be filched, so as to finance the Revolution. An eccentric English aristocrat with a taste for charades sees through the false lady, but out of a liking for a good joke, decides to help her along her path. He marries her and then dies, leaving the former Annette Boudin a wealthy lady free to dump her anarchist backers and become a pillar of the British establishment. The twist in the tale is that Armand Denis, the handsome lover who had drawn her into a life of dissimulation in the first place, turns up at Lady L.'s palace in the Home Counties on the day of a fancy-dress ball. She can't bear to let the love of her life escape her again. She sets a trap, has him hide inside a man-size trunk to escape the police, turns the key and leaves her most precious treasure locked inside it for ever.

Lady L. could be read as a message to Lesley not to keep her husband boxed in (which is how Silvia Agid, wife of Gary's school chum René, interpreted it later on, when the novel appeared – much altered – in French). Lesley could hardly avoid feeling targeted, as the décor of the pavilion where the coffin-trunk is kept is calqued on the furnishings of her former London home, and the cat-faced portraits on Lady L.'s walls are copies of Lesley's humorous artwork mentioned, no doubt as a clue, in her own book on Gary.[8] But it is as much a homage to Lesley and her mother, to their homes in Chelsea and Richmond, and to their very British pretensions to class, as it is an attack on them. In a strange way, too, *Lady L.* is Gary's farewell to Britain: just as the gazebo in which the oriental trunk with its precious corpse is stored is about to be demolished to make way for a bypass (thus prompting Lady L.'s explanation of why the place is of such importance to her), so Gary's 'RAF style' was about to be replaced by American English. His intense pursuit of opportunities to be born again is paralleled by an equally frequent use of fiction and memoir as ways of taking leave of former selves. *Promise at Dawn*, which he wrote immediately after *Lady L.* and tells the highly decorated story of his childhood and young manhood up to the end of the war, begins and ends with assertions that 'It's over' and 'I've done with life'.[9]

Lady L. is not only a novel in English, but an English novel through and through. Gary's light treatment of a serious subject fits into the genre that Graham Greene called 'entertainments', and which others, such as Muriel Spark, honed into gemstones of irony and malice. Gary's first adventure in writing 'like another' was remarkably successful and produced a much tighter, neater work than any of his French novels after *A European Education*. *Lady L.* is less verbose and repetitive than *The Roots of Heaven*, presumably because Gary was writing in a borrowed language; he probably benefited from stylistic advice from Lesley Blanch and no doubt from a copy-editor too (whose role is traditionally far more extensive in an American than in a French publishing house). It is not quite as significant a new work as Nabokov's *Pnin*, which appeared the same year; but it is just as funny, contains just as many complex Anglo-Franco-Russian puns and deals with a subject not obviously less important than the life of a potty academic: the relationship between idealism and terror, between false hopes and the horrors they bring.

Lady L. is also, from start to finish, a spirited defence of deception and artifice as sources of truth. The tulips and roses in the vase remind Lady L. of Matisse and the English sky looks to her 'rather like the dresses her granddaughters were wearing'. The purpose of nature, she clearly believes, is to come up to the standards set by art. Lady L. is a long-prepared and long-perfected performance of herself and a full-blown mystification of British society – and thus a mirror of the book in which she appears. 'For a writer of fiction, realism consists in not getting caught out,' Gary had declared in the first of his 'false interviews' with François Bondy a few months before publishing *Lady L.*[10] Similarly for the first of Gary's characters whose life is a fiction: the 'realism' of Lady L., on which her whole life depends, is the art of not getting caught out. Success can be her only morality and her sole virtue is sufficient talent to get away with pretending to be someone else.

Lady L. is an ironical personification of a quality that in French is called *roublardise* – the exercise of cunning and deception in defence of one's own interests. She isn't an anarchist in the way that her mentors had been, but in her pursuit of self-interest, her complete lack of scruple and her vision of life as a game to be played, she is anarchism incarnate. Lesley Blanch was probably only a secondary inspiration for *Lady L.*: the novel and its main character have more to tell us about Romain Gary.

Gary's second English-language novel is another polished pastiche of Graham Greene. Set in a generic Latin American statelet, *The Talent Scout* exploits an anti-clerical quip. The dictator of the day, Almayo, is an indigenous Cujon (another one of Gary's onomastic inventions) who, having learned from his missionary mentors that earthly powers are granted not by God but by the devil, seeks to sell his soul to the Evil One, as material goods seem much more enticing than eternal life. He's convinced that among the jugglers, ventriloquists, music-hall magicians and other vendors of illusion on the international cabaret circuit there must be one who can make the devil appear, and he has his agent (the 'talent scout' of the title) round up the very best and bring them to perform in the nightclub that is the source of his fortune and the centre of political life in the fly-blown capital of his state. Gary adds to this farcical set-up a conventional Third-World coup that gets the group of performers into dire straits, giving each the prompting and the opportunity to tell his own story; and he also adds the character of Nancy, a wholesome idealist from Iowa who, out of the kindness of her heart, has ended up as Almayo's drug-dependent moll. The point of the tale is that Greene is wrong to think the devil exists: there's no one there to buy your soul even when you do your best to put it up for sale. All the evil that you'll ever need can be found in men's souls without intervention from below.

The Ski Bum, Gary's third English work, is the most substantial and original of the set. The Swiss Alps replace Morel's African bush and Rainier's hilltop in Provence as the physical location that hints at the possible existence of a higher plane of life. American dropouts addicted to high-altitude skiing gather to pursue their isolation from the messy, complicated, everyday world below. In the summer they come down to the valleys seeking work to fill in the months before winter snows allow them to earn their crust again by giving wealthy tourists skiing lessons. That's when the awkward contact between the almost wordless Lenny and the beautiful, idealistic Jess Donahue gets the romantic plot into gear. The idealism of the 'ski bums' is expressed by the kind of cynical back talk that Gary had first invented with La Marne in *The Colours of the Day*; but Lenny can't avoid falling in love when he meets Jess, even though he thinks it the stupidest thing to do. *The Ski Bum*, which came out in 1965, portrays teenagers' disaffection with consumer society, and catches the mood of disappointment and desperation that Perec described with such different tools in *Things*, published in France in the very same month. Gary's novel, however, is broader in scope and lighter in tone, and incorporates a romantic plot as well as a crime novel wrapped around the character of Jess's father, a diplomat driven to drink by his experience in Bulgaria (see p. 127). The most ambitious of Gary's English novels, and also one of the most widely sold of all his books, *The Ski Bum* is a good example of what is best in Gary's work – dialogue, contemporaneity, sympathy with dropouts and bums, and narrative energy – while also exhibiting several of his less endearing quirks: too much plot, too many separate issues and an inconclusive ending.

The last of Gary's English fictions, written after he had left the USA and his marriage with Jean Seberg had collapsed, is a metaphysical science-fiction thriller. Devices and motifs borrowed from Ian Fleming and Len Deighton barely mask an attempt to talk directly about spirituality. The 'gasp' of *The Gasp* is man's last gasp. The conceit of the plot is that what departs the body in the moment of death is a force greater than any other. A French scientist has invented a means of capturing the 'soul-force' and can transform 'the last gasp' into electrical power. As a moral anarchist, he's prepared to provide his formula to every power on earth, even-handedly, thus confounding all the secret service operatives on his tail. The adventure culminates in Hoxha's Albania (in the version published later in France the name of the Albanian dictator is masked, no doubt to assuage the sensitivities of the Stalinist enthusiasts who still thrived on the Left Bank),[11] where global evaporation is averted by a sterling member of MI5 and a concentration of Universal Soul materialises in the shape of Jesus Christ.

The Gasp was written just as France was adopting its controversial policy of replacing oil-fired by nuclear power stations and it plays on legitimate public anxiety about the atomic future. But its satire of technological thoughtlessness is only a thin cover for an unusually explicit sermon about the nature of man. Gary wants to reiterate his old-fashioned belief in the human soul and to declare it out of bounds for commodification. Hastily written, and hardly improved by its later revision in French as *Charge d'âme*, *The Gasp* does not show Gary at his best. On the other hand its over-insistent moral argument makes it clear that he did not write it just to turn a fast buck and later claims made by Lesley Blanch (repeated by Anissimov) that Gary's English-language career was a purely commercial venture are clearly mistaken.

Gary's English curriculum is lighter in every way than his first run at mastering the novel form in French, but there was something inevitable about it ending with a defence of human souls. He hadn't dared to use the word in *The Roots of Heaven*, but what Gary really meant in that flawed masterpiece by the slogan of 'the human margin', as well as by the allegory of elephants roaming free, was that human life demanded more than material goods because it was more than a material phenomenon in itself. When asked in a radio interview why he had set his elephant story in Chad, Gary explained that the huge skies of Africa always hinted to him that there was something else, beyond and above the mortal world, and that the setting itself said something to him about the subject of his novel. In the English novels, too, when Gary talks of the individual, or of freedom, or of the soul, he means to express a deep, irrational conviction that our human forms are inhabited by an immaterial force, which never can be suppressed or enslaved. Gary's beliefs were antithetical to the fashions of thought current in French intellectual circles in the 1960s. Anti-humanist 'new novelists' like Robbe-Grillet were just as allergic to intimations of immortality as the hard left of the French Communist Party. It's not really surprising that Gary found a wider readership in the English-speaking world, which never really abandoned the nineteenth-century humanist ideals that make Gary such an awkward fit in the literary history of France.

Gary's career as an English-language novelist, which stretches from 1958 (*Lady L.*) through the 1960s (*The Talent Scout*, 1961 and *The Ski Bum*, 1965) to the early 1970s (*The Gasp*, 1973) and incorporates the complete rewriting of *A European Education* (1960), the longer English version of *Promise at Dawn* (1961), and the English-language versions of *The Dance of Genghis Cohn* (1968) and *White Dog* (*1970*), came to an end at exactly the moment of his next self-renewal as Émile Ajar (*Gros-Câlin* came out in 1974). This is not merely coincidental: the birth of Ajar was undoubtedly responsible for the end of Gary's writing in English. From 1974, all Gary's subsequent novels were translated into English from French by another hand, not by his own, as if the invention of the special dialect of Ajar's French had robbed him of the need, or perhaps the ability, to write in any other tongue. An alternative view would be that Gary's extraordinary success in writing fiction that passed muster in English delayed his discovery of a tongue that was completely his own.

21

A Pen for Hire

The role of Consul General is essentially representative. Routine consular matters – replacing lost passports, issuing visas, fishing drunks out of jail, arranging legal assistance or forwarding death notices to families in France – are handled by subordinates. Gary's job in Los Angeles, from 1956 to 1960, was to establish cordial relations with the French community organisations in his region; to represent French interests in as many public places as he could, from Chambers of Commerce to Rotary Clubs; to preside at receptions and inaugurations of French cultural events; and to promote the good name and the public image of France. He turned out to be very good at this, and his charm and fluency got France more favourable coverage in the Californian media than it had had for years. The same qualities also helped him get on well with the Hollywood crowd, which at that time included a number of celebrated French film makers, some of them naturalised Americans, such as Jules Dassin and Jean Renoir. But what made Gary's tenure really swing was his rapid emergence as an American celebrity in himself. The Consul General had more than diplomatic prestige. He was rapidly becoming a popular novelist and a public figure, with name recognition that many lesser celebrities could only envy, or admire.

The consulate general was located at 1919 Outpost Drive,

off Hollywood Boulevard. Romain Gary and Lesley Blanch lived in it together, but led quite separate lives, as they always had done. (Gary could never bring himself to use the familiar form *tu* with his wife, whom he always addresed as *vous*[1] – as Sartre did with Simone de Beauvoir.) Lesley had begun work on her next book, *The Sabres of Paradise*, a romanticised biography of Shamyl, the central figure of Tolstoy's last work, *Hadji Murad*. She wrote in her study, or on carpets laid over the lawn in the yard, with her cats all around and music from the Near East on the gramophone. She affected to care not a fig for Gary's sexual and occasionally romantic escapades. She strove to be a suave and effective hostess, however, and was delighted to rub shoulders at the consular table with many glamorous and world-famous guests. She seems to have continued to act as Gary's domestic minder, but Gary no longer had any intention of treating her as his wife.

On a short trip to London in autumn 1955, just after Lesley had agreed to accompany him to Los Angeles, Gary had dinner with the Koestlers (he had known Arthur since November 1945, when both men were briefly famous as writers in France), and on that occasion met Elizabeth Jane Howard, the long-suffering wife of the English writer Kingsley Amis. The next day Gary got back in touch with her and made an offer: come with me to LA, he said, and be my official mistress, a station in life that the French authorities would recognise (a blatant fib). Somewhat bewildered, Elizabeth agreed to spend a week with Gary in Paris on a trial run, but neither really fell for the other and she returned to London relieved that she wouldn't have to change her life.[2]

On arrival in Los Angeles Gary quickly seduced his married secretary, Odette de Bénédictis. He also rented a separate apartment in Laurel Lane, less than a mile away, to use as a writing retreat, as well as to bed prostitutes. On the liner taking him back from Le Havre to America after the Goncourt Prize in January 1957 he had an affair with a Belgian model, Romy van

Looye, and for a short while thought he would resign his post and settle down with her in France. He even asked René Agid to set aside a wing of his house for him to live in with the new love of his life; but the affair petered out.[3] Not long after, on one of his tours to consular offices in Texas, New Mexico and Arizona, Gary unwisely crossed a state line with a teenage prostitute in his car (she was almost certainly a police informer too) and was arrested for statutory rape.[4] Had he not had diplomatic immunity, he could have been put in jail.

Gary's excuse for all this whoring was that he had married Lesley ten years too late and, that as he was now over forty, it was time he had a child. However, his paternal urges were expressed in actions more characteristic of a drugged stoat than a senior diplomat. On one occasion he hurt himself quite badly from a fall he took when chasing a girl up the stairs.[5] Lesley recommended he should keep away from starlets and choose a solid peasant girl to bear him an heir (she lived in an Old Russian fantasy world even while making great strides towards her own Hollywood career). Gary did nothing of the sort, of course. He had a fling with Veronica Lake and who knows who else on the Hollywood scene. Lesley and Odette, who framed Gary's day, from office work to official dinners and literary dictation, were tolerant of the Consul General's sexual gluttony to an extraordinary degree, but the atmosphere at Outpost Drive could hardly have been serene. Blanch describes Gary in ever less flattering terms in the years they spent together in California; and in her testimony to Anissimov, Odette is also highly critical of Gary's personal behaviour, especially with respect to money. Now that he was rich, he became stingy, withholding tiny pay rises from his closest collaborators and also berating Lesley for spending too much on running the house. He was imperious in his demands – for dictation, unpaid overtime, 'quickies' – but gave little in return.

Gary had been a diplomat for more than ten years. In the

memory of those who were closest to him in LA, however, he had none of the social graces conventionally associated with his profession and rank. At table, he used his fingers and made a mess all over his face, and even the saintly Odette refused to sit opposite him at meals.[6] Gary made no effort to hide his yawns when bored by guests at the consular dinner table – when they were 'routine people' from the French community or the Chamber of Trade. He would ignore the conversation, pick at his food, get up and quit the room without taking his leave. 'His indifference to the reactions of others sometimes bordered on ruthlessness,' according to his increasingly irritated wife.[7] But when he had an audience that mattered to him – a pretty girl, a film producer, or network TV – he could turn on charm like a tap.

Accusations of oafishness seem strange when addressed to a man who paid such careful attention to his outward appearance, who had regular manicures and tailor-made suits, and who had begun to touch up the greying hairs on his still copious mane with jet-black dye. It is possible, of course, that Gary's newfound wealth and prestige went to his head, and that he let himself slide into boorish sloppiness at home. Lesley was increasingly fed up with the man and Odette was frankly exploited by him. Their retrospective accounts of Gary's life in LA, irreplaceable as they are, may be more or less heavily coloured by what happened next.

If Gary's manners at the consulate general seem to fall well short of the diplomatic norm, his position and prospects within the service – called 'The Church' in Foreign-Office insiders' talk – also seemed limited and cramped. He had been recruited by an unconventional procedure in the emergency circumstances of 1945 and, although he was one among several score to whom that had happened, he could never be considered an entirely normal diplomat. He had been extremely unhappy in two of his postings – Berne and London – and had inadvertently made a lifelong enemy of the powerful Jean Chauvel.

Although he had learned a great deal from Sofia and New York, the latter posting in particular had really got in the way of his writerly work. Was it all worth it? Gary's mercurial temper made him both utterly faithful to his patron and protector, Henri Hoppenot, and also prone to handing in his resignation on the spur of a bout of spleen. He had nearly done so in Berne, but now he was in Hollywood, on an extremely lucrative track, he toyed more and more with the idea of getting out and paid progressively less attention to his diplomatic career. Towards the end of his tour of duty, in fact, he barely did his job at all and left the running of the consulate to other members of the team. All the same, he was still very nervous about leaving 'The Church' to go freelance and live by his pen. For that, he needed to be very sure of his ground.

With film rights to three of his novels sold and one of them in production, and with *Lady L.* providing acknowledged proof of his ability to write in English with style, Gary had two obvious ways of milking his position in the United States: by working directly for Hollywood, as a scriptwriter or consultant; and by writing for American magazines. He did both with his customary energy and talent, became a very well-paid writer indeed and, fairly soon, a man of considerable financial means. The work that guaranteed his independence, however, made almost no contribution to his literary oeuvre and from all but a financial point of view it could be considered a waste of his creative time.

Gary kept his distance from the many film adaptations of his own novels, but spent a lot of time doctoring scripts for Hollywood producers, for significant fees. Almost none of these made it to the screen. His experience as adapter and adaptee also led him to want to be a film director himself and he wasted yet more of his time making two feature movies generally reckoned to be abysmally bad. The sorry story of Gary's cinematic career can be found in chapter 24.

Gary's career as a journalist began as a natural extension of his role as a spokesman for France in the United States and was conducted mainly in English. His first commission was an article about de Gaulle's return to power in May 1958, for *Life* magazine. As a serving diplomat, Gary had to clear the text with Paris and that is why the piece is, at bottom, a restatement of the official position. Of course, it has colour, fluency and persuasiveness far beyond any press release from a government information bureau, and it also expresses Gary's personal obsession with the courtly grandeur of the man he admired as a myth. Once Gary had left the Diplomatic Service, however, he took on far less lofty subjects for American magazines. 'I know a place in Paris' (1965), 'Flamboyant Guadeloupe' (1967), 'Penang: Tiger, tiger burning bright' (1971), 'The Oriental Hotel of Bangkok' (1972) and 'Singapore' (1973) in *Holiday* magazine and in *Travel & Leisure* are just feature articles of no special quality or interest. Gary also continued to write political journalism sporadically, for *Life* and, on one occasion, for the *New York Times*, on issues as burning as the generals' revolt in Algeria in 1961, the defeat of de Gaulle in 1969 and the Vietnam War in 1970. But as he became a sought-after commentator on French affairs in the United States, he began to 'repatriate' his journalistic talent by commenting on American matters in France, with an obituary of Gary Cooper in 1961 for *Le Nouveau Candide*, followed by articles on the UN, the Kennedys and race relations in the same journal. In the brief interlude between the end of his marriage to Jean Seberg and the birth of Émile Ajar, Gary became a columnist in the French press, writing several pieces for *Le Monde* and *Le Figaro* before starting an irregular 'Journal d'un irrégulier' in the mass-circulation *France-Soir*, giving vent to a progressively grumpier view of the world. Once the Ajar adventure got off the ground in 1973–74, however, he dropped his bilingual journalistic activities for good. He wrote almost nothing for the press in the last seven years of his life.

The political journalism has not aged well. The articles are recent enough to sound old-fashioned rather than truly historical and the warnings they utter sometimes seem off target. Gary was a proficient and professional creator of copy – fluent, on time, readable, provocative but not revolutionary – but his unique imagination and power of divination only really came into play in his fiction, not in his non-fiction prose. The journalism in English and in French kept his name in public view and probably increased sales of his novels by the celebrity effect, but was taken by the literary establishment to be evidence that he was not really a writer, only a hack. The articles, in sum, did nothing to enhance his reputation as a novelist; worse than that, they probably ensured that a generation of intellectuals did not even think to read works by one of the most innovative and important French writers of the time.

22

'It's Over . . .'

Promise at Dawn, 1958–1960

Gary was a great traveller throughout his life, but he detested conventional holiday tourism, especially the cultivated kind. He resisted being dragged off to see the sights, and avoided museums, art galleries and concert halls. When he yielded to Lesley Blanch's pressure to take a Christmas vacation in Mexico in 1958 he went into a kind of trance, stayed in his hotel bedroom and began to write, at great speed, a memoir of his early life. *Promise at Dawn* is the fruit of that uncooperative and glum anti-holiday, and it turned out to be Gary's most successful work by far. It has never been out of print, in English or French, for the past fifty years; it is also responsible for much of readers' fascination with Gary's complicated biography, and the source of infinite layers of confusion about the relationship between his life and his art.

All Gary's French novels have a love interest, in conformity with his aim of being a popular novelist as well as a serious one. *A European Education* describes the birth of love in two teenagers in the harsh circumstances of guerrilla war; *The Company of Men* also portrays a teenage crush between Luc and the consumptive Josette; even the satirical *Tulipe* and its remake as *L'Homme à la colombe* has a conventional boy–girl relationship (between Tulipe and Leni, and between Johnnie and Frankie respectively) to naturalise this otherwise quite unconventional tract. Love is a more central issue in *The Colours of the Day*: Rainier's passion for Ann Garantier conflicts with the demands of his idealism, yet love seems the higher value, since the purpose of the fight is to preserve man's freedom to be. The conflict is resolved in favour of honour, since, as in the snippet of Lovelace that Gary uses for an epigraph, *I could not love thee, Dear, so much / Loved I not Honour more.*[1]

In *The Roots of Heaven*, Minna's love for Morel is even more abstract – it is driven by her aspiration towards an ideal, not by anything so ordinary as sexual desire. Until 1958, sentimentality remained secondary to the intellectual and moral programme of Gary's plots. But in *Promise at Dawn* the central issue is love, though of an unusual kind: a mother's love for her son, and his charming, desperate and highly ambiguous attempts to respond in kind.

It is probable that Gary's proximity to Hollywood, his growing contacts with the film industry and his nimble-minded appropriation of its conventions and themes were responsible for his adoption of the copper-bottomed cliché of 'a boy's best friend' for the design of what purports to be a memoir of his life. Few and far between are French novels or memoirs in which mother love plays much of a role (Proust's *Remembrance of Things Past* being the only really important instance); but American fiction and film dealing with the powerful tribe of Jewish mothers are ten a penny, and must count among the most reliable vehicles of Californian schmaltz.

If it seems cynical to speculate on sources for Gary's hymn to 'Nina' other than the real life of Mina Kacewa herself, it is worth remembering that *Promise at Dawn* is the only one of Gary's books to portray a mother, that the only mother he ever portrays is his own. Motherhood and mother love are not central or even marginal themes of Gary's writing, they are almost entirely absent from his copious, imaginative and obsessively repetitive reinvention of the world. But as we have seen on p. 57 and elsewhere, fathers abound in Gary's fiction. In *A European Education* he provides his alter ego Janek with no less than three father figures (Dr Twardowski, his actual father, Dobranski, his adoptive father and mentor in the Maquis and, behind him, Dobranski's intellectual mentor, Professor Kreczmar). Similarly, the fourteen-year-old hero of *The Company of Men* has a real father (deceased), an adoptive father (the Fagin-like Gustave Vanderputte), and a paternal stand-in, the restaurateur Baju. In *The Colours of the Day*, Ann Garantier trails her depressingly intellectual father behind her and in *The Roots of Heaven* there are 'fathers' galore, be they religious (Fargue, Tassin) or mythological (de Gaulle). Of mothers, however, there are none in any of these books, save for one purely formal invocation, in *A European Education*, somewhat expanded in the revision of the text, which followed directly on from the writing of *Promise at Dawn*. In his memoir Gary insists that his mother was the most important person in his life, that what he became was her creation and that a mother's love is the fundamental, formative experience of life. The contradiction between the assertion of the memoir and the evidence of the fiction cries out for an explanation.

Had *Promise at Dawn* opened some kind of floodgate in Gary's heart and mind, had his work after 1960 become spotted with loving mothers and doting sons, the earlier fiction could be seen as a form of repression or an emotional avoidance technique. But there is no change in this domain until 1975. Gary's English fiction of the 1960s, as well as his many novels under the name of Gary in French, are just as bereft of motherhood as the work done prior to the composition of *Promise at Dawn*. *Lady L.*, which was written immediately prior to *Promise at Dawn*, does, it is true, give its eighty-year-old heroine a brood of descendants, but we learn only of her disdain for the stuffed shirts of Old England she has spawned and nothing of their feelings for her. Genghis Cohn, in both of his main appearances, and Fosco Zaga in *The Enchanters* and the characters of *Direct Flight to Allah*, *The Way Out* or *The Kites*, don't have any mothers at all. All Gary's fictional characters bar one, namely Momo in *Life Before Us*, have male ascendants only and seem to have emerged fully formed from a gooseberry bush or, more likely, been found in a rush crib floating down the Nile.

Promise at Dawn inverts the underlying parental model of Gary's fiction: absent motherhood is replaced by a domineering, passionate, all-invasive mother, and the multifarious fathers of the novels are replaced by an absent father, a non-father, a 'stranger' whom the narrator-protagonist barely knows. Unsurprisingly, Mother Nina thus takes on most of the traditional qualities of fatherhood. It is she who imparts to the boy his sense of values, including honour, and it is her eye, implanted in the boy's psyche in an almost explicit parody of a Freudian super-ego or the Lacanian '*non du père*', that keeps the rowdy youngster from straying too far from the righteous path (for example, from becoming a gigolo, or from giving up the fight).

Many of Gary's works are transparent dialogues with one or more of the classics of nineteenth-century European fiction – Gogol's short stories, Dickens's *Oliver Twist*, Dostoevsky's *Notes from the Underground*, Conrad's *Under Western Eyes*, *Heart of Darkness* and *Lord Jim*. The writer didn't make a secret of it, even if few readers seem to have noticed. 'What I'm after', Gary wrote in *A Quiet Night*, 'is a form of originality without perceptible influences – except for Gogol, often, and Conrad, for *The Roots of Heaven* – by using different languages and cultures – Russian, Polish . . .'[2] *Promise at Dawn*, which is still often described as an unprecedented innovation in the writing of autobiography in France,[3] is no less intertextual than Gary's other fictions. It is his response to one of the most widely read books of the twentieth century, Maksim Gorky's *Mother*.

Written and first published in New York in 1905, *Mother* is an autobiographical account of the author's young life in the rough environment of provincial Russia. The boy's first memory is of the death of his father: he is brought up by a mother much abused by her relatives, by history, by the authorities and the bosses, but who ensures that her one treasure, her son, grows up almost decently. Overlong, cloyingly sentimental and sermonising, *Mother* was received over many decades, in many languages, as a moving exposé of the horrors of capitalist exploitation and as a son's loving tribute to his mother. Its style of description and narration were adopted as models by Socialist Realism, and the book was thrust down students' throats by more or less sincere left-wingers throughout Europe and America until well after the Second World War. The miserabilist passages of *Promise at Dawn* – the chapters on poverty and making ends meet in Wilno and Warsaw – are calqued directly on it. That is not to say that the whole story of Gary's early life is fiction. But insofar as Gorky's righteous anger with the injustices of the pre-revolutionary world matches Gary's anger and thirst for justice in a world that treated his mother so poorly, *Promise at Dawn* is an American answer to the gold standard of Bolshevik literature.

Gorky is frequently invoked by name throughout Gary's work but the most significant reference occurs towards the end of *Promise at Dawn*. Gary entrusted the manuscript of his first novel, *A European Education*, to Moura Budberg, 'the friend of Gorki and H. G. Wells', and it was through her that he found a publisher for the work that would launch his career.[4] Gary's memoir thus comes to a circular close. His response to Gorky's *Mother* turns out to have been composed by a writer whose start in literary life was given him by the fading halo of the Old Bolshevik himself.

Gorky's stage play, *На Дне* (On the Bottom, 1901), usually translated as *Lower Depths*, presents a small set of characters at the ends of their tethers, living in the airless basement of a boarding house. A stark portrayal of poverty and of the bankruptcy of the old world of nineteenth-century Russia, *Lower Depths* is the source of one of Romain Gary's strangest characters, the Baron, played in Renoir's later film version (1936) by Louis Jouvet, a man whom Gary admired no end. Gorky's Baron is a penniless profligate who has lost everything. Gary's Baron, who first appears as Papski in *The Company of Men*, but then recurs, like a movable prop, in *The Colours of the Day*, *Europa* and many other texts, is an impeccably smart, almost wordless dummy in a permanent alcoholic haze. He speaks only to request the toilet, but otherwise sits bolt upright, gazing on the world with a benign, bemused and possibly meaningless stare. What does he represent? Gary said he didn't know, but could not leave this puppet out of his vision of the world, because he kept coming back in.

Promise at Dawn starts and ends at Big Sur, on the beach, as the narrator-hero merges into the ocean swell at the end, not the start, of his 'life'. The entire narrative is an immense flashback to a story located firmly in a past whose future is known, and at the brink of its end. Gary's life between 1945 and 1958 is covered only by implication and with a few references to his present existence as a diplomat and famous writer, and it is that life which is treated as near its necessary end. What remains unclear to the reader was whether the narrator simply expected to rise no more and to remain the figure he had become (which is one way of understanding the assertion that his life is at an end), or whether he expected his life to end soon in another, more literal sense. In retrospect, however, it is clear that the 'Romain Gary' who had come to fulfil his mother's unrealistic expectations of him (namely, to become an ambassador and a new Victor Hugo) was now complete and entire, and thus free to start on the next one of his lives (and had in fact already done so, as a novelist in another tongue). Entertaining, sentimental, witty and astute as it is, *Promise at*

Dawn is as much an *act* in Gary's life as a recreation of it. Its function is to say farewell – to Mother Nina and to the boy Roman, but also to 'Romain Gary' as he had been constructed up to then.

The heroine of the tale is the ultimate figure of the Jewish mother whose hyperbolic imagination and blithe disregard for mere truth signal and justify the book's own cavalier treatment of history and reality. But 'Nina' is not the only mythical figure to be constructed by the well-paced anecdotes of *Promise at Dawn*. The book serves just as much to create the legend of Romain Gary. The techniques Gary uses here are not identical to those deployed in *The Roots of Heaven*, but the overall effect is the same: to make legends out of characters and a myth out of a tale.

Because so much has already been said in this book and by others about Gary's tendency to decorate the record and to lie outright, it is worth stating clearly that the broad narrative of *Promise at Dawn* is true. Gary did grow up in Wilno and Warsaw, he did emigrate to France at the age of fourteen, did do his service in the Air Force and fight his way through World War Two. His memoir is not at all an 'alternative autobiography' or an exercise in what would later come to be called autofiction. It has a complicated relation to historical veracity, but it is not pure invention by any means, or a complete farrago of lies.

Chapter 32 of the English edition offers a curious example of Gary's characteristic *mentir-vrai* (truthful lying) in *Promise at Dawn*. It tells the almost independent story of Jan Zaremba, a middle-aged, dapper and prosperous Polish painter who alights one day at the Hôtel-Pension Mermonts in Nice, stays the whole year and tries to persuade the now ageing Nina to be his bride. Zaremba is an orphan who has never got over the absence of maternal love and the narrator, though only seventeen at the time, quickly realises that the quiet, moustachioed gentleman seeks a mother more than he seeks a wife.

Young Romain, the manifest object of all Nina's love, is thus Zaremba's only rival and the whole delicate process of wooing the foul-mouthed, domineering landlady is conducted through the boy, with gifts of clothes, toys, a wristwatch and suchlike. It fails, of course; and the shy artist departs in the morning without even saying goodbye. There is no reason to suppose that such an episode ever occurred: the anecdote has to be treated as a fiction. The physical appearance of Zaremba, however, is borrowed from that of a well-known Russian painter who was resident at that time in Nice, Maliavin, court painter to the Swedish royal family. In addition, his name is common among the Polish minority in Wilno, and the manner of his arrival, the length of his stay and the year to which Gary attributes it (1932–3) corresponds to the real visit of his uncle Borukh to the Hôtel-Pension Mermonts.

To call *Promise at Dawn* a seductive work is not to use a figure of speech. Teenage girls all over the world fell in love with the author they thought they had got to know from reading the book by torchlight in their dormitories or under their sheets. Fan mail poured in – and Gary replied to those that seemed to hold the best prospect for his particular tastes. At the other end of the spectrum, scholars trying to use *Promise at Dawn* to understand the life and mind of Romain Gary can quickly end up not charmed, but angry and confused. Some anecdotes are flagrant borrowings from literary sources and others are manifest nonsense, such as the one nearly all first-time readers remember most clearly: when Gary left for England, his mother, already very ill, wrote a whole stack of letters and postcards to her son ahead of time and arranged to have them mailed to him every couple of weeks by a friend who had taken refuge in Switzerland. As a result, Gary believed his mother was still behind him throughout the most dangerous part of his life and only when the war was over did he learn that she had died long before. The English edition even adds evidence by including as an end-piece a facsimile of one of

'Nina's' missives, ending with the exhortation: будь сильный и крепкий, (be strong and resolute). However, the plot-device of 'letters sent from beyond the grave' has a distinguished literary pedigree. In Balzac's *L'Envers de l'histoire contemporaine*, a daughter condemned to the scaffold writes a series of post-dated letters to her imprisoned mother recounting the progress of an inexorable disease, so that she would accept her daughter's death as a natural and not a shameful one.[5] As Anissimov points out, Nabokov's Russian novel *Подвиг* (1932; in English translation *Glory*, 1971) also contains a very similar plot. Yet almost all Gary's readers seem to fall for this deception and to treat it as one of the most moving parts of the whole text.[6]

In point of fact, some time in spring 1941 Gary, who was then on active duty in Bangui in Central Africa, received a letter from his friend René Agid telling him that Mina had died from stomach cancer in Nice on 16 February 1941.[7] Why, then, did Gary concoct an implausible tale that seems at least half borrowed from his own short story, 'All Is Well on the Kilimanjaro', if not from a whole literary tradition? To take another flagrant example of fiction passed off as historical fact: Gary tells us that he was on the tarmac at Hartford Bridge, in helmet, goggles and gloves, just after surviving 'a particularly lively mission', when an orderly handed him a telegram from a publisher saying he was having his book translated and would publish it as soon as he could. However, in June 1944, which is the only possible date for this episode, Gary had been working at a desk job at HQ, according to a note in his military record: 'Posted S.A. du Q.G. 16/5/44' (meaning: 'Transferred to the Archive Service of the Free French Headquarters on 16 May 1944').[8] The effect of these two changes to the record is clear: the first hypes the sentimental impact of the mother, and the second intensifies the heroic figure of the son. Both also show that Gary now had a firm grasp of how to draft scenes that Hollywood could put on screen. The best way to become a legend, after all, is to have someone else act the role you've written for yourself.

The problem with *Promise at Dawn* is not that it contains a number of inaccuracies, some of which may be intentional and others that are almost certainly ordinary mistakes. The problem is that it reads like a novel but seems to be about the man whose name appears on the cover. The 'autobiographical pact' as imagined by Philippe Lejeune is to take the first person of a narrative as the name of a real person if his or her name is on the cover or title page of the book, and thus to expect that, as in normal conversation or correspondence, that real person is doing his or her best to tell the truth.[9] Gary subverts that pact without saying what he is doing. The moral issue wouldn't arise if *Promise at Dawn* were considered a novel: first-person novels are not blamed for being untrue. To turn the memoir into a novel, and to get Gary off a moral hook of his own making, all you have to do is to treat 'Romain Gary' as a character, not a person. That's exactly what Gary was trying out. He was seeking to create a *character* called Romain Gary. Morality, in this artistic endeavour, consists in not getting caught, as Lady L. had been made to say. For most people, most of the time, the trick worked, and still works. The most outlandish excesses of Gary's invention – such as the list of objects he swallowed for love of Valentina – can be put down to the author's comic talent and self-guying wit. And most of the amendments to the historical record – such as Gary's mother's name – are not visible to the untutored eye.

This does not resolve the ultimate mystery of *Promise at Dawn*, which is close to the heart of the still unsolved mystery of Romain Gary. Why should he have *wanted* to become a character in a novel of his own invention? What strange idea of art led him to try to create a literary double who could do nothing but plague him in real life? Many of Gary's favourite authors had played with the theme of the 'double', the eerie romantic idea that someone else might be the 'real you', or else the usurper of your identity: Grabinksi in *The Grey Room*, Dostoevsky in *The Double*, not to mention Gombrowicz and his multiple exercises with alternative identities. But not one of them had gone so far as to imagine he could voluntarily create his own double *for real*. All the same, the mystery of Gary's alternative selves is more likely to be solved by reading European fiction than by pretending to put the man on a psychiatrist's couch. *Promise at Dawn*, despite its superficially autobiographical nature, is the first major experiment by Romain Gary in creating a character who is his own invention. That's not to say it is dishonest. It's a novel. By giving the world an unforgettably charming and successful hero called 'Romain Gary', it left the ex-diplomat whose legal name was Romain Gary entirely free to be someone else.

23

Celebrity Spouse
On the Road, 1960–1979

Promise at Dawn was written very fast – 'at white heat', according to Blanch – and completed before the end of 1958.[1] By January 1959 it was already in galley proof, but Gary wasn't keen to see it published straight away. As he wrote to Joe Barnes, he felt 'somewhat reluctant to bare my soul and my ass to the populace while I am still parading abroad in diplomatic disguise'.[2] In fact, the book, which would turn out to be a colossal success, was held back for nearly eighteen months, until May 1960, which was not a date chosen by chance.

In 1958 the French Fourth Republic collapsed, Charles de Gaulle returned to power and a career diplomat, Maurice Couve de Murville, was put in charge of foreign affairs. The Consul General soon sensed that it was only a matter of time before the strait-laced chief of French diplomacy would put him out to grass. In addition, the public position of de Gaulle over the Algerian question meant that Gary had to defend a policy he could hardly agree with in private. He preferred to serve de Gaulle henceforth by preserving the myth of the man who saved France. However, as he would now never get to be an *ambassadeur de France*, Gary could begin to count his autobiography as a kind of farewell to his life as an unconventional servant of the French state. As soon as he got back to LA from Paris after the launch of *Promise at Dawn*, Gary requested leave without pay for an indeterminate period. However, in the year that had elapsed between the completion of his embellished account of his mother's love and its release to the world, a more intimate and important change had intervened: Romain Gary had fallen in love.

The object of his new passion was an American blonde who'd only just turned twenty-one and, with her wide-eyed beauty, she looked even younger than that. She'd turned up at the Consul General's table in LA as the spouse of young French lawyer-cum-impresario, François Moreuil, who'd been invited to dine almost as a matter of course. In November 1959, when Gary set eyes on the waif-like girl already famous for being Joan of Arc, any pretence of diplomatic propriety evaporated like the morning haze. She was thunderstruck and so was he. Despite initial concern about their different backgrounds and ages, Gary committed himself to a passionate and profound affair.

Romain Gary was one among thousands who fell in love with Jean Seberg, of course, and far from the only man she'd taken a fancy to in her short life to date. However, the relationship that began almost at first sight had a different quality from those that either of them had been involved in before. It's not hard to see the power Seberg had to wrench Gary away from his soulless routine of one-hour stands. She was the worldwide incarnation of a French national icon of resistance and valour, yet she was American to the core – an emblematic conjunction of two of the identities closest to Gary's heart at that time. Not only was she young, but her screen image, forged when she was only sixteen, had granted her a lasting aura of being younger still. What Gary did not know when she cast herself at his feet was that Jean was destined to lose her mind. She had perhaps already started her slide into paranoia, but as she was madly in love, a touch of real madness must have seemed like icing on the cake.

The well-publicised liaison between Romain Gary and Jean Seberg that ensued thus had a hidden similarity to the first and only other great love affair of Gary's life, his youthful infatuation with Ilona Gesmay, who Gary did not yet know had gone completely insane (see p. 67). But Lesley Blanch thought that it was Gary who had now gone mad. She had never arched an eyebrow at her husband's previous skirt-chasing exploits, but she saw Jean as a threat – to herself, most of all, but also to Gary, who, she thought, was crazy to try to remake his life with an unstable teenage star. But Gary was adamant: he wanted a divorce. He wanted a divorce so as to marry Jean. Jean wanted to marry her diplomat so as to effect a reconciliation with her conventional Lutheran parents (her father owned a drugstore in Marshalltown, Iowa). Her divorce from François Moreuil for mental cruelty was easily arranged in the USA, but it turned out to have no legal validity in France; so Moreuil divorced her under French law, citing Gary as co-respondent. Things then got very confused, and it is not easy to sort out who, among the lovers and spouses, was the maddest of the three. Gary dashed back and forth between America and France, denying, asserting, and retracting this and that; Jean smashed up the dashboard of a taxi with her shoe and had to be hospitalised in Paris until she calmed down; Lesley squatted at Roquebrune and hired lawyers.

All the while, *Promise at Dawn* sold tens of thousands of copies in France, was bought for translation into dozens of languages, including Polish, then appeared in Gary's own English version – with a chapter added – in the USA, where the film rights were acquired for a princely sum. Gary's career as a diplomat petered out as expected and he finally left LA in June 1960, without even saying farewell to his staff, like a dog with his tail between his legs, or alternatively, in the view of Lesley Blanch, like a mad Roman emperor who'd lost all contact with the real world. His disappearance before the great reception on 14 July, for which hundreds of invitations had been sent out over his name, saddened and angered many people, and seemed to confirm either that the Consul General had no manners at all, or that he had finally gone out of his mind.

Gary's devotion to Jean was sexual, emotional and also, to an important degree, moral and ideological. Far from being a heartless femme fatale, Jean was moved by the sight of suffering and injustice wherever she saw it, and put much of her energy, and a large part of her earnings, into good causes, most notably civil rights for American Blacks. Gary had been fighting racial discrimination through antiphrasis and clever quips ever since he'd composed *Tulipe* in London in 1945. Jean's passionate concern for racial justice bound him to her profoundly. Her physical resemblance to a Nazi-era icon of blue-eyed womanhood made such commitment all the more precious.

Jean was the main reason why Gary gave up America and returned to France. Although her first big role had been in an American blockbuster of dubious quality – Preminger's *Saint Joan* – her standing as an actress was far higher in France than in the USA. She'd played in *Bonjour Tristesse*, an adaptation of Sagan's novel that had met with Truffaut's approval, and was picked by Jean-Luc Godard for the female lead in his radically innovative 1959 movie, *Breathless*, which launched the New Wave.

The move back to Paris for the sake of Jean's career cut across Gary's own development as a writer of English, and prompted a bizarre and devious scheme for reasserting himself as novelist in French: he began to have French versions of his American fiction produced in complete secrecy by a distinguished translator working directly for Gallimard. The first translation, *Lady L.*, was done in 1961, but so heavily rewritten by Gary that it did not come out until 1963. The second was *The Talent Scout*, which didn't come out (as *Les Mangeurs d'étoiles*) until 1966, when *The Ski Bum* had already appeared in the USA; that third English-language novel was also utterly transformed when it finally appeared as *Adieu Gary Cooper* in 1969. These translations allowed Gary to appear to continue to produce one new book a year throughout the 1960s (the other years were taken up with memoirs and essays), but the fact is that he wrote no new fiction in French apart from a few short stories for all the years he was living with Jean – until he went to Warsaw with her for the launch of the Polish edition of *Promise at Dawn*.

Romain Gary's adoration of Jean lasted about five years and it disrupted every aspect of his life. He took his leave from 'diplomatic disguise' in 1960, just as he became the legendary hero of *Promise at Dawn*, and thereafter masqueraded as a celebrity spouse. The jealous husband of a star can have no peace: he must follow his beloved wherever she goes, and that means all over the place. Neither Romain nor Jean had a home of his or her own when they agreed to live together. First, from September to December 1960, they rented a flat in the very upper-class Île Saint-Louis, then went to New York for the end of the year. From there, they set off on a grand honeymoon that took them to India, Hong Kong, Indochina and Japan, where Jean was fêted by the moguls of the cinema world. They were back in Paris in March 1961 and rented a flat at 108 Rue du Bac, at the smarter end of the Latin Quarter, a few minutes' walk from the offices of Gallimard, where Gary still had a cubbyhole to call his own. Shortly after moving in, they learned that a vaster, ten-roomed apartment was for sale in the same block and, despite Gary's recent disasters on the Paris Bourse, they were still rich enough to buy it outright. They spent a few months there while it was being modernised, but in autumn 1961 Jean went off to Africa to shoot *Congo Vivo* on location. The team quickly returned to Rome to complete the shoot, and Gary joined his wife there in October and took her on to Venice, with the paparazzi scuttling behind.

In December they spent time with Gary's school friend, Roger Agid, at Saint-Paul-de-Vence on the Riviera. Jean was now pregnant and was desperate to keep her condition out of the news, so her parents would not find out. After a short break at Rue du Bac, Gary and Jean set off again by car, first for Toulouse to see René Agid, recently appointed to a chair of medicine at the university, then on to Sitges, in Spain, which they did not like; soon they were in an apartment in Barcelona. Gary moved back and forth between Barcelona and Paris in the spring of 1962, with a side trip to Cannes in May, as he was a member of the jury at the Film Festival. Back in Barcelona in June, which was when he probably first saw his son, Gary took Jean and Alexandre-Diego to Palma de Mallorca for part of the summer. For the months of September and October 1962 the couple rented a luxurious villa in Nice, then returned to Paris for the disastrous première of Gary's play, *Johnnie Cœur*. Jean meanwhile had begun shooting a film in Switzerland and Gary was with her in Lausanne in January 1963. In February they were off to another film location in Marrakech; after a dreadful sea crossing from Morocco to Spain, they at last spent a few weeks 'at home' in Rue du Bac. Before long, of course, Jean was on the road again, to Georgetown, MD, to star in Robert Rossen's *Lilith*. Gary joined her there and went on with her to Long Island, NY, for the final shots. It was when they were there that they got a call inviting them to luncheon at the White House with JFK. So they caught the next plane to Washington, DC, and made their way back to Paris from the capital. But they could barely have had time to change suitcases before they flew the nest again for a tour of Spain, via Toulouse (as always, to see René Agid), Barcelona, Formentera and Mallorca.

They returned to Paris in time to make a quick trip to London before at last getting married, now that Gary's divorce from Lesley had come through. To do this without the press in attendance, Gary pulled strings with a former member of the Free French forces, Noël Sarrola, to perform the ceremony in the Corsican village of which he was mayor, and had a fellow Companion, General Feuvrier, act as witness.[3] Romain and Jean flew to Ajaccio and were married at Sarrola-Carcopino on 16 October; then caught the ferry to Nice, where they spent time with Gary's cousin Dinah[4] before catching the train back to Paris. But Gary was in Nice once more three weeks later, to address the annual congress of the UNR, which was what the ruling (Gaullist) party called itself that year.[5] After a few days at Rue du Bac, Gary was off on a very long flight to Lima, Peru, to do a story for an American magazine. Oddly enough, he'd already written and published 'Birds in Peru' (which may be why he accepted the commission in the first place).

The year 1964 seems to have been a little less dispersed, to judge by the not entirely consistent narrative given by Anissimov. No journeys are recorded for the first six months, but for July and August Gary rented Los Almendros, a huge villa at Puerto Andraitx on Mallorca. Returning to Paris in September, he hired a part-time secretary, Marjorie Brandon, and in December the establishment – now comprising Romain, Jean, the baby, the baby's nanny, Eugenia Muñoz Lacasta, and Marjorie – took up residence in Cannes while Jean acted in *Moment to Moment* at various locations on the French Riviera. Gary, Jean and the baby stayed at the Carlton, Nice's swankiest hotel, but the 'staff' were lodged elsewhere. Gary paid for Marjorie's lunches in the grand dining room – but she was not allowed to sit at his table.

The weather being too poor for filming, the entire production upped sticks and moved to LA, where the full tribe, now incorporating Jean's new secretary, Cecilia Alvarez, took up residence in a rented villa. It didn't last long – in February 1965 they were back in France, before another of Jean's unimpressive films, *Un Milliard dans un billard*, took them to Geneva and Lausanne in March. From April to July they appear to have been mostly at Rue du Bac, but in August Gary rented a holiday home at Saint-Jean-Cap-Ferrat, to get Jean away from some of her bad acquaintances in Paris. But it was a miserable stay and Gary ran back to Paris after two weeks. He was in such a bad mood that he even kicked his dog, who retaliated by peeing on his trouser leg.[6]

Reunited in Paris for a brief week or two, the establishment set off again in the autumn for LA, where Jean was playing in *A Fine Madness*, and at the end of the year they went to Marshalltown, Iowa, to spend Christmas with Jean's parents. Back to Paris in early 1966, they had a few weeks at home before starting off on a different kind of trip. Gary had been invited to speak at the Centre for French Civilisation at the University of Warsaw – a centre that had been set up for its first director, Michel Foucault, whose declarations about the 'end of humanity' raised Gary's ire almost as much as the theoretical pronouncements of Alain Robbe-Grillet. They spent two weeks in Poland, visited Krakow, then went on to Budapest before returning to Paris by train. Shortly after, they took a brief holiday in Nice, once again as guests of Roger Agid. But the road show was far from over.

In May 1966, they were accommodated in a grand hotel in Athens, Greece, during the filming of *Route de Corinthe* (also known as *Who's Got the Black Box?*), in which Gary himself got to play a bit part, as an aeroplane passenger dressed up as a Russian Orthodox priest. When that was over they moved on, via Paris, to Mallorca again, where the house Gary was having built was almost complete. But it wasn't a long summer break (break?) because Jean had a smallish role in a French film, *Estouffade à la Caraïbe*, which began shooting in mid-August, in Colombia. Gary travelled with her, but didn't stay long. His marriage was in trouble and he started looking around for other ways to cope. He was not about to abandon Jean; in fact, he had plans to help her with her career and to put her on a healthier track. His preliminary step was to get himself an unpaid job as adviser to the Minister of Information, Georges Gorce, with responsibility for generating ideas about cultural policy. What he really had in mind, however, was to become a movie director himself and he managed to find a producer prepared to finance an adaptation of his own short story, 'Birds in Peru', starring Jean.

Jean Seberg and Romain Gary in *Route de Corinthe*

Gary's directorial debut turned out to be a flop, however, as we shall see in chapter 24. So once the movie was finished, the writer set off on a long tour of the Far East, without Jean: Honolulu, Manila, Hong Kong, Calcutta, Tehran, Guam, Phnom Penh, Angkor Wat . . . (Anissimov lists the destinations in that order, but if Gary did travel from Calcutta to Phnom Penh by way of Tehran and Guam, his travel agent must have been out of his mind.) He was back in Paris in March 1968 just in time to hear that Jean's brother David had died in a car crash in Marshalltown. He turned round and caught the first plane out to the States, so he could be at Jean's side at the funeral. Then he travelled with her back to Washington, DC, where she was shooting *Pendulum*, and on to LA, where they rented a villa in Coldwater Canyon.

Once the student riots broke out in Paris in May, however, Gary flew straight back to see what was going on. After the huge demonstrations in support of de Gaulle on the Champs-Élysées, which brought 'the events' to a close, Gary, disgusted at finding himself a member of the majority, flew straight back to LA – but the villa had become a madhouse, with Jean's Black Power friends taking her for a ride. He turned again, more like a yoyo than Dick Whittington, and landed back in Paris in July, where he collapsed from exhaustion and signed himself in to a private clinic for a rest cure. By the time he was out, Jean had moved on to Oregon to film a musical, *Paint Your Wagon*. Press reports suggested she was having an affair with Clint Eastwood (which was correct)[7]. Gary dashed to Orly Airport and flew to the West Coast to confront the man. Only a duel would satisfy his honour, the suddenly Polish gentleman declared: kitchen, first light, bare fists. Eastwood couldn't see the point of getting a black eye just for Jean (and anyway, it would hold up the shoot and cost him a fortune), so he backed out. He also dropped Jean when the location shooting was over. Gary returned with his honour unsatisfied to Paris, then on to his new home on Mallorca, where he stayed until December 1968, writing *White Dog* for the most part. He made it back to Rue du Bac for Christmas with Diego, who'd been living there all this time with his adoptive mother and full-time nanny, Eugenia.

Romain Gary was forced to take his distance from Jean when she fell under the spell of a particularly nasty ex-convict and drug addict turned Black Power leader. For love of her he'd let his life descend into even greater chaos than before, he'd had to cope with the hostility of many of his old friends (including a long separation from René and Silvia Agid), but Hakim Jamal was an adventure too far.[8] Fatally attracted towards a man who treated her like shit, Jean gave away huge amounts of money to 'charities' ostensibly connected to the emancipation of American Blacks, but which in fact served to fund racketeering and the feathering of individual nests. Even when having an affair with Carlos Fuentes in Durango, it seems, Jean was kept on a string by Jamal. Reasonably enough, the FBI kept Seberg under surveillance: she was in a liaison with a convicted murderer and notorious drugrunner who also extorted money to buy guns for Black Power activists. She was even inveigled into buying weapons and vehicles for Mexican insurrectionists during a short infatuation with a handsome bandit. Current anti-terrorism laws would have had Seberg behind bars in a trice, but in the 1960s the authorities had fewer direct means to act, and used first intimidation and, later on, calculated leaks to limit the damage Seberg could do. She was made aware that she was under surveillance and that her phone was being tapped. Unfortunately, these methods, which might have made a more rational person pull back from outright support for crime, persuaded Seberg that her paranoia was objectively grounded. Gary felt obliged to take cover, to protect himself and his son. By 1965 the marriage was on the rocks and by 1968 it was at an end. The divorce took some time to come through and became final in 1971.

After the divorce the grand apartment at Rue du Bac was divided in two, and Gary and Jean became neighbours. Throughout the 1970s Gary watched over his ex-wife with paternal solicitude, doing the little he could to save her from self-destruction. The character of Nancy in *The Talent Scout*, written in 1960, shows that Gary knew early on what lay in store. More than once he bailed her and her subsequent husbands and lovers out of trouble.[9] The love affair was long over, but Gary's tragic commitment to a difficult, dangerous and unstable woman never wavered. He'd got into the mess with his eyes open and he stuck with it to the end.

Jean eventually became incapable of caring for herself, let alone anyone else, and Alexandre-Diego, born 1962,[10] was in Gary's sole charge. He was brought up almost entirely by Eugenia Muñoz Lacasta, the Spanish housekeeper whom Gary hired in 1960 to look after his apartment in Rue du Bac. She spoke to the infant in Spanish, which naturally became the child's mother tongue.

In 1969, after an affair with the Mexican revolutionary who replaced Fuentes in her bed, Jean became pregnant. The Hollywood press printed rumours planted by COINTELPRO, one of the many 'black propaganda' agencies in the murky world of US security, that she was about to give birth to the child of a Black Panther leader. Apparently the spooks thought that this would discredit Seberg, though it is hard to see why, given her public support of the Black cause. Reciprocally, Seberg took the press campaign as a form of persecution, and plunged into self-pity and paranoia. Gary took Jean's side, denounced the manipulations of the FBI and, although separated from his wife, claimed the child was his. The infant was born before term and lived only a few days. To prove that Jean had not been impregnated by a Black, the infant's coffin displayed in Marshalltown, Iowa, had a special glass lid fitted, for all to see that the tiny corpse inside it was white. This final ghoulish act was as irrational as all the others: the offspring of mixed black–white parents may just as well look white as black, and the glass lid proved nothing about the infant's biological father. There's no doubt that Jean and Gary suffered intensely from this deplorable episode, but between them they turned an awkward problem into an emotional disaster. Their lunatic contortions were crowned by naming the baby 'Nina', which, as Jean surely knew,[11] was not Gary's mother's name, but the name of the heroine of *Promise at Dawn*.

The preceding narrative of picaresque instability punctured by comic interludes is only an overview of Gary's public and publicised movements. At some point in this hectic decade he also acquired a flat at 54 Rue Moillebeau in Geneva, and a Swiss residence permit. By spending more than half the year outside his own country, and a certain number of days each year in the canton of Geneva, Gary became non-resident in France for tax purposes, and a Swiss taxpayer into the bargain. And in those days that really was a bargain, of the sort only rich people could afford. Consequently, there were many shorter trips to Switzerland slotted inside the other travels listed above. Sometimes he holed up in his small apartment to write; sometimes he stayed with an old friend he'd first met in Beirut during the war, at her lavish estate at Versoix. Of Gary's visits to Geneva only one thing is almost certainly true: unlike the alcoholic ex-diplomat Allan Donahue in *The Ski Bum*, he wasn't involved in smuggling gold.

The most paradoxical part of Gary's life on the road in the 1960s was his substantial involvement with Spain. His first contact with the country came through Eugenia Muñoz Lacasta, the housekeeper he hired to look after his apartment at 108 Rue du Bac. Thanks to her, Jean was able to hide first in Sitges, then in an apartment in Barcelona during her confinement. That was why Gary's only child was born in Spain: but the birth of Alexandre-Diego marked the beginning of a long connection between Romain Gary and a Phalangist state that still raised the hair on the backs of most people's necks.

In 1962 Spain was not a democracy and hardly counted as part of the modern world. General Franco had been in power for twenty-five years and thrown a dark cloak of conservatism and religiosity over the land. Free speech did not exist; all forms of regionalism were firmly repressed; you could even be arrested for baring a few centimetres too much flesh on a beach. Spain was among the very poorest countries in Europe and its main export, apart from oranges to Scotland to make Dundee marmalade, was human labour. In France and Switzerland, particularly, but also all over the developed world, Spanish labourers filled those menial jobs – street-sweeping, house-cleaning, machine-minding and so forth – that would soon come to be taken over by Algerians, at least in France.

Despite the debt he owed Hitler in his original seizure of power, Franco made Spain neutral during World War Two. The country was therefore not among the victors or the defeated in 1945, and remained politically and economically isolated for decades thereafter. It had no extradition treaty with its immediate neighbour France, nor did it have any with Britain, West Germany or the United States. It thus became a safe haven for former Nazis and such unsavoury characters as the head of the wartime 'Commissariat for Jewish Questions' in France, Louis Darquier de Pellepoix.

The Spanish economy remained in a time warp and the only kind of modernisation that occurred was in the development of the seaside holiday trade. On the Costa Brava and in the Balearics, box-like hotels were constructed all along the seafront, and charter flights began to fill them with mostly working-class families from Bolton and Wuppertal. To cater for them, fish-and-chip shops, hot-dog stalls, tatty souvenir stands and discos soon arose. Spain was a package-holiday destination at the very bottom of the market, before Yugoslavia, Greece and Turkey muscled in on the same act.

The lack of extradition made Spain a Mecca for hoodlums of all kinds; in Britain, in the 1960s, the Mediterranean seaside was commonly known as the Costa del Crime. After Algerian independence was granted in 1962, the leadership of the OAS (desperadoes who had opposed independence and brought bombs and assassination attempts to mainland France) naturally found refuge there too. In sum, Spain in the 1960s was not at all like the vibrant and wealthy democracy it has become over the last thirty years. It was the armpit of Europe – poor, cheap and desolate, overrun by hordes of northern Europeans out for a good time in the sun.

The plot of land that Gary purchased on Mallorca and the house he had built were a cut above the main run of Spanish tourist sites. With its three-storey turret, its vast veranda and pool, with views out to sea and over what was still the little fishing port of Puerto Andraitx (now a mass of concrete and high-rise apartment buildings), the villa he named Cimarrón was a millionaire's retreat. Except that, given the peseta's disastrous rate of exchange, it cost a lot less than the real millions Gary would have needed to buy a replacement for Roquebrune on the French Mediterranean coast. The plot had been found for him by the same old school friend who'd put Roquebrune in his way, Sacha Kardo-Sissoeff, who had ended up in seaside exile in Mallorca himself. It must have looked like a sweet deal, as Gary now needed a home outside France to maintain his non-resident status; the small flat he had in staid and quiet Geneva bored him out of his mind.

Perhaps the best that can be said of Gary's adoption of Puerto Andraitx as another home is that it contributed to the radical provocativeness that came to be his hallmark in the last decade of his life. Cimarrón demonstrated that he was a vulgar plutocrat with no political sensitivity and no memory of the past, exactly the opposite of what his books show his writerly self to be. He seems to have enjoyed displaying himself in ever more tasteless ways, in a bright yellow beach robe decorated with his 'trademark' of elephants, or in full leather gear astride his Harley Davidson motorbike. The house was big enough to accommodate several guests and Gary played the lavish host many times. Save that he mostly ignored the people he invited, prowled around looking glum and subjected everyone to the various strange diets he took up to keep himself in shape.

The Mogul. Cimarrón, around 1975

Many other literary tax exiles had lived on the Med – Maugham at Cap Ferrat, Burgess in Monte Carlo, Graham Greene in Antibes. Robert Graves had ended up in Mallorca, it's true, and in his wake came other writers like Harry Mathews. But Gary was not part of the penniless literary fraternity, such as it still existed on the island. He was part of the celebrity set and his best friend in the sun was the genial, outsized Russian actor-director, Peter Ustinov.

None of Gary's books is set in Spain and the only one to be set on an island is *The Guilty Head*, located on Tahiti, where Gary also owned a plot of land. Cimarrón functioned as a home base for part of the year from 1965, but it seems to have had no impact at all on Gary's imagination: when he was there, his mind was always somewhere else. In the 1970s, when he regularly spent about four months out of every twelve on Mallorca, he liked to describe himself as a 'citizen of the Rue du Bac'. It doesn't seem he ever thought of himself as a Balearic islander, or as a citizen of Franco's Spain.

The fact that Gary managed to write anything at all in the 1960s, as he traipsed from VIP lounge to grand hotel, hopped between rented houses and the three different properties he owned, juggled staff salaries, expenditures and accounts in Spanish, French, Swiss and American currency, looked after an increasingly difficult and paranoid wife and worried about his child, must be counted an extraordinary achievement in itself. The fact that he managed to write two significant works in English – *The Talent Scout* and *The Ski Bum* – as well as two bilingual works of huge importance in two distinct cultural environments – *The Dance of Genghis Cohn* and *White Dog* – is breathtaking. The failures and serious flaws of other work he did in that decade – his play, his movie and his long essay on the art of the novel, *Pour Sganarelle* – have to be weighed against his triumphant skill as a novelist and storyteller, and put in the context of a chaotic life without any routine or order for more than a few weeks at a time. Gary's energy, industry and artistry would have been admirable had he sat at home all those years chewing the end of his pencil. As it is, they are beyond easy comprehension.

Promise at Dawn begins and ends in a mood of serenity. In it, he recalls his bitter disappointment as a child at never learning to juggle more than five oranges: 'but no matter what I did, the sixth and last ball remained beyond my reach'.[12] He also says that around the age of forty 'the awful truth dawned on me, and I realized that the last ball did not exist'. But such mature wisdom does not seem to be borne out by Gary's life after the launch of his childhood memoir. What he then undertook were multiple existences as playwright, celebrity, man of property, film director, essayist and novelist too, as if to prove that he could win *every* prize. Life is short.

Why not do as many different things as you can? The least we can surely say about Gary's style of life as the husband of Jean is that it must have been a lot more fun than doing crosswords in a deckchair on the beach.

24

If at first you don't succeed . . .

Gary on Stage and Screen, 1945–1974

Romain Gary's involvement with film reached its peak in his years with Jean Seberg, but in that period, as in all others, it was not a great success. In fact, film work seems to have been the default for an altogether different ambition that Gary cherished from his earliest days – writing for the stage.

The attraction of the theatre may have been financial in the first place, as it was for many nineteenth-century novelists (Balzac, Flaubert and Henry James all tried their hand at the stage, with mediocre results). Gary's theatrical avocation may also have been inspired by the example of Sartre and Camus, who achieved great prominence and wealth as playwrights in the immediate post-war years. Whether it was also inspired by the theatrical career of Gary's mother is hard to say: just as plausible is that Nina's life at the 'Théâtre français de Moscou', mentioned repeatedly in *Promise at Dawn*, is a back-projection of Gary's own dreams for himself.

There is no trace of Gary trying to make a play out *A European Education*, but in October 1945, the first thing he did with *Tulipe* once it was typed was to send a copy of it to the legendary director, Louis Jouvet, hoping he would see some merit in it as the basis for a play. When Gary arrived in Sofia a few months later, he rewrote his parable as a stage play, which he then also mailed to Jouvet. The director's polite, lengthy reply served only to say: no way. 'I fear your play will weary the audience . . . As it stands I do not think the audience will be able to follow the adventures of Tulipe . . . I think it would be a good idea to invent a more rigorous and obvious plot, and to cut the play down in size . . .'[1] Gary's reply sounds like a letter from a schoolboy:

> Put simply, *Tulipe* is a satire of idealism – the tragedy of which is the fact that you cannot not be an idealist . . . It would be easy to merge the 'interludes' into the main text (I confess I was thinking mainly of the American version when I wrote them) and to make Tulipe's character more precise in the last scenes, to scale the play down to two acts and to change the ending. But I must say that I did not quite understand whether after making the changes you suggest you would even *consider* putting my play on?[2]

Gary got down to revision almost straight away and by the end of the summer sent Jouvet version two of the play, now a 'comedy in two acts' called *Le Radeau de la Méduse* (The Raft of the Medusa, after Géricault's painting of a historical shipwreck remembered for the barbaric things the survivors did to each other to survive). He got no reply, as Jouvet was on tour, so in January 1947 he sent him another copy of *Le Radeau* which elicited a long, superficially friendly, but rather cruel reply. Jouvet was looking for traditional theatrical values – character, action and a coherent relationship between the two. Gary's work has nothing of this kind – like the novel version, the play *Tulipe* is a sequence of sketches with characters who are merely alternative voices for Gary's own quips. Jouvet had the cheek to suggest that Gary had not yet separated himself sufficiently from his inventions, that he did not yet know how to write . . . and looked forward to a long face-to-face conversation, which might then enable Gary to produce a real play. Gary wasn't interested in a sermon on theatricality from Jouvet, so he accepted defeat and on 1 May 1947 wrote that he was putting *Tulipe* back in his bottom drawer. 'It will re-emerge one day, I hope, in the shape of an even more incoherent farce. I hate works that are "well-made".'[3]

Despite rejection by a director he admired and hoped to seduce ('the idea of your remaining unused by modern writers has become a kind of obsession for me,' he wrote), Gary gave up neither his theatrical ambitions nor *Tulipe*. He even carried on hoping that Jouvet would back him and wrote another play for the director, which he mailed to him in April 1950, but which got no nearer to production than any of Gary's previous efforts for the stage. *La Tendresse des pierres* (*The Soft-heartedness of Stones*) is a farce with four main characters: Florian, Lily, the Baron and a young simpleton.[4] These characters reappear in Gary's later work, notably in *The Dance of Genghis Cohn*, but the Baron was already a self-quotation, from *The Company of Men*. As for the title, it re-emerges as the French name of *A Quality of Despair*, the book Jess Donahue writes, in Gary's self-translation of *The Ski Bum*; then it became attached to the novel we now know as *Life Before Us*, by Émile Ajar. Impenetrable as it is, the idea of *stones that weep* seems to lie somewhere deep inside Gary's head.

Once Gary had published the second version of the *Tulipe* material as *L'Homme à la colombe* in 1958, he sought once again to put it into dramatic form. Try, and try again . . . and *Johnnie Cœur*, as the adaptation was called, did indeed get on stage. François Perier directed and performed the lead role in a production at the Théâtre de la Michodière in October 1962. It was panned in no uncertain terms in *Le Figaro* and *Le Parisien libéré*, and in *Le Monde* Bertrand Poirot-Delpech declared that it was not a play at all, just an illustrated conversation piece.[5] *Johnnie Cœur* closed at the end of its first week.

Despite this disaster, Gary went on to write a stage version of *The Company of Men*, first called *Dans la Nature*, then retitled *La Bonne Moitié*. Gary was not given a second chance to put a play on the Paris stage. After so many years of fruitless effort, he finally abandoned his theatrical ambitions and had the adaptation published in book form in 1979.

Gary beavered away at many other projects for the stage in the course of his life: a translation from Polish of a play about the novelist Balzac, a translation into French of a play by Bruce Friedman, drafts of adaptations of various of his own novels (*The Dance of Genghis Cohn*, *King Solomon*), and at least one original and independent comedy that is not bad at all.[6] *A Night in the Life of Harry Smithowitz* is a screwball comedy rather funnier than many a Hollywood movie. Harry and Marge Smith(owitz) return to Oatsville, Iowa from a European vacation to discover that their daughters have filled the house with their friends, to wit: the Soviet naval attaché, who thinks he's in a hotel annexe; the only Black family in town, whose own house has just been burned down; a grinning Vietcong, who lives in the guest bedroom, and in the basement an American beatnik by the name of Foulsome. The play is a fond satire of Jean Seberg and her notorious generosity towards every humanitarian cause she came across. The lunatic set-up allows for Feydeau-like stage business and some first-rate quips against bleeding hearts. But like nearly all Gary's theatrical work, it was never produced on stage and never published. He had a gift for storytelling in prose, for narrative that reads almost as if it were being spoken aloud. He never found the trick or the talent for telling stories through the voices and actions of others – on stage, or on screen.

Gary's career in the movies began in New York, when he sold the film rights to *The Colours of the Day*. The utterly mediocre and now unwatchable film that was eventually made from it bears little relationship to his original work.[7] However, before that film was even made, Gary scored a huge financial coup by selling the rights to *The Roots of Heaven* to Twentieth Century-Fox for the princely sum of $135,000. But it was a disaster from all other points of view. William Holden, who was in real life an impassioned activist on behalf of African wildlife, was originally cast to play Morel. John Huston was hired to direct the film and he recruited a whole set of big names to the cast – among them Errol Flynn, Orson Welles and Juliette Greco. But Holden had unfulfilled obligations to Paramount, who refused to release him. With the other talent under contract and an inflexible start date for shooting on location in Africa, Fox ended up casting Trevor Howard as Morel. Howard was a British character actor without much name recognition in the USA, so Errol Flynn, in the role of the exiled American soldier Forsythe, found himself billed as the star. Huston arrived in Africa with producer Darryl Zanuck, and the 140-degree inferno quickly took a heavy toll on the cast and crew. One actor collapsed with sunstroke, and everyone else except Huston and Flynn, who had each brought prodigious amounts of alcohol to consume, soon suffered from amoebic dysentery. With the frequent production delays, Huston went big-game hunting. He and Flynn started arguing on set and Flynn dared the director to fight him. Flynn had been an amateur boxer, but he was long past his prime. Huston, who had actually been a professional boxer in his youth, flattened the actor with one punch.

The screenplay of *The Roots of Heaven* was Gary's first exercise in the strange art of adaptation, but his initial version was completely rewritten by the famous British travel writer, Patrick Leigh Fermor. Gary also visited the shoot for a few days, but made no attempt to get involved. Just as well. Despite the huge amounts of money spent on it, the panoramic format used and the appeal of its subject, the film was a mess. It was screened in 1958, coinciding with the US launch of the English translation of the novel, but had a very short run.

Gary's next coup was to sell film rights to *Lady L.* to MGM in 1958, even before the novel was out, for the reported sum of $100,000. But the studio took a long time to make it. Originally billed as a vehicle for Gina Lollobrigida and Tony Curtis, it turned into a film adapted and directed by Peter Ustinov, starring Paul Newman and Sophia Loren. First shot as a long movie, it was shortened by thirty minutes before release, producing a fairly incomprehensible and silly sex comedy bearing only a generic relationship to the original novel. By the time it was made, in the early 1960s, Gary had become a frequent visitor to film shoots as the accompanying spouse of Jean, and had learned not to interfere. Although he counted Peter Ustinov among his friends (and saw him quite frequently in Mallorca once he had built his house there), he did not go even once to see *Lady L.* being made at the Studios de la Victorine in Nice or on location in Geneva. *Lady L.* was screened in 1965 and, like all the other adaptations of Gary's work, it fell completely flat.

However, Gary was now a bankable name and able to charge high fees for his services. He rapidly became a Hollywood professional, hiring out his pen to adapt and improve stories and film scripts by others. According to Jean-Marie Catonné, Gary obtained substantial fees for work on the script of *Seven Women* (John Ford, 1966) and on *The Horseman*, adapted from a novel by Joseph Kessel (John Frankenheimer, 1971), but his name does not appear on the credits.[8] He is believed to have doctored many other scripts that have disappeared. The only finished film in which he gets a writing credit was *The Longest Day* (Ken Annakin and others, 1962), a big-budget retelling of the D-Day landings based on the book by Cornelius Ryan, with almost every box-office star of the day in the cast, from Arletty to John Wayne. Gary acted as 'dialogue consultant', using his memory of RAF jargon to perfect the lines spoken by British airmen in the film. There is obvious irony, but also a secret triumph, in the fact that Richard Burton, in the role of a crashed pilot dying in a French farmyard, utters his last reflections on what it means to be an Englishman in words honed by a Yiddish-speaking Pole.

A movie entitled *The Ski Bum* was made by Bruce Clark in 1969 and released in 1971. Gary's name does not appear on the credits and the synopses available of this now unfindable film suggest it has at best a tangential relationship to Gary's novel. It does not seem related to *Millions of Dollars*, Gary's own unpublished adaptation of the novel, to be found in the Library of Congress in Washington, DC.

Promise at Dawn had an altogether different career. Almost as soon as it appeared in the USA in 1961 it was adapted for the stage by a prolific commercial playwright, Samuel Taylor. *First Love* opened at the Morosco Theater on Broadway on Christmas Day 1961, and got respectful but not enthusiastic reviews. It does not seem to have been revived since then.

Gary's memoir was also made into a film, but unlike all previous adaptations, *Promise at Dawn* was shot and released in French. Directed by the Franco-American Jules Dassin, it hews to Gary's text as much as can be expected from commercial cinema. Krakow replaces Wilno for no obvious reason; Nina, played by Melina Mercouri pretending to be Jewish and not Greek, is a lapsed star of the silent screen, and Ivan Moszhukin is treated as Gary's real father. The fanciful anecdote of letters written by Nina to be sent to her son after her death becomes the main story of the film. Gary took no part in the adaptation and did not visit the shoot, but in October 1969 he attended a private showing of the film before its commercial release. He came out of the screening room in tears. In the movie, the character of Romain Gary as a little boy declares: 'Mummy, I do not want to be a Jew!' In interviews thereafter Gary frequently returned to this invention, to complain, often vociferously, that he had never said anything of the kind, in *Promise at Dawn* or in real life. In his view it was a calumny. He avoided meeting Jules Dassin ever after, for fear he would have to teach him a lesson with his fists.

But by that time Gary had become a film director himself. Film has always had a higher cultural status in France than elsewhere, and in the wake of the French New Wave of the 1960s, many *auteurs* moved easily between book and screen – Robbe-Grillet being a notable example. But Gary's main motivation seems to have been to give Jean Seberg a better chance of displaying her talents than the second-rate movies she was playing in currently – most of them potboilers cooked up by studios in Paris and Hollywood, of no artistic significance whatever (a list of these movies can be found in Appendix IV). All the same, Gary's choice of project was bizarre and, to a degree, quite perverse. 'Birds in Peru' certainly had a promising record to date: written in 1962, it was translated into English by Richard Howard and published in *Hissing Tales* two years later, when it also appeared separately in *Playboy* magazine (under the title 'A Bit of a Dreamer, a Bit of a Fool'), and was selected as the best short story of 1964. This haunting and disturbing tale deals with female frigidity and nymphomania, and although it is not directly autobiographical, it clearly represents some kind of reaction to the difficult relationship that he had with Jean. To put it on the screen as a general-release film would be difficult, as the story involves actions normally restricted to pornographic movies; screening it with Gary's own wife as the lead actress under her husband's direction and gaze was to ask for serious trouble.

Produced by the distinguished cinematographer Jacques Natteau, who had been behind the camera for one of the better adaptations of *Les Misérables*, *Birds in Peru* was written, adapted and directed by Romain Gary. It was shot in Paris at the Boulogne-Billancourt studios, then at Huelva in Spain, in the later months of 1967. The few people who have seen it count it a very bad film. It is also pornographic: Jean Seberg mimics some kind of orgasm with four different partners in short sequence. Only her face can be seen in the sex shots, but in other sequences she is shown from behind without any clothes.

The original text of 'Birds in Peru' deals with delicate topics in language that is restrained and suggestive, but never crude. The events are admittedly bizarre (close to madness, in Gary's view), but their impact becomes altogether different when transferred to the screen. Gary expected the film would be banned by the censorship board – and it was, by nine votes to one. Gary, who at that time occupied a minor government post, asked the Minister of Culture, Georges Gorce, to overrule the film board's decision, which he did. Two particularly pornographic scenes were cut, the film was given an 'X' rating (forbidden to under-eighteens). *Birds in Peru* was screened at the Cannes Festival in May 1968, then in three cinemas on the Champs-Élysées. It was panned by the critics and withdrawn very soon. Released by Universal in the USA the following year, it earned this thumbs-down from Roger Ebert in the *Chicago Sun-Times*:

> The story goes that Gary wanted to direct this movie because he was so displeased by the two previous movies made from his books, *Lady L.* and *Roots of Heaven*. Those were stinkers, yes. So Gary took his short story *Birds in Peru* and directed it himself this time. Now there are three stinkers made from his work.

The screenplay for *Birds in Peru* is somewhat different from the short story, as it includes a recurrent plot device first found in *The Colours of the Day* and reused again in *The Way Out*: that of the self-commissioned murder, or suicide by proxy. As Ebert explains:

> The story involves a frigid beauty who arrives in Peru in the midst of a round-the-world trip in search of fulfilment. She is accompanied by her husband and his chauffeur, who complete a masochistic ménage à trois. The morning after the carnival, we find her on a beach with the bodies (some dead, some alive) of the lovers who tried and failed last night. She wanders away in shock. Arrives at a bordello on the seashore. Makes it with the madam and one of her customers. Wanders away again. Meets a sensitive young artist. Waits with him for her husband and the chauffeur to arrive. When they do, they will kill her. Then the chauffeur has instructions to kill the husband. There is a houseboy involved, too, whose function is to look startled and run places.[9]

Filmed more as a series of tableaux than as a drama, with wooden dialogue and close-ups held on Jean's face (and on her buttocks) for seemingly interminable minutes, *Birds in Peru* demonstrates only that Gary had no greater gift for expressing himself in film than he had for theatrical composition. It also failed in its primary aim of relaunching Jean as an international star. On the contrary: having his wife parade her nymphomania in public probably both hastened the end of the marriage and increased the general reluctance in Hollywood and elsewhere to hire such a fragile and dangerous person.

There is something equally distasteful about Gary's second and last attempt to make a film. It was undertaken in 1971 with a similar aim – to help Jean, now divorced, to restore a career that was on the skids. But like *Birds in Peru*, it also exploits Jean shamelessly. In real life, Gary's ex-wife was increasingly dependent on drugs and alcohol. The movie Gary had her star in, entitled *Kill! Kill! Kill!*, is a violent denunciation of the drug trade.

From an original script by Gary that has never been published, *Kill!* was financed by the producer Alexander

Salkind – another Polish émigré settled in France, who would soon make a fortune with *Superman* in 1978. With such backing, Gary was able to hire an expensive cast of stars – James Mason, Curd Jürgens, Stephen Boyd and Daniel Emilfork, alongside Jean Seberg, of course – and to whisk them all off to Spain and Afghanistan for most of the shooting. Mason plays the role of a hit man for a global drug-crime fighting unit and he methodically shoots down some of the world's leading drug barons for the safety of us all. Jean Seberg plays his bored wife who darts off to Afghanistan and falls into the arms of a renegade assassin who has severed his ties with the Interpol crime unit and is on a mission to root out a double agent. The narrative suspense is supposed to be provided by the mystery as to who the double agent really is – but the solution is obvious from the start.

Gary's distaste for intoxicating drugs of all kinds, including alcohol, was long-standing and entirely sincere; his hatred of drug dealers knew no bounds, and he was particularly horrified by the tolerance shown in America and increasingly in France towards drug usage by the young.[10] However, *Kill!* is not just a naive expression of this altogether laudable campaign, but an excuse to show Jean on set just what he wanted to do with her suppliers: shoot the lot of them. It's a violent movie, but alas, an unconvincing one, failing to horrify us with its conventional bath of synthetic blood. Over-plotted, clumsily acted and badly edited, it really has to count as one of the worst movies ever made. Gary made no more films. Nobody in his right mind would have funded him to do so in any case.

Two more adaptations were made of Gary's works in his lifetime. Simone Signoret played Madame Rosa in Moshe Mizrahi's version of *Life Before Us*, which won an Oscar for Best Foreign Film of 1978, but Gary was unable to claim any credit since at that time he was not supposed to have written the book. Mizrahi recalls that when the screenplay was complete, he sent a copy to Émile Ajar through his agent and got back a handwritten letter from him praising the result.

> When the movie was finished, there was a private screening, to which Ajar was invited. I sat in a cafe nearby and saw Romain Gary walking around restlessly. At the time there was already a rumor in Paris that Gary and Ajar were relatives. That evening a messenger brought a letter signed by Gary, in which he wrote that Ajar was lucky to have found such a good director to adapt his book. When Romain Gary committed suicide and his will became public, including his confession that he was Émile Ajar and his apology for the deception, I said to myself: You idiot, how could you not notice that the two letters you got – one from Ajar, the other from Gary – were written in the same distinctive hand![11]

Clair de femme, on the other hand, was fully attributable to Gary and in August 1979 he attended the private screening with his new companion, Leïla Chellabi, who would be the last woman to share his apartment at Rue du Bac. Directed by the already celebrated Costa-Gavras and starring Signoret's long-standing partner, Yves Montand, *Clair de femme* could have been a very good film indeed. But long experience of being turned into rubbish in the cinema made Gary very apprehensive. This in turn made Costa-Gavras so nervous of what the author might think that he left the screening so as not to have to face Gary when the lights went up. But for once, Gary was entranced. He went straight home after the show and rang Costa-Gavras to say, this is the first time I can say I couldn't have made a better film of it myself.[12]

Gary's work has continued to be attractive to film-makers over the last thirty years. The most notable posthumous adaptation is Sam Fuller's 1982 version of *White Dog*, a violent, stripped-down but also rather sentimental version of the animal anecdote at the heart of Gary's memoir. The French-Canadian version of *The Way Out*, however, like *Les Faussaires*, adapted from *The Guilty Head*, has never had an international release. *The Dance of Genghis Cohn* and *The Kites* have both been done as television dramas, the first in Britain in 1993 and the second in France in 2007. A movie based on the last Ajar novel, *King Solomon*, adapted and directed by Nathalie Donnini, is currently in production in France. Gary's career as a resource for the cinema is still a work in progress; perhaps it will come to rival his literary exploits one day. After all, nothing is impossible.

25

Cultural Legitimacy

Pour Sganarelle, 1965

In the early 1960s Romain Gary was a very famous writer. *A European Education*, *The Roots of Heaven* and *Promise at Dawn* were in every bookshop and on most French families' library shelves. Each one of his three great successes had already sold more copies than the literary production of Alain Robbe-Grillet, Samuel Beckett, Nathalie Sarraute and Michel Butor combined, but at the moment of French literature's greatest international prestige, the ex-diplomat turned celebrity didn't have a tenth of the cultural legitimacy enjoyed by its stars. He was a brilliant, seductive, entrancing teller of tales, whereas the avant-garde was doing its best to tear narrative interest out of literature altogether. Sarraute's earlier essay on 'The Age of Suspicion' had relegated storytelling to the cinema (a medium more suited to mass entertainment, she suggested), and dismissed conventional novelistic psychology, in the manner of Dostoevsky or Dickens, as no longer tenable in the modern world. The writing of Romain Gary, far closer to Dickens than to Robbe-Grillet, was out of phase with literary fashion. Ambitious young writers as yet unpublished, like Georges Perec and Renaud Camus, who both lived on Rue du Bac at that time, recognised Gary in the street and comforted themselves with the thought that they'd just seen one of the writers they would never need to read.[1]

Gary was a popular novelist but not a fashionable one; he tackled issues that were topical, but also traditional ones. Now that the formal innovations and subversive conventions of French writing in the 1950s and 1960s have settled into their place in the history of literature, Gary's temporary isolation seems in retrospect to be not an injustice at all, just the natural consequence of his literary project. But Gary was also vain. He really wanted the critical recognition that was denied him in his own time.

For the preceding twenty-two years, from 1938 to 1960, Gary had only ever been an occasional visitor to Paris, with no permanent perch, merely a minuscule office in the rabbit warren of Gallimard's main building in Rue Sébastien-Bottin. His circle of acquaintances spanned the globe, but in Paris it consisted essentially of a few old friends from school in Nice, a few surviving comrades from the Free French, his contacts at Gallimard and a mere handful of writers, such as Albert Camus and André Malraux. The former died in a car crash in 1960; the latter was now Minister of Culture, far outside (and far above) the opinion-making groups of Saint-Germain-des-Prés. In a peculiar sense Romain Gary, one of France's best-selling and most lavishly rewarded writers, was utterly isolated when, on his resignation from the Diplomatic Service, he settled down in the heart of the Latin Quarter, which was seen the world over as the place where modern culture was being made.

Gary set out to win cultural legitimacy, to use Bourdieu's term, that is to say, intellectual respect. The obvious tool to use was the essay, just like Sartre (*What is Literature?*), Robbe-Grillet (*For a New Novel*) and Sarraute (*The Age of Suspicion*). Like his predecessors, he too would point out where everyone else had gone wrong and where the real future of the modern novel lay. The conception, intention and application of the project which turned into *Pour Sganarelle* (1965) was entirely Parisian and unrelated to Gary's concurrent careers as English novelist, unrecognised playwright and incipient movie mogul. It has to be said that *Pour Sganarelle* is not a good book. No English-language publisher would have let it through without savage editing. Gallimard must have known what effect this meandering, unsupported and often ludicrous rant would have on the writer's French career, and their complaisance may not have been intended as a kindness to Romain Gary.

Pour Sganarelle is unreadable by all but the most assiduous of Gary's fans.[2] Newspaper critics decided not to review it and his profession of novelistic faith made no impact at all in the public sphere. Readers who picked it up off bookshop shelves expecting to plunge into another ripping yarn by the author of *Promise at Dawn* were bewildered. The book's sales were minimal, but its impact on Gary's reputation was severe. It made booksellers wary of new titles by Gary and they cut down their standing orders (the *offices* in French book trade slang) for his subsequent books in case they turned out to resemble the five-hundred-page flop of *Pour Sganarelle*.[3]

Gary had no experience of literary criticism, no interest in literary theory and no real talent as an essayist either. He had read widely in European fiction of previous centuries, but had little familiarity with contemporary French literature. He was too fluent and too idle to bother with checking facts, and he quoted from a memory that was far from perfect. He was just as inclined to invent characters (such as Hossémine, the 'authority' on Cervantes) in literary polemic as he was when writing fiction. He was similarly inclined to misquote and misattribute throughout his work: 'The power of screams is so great that it will break the harsh fate imposed on man', the epigraph to *Tulipe*, for example, is not from Kafka, as Gary thought, but from the Zohar![4] This ragbag of opinionated bunkum was written when Gary was shuttling between shooting locations as a celebrity spouse and tripping off on his own on highly paid reporting jobs for American magazines. Its chaotic shape is a fair reflection of the nomadic, disorganised existence the author led. However, despite its disabling flaws, *Pour Sganarelle* is an important work. Clumsy, confusing and mistaken as it often is, Gary's one long essay on the art of fiction lays out a unique and serious set of ideas about the nature of literature and the task of the fiction writer.

The nub of Gary's argument is an opposition between what he calls 'totalitarian' fiction and the 'total' novel. The terminology is unfortunate because other writers of the period used 'totalitarian' in much the same sense that Gary meant by his term of 'total'.[5] His central argument could be more comprehensibly formulated as a defence of the grand tradition of the all-encompassing, encyclopaedic novel of Balzac and Tolstoy (the 'total' novel) against twentieth-century modernist fiction, which presents man's plight in terms of an exclusive ('totalitarian') principle. Kafka, Céline, Sartre and Camus are for Gary all guilty of self-deception by declaring man to be condemned entirely to absurdity (Kafka), squalor (Céline), revolt (Camus) or nothingness (Sartre) while writing about human life from *outside* the prison house they claim we all inhabit. Gary's aim is to bring attention back to the novel as the art which can encompass *everything*.

If that were all, and if it had been backed up with demonstrations of the greater power of more ambitious, humanistic writing than was current in 1960s France, his work would probably now be seen as a precursor of Milan Kundera's *The Art of the Novel,* which similarly places Cervantes at the fountainhead of Western storytelling, and a prophetic intuition of what Georges Perec would seek to achieve in *Life A User's Manual* in 1978. In fact, Gary recognised the real power of that encyclopaedic, comic and human novel when it appeared, and drew particular attention to it in a radio broadcast: 'It's a huge book, every page of it shows the author's talent, and I was really pleased to see [*putting on a comically pompous voice*] that I am not alone! Ha! Ha!'[6]

Where he was alone, however, and perhaps will for ever

remain so, lies in the more recondite arguments of *Pour Sganarelle*. The invention of the novel, Gary said, was in essence the invention of a character, and the character at the heart of all 'total' fiction was what he called a Sganarelle, after Don Juan's cynical, ironic and immortal valet. The Sganarelle of the *commedia dell'arte* and its various transpositions to other theatrical traditions has little to do with Gary's use of the term, and his alternative characterisation of Sganarelle as a picaro is similarly out of kilter with literary history: but we have to let these very approximate invocations of tradition pass, so as not to miss the bizarre argument they are intended to prop up. Gary's Sganarelle is not just the named character at the centre of an episodic, self-perpetuating, always unfinished and open work, but the name also of the *author*, who is as much a creation of the novel as the novel is the creation of an author. The 'total' novelist (Cervantes, Tolstoy . . .) does not use fiction just to represent himself, but to invent a whole world, of which the novelist is necessarily a part. The novelist is an invention of the text in exact parallel to the novelist's invention of the text.

This fits well with the emerging work of the Konstanz School of literary criticism and theory, of which Gary would have had no knowledge. Wolfgang Iser and Hans-Robert Jauss argued that a narrative text designates through its manipulation of point of view an empty space in the work, which they call the 'reader position', of which the inescapable corollary is an 'author position', often called 'the implied author'.[7] The relationship of this 'writer in the text' to the historical person who actually wrote it is indeterminate – it can range from complete identification to straightforward antagonism. That's also what Gary says at the start of *Pour Sganarelle*: you can write to represent yourself, but also against yourself, to explore what it would be like to be opposite, or different. But where Gary's grappling with elements of literary theory veers off into previously unimagined terrain is in his assertion that the novelist's true task is to become the exclusive property of his own work – to become the 'implied author' not at a theoretical level, but for real.

This is close to madness and it did bring Gary to the brink ten years later. But the idea of making the writer the child of his text is tied by a hundred threads to all other aspects of Gary's life and work: the legendary subjects of his novels, his taste for frauds and mystifications, the total immersion he experienced when in creative frenzy. It also comes very close to explaining his rejection of his own paternity, as well as his sometimes alarming changes of costume and appearance. Gary wanted to be everyone because that was what a real writer – a 'total' novelist – was there to do. Which is the cause, and which is the consequence? Does the literary theory of *Pour Sganarelle* rationalise Gary's peculiar character and tastes, or do Gary's bizarre achievements as a multiple author and 'mobile personality'[8] spring from a coherent, marginally insane theory of literature? *Pour Sganarelle* brings us back to the same question as *Promise at Dawn*. The 'Romain Gary' whose story the latter book tells is manifestly a fiction, but bears the same name as the man who wrote it. But Gary is not 'hiding' a 'real self' behind the rearrangement of his own story. He is turning himself into a legend, because legends are those narrative ideals that give men aspirations to a higher moral plane. 'Romain Gary' is the character Gary designed so as to become something *more* than what he was. *Pour Sganarelle* hypothesises an entire art of fiction writing whose sole purpose is not to transform, but to create its own author. When the hot air is dissipated and the excess verbiage cut away, Gary's literary manifesto is entirely consistent with his practice as a novelist, and in no work was he a more skilful novelist of the kind he proposes than in *Promise at Dawn*.

Two important subsidiary arguments are worth rescuing from *Pour Sganarelle*. First, Gary attacks the idea of the *chef-d'oeuvre*, the perfect, closed, self-sufficient masterpiece, which serves as the ultmate yardstick of literary merit. Aesthetic perfection, which is only a critical hypothesis, not a demonstrable achievement, is a mere mask for something else – the detachment of the work from the world. But as the world is unfinished, and as literature always seeks to create its own parallel world, important works of verbal art are also always left in an unfinished, open and potential state. Gary takes the side of those 'baggy monsters' of the nineteenth century – Balzac, Dickens, Dostoevsky, Tolstoy – against the aesthetics of the classical period, oddly resurgent in the narrower ambitions of the 'New Novelists' of his own day. On the broader international front, Gary was far from alone. Grass, Burgess, Bellow, Mailer, Roth are all 'total' novelists in the sense Gary gave to that term, but as they were little known in Paris in 1965, they were not available to back the one-man band that Gary played in *Pour Sganarelle*.

The second repeated argument is that no individual literary work makes any difference to the real world, but that literature, in its totality, nourishes human culture, which really does make a difference to the state of the world. The ideological content of a novel is therefore irrelevant to its role. Gary argues with flashes of brilliance that Albert Camus and Jean-Paul Sartre did not win readers with their ideas, but with their art. Like all true writers, they contributed to culture through their artistry alone. There are incontrovertible examples supporting this view among the great nineteenth-century novelists: Balzac's defence of monarchy and Catholicism, Flaubert's anti-democratic scorn, Dostoevsky's Slavophile propaganda are irrelevant to their literary achievements, and it is because of their art, not because of their now obsolete ideas, that they still have readers and thus contribute to the ocean of our culture today. What's wrong with Socialist Realism and 'Committed Literature' is not that the ideologies they implement are untenable. It's because these literary doctrines are based on a mistaken idea of what literature is.

Good ideas don't improve a bad novel one bit; but most outmoded ideas don't do much harm in the long run to a great work of art. Sartre's position was the exact opposite. Gary was far from alone in thinking it wrong, but one of the very few who dared say so out loud. Understandably, nobody was listening. Sartre had just acquired literary sainthood by *turning down* the Nobel Prize.

V

All of the Above

26

‘The problem is the human race’

Genghis Cohn and *White Dog*, 1966–1970

The two main books that Gary wrote as his marriage to Jean Seberg fell apart are both comical, serious onslaughts on false ideals, and both are hybrid works – half-fiction and half-memoir, written half in English and half in French. *The Dance of Genghis Cohn* uses vulgarity and coruscating wit to defeat the greatest obscenity of twentieth-century history, the slaughter of the Jews by Nazi Germany. *White Dog* uses a different but equally savage kind of humour to mock racism and celebrity culture in America. Both books are meditations on the fearsome consequences of having ideals.

The French and English versions of *The Dance of Genghis Cohn* and *White Dog* are significantly different from each other. In both cases the French appeared first as a published book and the subsequent English ‘translations’ incorporate material drawing on the original reception of the work in French. But the relations between the two versions of each book are not as straightforward as their copyright pages make them seem. The manuscripts of *Genghis Cohn* suggest that Gary began writing this vicious screwball comedy in English, then switched to French halfway through. He had the published French version quickly back-translated by Camilla Sykes, but then rewrote her plain but by no means incompetent version from top to bottom, adding chapters, Yiddish jokes and topical references, including one of the funniest remarks ever made about de Gaulle.[1] The English version of *White Dog* was published in *Life* magazine a few months after the French original was out,[2] but its composition may actually have preceded the drafting of it in French. In both books, however, a third language enriches the mix, for reasons that are amusingly divergent. Genghis Cohn, a Holocaust unsurvivor, quips in Yiddish, naturally enough, seeing he is the ghost of a pre-war Jewish stand-up comedian from an imaginary but perfectly named Warsaw cabaret, the *Schwarze Schickse*. So does the 'real' Jean Seberg, in *White Dog* – because she'd mixed with so many Jewish producers in Hollywood!

Genghis Cohn is the *picaro* that Gary had promoted as the central figure of fiction-writing in *Pour Sganarelle*. This constantly mutating character had first dropped in on *The Ski Bum*, disguised as a wise-cracking member of the high-altitude skiing dropout fraternity. His later adventures in Tahiti are sketched out in a passage of *Pour Sganarelle*, which sets the scene for a later novel, *The Guilty Head*, usually considered a sequel to *The Dance of Genghis Cohn*, but clearly imagined ahead of it.[3] In his star turn, at the centre of *The Dance of Genghis Cohn*, he is of course dead, but this is not a problem for a Jewish picaro. Having dropped his trousers and shown his backside to his Nazi executioner in 1943, Cohn becomes a dybbuk lodged in the psyche of his murderer, a revenant exercising exquisite torture on a man who is now, in 1966, a respectable Commissioner of Police in the Bundesrepublik. With a name that makes him half-Tartar and half-Jew, just as Gary wished himself to be, Genghis Cohn is immortal, irreverent, indelicate, subversive and angry. 'You know what the *ganif* made me sing?' Commissioner Schatz grumbles to his lieutenant, Guth. '*El molorakhim*.'

> 'It's their funeral chant for the dead . . . He was sitting on my bed, his arms crossed, with a terrifying, mad gleam in his eye. After that, he made me sing *Yiddishe Mamme*. The son of a

bitch, he had no tact whatsoever [. . .] Then, just as the night was ending, he jumped from the bed, forced me to my knees, and made me recite the *Kaddish* . . . In my own house, in a nice German neighbourhood! Real *hutzpeh*, I call it. *Tfou, tfou, tfou.*' [. . .]

'On your knees?' repeats Guth. 'He made you recite the *Kaddish* on your knees? That's odd. I thought Jews didn't go down on their knees to pray.'

Schatz looks around suspiciously and lowers his voice. '*We made them kneel*' he mutters in a confidential tone . . . [4]

The French version of the novel is dated 'Warsaw, 1966' but as it incorporates references to the *Sunday Times* of 16 October 1966, Warsaw, which Gary visited in March of that year, must be reckoned the place where the idea for the novel arose, not the place where it was written. It is also the place where the French version ends, in an alarming breakdown of the boundaries between fiction, dream, memoir and report. The former *Hauptjudenfresser* Schatz has begun to wonder if his own persecution by the ghost of a murdered Jew was not the real story at all. What if he were himself a figment of Cohn's imagination? More likely, they are both dybbuks living in the mind of a novelist, who is preparing to evacuate them both by writing a book . . . Are they all just part of therapeutic exercise? At this point the novelist himself appears on the scene, and passes out in front of the Warsaw memorial to the Ghetto Uprising. As he comes round, he swears in Polish: *kurwa mac!* 'We didn't know your husband spoke the language of Mickiewicz,' says a passer-by. 'He studied humanities here, in the ghetto . . .' says Jean Seberg, who actually was in Warsaw with Gary in real life as well as in this passage.

'Ah! We didn't know he was a Jew . . .!'

'Nor did he.'[5]

This framing tailpiece, which is entirely missing from the English-language version of the text, makes Gary's pioneering and excessive Holocaust comedy easy enough to categorise in French. It becomes a novel of the rediscovery of roots, one of the earliest examples of the 'return to Jewishness' or the 'return of the repressed' that became such a marked feature of memoir and fiction writing in France in the following years, starting almost immediately, with Patrick Modiano's *La Place de l'Étoile* (1968).[6] It is also one of the major pegs on which Myriam Anissimov hangs her highly focused life of Gary as a 'shameful Jew', to the exclusion of all his other contradictory identities. But as this passage is by Gary, not by an Elie Wiesel or a self-analytical Perec, the writer's rediscovery of Jewish identity is constructed out of almost entirely imaginary facts.

Gary probably did not visit the memorial to the Ghetto Uprising in 1966. He certainly did not do so in the company of his Orbis tour guide, Jolanta Sell, whose real task (as a functionary of the Ministry of Culture) was to keep close watch on distinguished foreign visitors at all times.[7] She did accompany Gary and Seberg to the Warsaw Historical Museum, which contains many photographs of the ghetto, its destruction and of the persecution of the Jews. But Comrade Sell's distinguished visitor neither fainted, nor wept, nor broke out in Polish curses.[8]

And of course Gary did not do his baccalaureate in the ghetto either: he went to the Kreczmar Gymnasium, in a different part of town. It is also untrue that Gary had been unaware of being Jewish prior to his encounter with the Holocaust in Warsaw in 1966. The transcribed Hebrew prayers in *A European Education* (1944), the farcical plot of *Tulipe* (1946), the whole plot of *The Company of Men* (1949), the character of La Marne in *The Colours of the Day* (1951) and the figure of Abe Fields in *The Roots of Heaven* (1956) all betray a sensitivity to the situation of Jews and to the meaning of the Holocaust that is quite incompatible with any notion of his having ever suppressed his self-identification as a Jew.

The 'return of Jewishness' at the end of *The Dance of Genghis*

Cohn is better understood not as a personal confession but as a strategic move. Gary had remarkable antennae that picked up the trend and direction of current affairs, and the intensity of his pursuit of imaginary truths makes him seem, at times, like an old-fashioned prophet. In the early months of 1967, as Gary rewrote his first English draft into French, the situation in the Middle East was growing ever more tense. By April, Egypt's Nasser was making terrifying threats and proposed to close the Straits of Tiran, so as to cut off Israel's access to the Red Sea. The likelihood of war grew greater every day. De Gaulle warned Israel not to attack first. Many otherwise thoroughly assimilated French Jews, notably Raymond Aron, wrote passionately on the meaning that Israel had suddenly come to hold for them. De Gaulle, who had presided over an explicitly pro-Israeli policy up to that date (Israel was equipped with French warships, Mirage jets, and AMX tanks), suddenly changed course and, by suspending arms shipments to both sides, effectively cut off Israel's military supplies. It is precisely at this point that Gary's novel appeared – about two weeks before the outbreak of the Six-Day War. Whatever the result of Israel's rapid victory on the situation in the Middle East, it had a galvanising effect in France. Pro-Jewish and pro-Israeli sentiment was widespread and passionate; mistrust of de Gaulle grew exponentially; and many dejudaised French Jews suddenly found themselves drawn back into a Jewish identity.[9]

The Dance of Genghis Cohn is neither a response to this situation nor a major factor in its emergence. It is an uncannily timely work, just a few weeks ahead of the event that made it topical – and also highly unfashionable. The mood of pro-Israeli, anti-Arab sentiment on the French left, which for a short while was indistinguishable from opposition to de Gaulle, made *The Dance of Genghis Cohn* seem an utterly tasteless, marginally anti-Semitic work. Making fun of the Holocaust was not allowed. According to *L'Express*, it was even 'an affront to the memory of those who died at Auschwitz'. Gary the indefectible Gaullist could not have chosen a better way to provoke an outpouring of hypocritical balderdash. He should have rejoiced at the way the French public proved his point about the lingering inheritance of anti-Semitism. Yet he felt offended by the hostility that his perfectly aimed squib aroused. The same kind of reaction spoiled his pleasure at the immense success of his later pseudonymous fiction, *Life Before Us*, 'that racist and anti-Semitic work as it has been called by people who can't tell racism and anti-Semitism when they see it because it's the air they breathe and you never notice your own bad smell'.[10]

On the literary level, *The Dance of Genghis Cohn* is a not entirely happy marriage of two plots. The more successful is the satire of undying anti-Semitism in supposedly denazified post-war Germany, where Gary had never been. It's in that part of the text that he scores all his direct hits with outrageously unfair witticisms at the expense of Schatz and his staff. 'The office is very clean: my friend has an obsession about cleanliness,' dybbuk Cohn tells us.

> He's constantly washing his hands: a nervous tic. He's even had a little sink installed under the official portrait of President Lübke. Every few minutes or so he gets up to make his ablutions. He uses a special powder for this. Never soap. Schatzchen has a real phobia about soap. He says some of the old wartime soaps are still around and you never know with whom you are dealing.[11]

The second level of the novel is a fantastical and allegorical tale about a series of unexplained murders, which Schatz is responsible for solving. The victims are all found with their trousers round their ankles and an expression of beatific bliss on their face. They have all been trying to satisfy Lily, the missing wife of a cartoonish aristocrat, who serves perhaps too explicitly as the figure of the Ideal, accompanied as she is by the gamekeeper Florian, who is Death. This second tier of narrative allows Gary to express his scorn for all attempts to serve transcendent ideals through art or war, while at the same time purporting to demonstrate the inevitability of man's quest to satisfy a higher calling. But the fantastical, exaggerated, cruel humour of Genghis Cohn at the expense of Nazis old and young and, it must be added, at the expense of Germans and Germany, is utterly precise.

In November 1967 de Gaulle gave a press conference where he talked of a whole range of issues, including, notoriously, the Middle East. When he referred to the Jews (not the Israelis) as 'a people of the elite, domineering and self-assured',[12] he unleashed a wave of panic among French Jews, who heard in the vocabulary of this throwaway subordinate clause the resurgence of the language of pre-war anti-Semitism. Raymond Aron was pitiless in his analysis of de Gaulle's gaffe and launched a passionate attack on him.[13] In his English re-creation of *The Dance of Genghis Cohn*, Gary could not refuse the gift his erstwhile leader had just given him. 'I've had my hour of fame and my minute of silence,' an exasperated Cohn declares. 'Even de Gaulle has called me his equal, or, in his own words: "A people of the elite, self-assured and domineering". He seems to have somewhat confused Auschwitz with Austerlitz.'[14]

It is not really surprising that the English *Genghis Cohn* had a better reception in the USA and Britain (and also Israel) than the French original did in France.[15] In fact, it quickly became one of Gary's greatest critical and commercial successes, and many of its witty jibes in semi-Yiddish have stuck in readers' minds, and in the language:

> 'Can you image?' mutters Schatz. '*Kush mir im tokhes*! Real *hutzpeh*!'
>
> There is a moment of silence.

'I didn't know you spoke Yiddish,' says Guth.

The Commissioner seems thunderstruck. 'Did I speak Yiddish?'

'That's what it sounded like to me.'

'*Gott in Himmler!*' says Schatz.[16]

But just as Yiddish haunts the German language as the absent Jews haunt post-war Germany, so other, perhaps strangely familiar, ghosts haunt Romain Gary.[17] One obviously repeated image in this moral farce is the photograph of a Jew having his beard tugged by laughing German soldiers. It appears to be a memory of a well-known photograph taken in 1939 at the time of the initial German occupation of Warsaw. 'And what do you think the Hasidic Jew is doing while being pulled by the beard, standing there all alone among the laughing, humorous German soldiers? *He is laughing too*.'[18]

'Plucking the Jew'. Warsaw, September 1939

Well, he isn't laughing and he is not a Hasid but a student, wearing a *Polish* student's cap. What was in Gary's memory is not this photograph, in fact, but a parody of it – from Ernst Lubitsch's anti-German comedy film, *To Be or Not To Be*, the first 'Holocaust comedy', scripted before the Final Solution had even been invented. Similarly, Gary's various evocations of Jewish survivors' hands reaching up from the sewers through the gratings in Nalewki Street are not based on historical records or even on Andrzej Wajda's harrowing film of the Ghetto Uprising, *Kanal* – but borrowed from Carol Reed's *The Third Man*, which has nothing to do with the Holocaust at all. Literature is not like *haute cuisine*. The result does not depend on the authenticity of the ingredients from which it is made.

De Gaulle's contentious phrase about Jews in November 1967 prompted the most interesting use Gary ever made of his self-image as a chameleon. In *A Quiet Night*, Gary mentions de Gaulle's gaffe which, he says, was really flattering.

> Because after all, France has been an elite nation, self-assured and dominating through the thousand years of its history and I said so moreover on radio without causing the slightest offence. But when the old man dropped his clanger, the 'disparate elements' I'm made of clashed with each other, and one of them, the Jewish element, required some clarification from the others. I went to see De Gaulle, on behalf of my 'disparate elements'. I said: '*Mon général*, there was once a chameleon and when you put him on green, he turned green, when you put him on blue, he turned blue, when you put him on chocolate he turned chocolate and then he was put on a tartan and he exploded. So, may I ask you to explain what you mean by "the Jewish people" and whether that means French Jews belong to a different people from ours?' He raised his arms to heaven and said: 'But Romain Gary, when one talks of "the Jewish people" one always means the Biblical kind.' He's a crafty one.[19]

It isn't likely that this interview ever took place. The fabricated anecdote could therefore be taken to mean that Gary's Jewish identity was fundamental to him. If wounded, then the 'chameleon', the 'man of many parts', might fall to pieces.

Although she does not use this anecdote, Anissimov pursues just such a reading of Gary throughout the nine hundred pages of her biography of the writer. The parable of the 'exploding chameleon' should, however, be read more sympathetically, and in conjunction with many other declarations by Romain Gary on the issue of identity and self. He firmly believed it was possible to be many things, to have many parts and to lead several lives. He was Jewish and French and Russian and Polish and a hero and a charlatan too. What raised his ire in de Gaulle's remark was that it implied that being Jewish was different from being a Frenchman, that the two categories, Jew and French, did not truly overlap. (It's a tendentious interpretation of de Gaulle's words, but that is how it was read at the time.) Gary invented his story of a challenge to the President to obtain reassurance that he could be not just a Jew, but a Frenchman as well, one hundred per cent. In his 'Letter to the Jews of France', written in 1970, Gary insisted that French Jews had the right to be completely French: 'being French' necessarily included the right to be pro-Israeli, pro-Palestinian, a penguin lover or a vegetarian, an Auvergnat or a torero. He was particularly scathing about 'moderates' and 'pragmatists' who urged Jews to keep a low profile in the wake of the Six Day War and not flaunt their support for Israel lest it provoke a new outburst of French anti-Semitism. 'To require an Arab, a Jew or a Black to modify his behaviour one way or another because of racism is a racist act.'[20] In fact, the 'chameleon' never exploded and Gary was never reduced to being anything so simple as a Jew. After the adventure of Free France, if not earlier on in his life, he was never ashamed of being Jewish. He also gave his chameleon parable a new skin from time to time: 'On a red carpet it turns red, on a blue carpet it turns blue, on a yellow carpet it turns yellow, and on a Scottish kilt, it turns . . . into a writer!'[21]

White Dog is not a fantasy, but a memoir of Gary's life between March and August 1968, a time during which he was a witness of the Watts riots in Los Angeles after the assassination of Martin Luther King in Memphis on 4 April, and of the student uprising in Paris in May and the triumphant return of de Gaulle in June. It was a busy time, but there is no record, outside this book, of its central narrative: Romain Gary's adoption and retraining of a seven-year-old German shepherd that had been brought up to attack Blacks. The parable is so apt for the expression of Gary's overall view of humanity that the story of Batka the dog could have been invented for him. Unless he invented it himself, which is most likely.

What makes Batka a fearsome problem is not his animal nature, but what humans have taught him. In the novel, Gary hires Jack Carruthers, a real-life animal trainer and zookeeper in Hollywood, to train Batka out of his humanly programmed reflex aggression towards Blacks. After much difficulty, Carruthers's Black assistant, Keys, finally succeeds. But the irony of the parable is that Batka is now reprogrammed – by an angry Black – to attack Whites. The only thing that is wrong with the dog can be laid at the door of humanity. What needs mending is the human dimension of human nature, not its animal side.

The background of the dog story is life with Seberg in the palatial residence Gary had rented in LA, overrun by various groups of militants and, on one spectacularly funny occasion, by a recognisable bunch of Hollywood celebrities, all eager to help The Cause and by doing so to help themselves. The narrator 'Gary' is simultaneously enamoured of Jean's aspiration towards doing good and entirely sceptical of her chances, for her celebrity status means that whatever she does only gets her more celebrity. A secondary consequence of her indiscriminate generosity is that it gets her involved with dangerous, criminal and utterly self-seeking men. *White Dog* is in this respect a sad and critical book, exposing the inevitable downward slope on which Seberg was set, and undermining the case for 'solidarity' even while it subscribes sincerely to that ideal.

Gary's sour, well-targeted fight against racial discrimination in *Genghis Cohn* and in *White Dog* asserts and seeks to demonstrate that to treat Jews and Blacks as they deserve, as full members of the human race, means treating them as the selfish, crooked, corrupt and brutal beasts that men and women actually are. Blacks and Jews are ordinary human beings. The problem is not with Blacks, or with Jews. The problem is the human race. What's the solution? To laugh out loud. 'As Montaigne said, laughter is a deeply human characteristic.'[22]

27

'A Mysterious and Astonishing Adventure'

Gros-Câlin, 1972–1974

The birth of Émile Ajar was a consequence, not a cause, of a new novel Gary wrote in 1973. Initially entitled 'La Solitude du Python à Paris' (The Loneliness of the Python in Paris), echoing the assonant title of a modern British classic, Alan Sillitoe's *The Loneliness of the Long-Distance Runner* (1959), it eventually acquired a name proposed by its publisher, Michel Cournot: *Gros-Câlin*. It's French baby-speak for a big hug from Mummy. Gary's suggestion for an English title, 'Big-Hug',[1] doesn't quite work for a British ear; 'Cuddles' would be a plausible alternative. It is a first-person narration – almost a diary – of a thirty-seven-year-old statistician's affection for a pet python that he keeps in his dreary Paris apartment. The hugs he gets are indeed rather large.

The narrator has been encouraged to make a book out of his unusual experience and the diary we read purports to be a treatise on the care of reptiles as domestic pets. This motivation is transparently fictional from the first page, and the novel quickly establishes itself as a story about the pursuit of affection and love. At bottom it is a simple tale of unrequited yearning for the kind of relationship expressed by the arithmetical impossibility of 2 = 1.

What makes *Gros-Câlin* different from other sentimental tales of loneliness or pet care is the language in which it is written. Somewhat like Anthony Burgess's *A Clockwork Orange* (1962), *Gros-Câlin* simulates a non-existent dialect whose peculiarities of vocabulary and syntax create the social, moral and emotional plight that is its true subject.

Crushed by solitude in the great city ('Outer Paris', with its ten million 'inhibitants'), obsessed by his need for companionship, Cousin takes timid, fearful steps towards a Black girl who works in his office in a leather miniskirt and thigh boots. By the time he's ready to invite her out with a spray of violets in a little jar (difficulties with word order are among the many springs of Ajar's linguistic charm), Mademoiselle Dreyfus has resigned her job and disappeared, allegedly to return to French Guyana. The distraught aspirant is thrown into ever greater entanglements with his pet python and goes to a brothel for relief. The manageress of the establishment – 'Madam Superior' – parades her new girls to allow Cousin to make a democratic choice, but lo and behold, the last of the line, and the most desirable by far, is Mademoiselle Dreyfus herself. An hour's joy is followed by a terminal confusion of man and reptile. Cousin, whose language defines him from the start as distinctly peculiar, goes completely insane.

Gary often said that for him, writing was 'just another way of bawling', and in *Gros-Câlin*, under the cover of linguistic invention, he bawls about his own plight after the collapse of his relationship with Jean. The book could not have been written except by a man deeply affected by loneliness and the absence of love. On the other hand it is so mercilessly comical about its own unbalanced protagonist that it could not have been written by a self-pitying depressive either. Sentimental and savage in equal measure, *Gros-Câlin* dances on the fine line between laughter and tears.

The name finally chosen for the protagonist is far from arbitrary. Pavlowitch observes that the hero of Svevo's *Confessions of Zeno* is called Cosini – but Gary assured him that he only read Svevo after writing *Gros-Câlin*.[2] Because Pavlowitch, who was Gary's cousin (more precisely, the son of his cousin Dinah), came to play the role of Ajar in public later on, and because this first-person narration was taken (briefly) to be an autobiographical account of the life of its 'author', the name 'Cousin' was seen for a time as one of Gary's sly provocations about the true authorship of the book. But that is unlikely. Gary's invention of the name probably has a literary rather than a personal source.

'Cousin' is a metonym of 'brother' (the masculine form of the noun makes this more obvious in French than in English) – and to a reader or writer steeped in Russian culture, as Gary was, 'Brother' echoes with meaning. Akaky Akakievitch, the central character of Nikolai Gogol's short story, 'The Overcoat', is a pathetic, inadequate, mouse-like clerk in St Petersburg (Cousin's job as a statistician in the French civil service is just an updating of the clerkly function), and he is mercilessly ragged by his superiors and colleagues:

> It was only when the jokes became too unbearable . . . that [Akaky] would say, 'Leave me alone! Why do you insult me?' and there was something touching in his words . . . so that one young man . . . who, following the example of the rest, had allowed himself to tease him, suddenly stopped as though cut to the heart . . . Some unseen force seemed to repel him from the companions . . . and long afterwards . . . the figure of the humble little clerk with the bald patch on his head appeared before him with these heart-rending words, 'Leave me alone! Why do you insult me?' and within these moving words he heard others: 'I am your brother.' And the poor young man hid his face in his hand; and many times afterward in his life he shuddered, seeing how much inhumanity there is in man . . .[3]

'I am your brother' – я ваш брат – is a line that has been appropriated by infinitely many social and literary causes, and under the disguise of 'cousin' it lends Gary's *Gros-Câlin* a moving memory of Gogol's protest against the 'inhumanity in man'. Cousin *is* our brother in his loneliness and yearning, but he is also engaged in a comical but thoughtful response to another, equally well-known story from Gogol's *Petersburg Tales*.

The basic plot of *Gros-Câlin* is borrowed from 'The Diary of a Madman'. Poprishchin, the narrator, is a lonely clerk who becomes entranced by his boss's daughter. Her inaccessibility drives the diarist into delusions. He discovers correspondence between her pet dogs and overhears them talking about him. Poprishchin's descent into lunacy is marked by the increasing incoherence of the dates of his diary entries (43rd April, 86th Martober . . .), and he is finally taken off when he believes he has become the King of Spain. At the asylum, which he takes to be the court in Madrid, he sees at last his own resurrection, and that of Russia herself, in the form of a winged troika rising and flying over the little *izba* with his mother looking out of the window . . . As submitted to the Mercure de France in 1973, Ajar's *Gros-Câlin* also ends in a resurrection: Cousin is cheered at the Science Museum by crowds who take pity on him at last, as he manages to utter the words: *Je . . . vous . . . aime . . .* This last chapter was cut by the publishers, who felt it added nothing to the comical and poignant story already told. It has taken more than forty years to get it into print.[4]

At the start of *White Dog*, Gary mentions that on a trip to Colombia (when Jean was shooting *Estouffade à la Caraïbe*) he acquired a twenty-three-foot-long python, dubbed 'Pete the Strangler', which he later donated to Jack Carruthers's exotic animal farm near Los Angeles. He often went back to commune with it through the wire of its cage.

> I would go in, squat on the pebbles, and face the other creature. We would stare at each other in absolute astonishment,

> often for hours, deeply intrigued and wondering, awed and yet incapable of giving each other any kind of explanation about what had happened to us, and how and why it had happened, unable to help each other with some small flash of understanding drawn from our respective experiences. To find yourself in the skin of a python or in that of a man is such a mysterious and astonishing adventure that the bewilderment we shared had become a kind of fraternity, a brotherhood beyond and above our respective species.[5]

Gros-Câlin explores the paradox of 'Pete'. Seeing yourself in another is narcissism, whether the other is a woman or a poodle, yet love is the drive to unite with something or someone who is not you. As nobody can ever actually know what it is like to be another (to be a python, or just someone else), love is at best an aspiration and a loved one is always inaccessible. A relationship between man and reptile simply takes the human condition to an illustrative extreme; in his very eccentricity Michel Cousin is Everyman. Gary evades the conclusion that loneliness is the necessary and tragic condition of the individual by insisting that there is something really hopeful about the inaccessibility of difference. What's expressed in the eyes of a snake is incommensurable with what a human being can feel. That confirms the existence of something we do not yet know, and we should not jump to the (narcissistic) conclusion that it is of no interest, or no better than what we already know about life. The incomprehensibility of otherness is a reason for hanging on to hope.

Cousin, a statistician, is naturally given to playing with numbers, but the arithmetic of his diary confession has a literary rather than a mathematical source. The narrator of Dostoevsky's *Notes from the Underground* rails against the limits and constraints of human life by arguing that 'freedom' ought to mean being free to disagree with the proposition that 2 + 2 = 4. Like the Crystal Palace and *l'homme de la nature et de la vérité*, the rigidity of arithmetic is an affront to the limitless perversity of human nature. The Underground Man wants to be free to make 2 + 2 equal anything he likes. What Cousin-Ajar aspires to is the impossible arithmetic of 2 = 1. So what he needs is for 'impossibility' to be abolished.

> *J'attends la fin de l'impossible. Nous avons tous et depuis si longtemps une enfance malheureuse.*[6]
>
> I'm waiting for the end of the impossible. We all had an unhappy childhood, from way back.

This expression of Gary's aspiration to a state beyond the common lot of humanity is closely entwined with two idioms of standard French, taken from the common stock of clichés that his mother respected and revered. To urge a sweating cyclist up the last hundred metres of the Col du Tourmalet, you can remind him or her that *impossible n'est pas français!* just as you would say, 'An Englishman Never Gives Up!' But if you take the expression not metaphorically, but metalinguistically, as '*Impossible* is not [a] French [word]', you have an interesting problem. You can no longer say 'impossible' in French, and yet the impossible remains the issue you want to overcome. So you give up speaking French? That's what Michel Cousin does in the charming, crazy, comically contorted syntax and vocabulary of *Gros-Câlin*. A pale English simulation of the second paragraph of the novel would go something like this:

> I should mention at this point that a large part of Africa is French-speaking and that famous works by scientists have shown that that's where pythons come from. I must therefore beg pardon for the mutilant abusages, insubordinations, boomerangs, jacks-in-the-box, sideswipes, squints and illegal immigrants that may be found in the language, syntax and vocabulary of the present work. What's at stake is hope, pots of gold over the rainbow at rock-bottom crises. It would sadden

> me greatly if I were to be bullnosed into using words and forms that had already been doing the rounds and failing to find a way out.

Like the proverbs and folk wisdom of any language, *impossible n'est pas français* goes with another French saying that has the opposite meaning: *à l'impossible nul n'est tenu* (nobody is required to do the impossible). Well, Gary did do the impossible – he juggled five apples, became an air force hero, an 'Ambassador' and Victor Hugo. Therefore he *was* the nobody who was required to do the impossible. Treating the metaphorical expressions in these proverbs as statements about the meanings of words makes sense of Gary's imaginative self-identification with characters like Gustave Vanderputte, a 'nobody' inside someone else's overcoat, or Lenny, the monosyllabic ski bum. With equal, irresistible and insane logic, these authorless truisms from the manual of French idioms mean Gary can be *anyone*.

Gros-Câlin is therefore not so much a new departure in Gary's thinking as a mature recombination of the themes and materials out of which all his work is made. Yet the degree of its linguistic inventiveness makes it not instantly recognisable as just another version of his standard wail on behalf of humanity. Although the main features of 'Ajarspeak' are not without precedent in Gary's writing, or in the French tradition, the particular dosage of each – and their combination within a work of moral seriousness – is quite unique.[7] Some of them play on the intrinsic features of French words, such as spelling and sound. There are puns for the eye: *dix millions d'usagés*, for *usagers* ('ten million second-hand items' for 'ten million users' of public transport); *dans mon fort intérieur*, for *for intérieur* ('in my inner fortress' for 'in my heart of hearts'). There are puns for the ear: *à des cris défiant toute concurrence* instead of *à des prix défiant toute concurrence* ('unbeatable crises' instead of 'never knowingly undersold'). There are many delightful malapropisms, such as *prénaturé* for *prématuré* ('pre-natural' for 'premature'). Gary-Ajar also plays with the technique of a children's word-association skipping-rhyme game, where the last syllable of a word (always stressed in French) is used as the first syllable of a completely different expression,[8] giving the comical sequence of *sans autre forme de procès de Jeanne d'Arc* (an overlap between *sans autre forme de procès,* ('without more ado') and *le procès de Jeanne d'Arc*, ('the trial of Joan of Arc'). To think of this inscription of Jean Seberg's first screen role in a work that laments the absence of her love as a merely coincidental effect of a childish punning game would be to mistake the nature of Gary's verbal art.

The idea of creating a new author also has long roots in Gary's past, but his previous attempts at self-invention as Jack Ribbons and Fosco Sinibaldi had come to not very much. Part of the reason for those failures was that there was nothing new in the works cooked up solely for the purposes of a literary joke. But as he wrote *Gros-Câlin* in the spring and summer of 1973, Romain Gary realised that his 'diary of a nobody' was well-suited to achieving the plan he had laid out in *Pour Sganarelle* to make the author the child of the work and not the other way round. The plot he invented carried a major risk of failure, and the most remarkable thing about it – full of significance for our understanding of literature and what Pierre Bourdieu dubs 'the literary field'[9] – is that it did not fall flat on its face.

In *Life and Death of Émile Ajar*, the testament Gary penned in March 1979, the writer claims that his main motivation for adopting another pseudonym was to make fools of the critics. He was fed up with being categorised and disregarded as 'Romain Gary'. He wanted to prove to the world that journalists and publishers are lazy, do not read the texts they review or select, and rely on prejudice and gossip for the opinions they impose on the community. But his comprehensible urge to get his own back on the chattering class is not what made him write the first Ajar novel, or to write it the way he did.

> It was only after I had finished *Gros-Câlin* that I decided to publish the book under a pseudonym, without telling the publisher. I felt that there was an incompatibility between the notoriety, the weights and measures, according to which my work was judged, 'the image I had been saddled with', and the innermost nature of my book.[10]

Pseudonymous writers and performers are ten a penny. Molière, Stendhal, Apollinaire and Jules Romains were really called something else; Joyce Carol Oates and Ruth Rendell write under different names for different works; Erich Kästner was also Berthold Bürger, Melchior Kurtz, Peter Flint and Robert Neuner; Jacques Tati, Charlie Chaplin, Edith Piaf and Stan Laurel, too, are all stage names. Using a pseudonym and keeping the *identity* of the real author out of the public domain is rarer but not without many precedents: the novelist Julien Gracq carried on teaching history at high school as Monsieur Poirier with very few of his students knowing he had won the Goncourt Prize. But writing under a pseudonym and *not telling the publisher* who the real writer is takes imposture into an altogether different sphere. Not only is it almost impossible to pull off, but in the unlikely event of success, it raises tricky issues about the ownership of copyright, not to mention the questionable legality of signing a contract with a false name.

Part of the linguistic texture of *Gros-Câlin* is clearly designed to provide internal authentification of Gary's authorship (and ownership) of the text. Maybe these touches were added after completion of the first draft, as would need to be the case if Gary's account of the birth of Émile Ajar quoted above is to be taken at face value. But it seems more likely that these features, designed for a practical, not a literary, purpose, were part and parcel of the conception of the text from an early stage.

Gros-Câlin is studded with hidden borrowings from other languages. The more visible imports come from English, in line with a long tradition of French linguistic humour, but Gary adds a special twist by getting either the English or the French wrong: he writes *atractive*, uses *convénient* in the English sense of 'convenient', and invents a false etymology of the word *prologomène* to make it mean a 'prologue' to 'men'. But alongside the flaunting of faulty English, Gary introduces a professional bleeding heart and petition-signer, Professor Tsoures, whose name means 'worries' in Yiddish, and a Polish dentist called Burak, meaning 'beetroot'.[11] He introduces himself to the narrator:

'Burak, Polish. I'm a dentist but wanted to be a conductor.'

'Nobody understands you better than I do . . .'[12]

Taken together with the numerous self-quotations – such as '*un homme avec personne dedans*' (a man with nobody inside), from *The Company of Men* – and flagrant allusions to the use of alternative identities and foreign languages – '*j'aspire à une langue étrangère*,' says Cousin (I aspire to a foreign tongue) – the presence of Polish, Yiddish and English in a French novel based on a Russian classic adds up to Gary's authenticating personal signature inside the text. If all evidence of Gary's invention of the Ajar mystification had come to be destroyed, it would still be possible to prove without a shadow of a doubt that the only person who could possibly have written *Gros-Câlin* was the former French Consul General in Los Angeles. Many other people speak English, or Polish, or Russian, or Yiddish and write well in French. But nobody wrote in French with witty ease and could also use English, Polish, Russian and Yiddish together at the same time – except Romain Gary. Obvious, when you think about it.

The plot to deceive Gallimard required an accomplice. Gary chose an acquaintance, Pierre Michaut, a French businessman with interests in Brazil, where he frequently went, to perform the first step in the deception. Michaut barged his way into the office of Robert Gallimard to hand him a packet that he claimed to have brought back from one of his frequent trips to Rio. It contained a manuscript by an unknown French writer who for legal reasons was unable to use his real name and unable also to return to France. In other words, 'Émile Ajar' was designed from the start to be treated as a pseudonym – but as the pen-name of *someone else*. The trick, the exploit, the pinnacle of a writer's achievement as projected in *Pour Sganarelle* would be to give that someone else a real – that is to say, legendary – life.

The publisher read a page or two and decided it was worth following the usual procedures for unsolicited manuscripts. He had it sent out to a reader. Next day he got some kind of an invitation to call on Romain Gary in his flat at 108 Rue du Bac. Gary was in the lounge with another man he had seen before but could not quite recall. 'Don't you recognise this gentleman?' Gary asked his old friend, pointing to Pierre Michaut.

> 'Romain! Don't tell me you played *that* trick on me . . .'
>
> 'Yes I did! And now you know, you're going to give me your word of honour that you'll never breathe a word of it to anyone!'[13]

Robert kept his word, as did the handful of other people who were 'in the know' – Gary's typist, Martine Carré, his ex-wife Jean and his son Diego, his lawyers and his cousin Paul Pavlowitch. As for the novel, it went out to one of the firm's team of 'screeners', who collectively deal with up to three thousand unsolicited manuscripts each year. Publishers' readers can tell after only a few pages whether they've got something worthwhile in front of them and they fill in their report forms with impressive speed, especially as they're paid at piece rate.

Gallimard's forms used a grading system: 1, for 'can be published as is'; 2, for 'interesting but not publishable'; and 3, for 'no interest'. Subdivisions of '1' are used to indicate how much editing would be needed to bring the work up to standard. Well-organised as it is, the screening process is a fairly blunt instrument for picking grains of wheat out of bushels of chaff. Gary's first reader could easily have missed *Gros-Câlin*. After all, no more than one or two of the two or three hundred new novels published in Paris each year begin life as unsolicited manuscripts sent in by a person unknown. The statistical chances of the story of the lonely number cruncher and his pet snake getting into print were several thousand to one against. Gary had the luck of the devil. His reader was Christiane Baroche, an insomniac scientist who went on to become head of a biological research laboratory and a distinguished writer to boot. She noticed straight away that she had something out of the ordinary on her late-night desk.

> I laughed, I grinned, tears came to my eyes, my heart was touched . . . In a word, I engaged with this novel in the way we're all engaged with human nature, which is as it should be . . . This book has a life of its own. To sum up: it's good for press.[14]

She gave it a grade of 1, with only one reservation: that the last twenty pages or so were not of the same quality as the rest.[15] Gary's novel – still called 'La Solitude du python à Paris', by Émile Ajar – went on for second reading by members of the firm's editorial panel, and for discussion and decision at their next meeting. Claude Faraggi and Colette Duhamel, the two panel members asked to write independent reader reports, agreed with Baroche that the book was publishable, but with rather less enthusiasm than she. However, Raymond Queneau, who chaired the panel and was in effective control of Gallimard's poetry and fiction lists, smelled a rat. The unknown author seemed to him to be engaged in pastiche and he saw in the book some kind of 'meeting point' of Ionesco, Céline, Roger Nimier and Boris Vian – that's to say, in simplified terms, a hotchpotch of absurdism, anger, sentimentality and linguistic playfulness. For all his literary erudition, Queneau didn't spot the references to Gogol and Dostoevsky; but he probably also thought that 'Ajar' was taking a poke at his own *Zazie dans le métro*, which, too, uses wrong spellings, solecisms, malapropisms and rough logic with great artistry and wit. The author, he surmised in his own reading note, 'seems pretty cocksure of himself and must be a pain in the ass. He's only a camp-follower, but, at that level, he's got definite talent. What will he write next? *That is the question*.'[16] He would not agree to having *Gros-Câlin* on his own list, but given its quality, he agreed to have the submission passed on to a wholly owned subsidiary of Gallimard, Mercure de France, run by Simone Gallimard, the ex-wife of his own CEO, Claude.

Gary knew from his friend Robert Gallimard that the family firm had decided not to publish Ajar but had passed it down the line to Mercure de France, so he called on Pierre Michaut to set Plan B into action. The businessman managed to bump into the brother of the man in charge of the literature list at Mercure de France, and told him that he'd brought back from Brazil a really interesting manuscript that Gallimard had considered but turned down. The bait was taken, one brother rang the other and the editor rang the number he had been given (Michaut's number) to find out more. Within a day, he had the manuscript of 'La Solitude du python à Paris' on his desk and plunged into it. He was so struck by the text that he rang Simone Gallimard at her country residence and insisted she read it as well.

This is how Ajar's 'breakthrough' occurred in the memory of Michel Cournot, a cinema critic and fiction writer who was at that time editorial director of the fiction list at Mercure de France.[17] According to Anissimov, however, Cournot was first alerted to the interest of the manuscript by his boss, Simone Gallimard, who had had her elbow nudged by Robert, Gary's friend and sole confidant of the hoax outside Gary's family circle. It doesn't really matter which version you believe. It is quite possible that Cournot discovered the brilliance and charm of Émile Ajar independently, without the benefit of the reading notes by Christiane Baroche, Claude Farragi, Colette Duhamel and Raymond Queneau; and quite possible also that Simone was alerted to the quality of this new text by both Robert Gallimard and Cournot. It's more than likely that Gary gave himself two throws of the dice to win an unlikely victory of an almost indescribably delicious kind.

Robert Escarpit once argued that there are no 'undiscovered masterpieces' rejected by incompetent publishers, because 'masterpiece' can only be defined as a work that has proved its ability to speak to a wide audience over a period of time.[18] The argument is circular and unconvincing, but it is probably true that among the huge mass of unpublished manuscripts there are few that are any good, seeing that only a minute proportion of the novels that make it into print ever gain more than a few hundred readers. But anything can happen. Gary's success in getting his python novel through the net could be taken to prove Escarpit's point that quality will out. But it could also be taken as a game Gary was playing without any stakes. In the case of rejection, which was by far the most likely outcome, he could have had endless fun embarrassing Gallimard for failing to recognise the style of one of its house authors. A rejection slip would have proved one of the points Gary later claimed to have been the object of the Ajar invention: to show that the literary world of Paris categorises works by the name of their presumed authors, without paying serious attention to what is in them. What made the deception innocent fun at this initial stage was that Gary couldn't lose. But it is clear that he had not yet bothered to work out how he would manage success.

Gary had his secretary Martine Carré and Pierre Michaut sign confidentiality agreements that were almost certainly unenforceable in law, but which could serve as protection if the whole deception backfired and his actual authorship of Émile Ajar came to be disputed. The 'affair', as it has come to be called, rested on a fundamental ambiguity. Gary wanted to create himself anew, as Émile Ajar, and to that end he did everything he could to cover up the fact that he had written Ajar's book. On the other hand he did not want to lose an iota of his *ownership* of Ajar's work and to that end he did all he could to document the fact that he had written it. You could call it just plain business sense. Or else see in it a dramatic demonstration of the universal duality of a writer's relationship to his work. It must live a life of its own; once put into the public space, it doesn't belong to the author any more, but to the reading public; but it is also, always, *my* creation and belongs to no one else. However, the main character of *Gros-Câlin* was its author, Émile Ajar, and that gave an unprecedented twist to what is otherwise an ordinary authorial plight. The set-up of the Ajar affair turned a conventional aesthetic and emotional issue into a commercial, legal and personal dilemma for Romain Gary. And it was handled in a way that turned an intoxicating prank into a dreadful nightmare over the following four years.

The name that Gary chose for his self-invention bears the mark of his ambiguity about the nature of the exercise. 'Émile' harks back to a classic of German children's literature, Erich Kästner's *Emil and the Detectives*, and suggests there is a mystery to solve;[19] 'Ajar' tells you that the door is half open (see p. 170 for other, less plausible, interpretations of the name), which indeed it is, through the polyglot jokes and the numerous self-quotations and internal allusions that authenticate Gary's authorship of the text.

'La Solitude du python à Paris' was finished in first draft in the summer of 1973 and was typed up by Martine Carré in the autumn of that year. It was submitted to Gallimard by means of the hoax described in late December, with a covering note signed 'Émile Ajar' addressed to Pierre Michaut, purporting to have been written in Rio de Janeiro on 20 December 1973. By 13 February 1974 Gallimard let 'Ajar' know – by a letter from Robert Gallimard to Pierre Michaut – that they had decided not to publish and had passed the typescript on to Mercure de France. Cournot let 'Ajar' know, via postbox Michaut, that Mercure was indeed keen to publish, subject to amendments, including especially the omission of the whole last part of the story. Gary-Ajar could not behave as anything other than the novice writer he was pretending to be, and he therefore signalled his acceptance of the proposed editorial cuts in another forged letter signed Ajar and addressed to Michaut, for onward transmission to Cournot. At this stage – March 1974 – Gary also accepted a new title, *Gros-Câlin*, as the best of the alternatives that Cournot had proposed for 'La Solitude du python à Paris'. In late April Mercure de France issued a standard book contract, which Gary had signed for him by Jean-Claude Viard, an acquaintance of his cousin Paul Pavlowitch, using the name Émile Ajar.

The several Ajar signatures on the various letters and the contract, in Gary's or another's hand, were all different. Nobody noticed.

So far, so good. Gary had a long-standing contract with Gallimard giving the publisher right of first refusal on all his books. That constraint had been respected: Gallimard had turned down 'La Solitude', leaving Gary free to publish elsewhere. The writer wasn't guilty of serious forgery either, since it was not *he* who had signed the contract with Mercure de France under a false name. The only offence committed so far was the forgery of Ajar's signature *by someone else*.

Gary's new publisher also asked 'Ajar' to fill in an author information sheet. This is what he sent in:

Name:	Raja (Ajar)
Given name:	Émile
Address:	c/o Pierre Michaut, 978 Nascimento Silva Rua, Appt Terreo Ipanema Rio de Janeiro Brazil
Date of birth:	14 February 1940
Place of birth:	Oran (Algeria)
Biography:	Medical school
Photos submitted:	None[20]

Around this time, Gary sent a message to his cousin Paul Pavlowitch to come to see him in Paris. Pavlowitch had known Gary since childhood and had always looked up to his flamboyant and famous cousin with admiration and pride. Gary had on occasions been very generous to him and his wife Annie. He'd let them live rent free in the maids' rooms on the top floor of 108 Rue du Bac for a couple of years; he'd funded the purchase of a set of old farm dwellings near Cahors, where they lived; he'd had them spend summer holidays at Puerto Andraitx and would loan his red Volkswagen to the younger man without a second thought. Pavlowitch had many talents, including nearly all those Gary lacked: he was clever with his hands, good at building and decorating tasks, and was more at ease in the countryside than in town. In fact, he'd spent the previous two years remodelling the tumbledown houses of the 'Gary estate' at Caniac-du-Causse. Neither he nor his wife had stable employment at that time.

When he called at Rue du Bac in April 1974, he found his cousin in Mephistophelian disguise – dressed entirely in black leather, with a clumsily black-dyed beard, and smoking a fat Monte Cristo no. 2 cigar.

Gary closed the double doors and, with a conspiratorial glint in his eye, asked straight off, 'Want to go to Brazil?'

It was an alluring prospect for the younger man. Rio! All he would need to do was to stay at Pierre Michaut's apartment in Ipanema and masquerade as Émile Raja, pseudonym Ajar, when journalists came to interview him. Gary had already cooked up a biography for him, it wasn't very difficult to remember: medical school, then a clandestine abortion operation that went wrong . . . He'd fled to Brazil after the woman died, and written a new novel called *Gros-Câlin* – the jacket design by Folon was already done and on the coffee table.

The Rio deception never happened and nobody met 'Ajar' before the book was published in September 1974. The early reviews of it were excellent, but few critics were completely taken in by the story of a book penned by an exiled French medic hiding under a pseudonym in Brazil. Many thought it must have been penned by a 'real writer', and some flattering names were bandied about as the probable originators of the hoax – Louis Aragon and Raymond Queneau among them. No professional critic suggested Romain Gary. Only Christine Arnothy, a French writer born and brought up in Hungary, where Russian language and literary classics had been obligatory school subjects since 1946, came near to the truth: Ajar, she wrote, had a Czech sense of humour and suffered Russian angst. '*Ajar, c'est Gogol, Ajar, c'est le Pouchkine des ténèbres de Paris . . .*'[21]

The book began to run off the shelves and soon rumour spread that *Gros-Câlin* was likely to be short-listed for the Renaudot Prize, traditionally reserved for a debut writer. Gary's sense of fair play was provoked. Moreover, both his friend Robert Gallimard and his Paris lawyer, Maître Bossat, took the view that the deception had now gone far enough. (Gary also had a lawyer in Geneva and an agent in New York who knew the real identity of Ajar.) He didn't mind hoodwinking the literary establishment in general – that was the whole point –

but he agreed it would be unfair to stop a young writer from winning the prize. (It was won in the end by Georges Borgeaud, who was, ironically, no younger than Romain Gary.) He therefore instructed his publisher to withdraw *Gros-Câlin* from all prize lists in 1974 – but to do so he had to have the instruction issued by Émile Ajar, who had to be someone else. Paul Pavlowitch would be the man. But he didn't need to come on stage yet. The letter to Simone Gallimard instructing her to withdraw the book was signed once again by Pavlowitch's friend Viard.

Pavlowitch himself didn't understand why Gary didn't just blow the story there and then, in October or November 1974. He had scored a tremendous victory, proved all the points that the hoax was designed to make and, in addition, won respect, admiration and a wide new readership for a novel that was deeply personal and absolutely central to his work. Why was Romain ashamed and afraid of saying he had written *Gros-Câlin*? The answer, Pavlowitch says, is buried with the man.[22] But it had also been given ahead of time, by Gary himself, in *Pour Sganarelle*. And it was given again later on, in *Life and Death of Émile Ajar*:

> *It was a new birth. I was renewing myself. Everything was being given to me one more time.* I had the perfect illusion of a new creation of myself, by myself.[23]

28

Belleville Rendezvous

Life Before Us, 1975

'Monsieur Hamil, can somebody live without love?'
'Yes,' he said, and bowed his head in shame. I burst into tears.

Émile Ajar,
Life Before Us, p. 3

The Ajar adventure began as a wonderful hoot and slowly turned into a murky farce. The success of *Gros-Câlin* in autumn 1974, combined with the hidden defeat of an author obliged to excise what must surely have been intended as his last word, spurred Gary on to write another Ajar novel straight away. This time it wouldn't be indebted to Russian classics, but to a much-loved modern French text everybody should know: *Promise at Dawn*, by Romain Gary.

The year 1974 was not just that of Émile Ajar's birth, it was also the one in which the Old Guard of the Free French, the only 'family' to which Gary ever felt he belonged without reservation, lost its hold on power in France. Valéry Giscard d'Estaing, the son of an official of the Vichy regime, was elected President, having squeezed out a Companion of the Liberation, Jacques Chaban-Delmas, for the leadership of the right. OPEC quadrupled the price of a barrel of oil, provoking the first worldwide oil crisis, which also brought to an end thirty years of full employment in France, the period known retrospectively as *les trente glorieuses*. One national aspect of this epochal change was the emergence of 'immigration' as a political issue. Giscard changed France's nationality laws, abolishing the right to French nationality of children born in France of foreign parents (*jus soli*, or *droit du sol*), and he tightened restrictions on immigration to the point of strangulation. Gary realised that if he were to live his life over again as a fourteen-year-old immigrant in 1974 he would be an illegal, without a chance of ever becoming French. As he had never really ceased to be that fourteen-year-old boy, he now acquired a new self-image as a clandestine member of the underclass, despite his grand flat, great wealth and worldwide fame.

In *A Quiet Night*, the fake interview with François Bondy that Gary published in 1974, he'd tried to explain – again – what it had felt like for him to be a Polish-Russian-Jewish immigrant in Nice in 1928 at the age of fourteen. 'I was then, in the south of France, the equivalent of an Algerian today.'[1] Gary didn't know any Algerian teenage immigrants, but his self-identification came from what current affairs made the topical victim class of the day. That is why Gary re-imagined the hero and narrator of *Promise at Dawn* – his *legendary* self – as Momo, a fourteen-year-old Algerian lad living, quite implausibly, in the traditionally Jewish quarter of Belleville.

Life Before Us[2] was written, like its model and predecessor (see p. 294) 'in a kind of frenzy', between December 1974 and March 1975, in alternation with *The Way Out*.[3] Some days Gary wrote as Ajar in the morning and as Gary in the afternoon, and just as easily the other way round. Like *Promise at Dawn*, which was mostly written away from home (in a hotel room in Oaxaca), Ajar's second novel was written in a borrowed room – the guest suite of the palatial residence of Gary's old friend, Roger Agid, brother of René, at Lorgues, on the French Riviera. It was still important for Gary to write *from a distance*, as he had done with his best early work, imagining Paris from the vantage point of Sofia, or New York from London and the

Home Counties from Los Angeles, in *The Company of Men*, *Tulipe* and *Lady L.* respectively. This time, since he was entirely free to decide where to go, he needed an excuse for isolating himself from his material. He hired Paul Pavlowitch to remodel and redecorate his grand apartment in Rue du Bac, which was therefore not habitable for a period of several weeks.

Gary's decision to cast this new-old tale as a first-person narration was both natural (all his best work is written in that voice) and strategic. Émile Ajar could not possibly be both a statistician in his thirties and a fourteen-year-old Algerian at the same time: this proved that his novels were not confessions (just as Arnothy had suspected), but works of imaginative literature. In other words, *Life Before Us* was designed as an answer to the query raised by Queneau on his reading of 'La Solitude du python à Paris': 'What will he write next? *That is the question.*'

The choice of Belleville as a location was made before Gary left Paris to write the book in the south of France. To prepare the work, he asked a friend of Jean's, who was Black, to give him a brief guided tour . . . of a quite different immigrant quarter! Caba took him to the Goutte d'Or, around the Barbès-Rochechouart metro station. They didn't stay there more than a couple of hours, just enough time for Gary to collect what he needed to create the illusion of authenticity in his description of Belleville. Of one thing he could be pretty sure: none of the fourteen-year-old Arab paupers of Goutte d'Or or Belleville was going to read him, or be affected by the missile he was aiming at a quite different target, or audience.

The language of the second Ajar novel is superficially similar to the comically incorrect dialect of the first, but it is rationalised by different means and exploited to a different end. Solecisms, malapropisms, spelling mistakes, misapprehensions about the true meaning of words, and radical ellipses where causes and effects are inverted – all these features, which are common to the two works, now function not as symptoms of an unbalanced mind, but as the speech of an intelligent but woefully undereducated child. *Life Before Us* is therefore a degree more seductive and facile than *Gros-Câlin*, which largely accounts for its even greater appeal to a wide reading public. Almost everyone likes to smile with indulgence at children's linguistic errors. It's almost impossible not to fall into the trap.

The central figure of the new novel is an obese, diabetic, senile ex-tart who has for years been running a clandestine home for the unwanted children of other women of the streets. Madame Rosa is Jewish and she survived deportation to a concentration camp during the Second World War. Warm-hearted, desperate for money, unable to keep order, terrified of the authorities in case they come to arrest her again, subject to lapses of memory and mental vacuity, Madame Rosa comes to rely on Momo to help her through the terminal phase of her life. Teenage Diego recognised her instantly – Madame Rosa was for him a barely masked portrait of his beloved nanny, Eugenia Muñoz Lacasta, who was now an old lady and suffered terribly from the long climb up the service staircase at 108 Rue du Bac. But behind Eugenia another 'original' is clearly visible: Mina Kacewa née Owczynska, in her one and only famous role as mother Nina, in *Promise at Dawn*. One of the child Gary's earliest memories of her, according to that cunningly plotted self-portrait, is of her acting the role of Rosa, in a play significantly titled *The Shipwreck of Hope*[4] – save that there is no character called Rosa in the dramatis personae of *The Shipwreck of Hope*![5]

Like the first Ajar novel, *Life Before Us* contains dozens of subtly hidden and outrageously obvious hints and clues to the identity of its author. The doctor who attends Madame Rosa is called Dr Katz, which is the first half of Gary's birth name, Kacew, when pronounced (as it should be) in Polish. Momo's real father, who turns up on his release from prison after serving his sentence for the murder of Momo's mother, then conveniently drops dead on being told his son has been brought up a Jew (which he hasn't), is called Youssef Kadir, containing the two syllables, *ka-* and *-sef*, of Gary's birth name, Kacew, when pronounced in French (as it often was). The three African brothers who work as removal men and also take Madame Rosa on her last outing (to the Marne, by taxi, in a parody of the exploit of Paris's six hundred Russian taxi drivers in 1914, who drove troops to the front for free to help stop the German advance) are called Zaoum (which is how the French transcribe the Russian word заум) in honour of the 'language without meaning' (*zaumny yazik*) devised by the Russian futurist poets. Momo for his part gives away a pet dog so it can have a better life elsewhere, repeating a plot element from *The Company of Men*, and in another reminiscence of Gary's earlier novel he dresses up an umbrella and calls it 'Arthur'.[6] His Moslem mentor, Monsieur Hamil, tells him about 'clowns dancing in the streets and happy giants sitting on floats' in a town called Nice, which makes Momo 'feel at home'. Readers of *Colours of the Day* might have noticed the connection. Momo also reckons that Jews are very obstinate, 'especially when they've been exterminated; those are the ones who come back most' – which suggests that he'd read *The Dance of Genghis Cohn*.[7]

These are much more than teases and more substantial self-inscriptions than the 'authenticating traces' that Gary left in the language of *Gros-Câlin*. They are provocations of the reader to find out just who the author is – as if Gary, like the child Perec, 'didn't know what he wanted or feared the most: to stay hidden, or to be found out'.[8] But these traces of authorship are also, undoubtedly, to some degree involuntary. Gary did not know how to write except by repeating himself, by obsessive reinvention of the small set of themes and fetish objects that structure his world.

Momo is not an immigrant (he was born in France), but he treats the French language as if he were learning a foreign tongue. He uses clichés and admits he doesn't know what they mean, or why things are expressed that way. He comments at length on the meaning of the new words he's learning. As his environment resounds with phrases in Hebrew and Yiddish as well as Arabic, he glosses foreign terms for his listeners' benefit, mimicking the role of the teacher that he so desperately needs. By the end of the narrative of his early life he promises to remember how to write certain words correctly and declares his intention to speak French henceforth like a grown-up. It's very charming. It's very clever. And it fooled almost everybody at the time.

The street-slang kiddy-speak Gary invented for Momo was taken by serious critics – including major literary figures like Michel Tournier and established scholars of the French language, in France and abroad – as the authentic tongue of contemporary Belleville.[9] It seems incredible now, but Gary's linguistic deceptions were treated as material for learned essays on 'substandard French' and skilfully analysed as expressions of the coming revolt of the marginalised underclass. These critics were not slapdash skim readers writing reviews on Latin Quarter napkins for the national press. They had read the text with great attentiveness to detail – but through spectacles designed for them by Gary-Ajar. The characterisation of the mythical author misled them entirely. The Ajar scam provides incontrovertible evidence of the power of book packaging to blind us entirely even to what we read with care. We can laugh now. But we should not laugh too loudly.[10]

Momo, like his author, is anything but a revolutionary. He wants most of all to assimilate into the society around him, to become an indistinguishable adult member of it, and he dreams of doing it in two ways.

> When I'm big I'm going to write my own *Misérables,* because that's what people always write if they have anything to say.
>
> When I write my *Misérables* I'll say everything I want to say.
>
> When I'm big I'll have all the security forces under my thumb.[11]

These were Gary's ambitions and he made them come true. He became a French writer and he joined the 'security forces' – not the police, in his case, but the Air Force. These dreams aren't ironical jokes about immigrant kids – they're Gary's own truth about how an intelligent and energetic boy from the underclass can respond to a difficult start in life. They run directly counter to the conventional assumptions of the French Left of the period, which still looked to the proletariat for the justification, promotion and execution of the Next Revolution. *Life Before Us* is a custard pie courageously thrown at the face of Political Correctness, far more effective than the paint bombs that the bizarre Jean-Edern Hallier threw that year at various members of the literary establishment. Placards, demos, and Molotov cocktails, Gary implies, are just beach balls for the offspring of the French middle class.

Gary upped the stakes with his second Ajar in other more practical ways too. Once he'd finished the book and come back to his redecorated flat, he decided to keep Paul Pavlowitch on as a 'family retainer' and asked him to play the role of Émile Ajar, initially in dealings with Simone Gallimard and Michel Cournot. At this stage the new novel was called 'La Tendresse des pierres' ('Stones that Weep' or 'Soft Heart of Stones'). Cournot read it in June 1975 and liked it a lot less than *Gros-Câlin*: too sentimental, he thought, and if he'd spoken American English, he'd have said: too much schmaltz. He was still dealing with Ajar via Pierre Michaut, but when he asked the frontman to take a set of questions and observations back to the writer in Brazil, Michaut told him that Ajar would soon be in Europe – not in Paris, of course, but in Geneva.

Gary prepared Pavlowitch for his new role. His real name was Hamil Raja. A girlfriend who was the daughter of a Swiss diplomat had managed to get him into Switzerland legally. He was prepared to meet Michel Cournot in Geneva to go over the manuscript of 'La Tendresse des pierres'. Simone Gallimard was over the moon at the prospect of meeting her new author, for she never suspected he didn't exist. The 'Geneva interview', designed as the first sighting of Ajar in flesh and blood, was a comedy of errors. Pavlowitch mistakenly gave Cournot the wrong telephone number of the apartment he was using, and the editor and the publisher who had come down specially to meet him went back to Paris, mission unaccomplished. Calls from Pavlowitch to Gary and messages forwarded by circuitous routes enabled the rendezvous to take place the following week, but with Cournot alone, as Simone Gallimard had other engagements. In an ill-lit, sparsely furnished garret borrowed from an old friend of Gary's, Cournot played the role of the kindly editor to perfection, but Pavlowitch outplayed him as Hamil Raja. Cournot went back to Paris delighted to have met an important new talent in the literary field. He had asked the man if his misuse of French vocabulary and syntax was intended or involuntary, and had got an ambiguous, evasive reply. But there certainly was something odd about the way Ajar *spoke*. Cournot didn't even begin to guess that it came from the fact that Pavlowitch was reciting lines he had been made to learn by heart.

After the immense exploit of writing two novels under two different identities and setting one of them free to exist in the world, Gary felt depressed, agitated and at a loose end in the summer of 1975. He went into one of his phases of flight and travelled, almost haphazardly, to Brittany, the Riviera, Mallorca (to stay in the house he had built and now sold, but was still able to use as a retreat) and south-west France, to see the young man who was now playing the role of his second self. On the drive from Toulouse airport to Caniac-du-Causse, Paul mentioned that his wife Annie had recently reread *The Ski Bum* and noticed that the heroine, Jess Donahue, was herself the author of a novel called . . . *La Tendresse des pierres* (*A Quality of Despair* in the English original). Gary, once again disguised as a pantomime pirate in full black leather gear, nearly jumped out of his seat.

'Shit! Are you sure?'

Gary, despite his 'total historical recall', had really forgotten that the title of Ajar Two was a giveaway to the authorship of the text. It had to be changed. But as there was still no phone line in the farmhouse at Caniac, after lunch they had to drive down to Cahors to call Cournot. Pavlowitch told 'his' editor that the title just had to be changed.

'Why?'

'Because . . . Because!'

Pavlowitch gave nothing away, save a few useless alternatives Gary had just cooked up – 'Heavy Shoulders', 'Nothing', 'First Steps', 'Madame Rosa', 'Momo' – and left it to Cournot to find a better one.[12] Which he certainly did: *La Vie devant soi* is a very good title for Gary's second Ajar novel, even if it is not his.

Life Before Us is full of racial jokes, or jokes about race. 'For a long time I didn't know I was an Arab, because nobody insulted me';[13] 'When it came to racism, [Madame Rosa] was okay. For instance, we had a little Moïse in the house, and she used to call him an Arab asshole, but never me';[14] 'They'd had a terrible time with racism [in Africa], but then came the revolution, which ushered in a regime, and after that they were all right. I haven't had any trouble with racism myself, so I don't know what I should look forward to. Well, I suppose the black people have other faults';[15] 'If the Jews and Arabs clobber each other it's because whatever you may say to the contrary the Jews and Arabs are no different from anybody else, which is the whole principle of brotherhood, except maybe the Germans, who are even more so';[16] 'In my opinion, Jews are people like everybody else, but that's no reason to be down on them';[17] and so on, again and again, on the old issues closest to Gary's anguished heart: relations with and between Jews and Blacks, Jews and Arabs, Jews and Germans, and the French.

Gary gets away with these and many other jokes about Jews and others by casting them as the naive expressions of an uneducated child. Through them he managed to create a totally inauthentic image of a racial melting pot in a poor quarter of Paris in which Blacks, Arabs and Jews get on in mutual respect and misunderstanding. Gary's first readers were enthralled by this vision of a multicultural community on their doorstep. A revelation![18] But some people can't take a joke, even at the primary level. *L'Express* complained that among the novel's supporters not one had noticed 'a slight but lingering smell of anti-Semitism wafting from these pages . . . Ajar may not have intended this, but he should not be amazed to find himself invited to a signing session at the next reunion ball of former members of the wartime *Milice*.'[19] But putting aside this crass misreading, reviewers who gurgled with delight at Ajar's racially mixed slum paradise were also missing the real joke. The Belleville of Madame Rosa and Momo is a fabrication, a fantasy, a counter-image of France as it really is, designed to entrap its readers into sentimental identification with an Ideal. The comedy of race in *Life Before Us* is funny, but also serious. True to the function of literature as laid down in *Pour Sganarelle*, Gary offers us not a reflection of reality, but its reinvention.

Life Before Us is also, centrally, a love story, of the same kind as *Promise at Dawn*. Momo recognises Madame Rosa's complete devotion to him and pays her back in kind. In a world where sex is just a business and the male organ is referred to as 'the enemy of the human race'[20], true love is completely disconnected from passion and put back in its proper place: between parent and child. It's a position Gary could only sketch out under the cover of being someone else twice over (Émile Ajar and Momo), and with the assistance of the grotesque, taken to an exacerbated extreme. Madame Rosa dies. Such is Momo's unwillingness to part with her that he sits by her side in the cupboard under the stairs which she had chosen as her last resting place. He lights her candles, recites the 'Shema Yisrael', dresses the corpse by putting clumsy make-up on her face and sits shiva by her side.

> I kissed her once or twice, but that didn't help either. Her face was cold. She was beautiful with her artistic kimono, her red wig, and all the make-up I'd spread on her face. I put on a little more here and there because she looked kind of gray and blue every time I woke up . . . I was afraid to leave Madame Rosa alone, because maybe she'd wake up and think she was dead if everything was black all around her . . . I took all the perfume that was left and poured it on her, but it was impossible . . . Then I painted her face all different colours to hide it as much as possible. Her eyes were still open, but with the red, yellow, green and blue around them they didn't look so horrible because there wasn't anything natural about them any more. Then I lit seven candles the way the Jews do and lay down beside her on the mattress.[21]

Kitsch? Sure. Convincing? Utterly. This is not what Gary did for his own mother, except in a way through the largely concocted stories of *Promise at Dawn*. But it is what he should have done. Literature is a fabulous consolation.

29

'In the Sombre Folds of Life'

Womanlight and *The Way Out*, 1975–1977

Life Before Us ends with a sentence that sums up what Gary had to say in the later period of his writing career: *il faut aimer*. Translated by Ralph Manheim, after a nudge from 'Émile Ajar', it comes out in English as 'it takes loving'.[1] But Gary's real meaning comes straight from the book Momo wanted to write – *Les Misérables* by Victor Hugo.[2]

> *Aimer ou avoir aimé, cela suffit. Ne demandez rien ensuite. On n'a pas d'autre perle à trouver dans les plis ténébreux de la vie.*
> Loving or having loved is enough. Ask for nothing more. There's no other pearl to be found in the sombre folds of life.[3]

Gary developed Hugo's message under his real name in two admirable, partly shocking and sentimental novels, *Clair de femme* ('Womanlight') and *Au-delà de cette limite votre ticket n'est plus valable* ('The Way Out', called 'Your Ticket is No Longer Valid' in the USA). The writing of *The Way Out* followed immediately on the composition of *Gros-Câlin*, and *Clair de femme* was written somewhat later (the books were published in 1975 and 1977 respectively), but their material, their manner, their purposes and meanings are inextricably linked to the literary project of Émile Ajar.

They are also in part the late fruit of the defeat of Émile

Ajar, which has not yet been fully explained. Behind Gary's extraordinary triumph in imposing a new author and a new book on the publishing world lay a tragic compromise. To preserve the pseudonym and the cover story that went with it, Gary-Ajar accepted the publisher's wish to cut the entire last chapter of *Gros-Câlin*. Yet that last chapter, which has Cousin return to the company of men with universal love, gives the true meaning of the book. It is the only place in Gary's oeuvre (apart from the entirely misunderstood epilogue to *A European Education*) where redemption happens – where, so to speak, Rainier can love Ann and live happily ever after, where Luc Martin can become a man of honour without committing a crime, where Lenny and Jess can find happiness together, where Tulipe can stop cheating and Morel can save the elephants. That's why Gary felt he had to be someone else to write a book that gives away the ideal to which he aspires, but which he had never previously allowed to interfere with his moral and emotional realism. Yet he'd given up his 'last chapter' without a fight. He hadn't had much of an option, as he'd snookered himself by pretending to be someone else. Even so, he must have felt ashamed. Or perhaps he took it on the chin and accepted that in literature he had no way of saying what he really meant. It would not stop him writing. But it meant he had to pursue a slightly different, more sentimental track.

Living at Rue du Bac on his own – 'cohabiting with Miss Solitude', as he put it in *A Quiet Night* – and trailing statuesque, lip-sealed escorts from Madame Billy's and Madame Claude's with him to dinner parties and receptions, from 1974 Gary pursued two literary careers while also putting himself about as a TV and media celebrity. In these extraordinarily creative years Gary dropped the 'attack mode' of *White Dog* and *Genghis Cohn*, and tried, at last, to deal with intimate issues of how the good life should be lived, especially when its end is on your mind.

Some episodes of *Clair de femme* take the carnivelesque strain of Gary's writing to a heart-wrenching extreme. Señor Galba, a cabaret artiste with a cardiac problem who does an act with animals, unsurprisingly drops dead in his hotel room. By way of a funeral dirge, his chimpanzee Jackson puts 'El Fuego de Andalusia' on the gramophone and dances the paso doble with a pink-dyed poodle in front of his master's corpse.[4] In another comical interlude Gary gives a self-mocking portrait of Russian-Jewish émigré kitsch, and a litany of meaningless intellectual party patter that would not be out of place in Nathalie Sarraute's *Fruits d'Or*.[5] But most of this short novel is not funny at all.

The hero and narrator of the tale, Michel Folain, is an airline pilot in grave distress on the night his wife Yannick has chosen to end her suffering from an incurable disease. He encounters a forty-three-year-old but already white-haired woman, Lydia, whose daughter died six months previously in a car crash that left her husband with Wernicke's aphasia, a pathetic disorder in which the mind works perfectly well, but is disconnected from the meanings of words spoken and heard. During the long, boozy night of anguish that the pair spend together, Michel expounds an entire theory of love. His passion for Yannick has been the source, the nourishment, the sole ground of his life and from that he generalises: there is nothing more to life than love, yet if it is to be any use, it has to give nourishment even when it is gone. That's why in the end Lydia backs off. She doesn't want to be the object of a cult with religious overtones; it's as if Michel wanted her not so much to replace Yannick, as to become a cathedral in which he can venerate love itself.

Clair de femme was written before Jean Seberg's death and is not directly autobiographical. Nor does it seem that the kind of love that Gary's hero enjoys, promotes and theorises – the stable love of a couple united until death do them part and beyond – was anything Gary ever experienced. That is not to say the book is insincere; rather, it elaborates Gary's aspiration towards a higher level of human existence, which now, in the autumn of his life, he was sure could only be reached through reciprocated and unwavering love between a man and a woman. What he believes is in the end identical to the yearning of Michel Cousin, in Ajar's *Gros-Câlin*: a world in which the 'arithmetic of the impossible' exists, where 1 + 1 does equal 1. Or, in a sentence from *Clair de femme* that could equally well belong to either book: 'When you're bawling about being lonely, you're bawling about love.'[6] According to Paul Pavlowitch, who by 1977 had been publicly identified as Émile Ajar, some critics even accused the old man of plagiarising his cousin Ajar in *Clair de femme* . . . [7]

In *A Quiet Night*, Gary berated himself through the borrowed voice of Bondy for promoting 'femininity' while behaving and looking the part of the most macho of male chauvinist pigs.[8] His answer to the criticism in the fabricated interview smacks of special pleading, but in *Clair de femme* it makes much better sense. Love – 'unselfish, loyal and benevolent concern for another', according to *King Solomon* – is what gives value to life, because it is an arbitrary and total gift of the self. Its miraculous paradox is that caring for another nourishes the carer as well.

In his works of the 1970s, under the name of Ajar as well as his own, Gary's main point coincides with the philosophical argument of Harry Frankfurt: in the absence of a transcendent source of value, there is only love to give a sense to our lives.[9] However, Frankfurt doesn't think that sex has anything much to do with love, whereas Gary obviously does. That is why inability to express male desire – to make loving a woman a physical reality – looms on Gary's horizon as a threat to the possibility of a meaningful life.

The Way Out confronts what it might mean to become impotent. As in *Clair de femme*, the hero-narrator has a number of features in common with Romain Gary – late middle age, good looks, a taste for paradox and irony, and former service with the Free French – but they do not add up to sufficient evidence to suggest that the central issue of the novel constitutes a personal confession. Jacques Rainier in his third manifestation (see p. 180 for his earlier appearances) is a businessman facing ruin as his relatively small enterprise is squeezed out of the market by bigger German firms and by an American predator. He sees himself as the image of France after the first oil crisis of 1974 – dependent on newer, younger nations that have all the sources of energy without which the 'old country' cannot survive. He is also deeply in love with a Brazilian woman nearly forty years younger than he is and anxious about becoming physically unable to satisfy her. Gary's display of technical knowledge in the various interviews his hero has with medical experts may or may not come from personal experience: to learn about chemical psychotherapy when writing *Hocus Bogus* he consulted Dr L. Bertagna, and to document himself on aphasia for *Clair de femme* he went to see Dr Ducarne at the Salpetrière Hospital in Paris.[10] He could just as easily have contacted one or more sexologists not for treatment but for up-to-date medical jargon on erectile dysfunction.[11]

Did Gary suffer from a decline in his sexual prowess around the age of sixty? After forty-five years of Stakhanovite service his organ might well have enjoyed a rest. In interviews Gary was studiously, even energetically, evasive. On occasions he counter-attacked and offered to demonstrate in public (but on radio) that Jacques Rainier's problem was not his; on other occasions he defended his right to privacy and declared with huffy pride that he was not in favour of full frontal exposure.[12] Gary always wrote about himself, but he always wrote about himself *as someone else*. The topic of male impotence was an effective tool in the larger literary strategy on which he was engaged, and in his last Ajar novel, *King Solomon*, he stated explicitly the real meaning the term had for him. 'It's impotence,' the narrator Jeannot says to his girlfriend Aline. 'You know, real impotence, which means that you can't do anything when you can't do anything, from one end of the world to the other . . . So when you can just slightly help someone to suffer . . . I do what I can. I feel a bit less impotent.'[13]

The Way Out is also part of the cover Gary designed to keep the identity of Émile Ajar deeply hidden. Read as a masked autobiography, the story of Jacques Rainier's impotence could be taken as a revelation that the old Romain Gary was indeed on his way out and could therefore not possibly be the inventive young Émile Ajar.[14] The unusually detailed descriptions of male physiology, supported by all the medical terminology of the day, did not lead readers to suspect that Gary's account of how to cope with a less than rigid erection was essentially metaphorical. If he was misunderstood on that level, he really had himself to blame.

The Way Out is a variant of a much earlier novel, *The Colours of the Day*, first published in 1952. In both novels a failing hero (Bauché in the earlier case and Rainier in the later novel) contemplates and sets in motion means to have himself assassinated. This is by far the strangest recurrent plot device in Gary's whole oeuvre. The justification for the masked suicide in *The Way Out* is that Rainier does not want his family to forfeit his life insurance, which excludes suicide. The means he chooses to get rid of his now useless self is equally far-fetched. He goes to see 'Lili Marlene', a successful madam with links to the underworld who had disposed of twenty-seven German officers with a hatpin and got the Resistance Medal for it. The old tart has a heart of gold and good insight into her old commander. Instead of having Rainier knifed by a slit-eyed torero, she hires a sultry hunk of a chauffeur (the self-same hand for hire) to take him and his Brazilian lover on a long honeymoon drive, and to provide whatever additional services might be called for.

Clair de femme and *The Way Out* are books whose many

strong lyrical passages lay out a conviction that love is all that makes life worth having. But the central couples cannot achieve meaningful lives despite their amorous passions. Rainier can only love his Laura by means of a substitute; and Michel Folain (whose attributes and attitudes overlap confusingly with Rainier's) loses his wife Yannick to a suicide designed to thwart the ravages of disease. Gary does not grant his aspiration to a life based on love the power to correct the dysfunctions of the real world. History and physiology have the last word. The Author cannot provide happy ends.

30

Hocus Bogus, 1976

Life Before Us was a runaway success from the moment it appeared in bookshops and could not but be short-listed for the Goncourt Prize. It became urgent for the publisher to have an author to show to the press, not only because there were lingering rumours that Émile Ajar did not exist and others that he was really someone else, but because it's not possible to stoke the fires of a best-seller without author interviews in the right places and a back story to go with the book being sold. Gary was an old pro and well aware of all that. The maestro thought he could easily pull all the strings with one hand.

At the time of the 'Geneva Interview' with Michel Cournot, Pavlowitch had supplied Simone Gallimard with a photograph of Émile Ajar – a snap of himself taken some years before on a Caribbean beach, looking like Tarzan. The image appeared in national magazines and newspapers in September 1975 and also, a little later, in a regional paper, *La Dépêche du Midi*, widely read in the region of Toulouse, even in small places like Caniac-du-Causse. In Gary's view this was his Golem's first mistake: Roger Grenier at Gallimard and the French-American writer Thérèse de Saint-Phalle, who had met Pavlowitch, could easily have recognised the person in the photograph. But they didn't. Jean Seberg did recognise the image – but she had known for some months who the author of the Ajar texts really was, because Gary had told her.

Cournot did his job promoting Ajar's second book and offered *Le Monde des livres* an exclusive interview with the author, which was accepted with alacrity, as both the editor, Jacqueline Piatier, and one of the senior journalists, Yvonne Baby, were most impressed with *Life Before Us*. Anissimov reports Gary's Swiss lawyer as telling her that he was furious with the initiative; Pavlowitch, on the other hand, says that Gary was keen on the idea, as it would give his fictional author more plausibility.[1] But whether Gary was keen or not, this would be a crucial step. Pavlowitch now had almost infinite power over his master. He could blow the game, or mess it up. He could complicate it, or carry it off. Gary had no way of determining what Pavlowitch would actually say, short of being there with him.

The interview with Yvonne Baby took place in a rented house on Voldumvej, in a pleasant, leafy area not far from central Copenhagen. Why choose Denmark? A colleague once surmised that the location was a literary-political provocation, because Céline, the rabid anti-Semite and collaborator, had holed up in Denmark after the war until his sentence for collaboration with the enemy had been suspended. A more plausible explanation is that Pavlowitch had been to Copenhagen before and quite liked the place. After all, he was getting a free trip, and Annie – Ajar's French girlfriend for the occasion – came too.

Simone Gallimard came first. A large and flamboyant lady, she burst on the scene with gushing delight at finally meeting a writer she was convinced was 'one of the real greats'. She stayed overnight in the same house, spent time with Pavlowitch and his wife the next day, could not get over how wonderful it was to be the publisher of such a genius, and left in a swirl of good feelings and outsize admiration. Annie went back to France at the same time. Pavlowitch was on his own for the key interview with the emissary from *Le Monde*.

'One can lie from the bottom of one's heart,' Pavlowitch comments. 'That's what happened to me.'[2] But as he fibbed his way through the day, he spun an altogether different biography of Ajar from the one that had been prepared for him. He dropped the name of Vilna, mentioned Nice and gave out the fatal clue that Ajar had been a medical student *in Toulouse*. He talked about his mother. He spun an inconsistent web of half-truths and the result was an article in *Le Monde* that hardly made sense. Roger Grenier later mentioned to Gary, in passing, how curious it was that the long article on that new writer Ajar said nothing at all.

As the book became an ever greater sales phenomenon, the identity of the author, which *Le Monde* had failed to explain convincingly, became an issue, a topic and fairly soon, an 'affair'. Hardly a day passed without some press item raising the question. Gary began to worry about the mounting pressure. He instructed Pavlowitch not to give any interviews in Paris. He wrote his cousin letter after letter with ever more complicated suggestions for deceiving the press, for staying hidden and for releasing flocks of wild geese. He seemed to be not well in himself, agitated, anxious, unstable. Through the autumn months he just couldn't keep still, and dashed back and forth between Paris and Geneva by train and plane at the drop of a hat.

What was Gary worried about? The success of *Life Before Us* proved a second time over everything he later claimed he was trying to prove with the invention of Émile Ajar. Why didn't he simply issue a press release and enjoy watching every face in the literary firmament turn as red as a *burak*? He was much too afraid to do that. But what exactly was he afraid of?

'You don't need reasons to be afraid, Momo.'

I've never forgotten those words, because they were the truest words I've ever heard.[3]

A jobbing journalist who worked for the weekly news magazine *Le Point* read Ajar's interview in *Le Monde* with some care. Stringers in Copenhagen and Paris had drawn a complete blank. Jacques Bouzerand was from Cahors and had been a student in Toulouse. So had this Ajar. But he'd done medicine. Did he know anyone who'd been in the medical school? Yes, of course – he'd had a couple of girlfriends who were medical students. He looked at the photograph again, then passed it round a few friends from his student days. 'But that's Alex!' they exclaimed. Of course it was! He'd known the man himself. And his real name was . . . Paul Pavlowitch! What's more, he'd gone on to marry the sister of his old girlfriend from medical school. Bouzerand rang Annie's sister, Suzy, who was delighted to provide her brother-in-law's address – but no, he didn't have a telephone. Apparently, he'd just published a book that was doing very well . . .

Bouzerand told his editor he was on the brink of a huge scoop and got leave to take a photographer with him on the next train to Cahors – the overnight express. He dropped in on his mother for breakfast and borrowed her car, and put his foot on the pedal until he came to a halt in front of the farmhouse at Caniac-du-Causse. He dropped off the photographer so he could hide in the bushes, just in case. Annie was putting out the washing. Of course she recognised Bouzerand.

'What are you doing here?' she asked.

'I've come to see Alex.'

'Fuck you!'

Paul Pavlowitch (who had used his middle name, Alex, during his student years) came out of the house in high fury and told Bouzerand he could not and would not say anything, and that if he didn't get off the premises right now he would go get his shotgun and blow his head off. Then things calmed down a bit, and the reporter and photographer were invited to stay for lunch. While Annie was busy in the kitchen, Bouzerand and Pavlowitch walked down to the village to use the only telephone for miles around, in a café beside the main highway. It was an antique wind-up device, but good enough to get through to Claude Imbert, editor-in-chief of *Le Point*, who was having lunch with the CEO of one of France's major investment banks.

Imbert told Pavlowitch that he had no choice. Now he had been found, his name would be published. *Le Point* would run a story and an interview. He had to come to Paris immediately. And he did, by the evening train, *Le Capitole*, with the journalist and the photographer quizzing him all the way in the first-class compartment they paid for.

Romain Gary was surprised to be woken so late by a ring at his door and bewildered to see Paul, who had the taxi drop him off a few blocks away, as if he were an undercover agent in a spy movie. Which is what he was, now. Gary didn't sleep much that night, going over and over again with Paul how he should behave at the luncheon next day with the journalist and his editor.

The interview with Émile Ajar alias Paul Pavlowitch appeared in *Le Point* on 10 November 1975. It kept Gary's identity hidden and it did not reveal Pavlowitch's name, though it was obviously known to the journalists involved and consequently to the rest of the press as well. But as misfortunes never happen alone, a strange rumour apparently originating in Sweden got about that the real Émile Ajar was Romain Gary. Claude Gallimard asked his cousin Robert if this was true. Robert kept his promise of silence and arranged a meeting between the head of the firm and the writer. Gary solemnly declared that he had not written Ajar's novels, and that any resemblance between them and his own works could be accounted for by the understandable influence that he had on his young cousin's style.

This conversation can be seen as the crucial moment in the transformation of the hoax into a kind of tragedy. What still might have been defused as a joyous if rather exaggerated lark was now the subject of a flagrant and most likely actionable lie. Gary had dug himself into a hole. He had no way back without dishonour and, for the would-be Polish *pan*, that meant no way back at all. He could only push ever on with more deceit.

One week later, on 17 November, the Goncourt Prize panel met and awarded their annual distinction to *Life Before Us* by Émile Ajar. *France-Soir* asked the famous writer Romain Gary what he thought of the choice. 'I liked *Gros-Câlin*,' he said, off the cuff. 'I haven't read *Life Before Us* yet. But I don't think the author will be able to stay anonymous for much longer.' It's like mother said: one lie leads to another and the second leads to hell. That night, he had dinner out with friends and as he was walking back to 108 Rue du Bac he saw a milling throng of journalists outside his front door. According to Anissimov, he only got back inside by throwing his weight around and the liberal use of his fists.[4]

In the following days, on the strong advice of Robert Gallimard and his lawyers too, Gary agreed to have Émile Ajar turn down the Goncourt Prize, as it cannot be awarded to the same writer twice. Allowing it to remain attached to *Life Before Us* would be tantamount to fraud. But by 21 November, when the refusal of the Goncourt became known, several daily papers let out the fact that Ajar's real name was Paul Pavlowitch, that he was a close relative of Romain Gary and was holed up in the apartment above Gary's own. Actually, he had already gone back to Caniac-du-Causse. As for Gary, he couldn't take the strain any more. He was on tranquillisers and his mind was a blank.

When Pavlowitch realised that the game was nearly up he dashed back to Paris to evade what he imagined would be a sudden swarm of television camera crews. Annie phoned Gary to tell him. Gary was in a weird state. 'They're everywhere . . . on the landing . . . in the yard . . . But I've got my revolver. It's a mess. I'm going to end it . . .'[5] Annie managed to make him see sense, for a bit. It was Paul they were hunting for, not him. Of course! But that meant Paul must not come to the apartment! He'll be skinned alive! Calls to friends succeeded in having Pavlowitch met at the station and steered away from Rue du Bac, and one disaster was thus averted. Gary sank back into drugged sleep.

Over the next day or two Pavlowitch got to see Gary (by going up the servants' stairs), got chased by motorbike-mounted paparazzi on the pavement of Boulevard Raspail (and hit one of them to the ground), and got himself, his wife and daughter to London to hide. He wasn't too sure whether he wanted to carry on playing his cousin's now sinister game, or stick the knife in, hard. Gary, for his part, put himself about, bursting into temper on radio when asked about his relationship with Émile Ajar, and handwrote a statement for *Le Monde*, which published it on 3 December 1975 in facsimile: 'I affirm that I am not Émile Ajar and that I had no part whatsoever in the works of this author. Signed: Romain Gary.' Then he ran away to his flat in Rue Moillebeau in Geneva, to write the most fantastical, amazing, lunatic and brilliant book of his entire career.

Hocus Bogus (*Pseudo* in its French edition) tells the story of the Ajar mystification much as it has been laid out in the preceding pages of this book. It was written at breakneck speed, in little more than six weeks, between late November 1975 and January 1976. Its title is so transparent as to make its meaning invisible if you are not in on the joke. An inspired, intoxicated, seemingly lunatic rant, *Hocus Bogus* is the first-person narration of a character called Paul Pavlowitch, a borderline schizophrenic under treatment in a psychiatric clinic in Copenhagen. He has a serious problem with his uncle, whom he calls Tonton (French kiddy-speak for uncle) and then Tonton Macoute, after the name of the feared secret police of Haiti's deranged dictator, François 'Papa Doc' Duvalier. 'Uncle Bogey' is a famous writer and deeply jealous of his nephew's breakthrough success. He may even be the *father* of Émile Ajar – he was a close friend of Pavlowitch's mother, Dinah, and since the old roué screwed any woman he got near, he probably had an affair with her too. Masquerading as the conscience of a schizophrenic pretending to be someone else in order to authenticate the real existence of a fictional author and the strictly autobiographical nature of his work, Gary can at last say what he means. *Hocus Bogus* is a confession. But it's not the confession of Émile Ajar and even less the confession of Paul Pavlowitch. If there is any place where the real Romain Gary is to be found, it's in this extraordinary book, under all these layers of disguise.

Hocus Bogus was published in November 1976, and made it perfectly clear that Émile Ajar was Paul Pavlowitch and that Paul Pavlowitch was mad. That explained several things: Ajar's use of a pseudonym, his fear of publicity, his weird way of making appointments with journalists, his withdrawal from the Renaudot Prize and later his refusal of the Goncourt, as well as the inconsistent elements in the author biographies put out by his publisher and the contradictions in published interviews. Clearly, Romain Gary was a victim of his unstable, mythomaniac, certifiable and already certified relative. He could not possibly be held responsible for the two moving, disturbing *human documents* that Ajar had given the world. He was clean.

Hocus Bogus put Romain Gary in a place of safety, which turned out to be a custom-built mezzanine somewhere between the eighth and ninth circles of hell. The double, treble, quadruple deception he had now perpetrated on his readers meant that the truth about Émile Ajar could never be told while he was alive. The only thing that really remained to be decided was the date.

The narrator of *Hocus Bogus*, who might be identified least misleadingly as Roman Kacew, the true author of *Gros-Câlin* and *Life Before Us*, is riven by anxiety and guilt. He creeps into the ward office one night to find out what the doctors have written about him.

> I shall refrain with hauteur from quoting one card in my medical file which is clearly anti-Semitic: it says I am Jewish. But I tried to find out if my feeling of unworthiness and guilt came from the fact that I was Jewish and had therefore not crucified Jesus, for which I've been blamed ever since by anti-Semites. Did I become a python so as to stop being Jewish?
>
> Dr Christianssen said I jerked off too much.[6]

On the basis of this passage and a few similar ones, as well as a great deal of other circumstantial evidence, Myriam Anissimov constructs her portrait of Romain Gary as the archetypal self-hating Jew. There is just one problem with this explanation of Gary's moral position, his bizarre sensitivities and his literary project. This is a *joke* about Jewish self-hatred. Gary certainly hated himself, but not because he was a Jew. He took a pretty dim view of belonging to the human race. The only advantage of being Jewish was that it entitled him to make anti-Semitic jokes. That's what's meant by the expression 'a Jewish sense of humour'. As Ajar-Pavlowitch-Kacew tells it:

> I got up and lit a hope, to make some light and see a bit less clearly. Sorry, a match. Never confess. I didn't switch on because the electrics stay on permanently, whereas a match goes out quite quickly, so you have to take another one, which gives a second hope and a second dose of relief, and so on. There are fifty civilisations in a box of matches, it's got fifty times more hope than a single throw of a switch. As soon as I lit the first match I stopped hallucinating and saw Christ. Beside him stood Momo, the Arab Jewish kid, Mohammed from the Goutte d'Or, good door, good whore – you know,

> the place in *Life Before Us*, that racist and anti-Semitic work as it has been called by people who can't tell racism and anti-Semitism when they see it because it's the air they breathe and you never notice your own bad smell. Mohammed, called Momo for the benefit of the French, was standing next to the Jew called Christ, the guy they call love and salvation so as to persecute the Jews and punish them, because a Jew invented Christian civilisation and Christians can't ever forgive that, as it puts them under an obligation. It's a clinical fact that Christians really hate the Jews to death for having made them Christian and lumbering them with duties they really don't want to have.[7]

According to Pavlowitch, the long anecdote that follows this passage, in which Momo dares Christ to perform a miracle, comes straight out of *Le Vin des morts*,[8] the still unpublished novel Gary wrote with such passion in his youth and finally abandoned in a Swedish summer house just before the outbreak of World War Two. *Hocus Bogus*, which announces solemnly at its end that 'This is my last book', would therefore also be Gary-Kacew's first. And from first to last the questions of whether Gary was proud to be a Jew or ashamed of it, whether he respected tradition or resented it, whether he believed in God or feared the Devil, are beside the point. He felt responsible. He felt implicated. He felt that the sins and crimes of others sullied him too. Taken beyond a certain point, fraternity with the human race can drive you mad. To be normal you have to stop noticing what's being done by other people just like you – Franco, Pinochet, never mind who. All men are your brothers. Especially *cousins*.

Gros-Câlin is about loneliness in the absence of love, *Life Before Us* is about loving in the absence of the person loved and *Hocus Bogus* is about caring for the whole world, to the point where the mind breaks. There is a logical progression from one book to another. A coherent ethical position joins them together as one of the most serious if bizarre statements of 'old-fashioned humanism' in literature.

The Ajar hoax thus really did serve a purpose. There is no doubt Gary would be less read today if he hadn't carried it off with such manic skill and intensity. But his complete success left him in an unprecedented position. His best work, his real work, was now, by his own actions, no longer his. His creature, Émile Ajar, was someone else and out of his control. Paul Pavlowitch was now accepted as a writer of great talent and was given a job as a desk editor at Mercure de France. Film rights to both Ajar 1 and Ajar 2 had been sold, but Gary could have no control over the screen adaptation of his work. *Life Before Us* was made into a movie by Moshe Mizrahi, starring Simone Signoret, and turned out to be the most successful film venture of Gary's career to date, except that he had no way of taking credit. Titled *Madame Rosa* for US release, it won the Oscar for Best Foreign Film in 1978; Signoret also won a César for Best Actress. As for *Gros-Câlin*, it was adapted by a team of Italian script doctors and filmed by Jean-Claude Rawson with a cast that was half Italian and half French.

Gary could not do the English translations of Ajar himself either. The American publishers hired the doyen of literary translators, Ralph Manheim, for this special task. Manheim had been in the world of literature a long time – he had translated Céline, when *Journey to the End of the Night* was the latest European sensation, and he'd done Hitler's *Mein Kampf* too. He was not easily swayed by the views of an upstart like Émile Ajar on contemporary American slang. Gary wrote to him under camouflage and managed to impose one or two changes, notably the last line of the book, but *Life Before Us*, alas, just isn't on the same wavelength as *La Vie devant soi*. After *Hocus Bogus*, Gary was dispossessed, hoist by his own petard and more alone than can easily be imagined. He could tell no one about his true plight. Pavlowitch was no longer under his thumb and had to be treated with caution. In these desperate circumstances of a huge success that was also a diabolical self-laid trap, Gary did not take out his old service revolver. Nor did he allow the black jaws of depression to swallow him whole, as he had in London in 1955. 'It was not incapacitating,' according to William Styron, 'and he had it under control, but he felt it from time to time, this leaden and poisonous mood the colour of verdigris . . . Nonetheless he was hurting.'[9]

Amazingly, almost unbelievably, he gave himself a new lease of literary life. In the short time he had left, between 1976 and 1980, he wrote two more exceptional books while also revising several of his earlier works to leave them in the best possible state. The Ajar hoax had stranded Romain Gary in an invisible machine that lifted him like a rocket into outer space.

Father and Son. Rue du Bac, 1979

31

Happy Ends

King Solomon and *The Kites*, 1977–1980

Shall quips and sentences and these paper bullets of the brain awe a man from the career of his humour? No, the world must be peopled.

SHAKESPEARE,
MUCH ADO ABOUT NOTHING, II. iii

The final Ajar novel, *King Solomon*, written in 1977, and *The Kites*, first drafted in 1978, are the crowning glories of Gary's double career. Both are romantic comedies in a Shakespearean mould – funny, diverse and perceptive, ending in marriage and the founding of a family. Both are intensely nostalgic works, summoning up directly and indirectly Gary's 'Russian origins' and childhood in Poland, his love of that sad land and his love of his French home town, Nice. Both are also centrally concerned with the experience of the Second World War and, in different but equally significant ways, with the plight and fate of Jews in that period. All Gary is here, together with, at last, fictional and historical demonstrations of men and women who rise to the challenge of leading a good life.

Gary's last great books are much more like each other than anything else. *Hocus Bogus* had left Ajar as free to be Gary as vice versa, and the writer made no effort at all to mask his true identity, under either name. When Vina Tirgendvadum ran a computerised stylometric analysis of *King Solomon* she found that it was indistinguishable from works by Gary, whereas the other three Ajars display significant variation from the 'Gary norm'. The scholar-linguist's conclusion is that it isn't possible to maintain a false stylistic identity for very long.[1] She missed the point entirely: Gary wasn't trying any more.

The sunny moral atmosphere of *King Solomon* and *The Kites* bears no relation to the quality or the events of Romain Gary's life after 1976. He was making astronomical amounts of money, but in all other respects he was in a mess. Ismail Kadare has often insisted that critics should not take the context of his writing too much into account when trying to get the measure of his work, because a writer's task is to rise above the context. Gary-Ajar's last double bloom is an excellent example of that.

In his last years, when he was not buried in writing, which he was for much of the time, Gary lived in a permanent state of anxiety and distress. He was terrified of being found out as a fraud. He had an entirely unreasonable terror of a tax audit and his appeal for clemency went as far as the President, who gave instructions for Gary to be treated with respect, but within the law. He took a heap of anxiolytic drugs and consulted one specialist after another. According to Anissimov, one of his doctors advised him to stop bedding more than one prostitute per day. Apparently he didn't take the advice. He could not treat Paul Pavlowitch as the retainer and pliant servant any more: since the publication of *Hocus Bogus*, Pavlowitch *was* Émile Ajar and had his unbearably overpowering 'Uncle' at his mercy. Gary travelled a great deal, to see friends or to get away from them, to see his lawyers, or to see nothing at all. His generation was nearing its end. Not his biological generation, but the generation that had made France what it was – the great men of *La France Libre*. De Gaulle died in 1971, André Malraux in 1976. The Order of the Liberation, whose members were falling off their perches day by day, asked Gary to write a commemorative volume about them before it was too late. He took an assistant, interviewed a number of survivors, sketched out possibilities, then gave up. This was not a book he could write. Gary took his failure badly. He was inclined to take everything badly, in any case. He was a borderline case by the age of sixty-five.

Yet Gary remained a fabulous performer when he was on radio or television, or talking to sympathetic journalists, especially in Polish. His interview with Jacques Chancel in 1978 is a gem, and his conversation with Leszek Kolodziejczyk in November 1980 is one the most revealing and warm-hearted that he ever gave. But he was in even better form at his writing desk. His last works are the best he ever did.

Gary's miseries were compounded by the rapid disintegration of Jean Seberg, to whom he continued to devote 'tender and paternal solicitude', in the words of his old friend William Styron. Styron was shocked and saddened when he saw Jean in the summer of 1978:

> All her once fragile and luminous blond beauty had disappeared into a puffy mask. She moved like a sleepwalker, said little, and had the blank gaze of someone tranquilized (or drugged, or both) nearly to the point of catalepsy.[2]

Jean had fallen prey to nefarious thugs who found it easy to separate her from what little money she had left. Gary had to pay off her debts (and her lovers) more than once. On 8 September 1979, Jean Seberg's body was found under a rug on the back seat of a car parked by the kerb in Rue du Général-Appert, a quiet residential neighbourhood near the Porte Dauphine. The smell of rotting flesh seeping out of the vehicle alerted passers-by. She had probably been dead for ten or fourteen days. Romain Gary then went off the rails. He called a press conference at which he accused the FBI of being directly responsible for her death. It's certainly true that COINTELPRO had schemed to discredit Jean Seberg in the eyes of puritans (and racists) by putting out stories that the child she bore in

1970 had been fathered by a Black (see p. 305). But that was nearly ten years before. Since then the FBI had surely lost interest in a woman on the skids, living permanently abroad and no longer in the public eye. Gary was distraught and angry, but his absurd accusations were akin to paranoia. The nastier critics claimed he was doing it just to keep himself in the news. What's more likely is that the state of permanent anxiety that the Ajar mystification had engendered made him prone to believing in conspiracies and plots.

Jean may have died by accidental overdose, from natural causes, by suicide or murder. The state she was in and the life that she led in her last months would have produced some overlap between these possibilities in any case. Gary had long known that she was unstable and dangerous, and he cannot have been entirely surprised by the outcome. He had taken steps to distance Jean from their son Diego, and the vacation that the two of them spent together at Styron's guest cottage in Connecticut in summer 1978, when Diego was at a nearby tennis camp, was one of the few occasions when Jean had access in those years.

In this gloomy, agitated, hyperactive last period of his life, Gary wrote his will many times over. He also wrote his stunning revelation of the Ajar hoax, *Life and Death of Émile Ajar*, to be published at the discretion of Claude and Robert Gallimard, after his own death. He took the legal step of emancipating Diego a year ahead of his eighteenth birthday. He put things in place. He left clear instructions for his funeral. He was resolved not to grow old and to exercise the right of self-determination – the right to 'dispose of himself', in the French translation of that historical phrase – that he had learned in his childhood and youth to be one of the basic Rights of Man.

King Solomon, allegedly written by the young Émile Ajar, is about a very old man, Solomon Rubinstein, whereas *The Kites*, written by a patently old Romain Gary, is centred on an adolescent boy, Ludovic Fleury. Solomon is a Russian-speaking Jew from Wilno and Sweciany who trained as a pianist but failed to equal the *other* Rubinstein and became a tailor instead. He grew immensely rich in pre-war Paris as a manufacturer of ready-made trousers, which made him the *Roi du Pantalon*. 'Pantalon' is also the French term for *pantaleone*, the clown of the old Italian *commedia dell'arte* – and old Solomon really is the King of Clowns, in Gary's special use of the term, as well as being a secular Jewish saint.

During the German Occupation of Paris, Solomon hid for four years in a windowless box room on the Champs-Élysées while his lover, the cabaret singer Cora Lamenaire, ran off with a handsome thug who worked for the Gestapo. At the Liberation the lover was shot as a collaborator and Cora's career came to an abrupt end. Solomon never forgave her treachery. She ended up working as a toilet attendant in a café, whereas Solomon pursued quite other interests. He funded a suicide helpline – a volunteer-staffed advice and support service for suicides, similar to the Samaritans in the UK. Solomon's telephone support also mimics the real *S.O.S Amitié*, which had started up in Paris in the 1960s; its New York equivalent too, had impressed the narrator of Ajar's first book, *Gros-Câlin*.[3] By 1978, with the rapid expansion of the French telephone service, *S.O.S. Amitié* was in the news and Jean Seberg volunteered to work for it. That helps explain why King Solomon selected his volunteers with the greatest care: most of the youngsters who offer their services, he explains to his driver Jeannot, get more out of listening to others' despair than the callers do. Knowing there are other people in worse trouble gives them a real boost.

This wise, serene and dapper old man pursues justice and goodness in numerous other ways too. He has baskets of fruit and bunches of flowers delivered by courier to lonely old folk around town. He collects old postcards from flea markets and keeps appointments broken by war, disaster or fickleness decades after their time. He combs the lonely-hearts columns in the press and selects the most desperate appeals for special help. A few years after *King Solomon* was published, Philippe Sollers 'discovered' the treasure house of human experience to be found in the personal ads of daily newspapers in his roman-à-clef, *Women*.[4] It looks like he'd been reading Émile Ajar.

Why does Solomon use his time and money to shower arbitrary acts of kindness on people he doesn't know? It's by way of protest against Him Upstairs, who signally fails to do the same. Solomon makes no discrimination among people in terms of who most deserves to be loved, because although he loves humanity in general, he can only care for individuals. And he is especially concerned with relieving the sadness of old folk, who have done nothing to deserve the humiliations to which the laws of nature subject them.

Solomon treats himself as a man with a future, he will not contemplate giving in to old age. But as is always the case in Gary's serious and comic work, Solomon's future is his past. He manipulates the young taxi driver he more or less adopts (and who is the narrator of the tale) into giving comfort to his old flame Cora Lamenaire. Jeannot, to whom Gary grants a few of the traits of Paul Pavlowitch (but only a few), is an autodidact handyman with a passion for learning the meaning of words from dictionaries large and small. Like Momo in *Life Before Us*, he treats French as if it were a foreign tongue and Gary turns this highly original device into the source of a great deal of ironical but also serious fun. Like the clichés, fixed expressions and proverbs that he had always honoured as the substantive trace of a whole civilisation, especially when turned upside down, dictionary definitions are 'ready-mades' available for wear. The same trick was used years later by the thriller writer Fred Vargas in *Seeking Whom He May Devour* which, like much modern popular fiction, is indebted to models invented by Romain Gary. [5]

Out of love for humanity in general, Jeannot ends up in bed with Cora, a bird-brained sixty-five-year-old performer of *chanson réaliste*, in scenes that are simultaneously grotesque and sentimental. To extricate himself from this entirely misunderstood relationship – Cora thinks he is doing it for her and to tell her it is only for the principle would be just too hurtful to her feminine pride – Jeannot firmly steers Cora back to Solomon. The old lovers finally forgive each other and, in a grand reconciliation scene at the Gare de Lyon thoroughly worthy of Hollywood, Saint Darby and his Joan depart in a first-class wagon-lit for their honeymoon in Nice. Jeannot for his part settles down with his bookseller girlfriend Aline and starts a family. I don't think Gary's tongue was in his cheek. In any case, it should not have been. Chad Varah, the English priest who started the Samaritans in 1953 with the financial backing of the very rich patrons of St Stephen Walbrook in the City of London, didn't retire until 2003. He was made a Companion of Honour – a distinction even rarer than Gary's own – and lived to the ripe old age of ninety-two. Loving care does seem to be good for one's health.

The Kites takes the same themes from the other end of life, and works through the same history of love and war, resistance and betrayal, and final reconciliation in family life, in forward movement instead of retrospection.

Gary never had a garden and most likely couldn't tell a hoe from a pair of secateurs. The flowers he cultivated were rhetorical ones, and when flowers occur in his work they serve symbolic roles. The desperate finale of *The Company of Men* takes place in a rose garden tended by a level-crossing keeper whose only aim is to keep history, morality, tragedy and heroism on the other side of his fence. This first *gulistan* in Gary's work is an image of a false paradise in which 'real men' cannot and should not seek to dwell. But it is an alluring vision all the same, and Madame Rosa, in *Life Before Us*, mutters again and again, as she falls into a terminal coma, *Blumentag* (flower day), as if it were either a vision of paradise, or an aspiration towards it. Momo translates it for us from Madame Rosa's Yiddish – but Gary writes in proper German.

In *The Kites*, Gary's last *gulistan* is a human garden of moral flowers: the character of a retired Norman postmaster and kite-maker whose name makes it plain from the start. Ambroise Fleury drinks the nectar of the gods (ambrosia, *ambroisie*) and lives in a flowered garden (*jardin fleuri*). Gary's long and rich experience of playing with names here reaches such a peak of clarity that few readers have ever seen through his artfully drawn clouds. Similarly, the novel's location near the Channel coast in Normandy reflects no personal memory or experience, but serves exclusively to justify a narration of what was, for him and his whole generation, the most significant encounter of Good and Evil in modern history – the liberation of France from German Occupation by Allied forces. Gary doesn't use the real name of the British officer who was first at the bar of the Café Gondrée, the first building to be liberated on D-Day: Colonel Richard Geoffroy *Pine-Coffin* would have been just too outlandish for serious fiction. In any case, Gary's last novel gives no hint about a coming funeral, only about the possibility of rebirth.

The three-rosette restaurant by the shore in which much of the action of *The Kites* takes place is not so much a glorified version of the Café Gondrée as a legendary transformation of a literary place – Les Routiers, the roadside restaurant run by Monsieur and Madame Baju in *The Company of Men*. In that early, important novel, Luc, the teenage hero, is taken in by these kindly people and fed back to good health by a method presented as quintessentially French. Le Clos-joli, in *The Kites*, is even more patently an insubmersible symbol of French tradition. Marcellin Duprat, the chef, will not close down just because there is a German Occupation; in fact, he feels it is his bounden duty to make sure German officers appreciate the true heights of French culture, and he gives private cooking lessons to the local commanding officer in the name of the *mission civilisatrice*. That makes him a collaborator and a true patriot at the same time, depending on what language you want to use. It is a memorable and entertaining vignette of the argument Gary pursued from his earliest work, *A European Education*, written during the war years themselves: there is no clear human borderline between the two sides. Fraternity means self-identification with *all* your fellow men.

The narrator-hero of *The Kites* is a fourteen-year-old boy, Ludovic Fleury, the nephew and ward of the eccentric kite-maker Ambroise. He falls in love with a daughter of the Polish nobility who spends her summer holidays in the nearby Manoir des Jars, along with her spendthrift father Stas, her mother Genia and her twin brothers, Bruno and Tad. The nod to *Emil and the Three Twins*, a children's classic by the peace campaigner Erich Kästner, is obvious;[6] the books Ludo reads at this time – Remarque's *All Quiet on the Western Front* and Henri Barbusse's *Le Feu* – are also both anti-war classics of the same era.[7] Lila is a flighty, evanescent, seductive and thoroughly irritating girl with little real talent for anything except being herself. Bruno, on the other hand, is a virtuoso on the piano, whereas Tad is a gifted scientist, a budding intellectual and a Polish nationalist. Their family name, Bronicki, is fake, but just a weak vowel away from *Branicki*, the name of a celebrated *szlachta* (noble) clan whose ancestor, Hetman Jan Klemens, built the city centre of Bialystok as well as the Branicki Palace, the Polish Versailles. He was ousted from the contest for the kingship by his brother-in-law, Stanislaw Poniatowksi, whose direct descendant, Michel Poniatowski, became a contentious right-wing French politician, Minister of the Interior from 1974 to 1977 and Giscard d'Estaing's chief of staff at the Élysée at the time *The Kites* was written.

Ludo loses contact with Lila during the war, just as Gary lost touch with his beloved Ilona. He and his uncle work for the Resistance in their different ways. Ambroise carries on making and flying the 'memorial' kites for which he was famous. But whereas before the war he had commemorated national figures – Rousseau, Voltaire, Hugo, Jean-Jaurès – on the windy beaches of Normandy (the world kite-flying championship is still held in Dieppe), during the Occupation he starts to rally support for the Free French. His provocations come too close to alerting the Germans and, after his workshop is trashed, he disappears.

Lila's two brothers follow different tracks in the great conflict. Tad becomes a German officer and Bruno ends up . . . in the RAF. As *The Kites* is a romantic comedy, as well as a serious work of imagination and history, both brothers land up in Cléry, the village by the sea where the Chateau du Jars, Marcellin Duprat's restaurant, and Ambroise Fleury's kite museum are all to be found. As for Lila, she cheats Ludo atrociously and, after seducing a German officer, works in a brothel in Paris under the secretly benign command of a secretly Jewish madam, Julie Espinoza, aka la Comtesse Esterhazy. Her life is rather less extraordinary than that of Countess Olga Csáky, whom Gary met many times at Roquebrune. A poor Jewish girl from the Hungarian countryside who by dint of good looks and ambition got to marry a nobleman who then became Foreign Minister, Olga knew what lay in store just a little ahead of everyone else. In August 1939 she got a paper divorce and certificate of conversion, took the Bugatti out of the garage, put her two babies in it and drove by herself . . . to London. There she married a British naval officer and turned herself into a member of the establishment. She lived a long and happy life as an Englishwoman, became a close friend of Lesley Blanch and took to grumbling about foreigners who didn't do things the same way as 'vee Breeteesh'.[8] Novelists have to work hard to compete.

Ambroise the kite-maker, on the other hand, found his way from Cléry to Le Chambon-sur-Lignon, where he joined forces with André Trocmé to save Jewish children from deportation.

He got caught, and was himself deported to Auschwitz and Buchenwald. Fleury was not Jewish in the least, nor was he a Protestant, like the real Trocmé, and even less a man of religious convictions. He offered his services *for a just cause*, for he embodies, even more than Solomon Rubinstein in *King Solomon*, Gary's concept of a secular saint.

Gary brings the 'Lila plot', the love story he had been trying to tell all his life, to a wrenching, truthful and entirely imaginary conclusion. Lila returns to Cléry. She has slept with German officers and is thus stigmatised as a 'fallen woman' in liberated France. She must have her head shaved. Ludo does not just forgive her her sexual betrayal; he forgives her her political betrayal too. He goes further: he insists on walking with his shaven-headed lover down the street and decides to marry her. Three weeks must elapse between posting the banns and the marriage itself. By then Lila's hair has grown back an inch or two. Ludo takes her once more to the barber who had shaved her head and asks him to do it again, to make her look smart for the wedding. Just like you did it the last time, he demands. The barber shakes with fear and embarrassment.

> 'It wasn't my idea, I swear it! They came and . . .'
>
> 'Let's not debate whether it was 'them', or 'me', or 'our lot', or 'the other lot'. It's always *us*. Get on with it.'[9]

This is the same point Gary made in *Tulipe* thirty years previously, but now the 'village next door' is much closer to home. In *The Kites* he has a broad canvas of historical memory and fantasy on which he can inscribe his central moral argument in the entertaining, attractive setting of an adventure story that turns out all right in the end.

It turns out even better than that. Ambroise Fleury has survived and, after a short spell working in the Soviet Union teaching kids how to fly kites, he makes his way back to Cléry, looking just like his old self. Only the German officers are dead. Everyone else is on stage for the finale. A baby is on the way. Let the bells ring and the curtain fall.

Romain Gary shot himself on 2 December 1980 with the Smith and Wesson revolver he had legally owned since 1960.

32

Last Rites

Romain Gary's funeral took place on Tuesday 9 December 1980 at the Church of Saint-Louis des Invalides, with full military honours. He was given his last adieu not as a Jewish immigrant who made good, as a literary celebrity, or as a con artist of genius who nabbed the Goncourt twice, but with all the pomp and circumstance appropriate to a Companion of the Liberation and a Commander of the Legion of Honour. His coffin, draped in the tricolour, was carried by eleven airmen in full-dress uniform. The 'Last Post' was sounded on French horns.

The form of the ceremony had been planned by Gary and his instructions were followed to the letter. Many people were shocked, expressed surprise, even hostility. It seemed bad form for a popular novelist (nobody yet knew that he was two popular novelists at the same time) to have his mortal remains treated like a national treasure. But Gary's purpose was not to show off even after his own demise. It was to express his true and final identity as a man who had been made by the adventure of Free France. As he had said so many times, Free France was the only clan to which he had truly belonged without reservation. It was in the Lorraine Squadron that he had learned the meaning of comradeship, fraternity and the brotherhood of man. 'My season was Free France,' he told Jacques Chancel in 1978. He had said the same thing in 1970: 'There were no French, Arabs, Jews or blacks in the Foreign Legion shock troops or in my "Lorraine" squadron.'[1] To be buried as a *Compagnon de la Libération* was also to assert in his final act his life-long aspiration towards a world 'where no woman, Chinese, Jewish, Indian or whatever would have to carry her child uphill on her back: for a world where no one would be left alone'.[2] Conventionally minded left-wingers who thought a full military burial something akin to a Fascist whim had understood nothing about Romain Gary.

The Polish singer Ana Prucnal came to the church and with her husky voice she sang 'Lilovy Negr', a haunting and risqué music-hall song by Aleksandr Vertinsky that had been one of Mina Kacewa's favourite tunes.[3] According to Anissimov, some members of the congregation took it for a Hebrew hymn.[4] Romain Gary was cremated at the Père-Lachaise cemetery in Paris and some weeks later his ashes were scattered in the Mediterranean Sea, beneath Roquebrune, by his former wife Lesley Blanch and his son Alexandre-Diego Gary.

Gary left only one suicide note, headed 'For the press':

> D Day
>
> No connection with Jean Seberg. Aficionados of broken hearts should apply elsewhere.
>
> You could put this down to a depression, obviously. But then you would have to concede that it's been going on all my adult life and has allowed me to complete my literary work.
>
> So why? Maybe the answer should be sought in the title of my autobiographical work, A Quiet Night, and in the last line of my last novel: 'because you can't say better than that'. I have at last said all that I have to say.
>
> Romain Gary[5]

'A Quiet Night' is a more complex expression in French: *La Nuit sera calme* translates literally as 'The Night Will Be Quiet', and it makes better sense in this context than the English title Gary chose. But behind both French and English lies the Russian bedtime wish, спокойной ночи, ([I wish you] a peaceful night). That is surely what *garrí* the wharfrat wished himself.

But he also left good wishes to us all. *Life and Death of Émile Ajar*, written in 1979 in view of posthumous publication, ends with an old trouper's jolly adieu:

> I had a great deal of fun. *Au revoir et merci.*

Too much interpretation has been applied to these last postcards from beyond the grave. They mean exactly what they say. Gary did suffer from depression, but that's not why he pulled the trigger. He brought all his work to the best close he could manage, then did what he had always planned to do. He did have a lot of fun being Émile Ajar, but when a great act is over, it's done. Gary was not an admirable person in all respects; and in some he was monstrous, even repulsive. As Pavlowitch puts it, he was 'not all of a piece'. There was far too much of him for that.

Appendices

Appendix I

Curriculum Vitae

GARY, ROMAIN

Airman, diplomat, writer, director, journalist, actor, etc.

Born Roman Kacew, 8 May 1914 (21 May NS), Vilna (Russian Empire), only son of Mina Kacewa née Owczynski, and Leiba (Arieh) Kacew, businessman

French citizen by naturalisation (5 July 1935)

Name of Romain Gary made official by decree in 1951

Married 1. Lesley Blanch, London (UK), 4 April 1945, divorced 1963; 2. Jean Seberg, Ajaccio (Corsica), 1963, divorced 1970. One son, Alexandre-Diego Gary, born 1962

Education

Primary school, Wilno (Poland)

Secondary: Michal Kreczmar School, Ul. Wylcza, Warsaw, Poland (1926–28); Lycée de Nice, France (1928–33)

Faculté de droit, Aix-en-Provence (1933–4)

Faculté de droit, Paris (1934–8)

Military Service

Air Officers' Training School, Avord (1938); served as corporal, then as gunnery and navigation instructor with rank of *sergent*, Salon-de-Provence, then Bordeaux (1938–39).

Joined RAF as a member of the Forces aériennes de la France Libre (FAFL), July 1940. Gunner in Bomber Squadron TOE5 July–September 1940. Promoted *adjudant* September 1940. Unit incorporated in the Lorraine Squadron (RAF 324 Squadron) in

1941. Active service in West Africa, Sudan, Syria, 1941–2. Promoted to rank of *lieutenant*, December 1942. Active service in the UK, 1943–4.

Head of Chancery Division, FAFL HQ, London, 1944–5. Promoted *capitaine de réserve*, June 1945. Demobilised November 1945

Career

Appointed to the French Diplomatic Service, October 1945

Sofia, Bulgaria: Second Secretary, with the rank of *administrateur de 3e classe*, 1946–8

Paris, Foreign Office: Central Europe desk, 1948–9

Berne, Switzerland: First Secretary, with the rank of *administrateur de 2e classe*, 1950–1

Member of the French Delegation to the Security Council of the United Nations, New York, 1952–4. Promoted to rank of *administrateur de 1e classe*, August 1952. Promoted *conseiller*, 1954

London, UK: attached to the Brussels Treaty Organisation, 1955

Los Angeles, CA: Consul General 1956–60

La Paz, Bolivia: Chargé d'affaires, French Embassy, 1956–7

Leave without pay from the Diplomatic Service, 1960 –

Consultant to the Minister of Information, Georges Gorce, 1967–8

Qualifications

Baccalauréat de philosophie (mention: *passable*), July 1933

Licence de droit, 1938

Languages

Russian (native, mother tongue), Polish (native, Eastern dialect), Yiddish (conversational), German (reading, speaking), French (quasi-native, slight accent), English (British, then American: quasi-native), Bulgarian (reading knowledge)

Military and Civil Honours

Croix de guerre avec palmes de bronze, November 1944

Chevalier de la Légion d'honneur, June 1945

Compagnon de la Libération, August 1945
Officier de la Légion d'honneur, August 1955
Commandeur de la Légion d'honneur, December 1971

Literary Awards

Prix des Critiques, November 1945 (for *A European Education*)
Prix Goncourt, 1956 (for *The Roots of Heaven*)
Prix Dourchon-Louvet de l'Académie française, 1956
Prix Goncourt, 1975 (as Émile Ajar, for *Life Before Us*)

Residences

Roquebrune (French Riviera), 1949–60
108 Rue du Bac, 75006 Paris, France, from 1961
54 Rue Moillebeau, Geneva, Switzerland, from 1965
Cimarrón, Puerto Andraitx, Mallorca, Spain, from 1965

Died 2 December 1980, in Paris, from self-inflicted gunshot wound.

Appendix II

The Works of Romain Gary

As explained in chapter II, Gary's bibliography is peculiarly complicated.[1] Table I is a first simplification – a list of Romain Gary's works in chronological order of first publication, using the titles under which they appeared in English. Works not yet translated are named by their French titles, save for *Womanlight* (the English title of the film version of *Clair de femme*) and *A Quiet Night*, which is the title Gary gave to his own unpublished English translation of *La Nuit sera calme*.

Table 1. Simple title list

Romain Gary	1	*A European Education*	1944
Romain Gary	2	*Tulipe*	1946
Romain Gary	3	*The Company of Men*	1949
Romain Gary	4	*The Colours of the Day*	1952
Romain Gary	5	*The Roots of Heaven*	1956
Fosco Sinibaldi	2.2	*L'Homme à la colombe*	1958
Romain Gary	6	*Lady L.*	1958
Romain Gary	7	*Promise at Dawn*	1960
Romain Gary	8	*The Talent Scout*	1961
Romain Gary	9	*Pour Sganarelle*	1965
Romain Gary	10	*The Ski Bum*	1965
Romain Gary	11	*The Dance of Genghis Cohn*	1967
Romain Gary	12	*The Guilty Head*	1968
Romain Gary	13	*White Dog*	1970
Romain Gary	14	*Trésors de la Mer rouge*	1970
Romain Gary	15	*Europa*	1972
Romain Gary	16	*The Enchanters*	1973
Romain Gary	17	*The Gasp*	1973
René Deville	18	*Direct Flight to Allah*	1974
Romain Gary	19	*A Quiet Night*	1974
Émile Ajar	20	*Gros-Câlin*	1974
Romain Gary	21	*The Way Out*	1975
Émile Ajar	22	*Life Before Us*	1975
Émile Ajar	23	*Hocus Bogus*	1976
Romain Gary	24	*Womanlight*	1978
Émile Ajar	25	*King Solomon*	1979
Romain Gary	26	*The Kites*	1980
Romain Gary	27	*Life and Death of Émile Ajar*	1981

The simple list is, however, not the list of works to which either the French or the English reading public had access in the order of their writing or first publication. Gary pursued a somewhat separate career in each language, partly through force of circumstance, partly through deception. Table 2 shows the quite different orders of publication of Gary's works in French and in English. Actual titles of first publication in each language are used. Key numbers refer back to the titles listed in Table 1.

Table 2. Gary's twin careers

Year	In French	In English
1944		1 *Forest of Anger*
1945	1 *Éducation européenne*	
1946	2 *Tulipe*	
1949	3 *Le Grand vestiaire*	
1950		3 *The Company of Men*
1952	4 *Les Couleurs du jour*	
1953		4 *The Colours of the Day*
1956	5 *Les Racines du ciel*	
1958	2.2 *L'Homme à la colombe*	6 *Lady L.* 5 *The Roots of Heaven*
1960	7 *La Promesse de l'aube*	1 *A European Education*
1961		8 *The Talent Scout* 7 *Promise at Dawn*
1963	6 *Lady L.*	
1964		
1965	9 *Pour Sganarelle*	10 *The Ski Bum*
1966	8 *Les Mangeurs d'étoiles*	
1967	11 *La Danse de Gengis Cohn*	
1968	12 *La Tête coupable*	11 *The Dance of Genghis Cohn*
1969	10 *Adieu Gary Cooper*	12 *The Guilty Head*
1970	13 *Chien Blanc*	13 *White Dog*
1971	14 *Trésors de la Mer rouge*	
1972	15 *Europa*	
1973	16 *Les Enchanteurs*	17 *The Gasp*
1974	18 *Les Têtes de Stéphanie* 19 *La Nuit sera calme* 20 *Gros-Câlin*	
1975	21 *Au-delà de cette limite* 22 *La Vie devant soi*	16 *The Enchanters* 18 *Direct Flight to Allah*
1976	23 *Pseudo*	
1977	24 *Clair de femme*	21 *The Way Out*
1978	17 *Charge d'âme* 25 *L'Angoisse du roi Salomon*	15 *Europa* 22 *Momo*
1979	4 *Les Clowns lyriques*	
1980	26 *Les Cerfs-volants*	
1981	27 *Vie et mort d'Émile Ajar*	
1983		25 *King Solomon* 27 *Life and Death of Émile Ajar*
2009		23 *Hocus Bogus*

But these longer lists still mask the full extent of Gary's writing life. Most of his works appeared more than once in editions not only translated or back-translated, but revised, readjusted, adapted to the stage, reworked or retitled. The following table lists all the publications in book form of Gary's works other than unaltered reissues or translations between English and French in which Gary had no hand. Editions under the same title in which some notice is given of changes made to the text are marked by an asterisk; in other cases revised editions appeared as if they were mere reissues, or, as in the case of *Les Clowns lyriques*, as if they were different books.

Table 3. Gary rewrites himself

Year	In French	In English
1944		1.1 *Forest of Anger*
1945	1.2 *Éducation européenne*	
1946	2.1 *Tulipe*	
1949	3.1 *Le Grand vestiaire*	
1950		
1952	4.1 *Les Couleurs du jour*	
1953		4.2 *The Colours of the Day**
1956	5.1 *Les Racines du ciel*	
1958	2.2 *L'Homme à la colombe*	6.1 *Lady L.* 5.2 *The Roots of Heaven**
1960	7.1 *La Promesse de l'aube*	1.3 *A European Education*[2]
1961	2.3 *Johnnie Cœur* 1.4 *Education européenne**	8.1 *The Talent Scout* 7.2 *Promise at Dawn*
1963	6.2 *Lady L.*	
1965	9 *Pour Sganarelle*	10.1 *The Ski Bum*
1966	8.2 *Les Mangeurs d'étoiles*	
1967	11.1 *La Danse de Gengis Cohn*	
1968	12.1 *La Tête coupable*	11.2 *The Dance of Genghis Cohn**
1969	10.2 *Adieu Gary Cooper*	12.2 *The Guilty Head*
1970	2.4 *Tulipe* 13.1 *Chien Blanc*	13.2 *White Dog*
1971	14 *Trésors de la Mer rouge*	
1972	15 *Europa*	
1973	16 *Les Enchanteurs*	17.1 *The Gasp*
1974	18.2 *Les Têtes de Stéphanie*	
	19 *La Nuit sera calme* 20 *Gros-Câlin*	
1975	21 *Au-delà de cette limite* 22 *La Vie devant soi*	18.1 *Direct Flight to Allah*
1976	23 *Pseudo*	
1977	6.3 *Lady L.* 24 *Clair de femme*	
1978	17.2 *Charge d'âme* 25 *L'Angoisse du roi Salomon*	
1979	3.2 *La Bonne moitié* 4.3 *Les Clowns lyriques*	
1980	5.3 *Les Racines du ciel** 7.3 *La Promesse de l'aube** 12.3 *La Tête coupable* 26 *Les Cerfs-volants*	
1981	27 *Vie et mort d'Émile Ajar*	
1984	2.5 *L'Homme à la colombe**	

Table 4. Short fiction by Romain Gary

Alongside his novels, Gary also wrote a number of short stories, constituting the least-known but arguably the most accomplished part of his fiction. Here I list all known short stories in chronological order of first appearance, using titles taken from published English translations, with works unpublished in English being left with the best-known of their French titles. With the exception of S1 and S2, published under the name Romain Kacew, and S3, under the name A. Cary, all Gary's short stories appeared under his own (adopted) name.

			Extracted from or inserted in
S1	*L'Orage*	1935	
S2	*Une Petite femme*	1935	
S3	*Géographie humaine*	1943	
S4	*Le Continent englouti*	1944	1 *A European Education*
S5	*Noblesse et grandeur*	1944	
S6	All Is Well on the Kilimanjaro	1945	
S7	Comrade Pigeon	1945	
S8	The Night of History	1945	
S9	*Sergent Gnama*	1946	
S10	*Le Blanc prophète de Harlem*	1947	2 *Tulipe*
S11	Glass	1951	
S12	The Lute	1954	
S13	Speaking of Heroism	1956	
S14	A Craving for Innocence	1956	
S15	*JE mange mon soulier*	1956	10 *Promise at Dawn*
S16	*L'Évasion du professeur Ostrach*	1957	5 *The Roots of Heaven*
S17	The Wall: A Christmas Tale	1958	
S18	A Humanist	1958	
S19	*Débuts dans la vie*	1960	10 *Promise at Dawn*
S20	Courage and Farewell!	1960	10 *Promise at Dawn*
S21	*La Lune*	1961	
S22	The Fake	1962	
S23	Birds in Peru	1962	
S24	The Oldest Story Ever Told	1962	
S25	Nature	1962	
S26	Decadence	1962	
S27	The New Frontier	1962	
S28	The Dance of Genghis Cohn	1967	16 *The Dance of Genghis Cohn*
S29	*Dix ans après*	1968	
S30	*Cet Amour que j'ai tant aimé*	1974	20 *A Quiet Night*
S31	*Anatomie du déclin*	1975	22 *The Way Out*

The publishing history of these pieces is uncommonly complicated. *Gloire à nos illustres pionniers* (Gallimard, 1962) contains sixteen of the stories in the order: S23, S12, S18, S26, S22, S25, S5, S7, S8, S17, S6, S13, S11, S14, S24, S27. The English version, strangely titled *Hissing Tales*, translated by Richard Howard (Harper & Row, 1964), omits S5 and re-orders the other fifteen thus: S14, S7, S17, S22, S23, S24, S25, S26, S18, S6, S8, S13, S12, S11, S27. *Gloire à nos illustres pionniers* has been retitled twice over, as *Les Oiseaux vont mourir au Pérou* (Folio, 1975), containing the full set of stories, and as *Une Page d'histoire* (Folio, 2002), containing only S12, S22, S5, S8 and S11. *L'Orage* (L'Herne, 2005) reprints S1, S2, S3, S9 and S29.

Several of the stories, all of which were written in French, had virtually independent careers in English translation: S7 'Comrade Pigeon' came out in *Penguin Russian Review* in 1948; S12 'The Lute' appeared in *Harper's Bazaar* in November 1954; S18 'A Humanist' in the *Saturday Evening Post* in 1963 then in Alfred Hitchcock's *A Month of Mystery* in 1969 and in *Boucher's Choice* in the same year, and again in an anthology, *The Cream of Crime*, in 1972; S22 'The Fake' appeared in *Ladies' Home Journal* in 1963, then in *Short Story International* in 1964 and again in 1978; S23 'Birds in Peru' was reprinted as 'A Bit of a Dreamer, a Bit of a Fool' in *Playboy* in 1964 then again in *Short Story International* and in *The Pocket Playboy* in 1973; S26 'Decadence' was collected in *Tenth Annual S-F* in 1965, then in *Suddenly: Great Stories of Suspense and the Unexpected* and in the same year as 'The Living Statue', in *Bizarre Mystery Magazine* and finally, as 'Decadence', in *Best Crime Stories* in 1968.

Republication of Gary's stories in magazines, serials and anthologies was less frequent in French, but there were several variations in titles and one of content. S5 '*Noblesse et Grandeur*' was originally titled '*Grandeur nature*'; S8 'A Night of History' was titled '*Une Page d'histoire*' in all French versions, but its setting was transferred from Bohemia (in 1945) to Serbia (in

1962); S12 'The Lute' originally appeared as '*Ainsi s'achève une journée de soleil*' but found its definitive title first in English translation ('The Lute'), which was used for all subsequent French editions ('*Le Luth*'); S13 'Speaking of Heroism' first appeared under the title '*JE rencontre un barracuda*' and became '*Je parle d'héroïsme*' only when collected in 1962; similarly, S14 'A Craving for Innocence' ('*J'ai soif d'innocence*') came out first as '*JE découvre un Gauguin en vrac*'. S18 'A Humanist' was originally called '*Les Belles natures*' but found its definitive title on first republication in the collection *Gloire à nos illustres pionniers*. Only one of these stories – S21 '*La Lune*', recently discovered in *Elle* magazine by Jean-François Hangouët – has never been republished.

Appendix III

A bibliography of Gary in English

Gary's use of pseudonyms is only one of the devices he employed to cover his tracks. Just as frequent are misleading implications on title pages about the linguistic status and origin of his books. Some books purporting to be translations were no such thing; in other cases books not labelled as translations had in fact been brought over from French into English, or vice versa. Gary's 'English bibliography' cannot therefore be established simply by looking at a library catalogue, or by consulting the books themselves.

Gary's American and British bibliographies have to be kept apart. Most of his books were separately typeset for American and British publication and brought out by different publishers; in some cases titles vary from one side of the Atlantic to the other; furthermore, a few of his books were published in English only in the UK, and several others only in the USA. Some of his translators were British (Viola Garvin, Jonathan Griffin (a close friend of Pierre Rouve), J. Maxwell Johnson, Barbara Bray and Barbara Wright), and others American (although Ralph Manheim was based in Paris and Cambridge, not in the USA). American publishers frequently used British translators and vice versa.

Copyright attributions have been included to show Gary's personal control of his English-language rights, which was extensive but not total. The two translations published under the name of Émile Ajar obviously fell outside Gary's sway, since he was not supposed to have written them, but the other exceptions to the general rule – *The Roots of Heaven*, *The Way Out* and *Europa* – have for the moment no satisfactory explanation.

Annotations included in the British title list have not been repeated in the US list. Titles are listed in chronological order of publication; the numbering refers to the list of Gary's works given in Appendix II, Table I.

In the United Kingdom

1. *Forest of Anger*. Translated from the French by Viola Gerard Garvin (Cresset Press, 1944). No copyright assigned.
3. *The Company of Men*. Translated by Joseph Barnes. Copyright 1950 by Romain Gary (London: Michael Joseph, 1950; paperback reprint: London: Mayflower Books, 1966).
4. *The Colours of the Day*. Translated by Stephen Becker. Copyright 1953, 1954 by Romain Gary. [Substantially corrected and altered by Romain Gary; somewhat closer to the later French revision, *Les Clowns lyriques*, than to the original *Les Couleurs du jour*.] (London: Michael Joseph, 1953; paperback reprint: London: Mayflower Books, 1966). [The UK reprint, but not the first edition, carries a notice stating that changes had been made in the course of translation and would be incorporated into future French editions.] (Reissue: London: White Lion Publishers, 1974).
5. *The Roots of Heaven*. Translated by Jonathan Griffin (translation © Michael Joseph, London: Michael Joseph, 1958). [Contains a notice stating that changes had been made by the author in the course of translation and would be incorporated into future French editions; the changes are less substantial than in *The Colours of the Day* and the main change – the division of the novel into four parts in lieu of the original three – was not carried over into the French 'definitive edition' of 1980.] (Paperback reprint: London: Penguin, 1960; reissue: London: White Lion Publishers, 1973).

6. *Lady L.* © Propintel SA. [written in English]. (London: Michael Joseph, 1959; paperback reprint: London: Penguin, 1965).

1. *Nothing Important Ever Dies.* © Romain Gary 1960. [A substantial revision of *Forest of Anger*, with two additional chapters, one cut chapter, and many changes in dialogue and the order of narration.] (London: Cresset Press, 1960; paperback reprint: Transworld Publishers, 1963). [This is the basis of the 'definitive edition' of *Éducation européenne* published in French in 1961, but by no means identical to it.]

7. *Promise at Dawn.* Translated by John Markham Beach. Copyright 1961 by Romain Gary (London: Michael Joseph, 1962). [John Markham Beach is another of Gary's pseudonyms. The English edition has an additional chapter not brought into French until the 'definitive edition' in the 1970s.]

8. *The Talent Scout.* Translated by John Markham Beach [written in English]. Copyright 1961 by Romain Gary (London: Michael Joseph, 1961; reprint: New English Library, 1964; reprint: New English Library, 1965; paperback reprint: Sphere Books, 1971).

• *Hissing Tales.* Translated by Richard Howard. © Romain Gary 1963, 1964 (London: Michael Joseph, 1964; reprint: New English Library, 1966).

10. *The Ski Bum.* Copyright © 1964, 1965 by Romain Gary [written in English]. (London: Michael Joseph, 1965; reprint: New English Library, 1967).

11. *The Dance of Genghis Cohn.* Translated from the French by the author with the assistance of Camilla Sykes. [Rewritten from top to bottom, with additional material, by Romain Gary]. © Romain Gary 1968 (London: Cape, 1969; Paperback reprint: Penguin, 1978).

13. *White Dog.* © 1970 by Romain Gary (London: Jonathan Cape, 1971; reprint: Chicago and London: University of

Chicago Press, 2004). [The English version is significantly different from the French and was undoubtedly written entirely by Romain Gary.]

17. *The Gasp: a novel*. Copyright © 1973 by Romain Gary [written in English]. (London: Weidenfeld & Nicolson, 1973).
18. René Deville, *Direct Flight to Allah*. Translated from the French by J. Maxwell Brownjohn (Collins, 1975). [No copyright assignment. Brownjohn did the translation without assistance from Gary. Gary's authorship is revealed on the back-panel copy of the British edition.]
21. *The Way Out*. Translated from the French by Sophie Wilkins. © English translation by Georges Braziller (London: Michael Joseph, 1977). [Gary does not appear to have had any involvement in the translation; but he did add an epigraph.]
22. Émile Ajar, *Momo*. Translated by Ralph Manheim. Translation © Doubleday and Co., 1977, 1978 (Collins Harvill, 1978). [Gary, masquerading as Ajar, corresponded with Manheim over some translation issues but was unable to exert much influence.]

25 & 27. *King Solomon*. With *Life and Death of Émile Ajar*. Translated by Barbara Wright. English translation © Harper & Row 1983 (London: Harvill, 1983).

23. *Hocus Bogus*. Translated by David Bellos. With *Life and Death of Émile Ajar*. Translated by Barbara Wright (London: Yale University Press, 2010).

In the United States

3. *The Company of Men, a novel*. Translated by Joseph Barnes. Copyright 1950 by Romain Gary (Simon & Schuster, 1950).
4. *The Colors of the Day*. Translated from the French by Stephen Becker. Copyright 1953, 1954 by Romain Gary (New York: Simon & Schuster, 1953; reprint: White Lion Publishers, 1976).

5. *The Roots of Heaven*. Translated from the French by Jonathan Griffin. Translation © Michael Joseph (New York: Simon & Schuster, 1958; reprint: White Lion Publishers, 1974).
6. *Lady L.* © Propintel SA (New York: Simon & Schuster, 1959).
1. *A European Education*. © Romain Gary, 1960 (New York: Simon & Schuster, 1960).
7. *Promise at Dawn*. Translated from French by John Markham Beach. Copyright 1961 by Romain Gary (New York: Harper, 1961; reprint: New Directions, 1987).
8. *The Talent Scout*. Translated from French by John Markham Beach. Copyright 1961 by Romain Gary (New York: Harper, 1961).
- *Hissing Tales*. Translated by Richard Howard. © Romain Gary 1963, 1964 (New York: Harper & Row, 1964).
10. *The Ski Bum*. Copyright © 1964, 1965 by Romain Gary (New York: Harper & Row, 1965).
11. *The Dance of Genghis Cohn*. Translated from the French by the author with the assistance of Camilla Sykes. © Romain Gary 1968 (New York: World Publishing Company, 1968; reprint: Schocken Books, 1982).
12. *The Guilty Head*. © 1969 by Romain Gary (New York: World Publishing Company, 1969). [The translation is by Romain Gary, who introduced substantial new material.]
13. *White Dog*. © 1970 by Romain Gary (New York: World Publishing Company, 1970; reprint: Chicago and London: Chicago University Press, 2004).
15. *Europa*. Translated from the French by Barbara Bray and the author. © Éditions Gallimard, 1972. Translation © by Doubleday & Co., 1978 (Doubleday, 1978).
16. *The Enchanters*. Translated from the French by Helen Eustis. English Translation © Romain Gary 1975 (New York: Putnam, 1975). [A shortened and expurgated version of the French. Gary presumably approved the changes.]

17. *The Gasp*. Copyright © 1973 by Romain Gary (New York: Putnam, 1973).
21. *Your Ticket Is No Longer Valid*. Translated by Sophie Wilkins. © English translation by Georges Braziller (G. Brazillller, 1977).
22. Émile Ajar, *Momo*. Translated by Ralph Manheim. Translation © Doubleday and Co., 1977, 1978 (Doubleday, 1978); reprinted under the title *The Life Before Us*, with an afterword by James Laughlin (New York: New Directions, 1986).
25 & 27. *King Solomon.* With *Life and Death of Émile Ajar*. Translated by Barbara Wright. English translation © Harper & Row, 1983 (New York: Harper & Row, 1983).
23. *Hocus Bogus*. Translated by David Bellos. With *Life and Death of Émile Ajar*. Translated by Barbara Wright (New Haven, CT: Yale University Press, 2010).

Other works in English

2. *Tulipe*. English version by Romain Gary, circa 1945, whereabouts unknown.
2.2. *A Man with a Dove, or, The Last Adventures of Frankie and Johnnie*. Translated by Joseph Barnes with revisions by Romain Gary, 1955. (Unpublished, Barnes Papers, Columbia University Library, New York).
10. *Millions of Dollars*. Film adaptation of *The Ski Bum* by Romain Gary. (Unpublished, Library of Congress, Washington, DC).
• *A Day in the Life of Harry Smithowitz*. Stage comedy, circa 1970. (Unpublished, IMEC, Fonds Gary).
19. *A Quiet Night*. English version of *La Nuit sera calme* by Romain Gary, circa 1974. (Unpublished, IMEC, Fonds Gary).
26. Extracts from *The Kites*, available online at http://www.geocities.com/p_leriche/gary/index.htm.

Appendix IV

A Filmography of Gary and Seberg from 1960 to 1972

Release date	Title	Director	Principal locations
1960	*Let No Man Write My Epitaph*	Philip Leacock	New York
1960	*La Récréation*	François Moreuil	Paris
1961	*Les Grandes personnes*	Jean Valère	Paris
1961	*L'Amant de cinq jours*	Philippe de Broca	Paris
1962	*Congo vivo*	Guiseppe Bennati	Italy
1963	*In the French Style*	Robert Parrish	Paris
1964	*Les Plus belles escro-queries du monde*	Claude Chabrol	Paris, Marrakech
1964	*Échappement libre*	Jean Becker	Barcelona, Granada, Germany, Greece, Italy, Marseille
1964	*Lilith*	Robert Rossen	Rockville, MD
1965	*Un Milliard dans un billard*	Nicolas Gesner	Switzerland
1965	*Moment to Moment*	Mervyn Le Roy	Mougins, Nice, St Paul-de-Vence

Release date	Title	Director	Principal locations
1966	*Estouffade à la Caraïbe*	Jacques Besnard	South America
1966	*La Ligne de démarcation*	Claude Chabrol	French Jura
1966	*A Fine Madness*	Irvin Kershner	Long Island and NYC
1967	*Who's Got the Black Box?*	Claude Chabrol	Paris, St Tropez, Athens
1968	*Les Oiseaux vont mourir au Pérou*	Romain Gary	Paris and Seville (Spain)
1969	*Pendulum*	George Schaefer	Washington, DC
1969	*Paint Your Wagon*	Joshua Logan	Oregon and California
1970	*Ondata di calore*	Nelo Risi	Agadir (Morocco)
1970	*Airport*	George Seaton	Minneapolis
1970	*Macho Callahan*	Bernhard Kowalski	Durango (Mexico)
1971	*Kill!*	Romain Gary	Spain, Tunisia, Afghanistan
1972	*Questa specia d'amore*	Alberto Bevilacqua	Parma, Rome

Works Cited

Place of publication is Paris unless otherwise stated.

I. By Romain Gary

(As Romain Kacew), *Le Vin des morts*. Unpublished manuscript, circa 1935. Private collection. Extracts published in Anissimov, pp. 106–7

(As Romain Kacew), 'L'Orage', *Gringoire*, 15 February 1935. Reprinted in Romain Gary, *L'Orage*, *L'Herne*, 2005, pp. 13–37

(As Romain Kacew), 'Une petite femme', *Gringoire*, 24 May 1935. Reprinted in Romain Gary, *L'Orage*, *L'Herne*, 2005, pp. 113–40

(As A. Cary), '*Géographie humaine*', *La Marseillaise* (London), 7 March 1943. Reprinted in Romain Gary, *L'Orage*, *L'Herne*, 2005, pp. 81–92

(As Romain Gary), '*Le Continent englouti*', *La France Libre*, issue 45, July 1944

'*Grandeur nature*', *La France Libre*, September 1944. As '*Noblesse et grandeur*' in *Gloire à nos illustres pionniers*

Éducation européenne, (1) Calmann-Lévy, 1945; (2) Gallimard, 1961. As *Forest of Anger*, London, Cresset Press, 1944. As *A European Education*, New York, Harper & Row, 1960

'*Tout va bien sur le Kilimandjaro*', *Cadran*, issue 12, May 1945, p. 22. Reprinted in *Gloire à nos illustres pionniers*

'*Citoyen Pigeon*', *Cadran*, August 1945. Reprinted in *Gloire à nos illustres pionniers*

'*Une page d'histoire*', *La France Libre*, December 1945. Revised version in *Gloire à nos illustres pionniers*

'Sergent Gnama', *Bulletin de l'Association des Français libres*, January 1946, pp. 11–13. Reprinted in Romain Gary, *L'Orage*, *L'Herne*, 2005, pp. 107–11

Tulipe, (1) Calmann-Lévy, 1946; (2) Gallimard, 1970

Le Grand vestiaire, Gallimard, 1949. As *The Company of Men*, New York: Simon & Schuster, 1950

Les Couleurs du jour, Gallimard, 1951. As *The Colors of the Day*, New York: Simon & Schuster, 1953

'Les habitants de la terre', *Revue de Paris*, January 1951. Reprinted in *Gloire à nos illustres pionniers*

'Ainsi s'achève une journée de soleil', *La Table ronde*, issue 78, June 1954, pp. 75–92. As *'Le Luth'* in *Gloire à nos illustres pionniers*

'Lesley est une sorcière', *Elle*, 7 March 1955. Reprinted in Hangouët, Jean-François and Paul Audi (eds), 'Romain Gary', *Les Cahiers de l'Herne* 85 (2005), pp. 263–7

Les Racines du ciel, Gallimard, 1956. As *The Roots of Heaven*, New York: Simon & Schuster, 1958

'Je rencontre un barracuda', *Elle*, 23 April 1956. As *'Je parle d'héroïsme'* in *Gloire à nos illustres pionniers*

'Je découvre un Gauguin en vrac', *Elle*, 30 April 1956. As 'A Craving for Innocence' in *Hissing Tales*

'JE mange mon soulier', *Elle*, 10 December 1956, pp. 50–1, 103. Incorporated in modified form in *Promise at Dawn*, pp. 58–60

'Les Hommes, ces éléphants', *L'Express*, 4 January 1957. As *'La marge humaine'* in *L'Affaire homme*, Jean-François Hangouët and Paul Audi (eds), Paris: Folio, 2005, pp. 17–31

(As Fosco Sinibaldi), *L'Homme à la colombe* (1958), Gallimard, 2004

Lady L., New York: Simon & Schuster, 1958. As *Lady L.* Gallimard, 1963

'Le mur', *Preuves*, issue 84, February 1958. As *'Le mur, simple conte de Noël'* in *Gloire à nos illustres pionniers*

'Les belles natures', *Preuves*, issue 84, February 1958. As 'A Humanist' in *Hissing Tales*

'The Man Who Stayed Lonely to Save France', *Life*, vol. 45, issue 23, 8 December 1958

'The Colonials', *Holiday* 25, April 1959; French translation in *L'Affaire homme*, pp. 51–63

La Promesse de l'aube, Gallimard, 1960. As *Promise at Dawn*, London: Michael Joseph, 1961

The Talent Scout, New York: Harper & Row, 1961. As *Les Mangeurs d'étoiles*, Gallimard, 1966

'*Gary Cooper, mon ami si timide*', *Le Nouveau Candide*, issue 3, 18 May 1961, p. 7

'The Triumph of Rudeness', *Holiday* 30, July 1961. French translation in *L'Affaire homme*, pp. 79–89

'*Gloire à nos illustres pionniers*' (1962). As 'The New Frontier' in *Hissing Tales*

'*Les Oiseaux vont mourir au Pérou*', in Gloire à nos illustres pionniers. As 'Birds in Peru' in *Hissing Tales*.

Gloire à nos illustres pionniers, Gallimard, 1962. As *Hissing Tales*, New York: Simon & Schuster, 1964

'*La plus vieille histoire du monde*', *Preuves*, issue 133, March 1962. Reprinted in *Gloire à nos illustres pionniers*

'Here is Might and Reassuring Promise', *Life*, 21 December 1962

'I know a place in Paris', *Holiday* 37, January 1965

Pour Sganarelle (1965), Gallimard, 2004

The Ski Bum, London: Michael Joseph, 1965. As *Adieu Gary Cooper*, Gallimard, 1969

Letter to the Editor, *New York Times*, 12 June 1966

La Danse de Gengis Cohn, Gallimard, 1967. As *The Dance of Genghis Cohn* (1968), London: Penguin, 1973

'*Questionnaire Marcel Proust*', *Livres de France*, March 1967, p. 18

'Flamboyant Guadeloupe', *Holiday* 42, August 1967

'Dear Elephant, Sir', *Life*, 22 December 1967

'*Dix ans après ou la plus vieille histoire du monde*', *Icare*, issue 44, winter 1967

La Tête coupable, Gallimard, 1968. As *The Guilty Head*, New York: World Publishing, 1969
'To My General, with Love and Anger', *Life*, vol. 66, issue 18, 9 May 1969
Chien blanc, Gallimard, 1970. As *White Dog*, New York: World Publishing, 1970
Trésors de la Mer rouge, Gallimard, 1970
'*Lettre aux Juifs de France*', *Le Figaro littéraire*, 9 March 1970; reprinted in *L'Affaire homme*, pp. 221–5
'Ode to the man who was France', *Life*, vol. 69, issue 21, 20 November 1970
'Penang: Tiger, tiger burning bright', *Travel & Leisure*, December 1971
'*Faux Romantisme et Avenir*', *Le Monde*, 11 December 1971
Europa, Gallimard, 1972. As *Europa*, New York: Doubleday, 1978
'*Ma haine des trafiquants de drogue est sans limite*', *Le Figaro*, 27 January 1972
'The Oriental Hotel of Bangkok', *Travel & Leisure*, October 1972
Les Enchanteurs, Gallimard, 1973. As *The Enchanters*, New York: Putnam, 1975
The Gasp, London: Weidenfeld & Nicolson, 1973. As *Charge d'âme*, Gallimard, 1978
'Singapore', *Travel & Leisure*, Autumn 1973
(As Shatan Bogat), *Les Têtes de Stéphanie*, Gallimard, 1974. (As René Deville) as *Direct Flight to Allah*, London: Collins, 1975
La Nuit sera calme (1974), Folio, 1980
(As Émile Ajar), *Gros-Câlin* (1974), Folio, 2003. Complete text, Jean-François Hangouët (ed.), Mercure de France, 2007
Au-delà de cette limite votre ticket n'est plus valable, Galllimard, 1975. As *Your Ticket Is No Longer Valid*, New York: Georges Braziller, 1977
(As Émile Ajar), *La Vie devant soi*, Mercure de France, 1975. As *Momo*, New York: New Directions, 1976

(As Émile Ajar), *Pseudo*, Mercure de France, 1976. As *Hocus Bogus*, transl. David Bellos, New Haven, CT: Yale University Press, 2010

Clair de femme (1977), Folio, 1982

'*Le Nouveau romantisme*', in *Clair de femme*, Cercle du Nouveau Livre, Librairie Jules Taillandier, 1977; reprinted in *L'Affaire homme*, pp. 283–97

(As Émile Ajar), *L'Angoisse du roi Salomon*, Mercure de France, 1978. As *King Solomon*, London: Harvill, 1983

Les Clowns lyriques (1979), Folio, 1989

Les Cerfs-volants, Gallimard, 1980

'*Si l'enfer pouvait avoir des murs . . .*' testimonial in the catalogue of the exhibition 'Résistance–Déportation' at the Musée de l'Ordre de la Libération, Paris, April–June 1980

Posthumous works and collections:

Vie et mort d'Émile Ajar, Gallimard, 1981. As *Life and Death of Émile Ajar*, transl. Barbara Wright in *King Solomon* and in *Hocus Bogus*

Ode à l'homme qui fut la France, transl. and ed. Paul Audi Paris: Folio, 2000

L'Affaire homme, transl. and ed. Pierre-Emmanuel Dauzat, Paul Audi and Jean-François Hangouët, Folio, 2005

L'Orage, Béatrice Vierne (ed.), L'Herne, 2005

II. By other authors

Achtouk, Olivier, '*Généalogie du roman: la paternité hugolienne à l'épreuve de l'écruture ajarienne*', in *Études Romain Gary I. Signé Ajar*, La Chasse au Snark, 2004, pp. 49–70

Anissimov, Myriam, *Roman Gary, le cameléon*, revised edition, Folio, 2006

Anonymous, *Guerilla Warfare in the Occupied Parts of the Soviet Union*, Popular Lecture Series, Moscow: Foreign Languages Publishing House, [June] 1943

Anonymous, *Poland Fights On*, London: Stratton House, 1942

Anonymous, *Preparatory Document for the International Conference for the Protection of the Fauna and Flora of Africa, Bukavu, 26–31 October 1953*, available online from http://app.iucn.org

Antelme, Robert, *L'Espèce humaine* (1948). As *The Human Race*, transl. Jeffrey Haight and Annie Mahler, Marlboro, VT: Marlboro Press, 1992

Arnothy, Christine, review of *Gros-Câlin*, *Le Parisien libéré*, 29 October 1974

Aron, Raymond, *De Gaulle, Israël et les Juifs*, Plon, 1968

Athill, Diana, *Make Believe. A True Story*, London: Sinclair-Stevenson, 1993

Audi, Paul, *Je me suis toujours été un autre*, Bourgois, 2007

——*L'Europe et son fantôme*, Léo Scheer, 2003

——*La Fin de l'impossible. Deux ou trois choses que je sais de Gary*, Bourgois, 2005

Aymé, Marcel, *Uranus*, Gallimard, 1948

Balzac, Honoré de, *Lettres à Madame Hanska*, Roger Pierrot (ed.), Delta, 1967

——*L'Envers de l'histoire contemporaine* (1848), Folio, 1984

Barbusse, Henri, *Le Feu* (1917). As *Under Fire*, transl. Fitzwater Wray, New York: Dutton, 1919

Bayard, Pierre, *Il était deux fois Romain Gary*, PUF, 1990

Beauvoir, Simone de, *Les Mandarins* (1954). As *The Mandarins*, transl. Leonard Friedman, London: Fontana, 1960

——*Le sang des autres* (1947). As *The Blood of Others*, transl. Yvonne Moiyse and Roger Senhouse, London: Secker & Warburg, 1948

Beckett, Eric W., *The North Atlantic Treaty, the Brussels Treaty and the Charter of the United Nations*, London: Stevens, 1950

Bellos, David, '*Petite histoire de l'incorrection à l'usage des ajaristes*', in *Études Romain Gary I. Signé Ajar*, La Chasse au Snark, 2004, pp. 29–47

——'*Le Malentendu: l'histoire cachée d'* Éducation européenne', in Jean-François Hangouët and Paul Audi (eds), 'Romain Gary', *Les Cahiers de l'Herne* 85 (2005), pp. 150–68

Bellos, David and Avram Offer, '*A Propos de l'acte de naissance de Roman Katzav*', *Le Plaid* 10 (2003), pp. 27–31

Berberova, Nina, *Железная Женщина* (*The Iron Lady*), New York: YMCA Press, 1981

Beresford, J. D., review of *Forest of Anger*, *Guardian*, 12 January 1945

Blanch, Lesley, *The Wilder Shores of Love*, London: John Murray, 1954. As *Les Rives sauvages de l'amour*, Paris: Plon, 1956

——*Around the World in Eighty Dishes*, New York: Harper, 1955

——*The Game of Hearts*. Harriette Wilson and her Memoirs, interspersed with excerpts from the *Confessions* of Julia Johnstone, her rival, edited and with an introduction by Lesley Blanch, New York: Simon & Schuster, 1955; London: Gryphon Books, 1957

——*Journey into the Mind's Eye*, New York: Atheneum, 1969

——*Romain, un regard particulier*, Arles: Actes Sud, 1996

Boisen, Jørn, *Un picaro métaphysique. Romain Gary et l'art du roman*, Odense (Denmark): Odense University Press, 1996

Bona, Dominique, *Romain Gary*, Mercure de France, 1987

Bondy, François, '*Le moment de vérité. Entretien avec Romain Gary*', *Preuves* 73, March 1957; reprinted in *L'Affaire homme*, pp. 35–48

Bonnier, Henry, '*Une Heure avec Romain Gary*' (1967), re-broadcast by France-Culture on 22 April 1995, Archives INA, Paris

Bory, Jean-Louis, *Mon Village à l'heure allemande*, New York: Maison française, 1945

Bosquet, Alain, '*Mémoire européenne*', *Le Quotidien de Paris*, 20 May 1980; reprinted in Jean-François Hangouët and Paul Audi (eds), 'Romain Gary', pp. 307–8

Boston, Anne, *Lesley Blanch. Inner Landscapes, Wilder Shores*, London: John Murray, 2010

Bourdieu, Pierre, '*Champ intellectuel et projet créateur*', *Les Temps modernes* 22, 1966, pp. 865–906

Bourin, André, '*Entretiens avec Romain Gary*', broadcast by France-Culture in six episodes between May and July 1969

Brenot, Philippe, *Le manuscrit perdu*, Le Bouscat: L'Esprit du Temps, 2006

Broché, François, *Les Bombardiers de la France Libre, Le Groupe Lorraine*, La Table ronde, 1979

Burgess, Anthony, *A Clockwork Orange* (1971), London: Penguin, 2000

Butor, Michel, *L'Emploi du temps*, Minuit, 1958

Calvino, J.-B., *Dictionnaire Niçois-Français* (1983), reprinted 1997

Camus, Albert, *La Peste* (1947). As *The Plague*, transl. Justin O'Brien, London: Everyman's Library, 2004

Carver, Robert, *The Accursed Mountains: Journeys in Albania*, London: John Murray, 1998

Castellana, Georges, *Dictionnaire Niçois-Français* (1952), reprinted 2001

Catonné, Jean-Marie, *Romain Gary/Émile Ajar*, Belfond, 1990

Céline, Louis-Ferdinand, *Voyage au bout de la nuit* (1932). As *Journey to the End of Night*, transl. Ralph Manheim, New York: New Directions, 1988

Chancel, Jacques, '*Radioscopie – Romain Gary*', broadcast live by France-Inter, 25 October 1968; '*Radioscopie – Romain Gary*', broadcast live by France-Inter, 10 June 1975; '*Radioscopie – Romain Gary*', broadcast live by France-Inter on 26 October 1978

Chellabi, Leïla, *Romain mon amour*, Novamuse, 1997

Coates-Smith, Michael and Jean-François Hangouët, 'L'Œuvre publié de Romain Gary', in Jean-François Hangouët and Paul Audi (eds), 'Romain Gary', pp. 334–56

Colquhoun, Robert, *Raymond Aron*, London: Sage, 1986

Conrad, Joseph, *Heart of Darkness* (1899), London: Penguin, 2007

——*Lord Jim* (1900), London: Penguin, 2007

——*Under Western Eyes* (1911), Oxford: Worlds Classics, 2008

Cournot, Michel, 'Ma Vérité sur l'affaire Ajar'. *Le Nouvel*

Observateur, 30 August 1990; reprinted in Jean-François Hangouët and Paul Audi (eds), 'Romain Gary', pp. 68–72

De Gaulle, Charles, *Lettres, Notes et carnets, 1966–1969*, Plon, 1987, p. 129 (letter to Romain Gary, 7 August 1967)

Descartes, René, *Méditations métaphysiques* (Meditationes de prima philosophiae, 1678), Florence Khodoss (ed.), PUF, 1956

Desforges, Régine, *A Paris au printemps* . . . Fayard, 2008

Dickens, Charles, *Great Expectations* (1861), London: Penguin, 2004

—— *Oliver Twist, or the Parish Boy's Progress* (1838), London: Penguin, 2003

Dostoevsky, Fyodor, *Notes from the Underground* (1864), transl. Mirra Ginsburg, New York: Bantam, 1992

—— *Crime and Punishment* (1862), transl. David Macduff, London: Penguin, 2003

——'Bobok' (1873), in *The Gambler and Other Stories*, transl. Jessie Coulson, London: Penguin, 1966

—— *The Brothers Karamazov* (1880), transl. David Magarshack, London: Penguin, 1982

—— *The Double. A Poem of St Petersburg* (1846), transl. George Bird, London: Harvill, 1957

Ebert, Roger, 'Birds in Peru', *Chicago Sun-Times*, 12 August 1969

Escarpit, Robert, *Sociologie de la littérature*, PUF, 1965

Fayol, Pierre, *Le Chambon-sur-Lignon sous l'Occupation*, Paris: L'Harmattan, 1990

Frankfurt, Harry, *On Bullshit*, Princeton, NJ: Princeton University Press, 2005

—— *The Reasons of Love*, Princeton, NJ: Princeton University Press, 2004

Fuentes, Carlos, *Diana the Goddess Who Hunts Alone*, London: Bloomsbury, 1996

Galbeau, Patrice, '*La Vie entre les lignes*', broadcast by France-Culture in five parts between September and December 1973

Gautier, Jean-Jacques, review of *Johnnie Cœur*, *Le Figaro*, 19 October 1962

Gogol, Nikolai, 'Diary of a Madman' (1835), in *The Collected Tales and Plays of Nikolai Gogol*, transl. Constance Garnett (revised), New York: Pantheon, 1964, pp, 453–73

——'The Inspector General' (1836), in *The Collected Tales and Plays of Nikolai Gogol*, transl. Constance Garnett (revised), pp. 597–675

——'The Overcoat' (1842), in *The Collected Tales and Plays of Nikolai Gogol*, transl. Constance Garnett (revised), pp. 562–92

——*Dead Souls* (1842), transl. Robert Maguire, London: Penguin, 2004

Gombrowicz, Witold, *Entretiens de Dominique de Roux avec Gombrowicz*, Paris: Pierre Belfond, 1968

Gorky, Maksim, *Culture and the People*, London: Lawrence & Wishart, 1939

——*Lower Depths*, transl. Lawrence Irving, New York: Duffield, 1912

——*Mother* (1905), New York: Appleton, 1907

Grabinski, Stefan, 'The Grey Room', in *Sarah's House*, transl. Wiesiek Powaga, London: CB Editions, 2007

Hallie, Philip, *Lest Innocent Blood Be Shed*, New York: Harper & Row, 1979

Hangouët, Jean-François and Paul Audi (eds), 'Romain Gary', *Les Cahiers de l'Herne* 85 (2005)

Hangouët, Jean-François, 'Le Don des langues', in Hangouët, Jean-François and Paul Audi (eds), 'Romain Gary', pp. 16–28

Hiller, Marta, *A Woman in Berlin*, transl. James Stern, New York: Harcourt, 1954

Hitler, Adolf, *Mein Kampf* (1926). As *Mein Kampf*, transl. Ralph Manheim, Boston: Houghton Mifflin, 1943

Hoffmann, E. T. A., *Der Sandmann* (1816). As 'The Sandman' in *Tales of Hoffmann*, transl. R. J. Hollingdale, London: Penguin, 2004

Howard, Elizabeth Jane, *Slipstream. A Memoir*, London: Macmillan, 2002

Huchon, Mireille, *Louise Labé. Une creature de papier*, Geneva: Droz, 2006

Hugo, Victor, *Les Misérables* (1862), Paris: Bibliothèque de la Pléïade, 1951, transl. Julie Rose, New York: The Modern Library, 2008

Huston, Nancy, *Tombeau de Romain Gary*, Arles: Actes sud, 1995

——'*Gary se traduit*', *Le Plaid* 7 (2001), pp. 3–14

Iser, Wolfgang, *The Implied Reader: patterns of communication in prose fiction from Bunyan to Beckett*, Baltimore, MD: Johns Hopkins University Press, 1974

Jacobs, Naomi, 'I woke up in the future', *Guardian Weekend*, 23 August 2008, p. 12

Jarocki, Robert, '*Pięć minut ambasadora. Rozmowy ze Stanisławem Gajewskim*', Warsaw: PWN, 1993, pp.174–9

Jauss, Hans-Robert, *Literaturgeschichte als Provokation der Literaturwissenschaft*, Konstanz: Universitätsverlag, 1967

Jelenski, Konstantin, '*Entretien avec Romain Gary*', *Livres de France* 18.3, March 1967

Kafka, Franz, *The Trial* (1925), transl. Mike Mitchell, Oxford: The Worlds Classics, 2009

Kästner, Erich, *Emil und die Detektive* (1929). As *Emil and the Detectives*, transl. Eileen Hall, London: Jonathan Cape, 1959

——*Emil und die drei Zwillinge* (1933). As *Emil and the Three Twins*, transl. Cyrus Brooks, London: Penguin, 1968

——*Romane für Kinder* II, Munich: Hanser Verlag, 1998

Kessel, Joseph, *L'Équipage*, Nrf, 1923

—— *L'Armée des Ombres, chronique de la résistance*, Jacques Schiffrin (ed.), New York: Pantheon Books, 1944

——*Le Lion* (1958). As *The Lion*, transl. Peter Green, New York: Knopf, 1959

Klein, Uri, 'Maker of Movies that Move Him', *Ha'aretz* online, 17 December 2009

Kolodziejczyk, Leszek, interview with Romain Gary (in Polish), *Życie Warszawy* 14 (1981), p. 7

Korbinski, Stefan, *The Polish Underground State. A Guide to the Underground, 1939–1945*, transl. Marta Erdman, Boulder, CO: East European Quarterly, 1978

Kott, Jan, 'A Strange Novel about the Polish Resistance' (in Polish), *Odrodzenie* 1 (1946), p. 11

Krefeld, Thomas, *Substandard als Mittel literarischer Stilbildung. Der Roman* La Vie devant soi *von Émile Ajar*', in Günter Holtus, Edgar Radtke (eds), *Sprachlicher Substandard III*, Tübingen: Niemeyer Verlag, 1990, pp. 244–67

Kundera, Milan, *The Art of the Novel* (1986), transl. Linda Asher, New York: Grove Press, 1988

Lacretelle, Jacques de, *Silbermann*, Nrf, 1922

Lalande, Bernard, '*Pour une lecture de* La Vie devant soi', *Le Français dans le monde* 158.1 (1981), pp. 37–40, 57–9

Lambermont, P. M., *Lorraine Squadron*, London: Cassell, 1956

Lapierre, Dominique, article on Matta in *Paris-Match*, 28 March 1959; revised version in D. Lapierre, *A Thousand Suns*, New York: Warner Books, 2000

Larat, Fabrice, *Romain Gary. Un itinéraire européen*, Chêne-Bourg: Georg, 1999

Lecarme, Jacques, '*Au-delà de cette limite . . . ou le nouveau ticket de Romain Gary*', in Mireille Sacotte (ed.), *Romain Gary et la pluralité des mondes*, PUF, 2002, pp. 111–28

Lejeune, Philippe, *On Autobiography*, transl. Katherine Leary, Minneapolis, MN: University of Minnesota Press, 1988

Lerminier, Georges, review of *Johnnie Cœur, Le Parisien libéré*, 19 October 1962

Lukas, Richard, *Forgotten Holocaust. The Poles Under German Occupation, 1939–1944*, Lexington, KY: University Press of Kentucky, 1986

Lynn, Andrea, *Shadow Lovers. The Last Affairs of H. G. Wells*, Westview Press, 2002

Maechler, Stefan, *The Wilkomirski Affair: A Study in Biographical*

Truth, transl. John E. Woods, New York: Schocken Books, 2001

Malraux, André, *La Condition humaine* (1933). As *Man's Estate*, transl. Alastair Macdonald, London: Hamilton, 1968

——*L'Espoir* (1937). As *Man's Hope*, transl. Stuart Gilbert and Alastair MacDonald, New York: Random House, 1938

Martin, Douglas, obituary notice for Anna Marly, *New York Times*, 13 March 2006, p. A19

Meurice, Paul, *Fanfan la Tulipe*, Michel Lévy, 1858

Mickiewicz, Adam, *Pan Tadeusz* (1834). As *Pan Tadeusz, or, The last foray in Lithuania*, transl. Kenneth Mackenzie, London: Polish Cultural Foundation, 1990

Minczeles, Henri, *Vilna, Wilno, Vilnius. La Jérusalem de Lituanie*, La Découverte, 2000

Modiano, Patrick, *La Place de l'Étoile*, Gallimard, 1968

Monney, Caroline, '*Vingt Questions à Romain Gary*', in Romain Gary, *Charge d'âme*, Cercle du nouveau livre, Librairie Jules Taillandier, 1978; reprinted in R. Gary, *L'Affaire homme*, pp. 302–8

Morel, Paul, review of *Johnnie Cœur*, *Libération*, 19 October 1962

Nabokov, Vladimir, *Подвиг* (1932); as 'Glory', in *Five Novels*, London: Collins, 1979

——*Pnin*, New York: Doubleday, 1957

Östman, Charlotte, *L'Utopie et l'ironie. Étude sur* Gros-Câlin *et sa place dans l'œuvre de Romain Gary*, Stockholm: Almqist & Wiksell, 1994

Ozick, Cynthia, *Heir to the Glimmering World*, Boston, MA: Houghton Mifflin, 2004

Pavlowitch, Paul, *L'Homme que l'on croyait*, Fayard, 1981

Payne, Robert, review of *The Wilder Shores of Love*, *New York Times* Sunday Book Review, 5 September 1954

Pépin, Jean-François, *L'Humour de l'exil dans les œuvres de Romain Gary et d'Isaac Bashevis Singer*, L'Harmattan, 2001

Perec, Georges, *W or The Memory of Childhood* (1975), transl. D. Bellos, London: Collins Harvill, 1988

——*Life A User's Manual* (1978), transl. D. Bellos, London: Collins Harvill, 1987

——*L.G. Une aventure des années soixante*, Paris: Seuil, 1991

Poirot-Delpech, Bertrand, review of *Johnnie Cœur*, *Le Monde*, 19 October 1962

Prescott, Orville, review of *The Wilder Shores of Love*, *New York Times*, 3 September 1954

Prial, Frank J., 'Gary won Goncourt 75 under pseudonym "Ajar"', *New York Times*, 2 July 1981, p. C11

Pruszynski, Ksawery, *Poland Fights Back*, London: Hodder, 1941

Pryce-Jones, Alan, review of *Forest of Anger*, *Observer*, 14 January 1945

Pszoniak, Wojciek, 'Romain Gary', *Kultura* 1981:1, p. 2

Pynchon, Thomas, 'Pros and Cohns', *New York Times*, 17 July 1966

——*The Crying of Lot 49*, Philadelphia, PA: Lippincott, 1966

Queneau, Raymond, *Zazie dans le métro*, Gallimard, 1959

Remarque, Erich-Maria, *Im Westen Nichts Neues* (1929). As *All Quiet On the Western Front*, transl. Brian Murdoch, London: Vintage, 1996

Rinaldi, Angelo (as Alexandre Sorel), review of *La Vie devant soi*, *L'Express*, 1 December 1975

Robbe-Grillet, Alain, *Pour un nouveau roman* (1961). As *For a New Novel*, transl. Richard Howard, Freeport, NY: Books for Libraries, 1970

Rosenthal, A.M. 'France Denounces Moves in U.N . . .', *New York Times*, 27 August 1953

Rosse, Dominique, *Romain Gary et la modernité*, Ottawa: Presses de l'Université d'Ottawa, 1997

Roumette, Julien, *Étude sur* La Promesse de l'aube, Ellipses, 2006

Rousset, David, *L'Univers concentrationnaire* (1946). As *The Other Kingdom*, transl. Ramon Guthrie, New York: Raynal and Hitchcock, 1947

Rudolf, Anthony, obituary of Pierre Rouve (Petar Ouvalieff), *Independent*, 17 December 1998

Sacotte, Mireille, (ed.), *Romain Gary, Écrivain-Diplomate*, ADPF, 2003

Sagan, Françoise, *Bonjour Tristesse*, Julliard, 1954

Saint-Exupéry, Antoine de, *Courrier Sud*, Gallimard, 1929

——*Vol de nuit*, Gallimard, 1931

Sarraute, Nathalie, *Fruits d'or* (1963). As *Golden Fruits*, transl. Maria Jolas, New York: Braziller, 1964

——*L'Ere du soupçon* (1954). As *The Age of Suspicion. Essays on the Novel*, transl. Maria Jolas, New York: Braziller, 1963

Sartre, Jean-Paul, *La Nausée* (1938). As *Nausea*, transl. Lloyd Alexander, New York: New Directions, 1964

——'*Érostrate*' (1939), in *Le Mur*, Gallimard, 1966

——'*L'Enfance d'un chef*' (1939), in *Le Mur*, Gallimard, 1966

——*Qu'est-que la littérature?* (1948). As *What is Literature?*, transl. Bernard Frechtman, New York: Philosophical Library, 1949

——*Réflexions sur la question juive* (1946). As *Anti-Semite and Jew*, transl. George Becker, New York: Schocken, 1948

——*L'âge de raison* (1945). As *The Age of Reason*, transl. Eric Sutton, London: Hamish Hamilton, 1947

Schmetz, Victor Martin, '*Henri Vandeputte romancier populaire: de la honte à la fierté*', in Jacques Mizzozi (ed.), *Le Roman populaire en question(s)*, Limoges: Presses universitaires, 1997

Schmitt, Eric-Emmanuel, *Monsieur Ibrahim and the Flowers of the Koran* (2001), transl. Marjolijn de Jager, New York: Other Press, 2004

Schoolcraft, Ralph, *Romain Gary. The Man Who Sold His Shadow*, Philadelphia, PA: University of Pennsylvania Press, 2002

Schwartz-Bart, André, *Le Dernier des Justes* (1959). As *The Last of the Just*, transl. Stephen Becker, New York: Atheneum, 1960

Segonzac, A. de, '*Rescapé de l'escadrille* Lorraine', *France-Soir*, 8 November 1945; reprinted in Jean-François Hangouët and Paul Audi (eds), 'Romain Gary', p. 127

Sellier, André and Jean Sellier, *Atlas des peuples d'Europe centrale*, La Découverte, 1998

Sillitoe, Alan, *The Loneliness of the Long-Distance Runner*, London: W. H. Allen, 1959

Sollers, Philippe, *Femmes*, Gallimard, 1983. As *Women*, transl. Barbara Bray, New York: Columbia University Press, 1992

Spitzer, Leo, '*Das Eigene und das Fremde. Über Philologie und Nationalismus*', *Die Wandlung* I (1945), pp. 566–94

—— 'The *Lettres portugaises*' (1954), in *Essays in Seventeenth-Century French Literature*, transl. David Bellos, Cambridge: Cambridge University Press, 1981, pp. 253–83

Stekel, Wilhelm, *Frigidity in Woman* (*Die Geschlechtskälte der Frau*), authorised English version by James S. van Teslaar, London and New York: Vision Press, 1953

—— *Impotence in the Male. The psychic disorders of sexual function in the male*, authorised English version by Oswald H. Boltz, London and New York: Vision Press, 1953

Stevenson, Robert Louis, *The Strange Case of Dr Jekyll and Mr Hyde* (1886), London: Penguin, 2007

Styron, William, *Darkness Visible* (1990), London: Vintage, 2001

Sudermann, Hermann, *Schmetterlingsschlacht* (1895)

Svevo, Italo, *The Confessions of Zeno* (1923), transl. Beryl de Zoete, New York: New Directions, 1930

Szafran, Maurice, *Les Juifs dans la politique française, de 1945 à nos jours*, Flammarion, 1990

Taylor, Samuel, *First Love. A Play in Three Acts Based on the Memoir* Promise at Dawn *by Romain Gary*, New York: Harper, 1962

Tirgendvadum, Vina, 'Linguistic Fingerprints and Literary Fraud', *Computing in the Humanities Working Papers (CHWP)* A.9, 1998

Todd, Olivier, *Malraux: A Life*, transl. Joe West, New York: Knopf, 2005

Todorov, Tzvetan, *Hope and Memory. Reflections on the Twentieth Century*, transl. David Bellos, London: Atlantic Books, 2003

Tolstoy, Lev, 'Hadji Murad' (1910), in *Ivan Ilitch and Hadji Murad and Other Stories*, Oxford: The World's Classics, 1935

Tournier, Michel, '*Émile Ajar ou la vie derrière soi*', in *Le Vol du vampire. Notes de lecture*, Paris: Mercure de France, 1981, pp. 329–44

Vaksberg, Arcadi, *Le Mystère Gorky*, Albin Michel, 1997

Vargas, Fred, *L'Homme à l'envers*, Viviane Hamy, 2002. As *Seeking Whom He May Devour*, transl. David Bellos, London: Harvill Press, 2004

Wiesel, Élie. *La Nuit*, Minuit, 1958. As *Night*, transl. Marion Wiesel, New York: Hill & Wang, 2006

References

Except where necessary, quotations have been given in English and, whenever possible, taken from the published English versions of Gary's works. All quotations in English from works by Gary and others not yet published in translation are my own.

Page numbers for works existing in English refer to the editions listed below:

1. *A European Education*
   As *Forest of Anger*, London: Cresset Press, 1944
   As *A European Education*, New York: Harper & Row, 1960
3. *The Company of Men*, New York: Simon & Schuster, 1950
4. *The Colors of the Day*, New York: Simon & Schuster, 1953
5. *The Roots of Heaven*, New York: Simon & Schuster, 1958
6. *Lady L.*, New York: Simon & Schuster, 1959
7. *Promise at Dawn*, London: Michael Joseph, 1961
8. *The Talent Scout*, New York: Harper & Row, 1961
10. *The Ski Bum*, London: Michael Joseph, 1965
11. *The Dance of Genghis Cohn*, London: Penguin, 1973
12. *The Guilty Head*, New York: World Publishing, 1969
13. *White Dog*, New York: World Publishing, 1970
15. *Europa*, New York: Doubleday, 1978
16. *The Enchanters*, New York: Putnam, 1975
17. *The Gasp*, London: Weidenfeld & Nicolson, 1973
18. (As René Deville), *Direct Flight to Allah*, London: Collins, 1975
21. *The Way Out.* As *Your Ticket is No Longer Valid*, New York: Georges Braziller, 1977
22. (As Émile Ajar), *Life Before Us.* As *Momo*, New York: New Directions, 1976
23. *Hocus Bogus*, New Haven, CT: Yale University Press, 2010

25. *King Solomon*, London: Harvill, 1983
27. *Life and Death of Émile Ajar.* Included in *King Solomon*, London: Harvill, 1983
• *Hissing Tales*, New York: Simon & Schuster, 1964

Page numbers for works not yet published in English translation refer to the following editions:

2.1. *Tulipe*, Paris: Calmann-Lévy, 1946
2.2. *L'Homme à la colombe*, Paris: Gallimard, 2004 (Collection L'Imaginaire)
9. *Pour Sganarelle*, Paris: Gallimard, 2004
14. *Trésors de la Mer rouge*, Paris: Gallimard, 1970
19. *La Nuit sera calme*, Paris: Folio, 1980 (*A Quiet Night*)
20. *Gros-Câlin*, Paris: Folio, 2003
24. *Clair de femme*, Paris: Folio, 1982 (*Womanlight*)
4.3 *Les Clowns lyriques*, Paris: Folio, 1989
26. *Les Cerfs-volants*, Paris: Gallimard, 1980 (*The Kites*)

Three frequently quoted books are referred to by the author's surname followed by a page number:

Anissimov: Myriam Anissimov, *Roman Gary, le caméléon*; revised edition, Paris: Folio, 2006
Blanch: Lesley Blanch, *Romain, un regard particulier*, Arles: Actes sud, 1996
Pavlowitch: Paul Pavlowitch. *L'Homme que l'on croyait*, Paris: Fayard, 1981

Quotations from Blanch are from the unpublished English-language original, but page references are to the French translation.

Also referred to by an abbreviated title is a special journal issue devoted to Romain Gary:

L'Herne: Jean-François Hangouët and Paul Audi, (eds), 'Romain Gary', *Les Cahiers de l'Herne* 85, 2005

Three sets of radio interviews are also referred to by the interviewer's name and date of broadcast. Transcriptions from the tapes at the Institut national de l'audiovisuel (INA) and translations are my own:

Bourin: André Bourin, 'Entretiens avec Romain Gary', broadcast by France-Culture in six episodes between May and July 1969

Galbeau: Patrice Galbeau, 'La Vie entre les lignes', broadcast by France-Culture in five parts between September and December 1973

Chancel: Jacques Chancel, (1) 'Radioscopie – Romain Gary', broadcast live by France-Inter, 25 October 1968; (2) 'Radioscopie – Romain Gary', broadcast live by France-Inter, 10 June 1975; (3) 'Radioscopie – Romain Gary', broadcast live by France-Inter, 26 October 1978

Archival sources are also referenced in abbreviated form:

Barnes Collection: Papers of J. Barnes, Columbia University Library, New York

Fonds Albert Camus: Fonds Albert Camus, Bibliothèque Méjeanne, Aix-en-Provence

IMEC: Fonds Romain Gary, Institut Mémoires de l'Édition contemporaine, Abbaye d'Ardenne, Calvados

Notes

An Introduction to Romain Gary

1 From the recollections of Victor Brombert, Paris, April 2003. Alain Aptekman, in a conversation in Paris in May 2003, confirmed Gary's continuing bitterness towards Sartre.

2 Anissimov, pp. 39–40. Anissimov's heroic endeavours to collect every scrap of documentary and hearsay evidence about the real life of Romain Gary deserve respect and gratitude.

3 *Entretiens de Dominique de Roux avec Gombrowicz* (Paris: Pierre Belfond, 1968). An English version (transl. Alastair Hamilton) was published as *A Kind of Testament* under Gombrowicz's sole name in 1973 by Calder and Boyars.

4 *White Dog*, p. 7.

5 *Par hasard* ('by chance'), pronounced with a French lisp.

Chapter 1 Self-Determination

1 *Promise at Dawn*, p. 29.

2 The date on Gary's birth certificate is in the Julian calendar, in use throughout Russia at that time. It is equivalent to 21 May 1914 in the Gregorian calendar used in the West. The original bilingual certificate (in Russian and Hebrew) is reproduced in *Le Plaid* 9 (2002), pp. 18–23 and further comments (in French) on its meaning can be found in David Bellos, Avram Offer, '*A Propos de l'acte de naissance de Roman Katzav*', (*Le Plaid* 10 (2003), pp. 27–31).

3 See Henri Minczeles, *Vilna, Wilno, Vilnius. La Jérusalem de Lituanie* (Paris: La Découverte, 2000) for an authoritative history of the town.

4 See André and Jean Sellier, *Atlas des peuples d'Europe centrale* (Paris: La Découverte, 1998).

5 Romain Gary, *Forest of Anger*, pp. 83–4.

6 Galbeau, episode 4.

7 *Promise at Dawn*, p. 85, and Anissimov, p. 62. Bordighera is also re-inscribed in *Direct Flight to Allah*, p. 111, as the site of a film festival. Devoted exclusively to comedy films, the Bordighera Film Festival awarded 'Golden Olives' during its relatively short existence from 1953 to 1964.

8 The divorce of Leiba and Mina Kacew was not formally granted until 17 October 1929, but the couple split up in 1925 (Anissimov, p. 55).

9 *White Dog*, p. 257.

10 *Tulipe*, p. 76.

Chapter 2 The Child

1 Recalled, not by chance, as one of the residences of 'King' Solomon Rubinstein, the hero of Ajar's last novel. See *King Solomon*, p. 27.

2 Information from the records of the Jewish community in Vilnius, supplied by the chief archivist, Galina Baranova, and also laid out in Anissimov, pp. 28–30.

3 *Promise at Dawn*, p. 73.

4 *Tulipe* (1946 edition), p. 26.

5 Nonetheless, the plot of *Europa* (1972) is explicitly based on chess; Gary accurately quotes Anderssen's 'Immortal Game' on p. 58 as well as a classic chess problem on p. 66.

6 Anissimov, p. 72.

7 *Promise at Dawn*, p. 9.

8 Ibid., p. 78.

9 Ibid., p. 35.

10 Ibid., pp. 36–7.

11 Anissimov, p. 90, quotes the wife of Stas Gajewski (whom Gary befriended in the 1970s) as recalling that the school he really attended was Gurskiego.

12 Conversation with Jolanta Sell, Warsaw, October 2003.

13 *Forest of Anger*, p. 30; *Éducation européenne* (1945 edition),

p. 34. In the 1960 version, Kreczmar becomes Lentowicz and the news-sheet becomes *Freedom*. The National Democrats in Occupied Poland did in fact publish a journal called *Walka*. See Richard Lukas, *Forgotten Holocaust. The Poles Under German Occupation, 1939–1944*. (Lexington, KY: University Press of Kentucky, 1986).

14 The poem was Lermontov's short lyric, 'Frond of Palestine' (Весьма Палестина).

15 Numerous Owczynskis lived in Warsaw at the time. Anissimov, p. 961, gives a few names; many more can be found in the Warsaw telephone directory. Gary's aunt by marriage, Maria, was also born Owczynska. It's not a rare name.

Chapter 3 The Cosmopolitan

1 Blanch, p. 60.

2 *King Solomon*, p. 238.

3 Dialogue from Pavlowitch, p. 103. The words in Russian mean 'understand?' and 'do you see?'.

4 'Here is Might and Reassuring Promise' (*Life*, 21 December 1962); French translation in *L'Affaire homme*, pp. 103–6.

5 Or perhaps with money inherited by Lesley Blanch. Like most marital wrangles, the argument about who really bought Roquebrune is hardly worth trying to sort out. The property became Lesley's as part of the agonising divorce settlement reached in 1963.

6 *Wiadomości Literackie* is a surprising choice for a teenager. It was a serious literary review and the organ of the 'Skamander' group of realist poets.

7 '*Le Nouveau romantisme*', an interview-preface to a book club edition of *Clair de femme*, in *L'Affaire homme*, p. 283.

8 Anissimov, p. 140.

9 Blanch, p. 47, gives an entertaining account of Gary's panicked meanderings around Paris in 1945.

10 *Życie Warszawy* 14 (1981), p. 7.

11 Mentioned explicitly in an interview with Henry Bonnier, '*Une Heure avec Romain Gary*', broadcast by France-Culture in 1967.

12 Robert Jarocki, '*Pięć minut ambasadora. Rozmowy ze Stanisławem Gajewskim*', Warsaw: PWN, 1993, pp. 174–9.

13 Anissimov, p. 276, treats Gary's Diploma in Slavic Languages from Warsaw University as a fiction because no documentary trace of it has been found.

14 *La Nuit sera calme*, p. 234.

15 'The Triumph of Rudeness', *Holiday* 30 (July 1961); French translation in *L'Affaire homme*, pp. 79–89.

16 Recollections of Sir Adam Robertson, All Souls College, Oxford, November 2002.

17 Pavlowitch, p. 107.

18 From an unpublished manuscript preface to an envisaged second edition of *The Dance of Genghis Cohn* (IMEC, Fonds Gary). However, in another draft of a similar text filed with papers relating to *A Quiet Night*, Gary recalls the same engraving hanging in the Wilno apartment of his *other* Uncle Borukh. Other scraps and drafts locate the apartment in Białystok, where (as far as we know) Gary never went.

19 *La Nuit sera calme*, p. 235.

20 His memory of these school classics grew so approximate as to make him attribute a famous saying by Montaigne to Rabelais, in *A Quiet Night* (*La Nuit sera calme*, p. 67).

21 Wojciek Pszoniak, 'Romain Gary', *Kultura* 1981:1, p. 2.

Chapter 4 The Cossack and the Cucumber

1 In recent correspondence with Jean-François Hangouët, Galina Baranova, an archivist in Vilnius, says that she is now certain that 'Troki was mentioned in the birth record of Roman Katsev by mistake'. The speculations that follow are not dependent on the veracity of the birth record, only on the fantasies that Gary may have built on the *name* of Troki.

[2] Adapted from http://philtar.ucsm.ac.uk/encyclopedia/judaism/kara.html.

[3] The majority of Karaites now live in Israel where they have their own religious courts. They are not permitted to marry Jews. About 1,200 Karaites are resident in the USA. Cynthia Ozick's *Heir to the Glimmering World* weaves a fascinating story around the mysteries of this ancient faith.

[4] From the recollections of Alain Aptekman, Paris, May 2003.

[5] It is fairly certain that he was not, since Karaites were not allowed to marry orthodox Jews; moreover, his name, Kacew, was the Russianised version of the more traditional name Katz, derived from an acronym which identified its bearer as a member of the Levite tribe.

[6] Minczeles, op. cit., pp. 113–17.

[7] *Colours of the Day*, p. 27.

[8] *Promise at Dawn*, pp. 73–4.

[9] Paul Audi, *Je me suis toujours été un autre* (Paris: Bourgois, 2007, pp. 241–7), takes Myriam Anissimov to task for making a similar suggestion about this passage. Audi doesn't explain why Gary fabricated a manifestly false account of his father's death, but argues that the story of his having died before getting to the gas chamber is a way of asserting that the Nazis did not have the last word on the matter.

[10] Romain Gary, 'Questionnaire Marcel Proust', *Livres de France*, March 1967, p. 18.

[11] Anissimov, p. 78.

[12] The photographic section of *L'Herne* shows Moszhukin in the role of Casanova beside an image of Gary in 1975 (figures 10 and 11). There really is a resemblance – but both men are heavily made up.

Chapter 5 The Student

[1] This strange phrase in ancient legal French means that the transfer of sovereignty occurs instantaneously upon

the moment of death of the previous monarch and is often translated as 'The King is Dead! Long Live the King!'. Misunderstood as an expression in ordinary French, it seems to say that 'the dead man grips the living by the throat'.

2 *Promise at Dawn*, p. 133.

3 Ibid., p. 149.

4 The character called Pech in the earlier versions of *A European Education* is renamed Hromada (and turned into a Ukrainian partisan) in the so-called definitive edition.

5 *Promise at Dawn*, pp. 242–3. The same claim is made in *White Dog*, p. 74; the price Gary says he paid for the sixteen-year-old-girl – a hunting knife, fifty yards of silk and five jars of Dijon mustard – should probably be taken as a joke about colonial mores, not as an instance of them.

6 Bourin, 19 June 1969.

7 Charlotte Östman, *L'Utopie et l'ironie. Étude sur* Gros-Câlin *et sa place dans l'œuvre de Romain Gary* (Stockholm: Almqist & Wiksell, 1994), p. 146.

8 Anissimov, pp. 106–7. Philippe Brenot, *Le manuscrit perdu* (Le Bouscat: L'Esprit du Temps, 2006) reprints the passages quoted by Anissimov, with blank pages indicating other parts of the text.

9 The back-panel copy of *The Ski Bum* and *Hissing Tales*, and the blurb of the Penguin edition of *The Dance of Genghis Cohn*, to take just three examples, all state that Gary *enlisted* in the French Air Force. The standard biographical blurb in current French paperback editions of his work uses the expression '*engagé dans l'aviation en 1938 . . .*', which is a little more ambiguous.

10 Anissimov, pp. 162–3.

11 *Promise at Dawn*, p. 175. The passage occurs in a somewhat different stylistic form on p. 240 of *La Promesse de l'aube*, 1960 edition, but with identical information.

12 Blanch, pp. 139–40.

Chapter 6 The Hero

1 Pavlowitch, p. 138; Dinah, Eliasz's daughter, had asked Gary not to include any mention of this profligate gambler in *Promise at Dawn*; Gary felt freer to use him after Dinah's death and did so in *Hocus Bogus*, pp. 111–13.

2 Romain Gary to Claude Gallimard, 10 June 1952, quoted in Anissimov, p. 234.

3 The British Library catalogue lists *Forest of Anger* as being 'by Romain Gary [psd. of Romain Kassef]'.

4 From Gary's war record (*livret militaire*), quoted by Jean-Marie Catonné, Colloque Romain Gary, Toulouse, 2 May 2007.

5 Bourin, 5 June 1969.

6 Bourin, 12 June 1969; *A Quiet Night*, p. 24.

7 Only foreigners can enlist in the Foreign Legion.

8 Romain Gary, letter to Kristel Kriland, 1 April 1939, quoted in Anissimov, p. 130.

9 '*Heureux ceux qui sont morts dans une juste guerre/Heureux les épis mûrs et les blés moissonnés*', quoted in full by Gary thirty years later in *La Danse de Gengis Cohn*, p. 267.

10 *White Dog*, p. 136.

11 Ibid., p. 114.

12 For a full history of the squadron and its aircraft, see François Broché, *Les Bombardiers de la France Libre, Le Groupe Lorraine* (Paris: La Table ronde, 1979). In English, see P. M. Lambermont, *Lorraine Squadron* (London: Cassell, 1956).

13 Testimonial by Romain Gary in the catalogue of the exhibition '*Résistance – Déportation*', Paris, 1980. Boston aircraft were not used for long-range missions over Germany, but for targets near the Channel. If Gary's bombs killed any babies, they were French, Belgian or Dutch.

14 Ops No. 70, 26 March, according to the official RAF record for 'F/O GaryR. serial no. 30349'; see chapter 11 for details of Gary's name changes during the war.

Chapter 7 The Novelist

1 Bourin, 5 June 1969.

2 The general frame of *A European Education* is nonetheless quite plausible. According to Stefan Korbinski, *The Polish Underground State. A Guide to the Underground, 1939–1945*, transl. Marta Erdman (Boulder, CO: East European Quarterly, 1978, pp. 89–91), in mid-1943 there were two fighting units of the Polish Home Army in the area around Wilno, each between thirty and one hundred men.

3 Bourin, 5 June 1969.

4 Leszek Kolodziejczyk, in *Życie Warszawy* 14 (1981), p. 7.

5 *Forest of Anger*, p. 21.

6 'Dobranski', with or without the accent over the 'n', is a Westernisation of the Polish spelling Dobrzański. The name is borrowed from Major Henryk Dobrzański (code-name Hubal), considered by some to be the founding father of the Polish partisan movement. See Richard Lukas, op. cit., p. 51.

7 *Guerilla Warfare in the Occupied Parts of the Soviet Union*, Popular Lecture Series (Moscow: Foreign Languages Publishing House, [June] 1943, p. 8). Other possible sources for Gary's vision of the partisan war include: Ksawery Pruszynski, *Poland Fights Back*. (London: Hodder, 1941); *Poland Fights On*, a news-sheet published from Stratton House in 1942; and reports in the numerous Polish newspapers published in London at that time.

8 *Forest of Anger*, p. 8.

9 See Robert Colquhoun, *Raymond Aron* (London: Sage, 1986, volume 1, pp. 211–55) for a fuller portrait of *La France Libre* and the sources of these details.

10 Kessel's first article in *France* is dated 4 March 1943; the concluding part of *L'Armée des ombres*, 'L'Évasion', was serialised in *France* from 12 July. The book itself appeared in French in Algiers and New York towards the end of the year, and was brought out in Britain in 1944 by the Cresset Press.

The back panel of the dust jacket of *Forest of Anger* is entirely devoted to Kessel's famous novel, as if it were a companion volume.

11 See Andrea Lynn, *Shadow Lovers. The Last Affairs of H. G. Wells* (Westview Press, 2002).

12 Maksim Gorky, *Culture and the People* (London: Lawrence & Wishart, 1939, p. 82). (The source was discovered by Jean-François Hangouët.) The mysterious life of Moura Budberg is the subject of Nina Berberova's *Железная Женщина* ('The Iron Lady', New York: YMCA Press, 1981). The investigative journalist Arcadi Vaksberg, in *Le Mystère Gorky* (Albin Michel, 1997), tears most of Berberova's account to shreds.

13 Public Record Office (Kew), dossiers KV 2/979–981, 'Soviet Intelligence Agents and Suspected Agents'.

14 See Rémi Kauffer's article at www.historia.presse.fr/data/mag/670/67004601.html for details.

15 Her constant refrain, 'Tango Milonga', can be heard at http://www.youtube.com/watch?v=OPju6wiGSRA.

16 *Forest of Anger*, p. 166.

17 Gary's narration of the event in *Promise at Dawn* is largely fictional, but in the English version only he gives a probably reliable detail: the message said that the book would appear 'within five months'. As it did appear in December 1944, the news must have reached him within a few weeks of D-Day.

18 *Forest of Anger*, p. 171.

19 Reprinted in *L'Herne*, p. 229.

20 Alan Pryce-Jones's regular books column in the *Observer*, 14 January 1945, puts it alongside a new work by Maria Kuncewiczowa as one of 'two Polish novels [that] also deserve praise . . .'; similarly, J. D. Beresford's round-up of new books in the *Guardian* on 12 January 1945 treats *Forest of Anger* exclusively as a story of the Polish Maquis.

21 Alain Aptekman recalls Gary explaining later on that Lesley had been his *marraine de guerre*. Anne Boston, *Lesley Blanch*

(London: John Murray, 2010, p. 60) also points out the incoherences in Blanch's account of her meeting Romain Gary.

22 Lesley Blanch, *Journey into the Mind's Eye* (New York: Atheneum, 1969, p. 274).

23 Conversation with Mike Csáky, London, 22 March 2006. Csáky spent most of his summer holidays as a child at Blanch's home in Roquebrune, with his grandmother Olga, and Lesley.

24 Anne Boston, op. cit., p. 42, also reveals that despite her lifelong interest in Russia, Lesley never learned more than basic expressions in that language either.

25 More than 100,000 'men of the woods' in Poland and Lithuania were captured and deported to Soviet prison camps between 1945 and 1953. See Minczeles, op. cit., p. 405.

26 For a full account of the history of *A European Education*, see David Bellos, 'Le Malentendu: l'histoire cachée d'*Éducation européenne*' (*L'Herne*, pp. 150–68).

27 The expression is from Ralph Schoolcraft, *Romain Gary. The Man Who Sold His Shadow* (Philadelphia, PA: University of Pennsylvania Press, 2002).

Chapter 8 Gary and Charles de Gaulle

1 Gary recalled his interview as taking place in St Stephen's House, but if this meeting did take place in August 1940 it would have been in Carlton Gardens, which was the Free French HQ from 23 July 1940.

2 Romain Gary, 'To My General, with Love and Anger' (*Life*, vol. 66, issue 18, 9 May 1969, p. 28); a more elaborate version of the same anecdote appears in *La Nuit sera calme,* pp. 22–3.

3 Anissimov, p. 161; *Promise at Dawn*, p. 96.

4 In *Promise at Dawn,* p. 256, Gary says the medal was pinned on to his breast by de Gaulle himself, 'some months later', at a ceremony under the Arc de Triomphe in Paris. This cannot be true.

5 Quoted from R. Gary, *Ode à l'homme qui fut la France*, Paul Audi (ed.) (Paris: Folio, 2000, p. 103).

6 Anissimov, p. 151.
7 *La Nuit sera calme*, pp. 215–17.
8 Olivier Todd, *Malraux: A Life* (New York: Knopf, 2005) gives the fullest account of a man who was, like Gary, and perhaps to an even more spectacular degree, a charlatan and a genius at the same time.
9 R. Gary, 'The Man Who Stayed Lonely to Save France' (*Life*, vol. 45, issue 23, 8 December 1958).
10 R. Gary, 'Ode to the man who was France' (*Life*, vol. 69, issue 21, 20 November 1970.
11 In the English version, Parts I, II and III.
12 Bourin, 12 June 1969.
13 Chancel, 1975.

Chapter 9 Gary's Politics

1 For a subtle reading of Gary's thinking about Europe as an idea and a potential political entity, see Paul Audi, *L'Europe et son fantôme* (Léo Scheer, 2003).
2 *The Enchanters*, p. 258.
3 *White Dog*, p. 67; troika bells, *White Dog*, p. 20.
4 *White Dog*, p. 215.
5 Ibid., p. 216.
6 Ibid., p. 31, compounds the deception, since some of it is true.
7 Harry Frankfurt, *On Bullshit.* (Princeton, NJ: Princeton University Press, 2005, pp. 66–7).
8 *La Nuit sera calme*, p. 67.
9 *White Dog*, p. 29.
10 Bourin, 5 June 1969.
11 Fabrice Larat, *Romain Gary. Un itinéraire européen* (Chêne-Bourg: Georg, 1999), treats Gary's Bulgarian experience as his 'education' in Communism and realpolitik.
12 Recalled in French transliteration as 'Dimitroff' in Gary's May '68 graffiti exercise, mentioned on page 123.
13 Anissimov, p. 286, tells the story of Nedi Trianova, obliged by the secret police to seduce Gary and to have him

photographed in a compromising position. In *A Quiet Night* (*La Nuit sera calme*, pp. 125–8), Gary tells the story (or at least, a story) of how he got out of the trap.

14 For almost identical comments about another Balkan country at a different time, see Robert Carver's *The Accursed Mountains: Journeys in Albania* (John Murray, 1998).

15 As far as I have been able to establish, Maynard Barnes was not related to Joseph Barnes.

16 Oral History Interview with Mark F. Ethridge (US envoy to the Balkans, 1945), Moncure, North Carolina, 4 June 1974 by Richard D. McKinzie. Truman Presidential Museum and Library, http://www.trumanlibrary.org/oralhist/ethridge.htm.

17 *The Ski Bum*, p. 38.

18 *Adieu Gary Cooper*, p. 76.

19 *La Nuit sera calme*, pp. 117–18.

20 Conversation with Diego Gary, 17 December 2008.

21 Régine Desforges, *A Paris au printemps . . .* (Fayard, 2008, p. 174).

22 *La Nuit sera calme*, p. 97.

23 Romain Gary, 'Les Hommes, ces éléphants', *L'Express*, 4 January 1957; as *'La marge humaine'* in *L'Affaire homme*, Jean-François Hangouët and Paul Audi (eds) (Folio, 2005, pp. 17–31).

24 'The Colonials', *Holiday* 25, April 1959; French translation in *L'Affaire homme*, pp. 51–63.

Chapter 10 Sex

1 The main exception is in *The Way Out*, where sex is described in considerable detail from the point of view of a middle-aged man suffering the onset of erectile dysfunction.

2 *Hocus Bogus*, p. 144.

3 *Gros-Câlin*, p. 201.

4 Blanch, p. 56 (published French version), quoted from the unpublished English original.

5 Jan Kott, 'A Strange Novel about the Polish Resistance', (*Odrodzenie* 1 (1946), p. 11).

6 Reminiscence of Professor Marina van Zuylen, December 2007.

7 *Clair de femme*, p. 179.

8 *King Solomon*, p. 84.

9 Blanch, p. 54.

10 Anissimov, p. 377.

11 *Roots of Heaven*, pp. 136, 215.

12 *Que de femmes se sont crues ainsi aimées, alors qu'elles n'étaient contre moi que l'absence de quelqu'un!*, *Les Enchanteurs*, p. 192. The passage, together with the long paragraph from which it is taken, is omitted from the English edition.

13 *The Guilty Head*, p. 15.

14 This supposed fact is mentioned in *The Colours of the Day*, p. 84 and also in *The Ski Bum*, p. 134.

15 Anissimov, p. 286; Anne Boston, op. cit., p. 87, says this particular lover was a Turkoman, which is not the same thing.

16 Carlos Fuentes, *Diana the Goddess Who Hunts Alone* (London: Bloomsbury, 1996).

17 English cannot quite reproduce the flagrant coyness of this statement: *Il fut l'amant discret de nombreuses femmes. Elles venaient s'offrir à lui fugacement et, sans leur présence, la venue du crépuscule lui était insupportable . . . Malgré ses innombrables conquêtes, Gary n'était pas un Don Juan, mais un homme pressé, timide, solitaire et angoissé* (Anissimov, p. 19).

18 *La Nuit sera calme*, p. 30.

19 Ibid., p. 30.

20 *White Dog*, p. 136.

21 These details confirmed by Nathalie Loiseau, press officer for the French Embassy in Washington, at a conference in New York on 5 May 2006. The incident was not reported in the press at the time but was no secret in the French diplomatic community.

22 Anissimov, p. 539.

23 *Trésors de la Mer rouge*, p. 102.

24 Quoted in Anissimov, p. 131, from an undated conversation between Variety Moszinski and René Agid. It's quite likely that Gary was actually trying to imitate his hero of the day, André Malraux, who had uncontrollable facial twitches.

25 Caroline Monney, '*Vingt Questions à Romain Gary*' (1978), in R. Gary, *L'Affaire homme*, p. 302.

26 *The Enchanters*, p. 140.

27 Blanch, p. 40.

28 Alain Bosquet, '*Mémoire européenne*' (*Le Quotidien de Paris*, 20 May 1980; *L'Herne*, pp. 307–8).

29 Nancy Huston, *Tombeau de Romain Gary* (Arles: Actes sud, 1995).

30 From the recollections of Alain Aptekman, Paris, May 2003, and Jean-Yves Pouilloux, Avignon, July 2003.

31 *La Danse de Gengis Cohn*, p. 231.

32 *La Reine des pommes* is the French title of Himes's *The Five-Cornered Square*. Carelessly, Gary did not bother to replace the French on p. 130 of the English translation.

33 Wilhelm Stekel (not Steckel), *Frigidity in Woman* (*Die Geschlechtskälte der Frau*). Authorised English Version by James S. van Teslaar (New York: Liverlight, 1936; new edition, London and New York: Vision Press, 1953); *Impotence in the Male. The psychic disorders of sexual function in the male* . . . (authorised English version by Oswald H. Boltz, 2 vols, London and New York: Vision Press, 1953). The first French translation of *L'Homme impuissant* appeared in 1972 and of *La Femme frigide* in 1973.

34 Lesley Blanch, *The Game of Hearts. Harriette Wilson and her Memoirs* (New York: Simon and Schuster, 1955). Wilson's memoirs seem to have been one of her favourite texts. She made Gary read it to learn English in 1944 – alongside John Donne! (Blanch, p. 29).

35 Conversation with Mike Csáky (Olga's grandson), London, 22 March 2006.

36 '*Le moment de vérité. Entretien avec Romain Gary*', (*Preuves* 73, (March 1957), in *L'Affaire homme*, p. 45). Much but not all of

this early exercise in ventriloquy was incorporated into *A Quiet Night* in 1974.

37 Blanch, p. 143.

38 Ibid., pp. 102–3.

39 The phrase, literally meaning 'your mother is a whore', is the first thing the narrator says when he recovers from the fainting fit he suffered after seeing the Holocaust exhibition at the Warsaw City Museum in 1966, in the French version of *The Dance of Genghis Cohn*.

40 Anissimov, p. 834, states that Gary made 'minor modifications' to *The Colours of the Day* when he republished it under its new title in 1979. In fact, there are huge differences, especially with respect to the French original; the rewriting began with the English translation in 1953.

41 '*JE mange mon soulier*', *Elle*, 10 December 1956, pp. 50–1, 103.

42 *Promise at Dawn*, p. 58.

Chapter 11 The Books Gary Wrote

1 The nearest to complete collection is at the Library of Congress, in Washington, DC. This is because the Bibliothèque Nationale in France did not acquire English 'translations' of Gary's novels, whereas the Library of Congress did purchase many of the French 'originals'.

2 *The Dance of Genghis Cohn* is a transitional text in this respect. The manuscripts suggest that parts of it were written in English first, then rewritten in French. Gary also referred to it on a radio programme as one of the novels he wrote in English. However, the finished French text definitely predates the English version, which Gary rewrote very liberally from a plain prose translation commissioned from Camilla Sykes.

3 Anissimov, p. 678.

4 '*Le moment exige que je fasse deux ou trois œuvres capitales . . . qui montrent que je suis plus brillant, plus jeune et plus fécond que jamais*' (H. de Balzac, *Lettres à Madame Hanska*, Pierrot

(ed.) Paris: Delta, 1967, III: p. 213, letter dated 26 June 1846).

5 Michael Coates-Smith and Jean-François Hangouët, '*L'Œuvre publié de Romain Gary*' (*L'Herne*, pp. 334–56), is the authoritative bibliography.

6 Leo Spitzer, '*Das Eigene und das Fremde. Über Philologie und Nationalismus*', *Die Wandlung* I (1945), pp. 566–94.

7 Interview with Henri Bonnier (1967), re-broadcast by France-Culture on 22 April 1995 (Archives INA, Paris).

Chapter 12 Games with Names

1 Romain Gary, Letter to the Editor, *New York Times*, 12 June 1966; replies from Pynchon and others, 'Pros and Cohns', 17 July 1966.

2 Douglas Martin, obituary notice for Anna Marly, *New York Times*, 13 March 2006, p. A19.

3 'Géographie humaine', *La Marseillaise* (London), 7 March 1943.

4 The cartoonist Folon inscribed one of his drawings hung on Gary's wall at Rue du Bac with a dedication to 'Romain Gary Cooper', presumably for similar reasons. See Pavlowitch, p. 94.

5 Gary wrote a touching obituary, '*Gary Cooper, mon ami si timide*' (*Le Nouveau Candide*, issue 3, 18 May 1961, p. 7).

6 *White Dog*, p. 139.

7 *Chien blanc*, p. 114.

8 Others have also pointed out that the imperative of *gor'et* is *gorí*, not *garí*. However, Gary frequently transliterates unstressed Russian 'o' as 'a', as in *kharacho* (for *khorosho*, 'good'), (*Clair de femme*, p. 100). It may be the trace of a Polish or Yiddish accent in Gary's memory of Russian, or just a personal transliteration convention.

9 Pavlowitch, p. 19.

10 In a 1978 interview with Caroline Monney (reprinted in *L'Affaire homme*, pp. 299–308) Gary dropped the 'burn' etymology of his name and attributed his adoption of it to

the fact that it was his mother's stage name (p. 300); the same red herring can be found in Pavlowitch, p. 19. In *Promise at Dawn* (1960), however, her stage name is said to be 'Nina Borisovska'.

11 Frank J. Prial, 'Gary won Goncourt 75 under pseudonym "Ajar"' (*New York Times*, 2 July 1981, p. C11).

12 Personal correspondence with Ralph Schoolcraft. Sinibaldi also used the name 'Paul Gary' at different times of his life.

13 Conversation with Diego Gary, Paris, 29 May 2006.

14 Romain Gary, *Gloire à nos illustres pionniers* (Gallimard: 1962, p. 7). The epigraph is dropped from the English translation.

15 *L'Homme à la colombe*, p. 87.

16 Victor Martin Schmetz, '*Henri Vandeputte romancier populaire: de la honte à la fierté*' in Jacques Mizzozi (ed.), *Le Roman populaire en question(s)* (Limoges: Presses universitaires, 1997).

17 *White Dog*, p. 146.

18 For further discussion of naming as a memorial device in Gary, see Pierre Bayard, *Il était deux fois Romain Gary* (PUF, 1990, pp. 9–20), and also Tzvetan Todorov, *Hope and Memory. Reflections on the Twentieth Century*, transl. David Bellos (London: Atlantic Books, 2003, pp. 213–27).

19 *Promise at Dawn*, p. 39.

20 Ibid., pp. 38–9.

21 My translation. The original is: я прошу вас покорнейше, как поедете в Петербуге, скажите всем там вельможам разным: сенаторам и адмиралам, что вот, ваше сиятельство, живёт в таком-то городе Пётр Иванович Бобчинский. Так и скажите: живёт Пётр Иванович Бобчинский. (*Ревизор* III.vii, ll. 64–9)

22 Jean-François Hangouët, '*Le Don des langues*' (*L'Herne*, p. 24 and note 81) is the first known mention of the resemblance.

23 The English version, but not the French 'original' of this story of a crate of Guinness buried with full military honours in a cemetery near Reading, has a giveaway footnote: 'The authenticity of this episode has been questioned

. . . The following persons can bear witness to its veracity . . .' The list of names that follows comprises only deceased members of the French and British forces.

24 *King Solomon*, p. 24.

25 *Les Couleurs du jour*, p. 27. My translation. Omitted from the published English translation, which served as the basis for a back translation, *Les Clowns lyriques*, published in 1979.

26 A. Cary, '*Géographie humaine*', *La Marseillaise* (London, 7 March 1943, p. 5); reprinted in R. Gary, *L'Orage* (Paris: *L'Herne*, 2005, pp. 83–92). 'Cary' is assumed to have been a misprint; but see p. 168 for an alternative hypothesis.

27 *The Colours of the Day*, p. 3; *White Dog*, p. 9; *Promise at Dawn*, p. 251.

28 For example, a letter to René Ziller quoted by Anissimov, p. 287.

29 *Promise at Dawn*, pp. 19, 21, 120.

30 *Les Cerfs-volants*, p. 370.

31 New York: Harper & Row, 1979. The French translation of Hallie's book did not appear until March 1980 and *The Kites* went to press in April of that year. Other sources for the story of Trocmé are listed in Pierre Fayol, *Le Chambon-sur-Lignon sous l'Occupation* (Paris: L'Harmattan, 1990).

Chapter 13 The Way Gary Wrote

1 *La Nuit sera calme*, p. 24.

2 Anissimov, p. 440.

3 '*Le Journal de Treize Heures*', 21 November 1975 (Archives INA, Paris).

4 Anissimov, p. 249.

5 Blanch, p. 15.

6 Anissimov, p. 325.

7 Bourin, 12 June 1969.

8 Elizabeth Jane Howard, *Slipstream. A Memoir* (London: Macmillan, 2002, p. 290).

9 'A daily evacuation', Blanch, p. 86.

10 Letter to Joseph Barnes, 30 August [1950] (Barnes Collection).

[11] The English version, which appeared in 1958, was amended quite substantially by Gary and is divided into four parts. What is here called Part III (as it is in all French editions) corresponds to Part IV of the English.
[12] Letter to Joseph Barnes, 9 August [1950]. (Barnes Collection).
[13] *Promise at Dawn*, p. 92.
[14] For a list of *gnamas* typical of today's Senegal, see http://www.au-senegal.com/art_en/cuisine.htm.
[15] *The Colours of the Day*, p. 177.
[16] *The Roots of Heaven*, p. 65.
[17] Letter to Joe Barnes, 1 November 1950; see also Anissimov, p. 229.
[18] The phrase disappears entirely in the English version of the passage (Penguin edition, p. 108).

Chapter 14 What Gary Meant

[1] For examples of Gary's sometimes hidden use of this adage, see Jean-François Pépin, *L'Humour de l'exil dans les œuvres de Romain Gary et d'Isaac Bashevis Singer* (L'Harmattan, 2001, pp. 81–102).
[2] *La Nuit sera calme*, p. 227.
[3] Paul Audi, *La Fin de l'impossible. Deux ou trois choses que je sais de Gary* (Bourgois, 2005).

Chapter 15 Gandhi's Ham Sandwich

[1] A. de Segonzac, '*Rescapé de l'escadrille* Lorraine', (*France-Soir*, 8 November 1945; *L'Herne*, p. 127).
[2] An unpublished English version is mentioned in letters to Albert Camus, 7 August 1945 (Fonds Camus) and to Louis Jouvet, 20 July 1946 and 17 May 1947 (*L'Herne*, pp. 80, 84), but it has never been found.
[3] Letter to Pierre Calmann-Lévy, 28 August 1945, quoted in Schoolcraft, op. cit. p. 33 and note 16.
[4] The silent version Gary is likely to have seen in Warsaw or perhaps in the first years of his life in Nice was made in

1925 by René Leprince. The first sound version, by Christian-Jaque, dates from 1952.

5 Uncle Nat's identity as a Jew masquerading as a Black is only made explicit in the 1970 revision of the text, but it can easily be guessed even in the 1946 first edition from the old man's Yiddish jokes.

6 *Tulipe* (1946), p. 45. This passage was cut from the second edition of *Tulipe* in 1970 for an obvious reason: the meaning of the term 'Palestinian refugee' had been transformed by the foundation of the State of Israel in 1948. In 1946, Gary meant to be comical about *Jews* leaving Palestine for their 'historic homelands' in Germany and Poland.

7 *Tulipe* (1946), p. 28.

8 Ibid., p. 58.

9 Ibid., pp. 69–70. The guessing game is reprised in *The Dance of Genghis Cohn*, p. 137, as ' a word of five letters . . . It begins with a J . . .'

10 Blanch, p. 37.

11 *The Gasp*, p. 224.

12 *La Nuit sera calme*, p. 228.

Chapter 16 Gary the Rat

1 The original epigraph from *Tulipe* is also omitted from the American translation, no doubt because *Tulipe* was not available in English (and remains untranslated to this day).

2 F. Dostoevsky, *Notes from the Underground* (1864), transl. Mirra Ginsburg (New York: Bantam, 1992, p. 10).

3 *The Company of Men*, p. 106.

4 Ibid., p. 233.

5 *Notes from the Underground*, p. 15.

6 Ibid., p. 16.

7 *La Promesse de l'aube*, pp. 22–3. My translation. The passage occurs only in the French version of the text. The same point is made by Pavlowitch, p. 66.

8 *The Company of Men*, pp. 100, 117, 36.

[9] Ibid., p. 52; *Le Grand vestiaire*, p. 71.
[10] *The Company of Men*, p. 92.
[11] Ibid., p. 97.
[12] Ibid., p. 186.
[13] Ibid., p. 63.
[14] Ibid., p. 68.
[15] Ibid., p. 179.
[16] Ibid., p. 108.
[17] Ibid., p. 45.
[18] Ibid., p. 47.
[19] Jean-Paul Sartre, '*Érostrate*', in *Le Mur* (Gallimard, 1939).
[20] René Descartes, *Metaphysical Meditations*, IX.25. Translated from the standard French translation of Descartes's Latin text. The wording of the standard English version, taken direct from the Latin, is less germane to Sartre's and Gary's use of the motif.
[21] *The Company of Men*, p. 27.
[22] The striking commonality of the theme of 'the view from above' in three works created almost simultaneously in three different countries can only be taken as a sign of the times. Gary, Aymé and Greene cannot have read each other in time to filch the formula from either of the others.
[23] K. Jelenski, '*Entretien avec Romain Gary*' (*Livres de France* 18.3, March 1967, p. 4).
[24] Avignon, L'Isle-sur-la-Sorgue, Cavaillon and Carpentras are the *arba'im kehilot*, the 'four towns' of Provence where Jews were protected by papal decree for hundreds of years. As with the Wilno of *A European Education*, Gary's choice of place is predominantly symbolic.
[25] *The Company of Men*, p. 210.
[26] Ibid., pp. 56, 166.
[27] *La Nuit sera calme*, p. 26.
[28] J.-B Calvino, *Dictionnaire Niçois-Français* (1983, reprinted 1997); Georges Castellana, *Dictionnaire Niçois-Français* (1952, reprinted 2001, p. 131) gives the spelling as *garí* and the meaning as *surmulot* (wharf rat).

Chapter 17 Diplomacy

1 Letter from Gary to A. Camus, London, 7 August [1945] (Fonds Albert Camus).

2 Anissimov, p. 305.

3 *La Nuit sera calme*, p. 143.

4 Letter to Joe Barnes, 9 August 1950 (Barnes Collection).

5 *La Nuit sera calme*, p. 262.

6 A. M. Rosenthal, 'France Denounces Moves in U.N . . .' *New York Times*, 27 August 1953.

7 The AEF (French Equatorial Africa) comprised Chad, Ubangi, Middle Congo and Gabon (today: Chad, République Centrafricaine, Congo-Brazzaville and Gabon), a crescent of savannah, desert and jungle with a land mass twice the size of Europe.

8 Extracted from *Preparatory Document for the International Conference for the Protection of the Fauna and Flora of Africa, Bukavu, 26–31 October 1953*. Available online from http://app.iucn.org.

9 *The Company of Men*, pp. 194–5.

10 The English version of 1958 divides Part I into two, thus making four parts in all. Part III of *Les Racines du ciel* thus corresponds to Part IV of *The Roots of Heaven*. In addition, chapter 33 of the French original was omitted from the English, whose chapters 33–8 correspond to chapters 34–9 of the original.

11 Galbeau, episode 2.

12 Ibid., episode 1.

13 See the article by Dominique Lapierre (*Paris-Match*, 28 March 1959); revised version in D. Lapierre, *A Thousand Suns* (New York: Warner Books, 2000).

14 Galbeau, episode 4.

15 *Eine Frau in Berlin*, transl. James Stern as *A Woman in Berlin* (New York: Harcourt, 1954). It has recently been reissued in German and English, and used as the basis of a film, *Anonyma, Eine Frau in Berlin*, directed by Max Färberböck, 2008.

Chapter 18 Masquerade

1 Orville Prescott, in the *New York Times*, 3 September 1954, and Robert Payne, in the *NYT* Sunday Book Review, 5 September, both gave it rave reviews.

2 Lesley Blanch, *Les Rives sauvages de l'amour* (Paris: Plon, 1956).

3 *Elle*, 7 March 1955; reprinted in *Les Nouvelles littéraires*, 6 December 1956 and in *Actualité littéraire*, February 1957; (*L'Herne*, pp. 263–7).

4 *The Game of Hearts*: Harriette Wilson's Memoirs, interspersed with excerpts from the *Confessions* of Julia Johnstone, her rival, edited and with an introduction by Lesley Blanch (New York: Simon & Schuster, 1955; London: Gryphon Books, 1957).

5 Galbeau, episode 2.

6 Blanch, p. 37.

7 See Eric W. Beckett, *The North Atlantic Treaty, the Brussels Treaty and the Charter of the United Nations* (London: Stevens, 1950).

8 Letter to Joseph Barnes, 25 April 1955 (Barnes Collection).

9 Anthony Rudolf, obituary of Pierre Rouve, *Independent*, 17 December 1998.

10 For an explanation of the pseudonym, see page 172.

11 Anissimov, p. 413, reproduces the document.

12 Letter to Barnes, 21 May [1955] (Barnes Collection).

Chapter 19 Top Prize

1 Anne Boston, op. cit., p. 112.

2 The anecdote was first told on television in *Lectures pour tous* in 1956. Repeated in 'Dear Elephant, Sir', an open letter to elephants accompanying a wildlife photo-reportage by Peter Beard (*Life*, 22 December 1967).

3 'Don't cry'.

4 *The Roots of Heaven*, p. 412.

5 The 'definitive edition' of the French text published in 1980

and currently in print puts the expression in proper German, '*Wein nicht*', thus making nonsense of the whole sentence. I take this to be the fault of a proofreader who thought he could spell. In the original edition, p. 441, the phrase is identical to that of the English text quoted here.

6 See http://www.imdb.com/title/tt0186803/plotsummary.

7 Telegram reproduced in Mireille Sacotte (ed.), *Romain Gary, Écrivain-Diplomate* (Paris: ADPF, 2003, p. 53).

Chapter 20 Changing Faces

1 *La Nuit sera calme*, p. 234; see also p. 343.

2 *Gros-Câlin*, p. 101.

3 *Promise at Dawn*, p. 252. The French version of this famous passage says: 'I was born' (*La Promesse de l'aube*, Folio p. 374). The English plural undoubtedly includes Gary's mother, who had died three years earlier.

4 *Life and Death of Émile Ajar*, printed as an appendix to *King Solomon*, p. 250; also as an appendix to *Hocus Bogus*, p. 186.

5 *The Enchanters*, p. 53.

6 For a rare personal account of such mental rebirth, see Naomi Jacobs, 'I woke up in the future', (*Guardian Weekend*, 23 August 2008, p. 12).

7 Barely a few months separate the publication of the French edition (1960) from the American one (1961). The English version was probably written before the French was published.

8 Blanch, p. 34; for examples, see Blanch, *Around the World in Eighty Dishes*.

9 This is my attempt to explain the force of the last words of the text, which are grammatically and stylistically odd: *J'ai vécu*. Gary's own English translation is just the plain 'I have lived' (*Promise at Dawn*, p. 263). What I think Gary meant to say through the French is only truly sayable in the first-person perfective past of the Russian verb 'to live': *Я пожил.*

10 '*Le Moment de Vérité. Entretien avec Romain Gary*', (*Preuves 73*, March 1957, p. 7, in *L'Affaire homme*, p. 46).

11 Some of them were in influential positions in academic and literary life in France. The journalist and novelist Robert Escarpit, for example, who was at the time also president of the University of Bordeaux, was a frequent visitor to Albania and a propagandist on behalf of Hoxha's paranoid Stalinist regime.

Chapter 21 A Pen for Hire

1 Anne Boston, op. cit., p. 69.

2 Elizabeth Jane Howard, op. cit., (pp. 287–91). Howard mistakenly recalls that *The Roots of Heaven* had just appeared in the UK, probably confusing it with *The Colours of the Day*. In Paris she saw the still incomplete manuscript of *Les Racines du ciel*, which makes the dating of this episode quite certain – late 1955.

3 More details can be found in Anissimov, pp. 409, 434.

4 Anissimov, p. 377, gives the details, but not her sources; Gary gives his own version of the episode in *A Quiet Night* (*La Nuit sera calme,* pp. 293–5).

5 Anissimov, p. 378.

6 Anissimov, pp. 380–1. Gary seems to have been a messy eater when he returned to Paris as well. See Régine Desforges, *A Paris au printemps* . . . (Fayard, 2008, p. 175), for a telling anecdote.

7 Blanch, p. 131.

Chapter 22 'It's Over . . .'

1 The epigraph appears only in the English edition. According to Blanch, p. 27, it was she who first alerted Gary to these lines, in London in 1943.

2 *La Nuit sera calme*, p. 255.

3 Julien Roumette, *Étude sur* La Promesse de l'aube (Paris: Ellipses, 2006, p. 15) calls it 'an autobiography that marks a

break with great modern autobiographies', but grants on p. 13 that 'Russian and Anglo-Saxon novels probably had more influence on Gary than French literature'.

4 *Promise at Dawn*, p. 251.

5 H. de Balzac, *L'Envers de l'histoire contemporaine* (1848, Folio edition, pp. 167–8).

6 Pierre Bayard, op. cit., pp. 34–44, gives a psychoanalytical reading of this anecdote.

7 Anissimov, p. 217.

8 Service Historique de l'Armée de l'Air, file G208A, document kindly provided by Jean-François Hangouët.

9 Philippe Lejeune, *On Autobiography*, transl. Katherine Leary (Minneapolis, MN: University of Minnesota Press, 1988).

Chapter 23 Celebrity Spouse

1 Blanch, p. 138.

2 Letter to Joseph Barnes, 15 January 1959 (Barnes Collection).

3 Anissimov, p. 522.

4 One of their Russian conversations is reproduced on p. 41.

5 In *A Quiet Night* Gary calls it the UDR (*La Nuit sera calme*, p. 152); the name change occurred in 1967.

6 Anissimov, p. 541.

7 Anissimov, pp. 591–2, provides more detail on the affair.

8 For a sympathetic account of Hakim Jamal and his affair with Seberg, see Diana Athill, *Make Believe. A True Story* (London: Sinclair-Stevenson, 1993). Jamal, real name Alan Donaldson, had an uncanny ability to seduce interesting women, including Athill. Unlike Seberg, however, Athill was sane enough to realise fairly quickly that Jamal was quite mad.

9 He was not above stooping to low tricks to do this. When the demented and violent Jamal reappeared at Seberg's clinic in 1972, Gary warned him that the police were about to swoop. However, Gary could get a diplomatic laissez-passer that would enable Jamal to leave the country, but only if he

used it within the following two days. Which he did. See Athill, op. cit. pp. 64–5.

10 Diego's birth was not declared until 1963, allegedly so he would not bear the stigma of being an illegitimate child. More secretly, it might also have been done to ensure that Gary's son had *faux papiers en règle* ('genuine false ID') like so many of his male heroes, from Luc Martin to Momo.

11 'Mina née Josel' is entered as 'husband's mother's name' on the marriage certificate of Romain Gary and Jean Seberg. Photocopy of the registry of marriages, Sarrola-Carcopino, Corsica, kindly provided by Jean-François Hangouët.

12 *Promise at Dawn*, p. 91.

Chapter 24 If at first you don't succeed . . .

1 Jouvet to Gary, 11 July 1946 (*L'Herne*, pp. 79–80).

2 Gary to Jouvet, 20 July 1946 (*L'Herne*, p. 80).

3 Gary to Jouvet, 1 May 1947 (*L'Herne*, p. 84).

4 Anissimov, p. 313.

5 Reviews of *Johnnie Cœur*: Paul Morel, *Libération*, 19 October 1962; Georges Lerminier, *Le Parisien libéré*, same date; Jean-Jacques Gautier, *Le Figaro*, same date; Bertrand Poirot-Delpech, *Le Monde*, same date.

6 All these typescripts are among Gary's papers at IMEC.

7 Nunnally Johnston, *The Man Who Understood Women*, starring Leslie Caron and Henry Fonda, was released in 1959, to little acclaim.

8 Jean-Marie Catonné, *Romain Gary/Émile Ajar* (Paris: Belfond, 1990, p. 254).

9 Roger Ebert, 'Birds in Peru', (*Chicago Sun-Times*, 12 August 1969).

10 He gave eloquent and virulent expression to these views in an article, '*Faux Romantisme et Avenir*' (*Le Monde*, 11 December 1971); and again in *Ma haine des trafiquants de drogue est sans limite* (*Le Figaro*, 27 January 1972).

[11] Uri Klein, 'Maker of Movies that Move Him', interview with Mizrahi, (*Ha'aretz* online, 17 December 2009).

[12] Leila Chellabi, *Romain mon amour* (Novamuse, 1997, pp. 109–110).

Chapter 25 Cultural Legitimacy

[1] Conversation with Renaud Camus, Paris, March 1998.

[2] Jørn Boisen, *Un picaro métaphysique. Romain Gary et l'art du roman* (Odense: Odense University Press, 1996) is the fullest attempt to get to grips with *Pour Sganarelle*. See also Dominique Rosse, *Romain Gary et la modernité* (Ottawa: Presses de l'Université d'Ottawa, 1997).

[3] Conversation with Roger Grenier, Paris, 5 November 2002.

[4] See the note by Jean-François Hangouët on p. 204 of *L'Affaire homme*.

[5] Georges Perec, for example, in his articles for *Partisans* in 1962–3, reprinted in *L. G. Une aventure des années soixante* (Paris: Seuil, 1991), which are themselves indebted to the literary terminology in vogue at the École normale supérieure.

[6] In the original, from Chancel 1978: *C'est un énorme livre, à chaque page on voit le talent, et ça m'a fait plaisir de voir . . . que je ne suis pas le seul! Hi hi hi!*

[7] Wolfgang Iser, *The Implied Reader: patterns of communication in prose fiction from Bunyan to Beckett* (Baltimore, MD: Johns Hopkins University Press, 1974); Hans-Robert Jauss, *Literaturgeschichte als Provokation der Literaturwissenschaft* (Konstanz: Universitätsverlag, 1967).

[8] The term is from Ralph Schoolcraft, op. cit.

Chapter 26 'The problem is the human race'

[1] Nancy Huston, '*Gary se traduit*' (*Le Plaid* 7, 2001, pp. 3–14), gives an incomplete account of the differences between the English and French versions of *Genghis Cohn*.

[2] *Chien Blanc* appeared in French in March 1970; *Life* of 9 October 1970 carried the whole novel in English.

[3] *Pour Sganarelle*, pp. 272–3.

4 *The Dance of Genghis Cohn*, pp. 26–7.

5 Ibid., p. 352, my translation.

6 The similarity in style and content of Modiano's breakthrough novel to *The Dance of Genghis Cohn* – and its great difference from all the thirty novels he has written since 1968 – could well be worth a closer look.

7 Telephone interview with Jolanta Sell, Warsaw, October 2003.

8 After his speech in French at the French Cultural Centre, Gary took and answered questions about his work in Polish, and impressed the audience with his fluency – and with his old-fashioned, unmistakably Yiddish accent.

9 See Maurice Szafran, *Les Juifs dans la politique française, de 1945 à nos jours* (Flammarion, 1990: pp. 149–172).

10 *Hocus Bogus*, p. 60.

11 *The Dance of Genghis Cohn*, p. 11.

12 The online archive of French television news at www.ina.fr/archivespourtous allows us all now to see and hear de Gaulle making the remark.

13 Raymond Aron, *De Gaulle, Israël et les Juifs* (Plon, 1968).

14 *The Dance of Genghis Cohn*, p. 190.

15 It was adapted for television in 1993 by Elija Moshinsky – in English, for the BBC.

16 *The Dance of Genghis Cohn*, p. 25.

17 One example of the German language haunting Gary himself is his famously ungrammatical declaration, *Je me suis toujours été étranger*. It is a word-for-word translation of standard German, *Ich bin mir immer ein Fremder gewesen*, ('I have always been foreign to myself').

18 *The Dance of Genghis Cohn*, p. 35.

19 *La Nuit sera calme*, pp. 233–4.

20 Romain Gary, '*Lettre aux Juifs de France*', (*Le Figaro littéraire*, 9 March 1970, in *L'Affaire homme*, p. 223).

21 *L'Affaire homme*, p. 285.

22 *The Dance of Genghis Cohn*, p. 35. The adage comes from Rabelais, in fact.

Chapter 27 'A Mysterious and Astonishing Adventure'

1 Pavlowitch, p. 280.

2 Ibid., p. 56.

3 *The Collected Tales and Plays of Nikolai Gogol*, transl. Constance Garnett (revised) (New York: Pantheon, 1964, p. 565).

4 Romain Gary (Émile Ajar), *Gros-Câlin. Roman. Nouvelle Edition* (Paris: Mercure de France, 2007). Admirably introduced and edited by Jean-François Hangouët.

5 *White Dog*, p. 5.

6 *Gros-Câlin*, p. 60.

7 For more details of Ajar's linguistic peculiarities, see David Bellos, '*Petite histoire de l'incorrection à l'usage des ajaristes*', in *Études Romain Gary I. Signé Ajar*. (La Chasse au Snark, 2004, pp. 29–47).

8 The most common is '*marabout, bout de ficelle, selle de cheval* . . .'.

9 Pierre Bourdieu, '*Champ intellectuel et projet créateur*' (*Les Temps modernes* 22, 1966, pp. 865–906).

10 *Life and Death* . . . in *King Solomon*, pp. 246–7.

11 The Polish idiom, *czerwony jak burak*, is the literal equivalent of 'red as a beetroot'.

12 *Gros-Câlin*, p. 99.

13 Detail and dialogue from Anissimov, pp. 717–18.

14 Reader report by C. Baroche, quoted by Anissimov, p. 718.

15 Conversation with Christiane Baroche, Paris, 9 February 2006.

16 Gallimard archives, quoted by Dominique Bona, *Romain Gary*, p. 322.

17 Michel Cournot, '*Ma Vérité sur l'affaire Ajar*' (*Le Nouvel Observateur*, 30 August 1990; *L'Herne*, pp. 68–72).

18 Robert Escarpit, *Sociologie de la littérature*. (Paris: PUF, 1965).

19 Erich Kästner is mentioned at length in the last Ajar novel, no doubt as a nod in the right direction. See *King Solomon*, p. 203.

20 Mercure de France archives, quoted by Anissimov, p. 724.

21 'Ajar is Gogol, Ajar is the Pushkin of the darker side of Paris . . .' (*Le Parisien libéré*, 29 October 1974; quoted in Pavlowitch, p. 59).

22 Pavlowitch, p. 58.

23 *King Solomon*, p. 250.

Chapter 28 Belleville Rendezvous

1 *La Nuit sera calme*, p. 26.

2 *Life Before Us* is not a good translation of *La Vie devant soi*, but a better one is hard to find. Dickens bagged *Great Expectations* and Kipling has first call on 'You'll be a Man, My Son'; a pun putting both of these heroico-sentimental antecedents into service might make the grade.

3 Anissimov, p. 736.

4 *Promise at Dawn*, p. 27.

5 *Le Naufrage de l'espoir* (*The Shipwreck of Hope*) is the French title of a very popular German play by Hermann Suderman called *Schmetterlingsschlacht* (1895) and known in Russian – the language in which Gary alleged to remember it – as бой бабочек (both titles meaning 'The Fight [sic] of the Butterflies'). It was filmed in Germany in 1925.

6 The name is most likely a reminiscence of Erich Kästner's story for children in verse and pictures, '*Arthur mit dem langen Arm*' (1930). See E. Kästner, *Romane für Kinder* II (Munich: Hanser Verlag, 1998, p. 7).

7 *Life Before Us*, pp. 25, 36.

8 Georges Perec, *W or The Memory of Childhood*, transl. D. Bellos (London: Collins Harvill, 1988, p. 7). The French original appeared in 1975, a few weeks before Ajar's *Life Before Us*.

9 Michel Tournier, '*Émile Ajar ou la vie derrière soi*', in *Le Vol du vampire. Notes de lecture* (Paris: Mercure de France, 1981, pp. 329–44); Bernard Lalande, '*Pour une lecture de* La Vie devant soi' (*Le Français dans le monde* 158.1, 1981, 37–40, 57–9); Thomas Krefeld, '*Substandard als Mittel literarischer Stilbildung. Der Roman* La Vie devant soi *von Émile Ajar*', in

Günter Holtus, Edgar Radtke (eds), *Sprachlicher Substandard III* (Tübingen, Niemeyer Verlag, 1990, pp. 244–67).

10 Further evidence that literary texts do not contain sufficient information to allow the identity (or the age, gender, skin colour, or creed) of the writer to be known has been provided by the discovery that Binjamin Wilkomirski's holocaust memoir, *Fragments*, was a novel by Bruno Grosjean, that the *Letters of a Portuguese Nun* that Rilke took as authentic were written by a French nobleman, and that Lousie Labé, the great woman poet of the French renaissance, was a quartet of men. See Stefan Maechler, *The Wilkomirski Affair: A Study in Biographical Truth*, transl. John E. Woods (New York: Schocken Books, 2001); Leo Spitzer, *Essays in Seventeenth-Century French Literature*, transl. David Bellos (Cambridge: Cambridge University Press, 1981) and Mireille Huchon, *Louise Labé. Une créature de papier* (Geneva: Droz, 2006).

11 *Life Before Us*, pp. 145, 157, 145.

12 Narrative and dialogue borrowed from Pavlowitch, pp. 98, 100. One of these titles, *Madame Rosa*, was used for the film version, starring Simone Signoret, and another, *Momo*, for the reissue of the English translation when the movie was screened in the USA.

13 *Life Before Us*, p. 3.

14 Ibid., p. 5.

15 Ibid., p. 27.

16 Ibid., p. 31.

17 Ibid., p. 37.

18 Gary's 'revelation' of ethnic harmony in the slums of Paris in *Life Before Us* has been shamelessly exploited by Eric-Emmanuel Schmitt in *Monsieur Ibrahim and the Flowers of the Koran* (first published in 2002), a feel-good morality tale whose success proves that you can go on fooling people for a very long time.

19 Signed 'Alexandre Sorel', the review was actually written by

Angelo Rinaldi (*L'Express*, 1 December 1975, quoted by Anissimov, p. 753).

[20] The expression was used (in French) by Russian aristocrats in the early nineteenth century as a disrespectful way of talking about Napoleon – as every reader of *War and Peace* knows.

[21] *Life Before Us*, p. 181.

Chapter 29 'In the Sombre Folds of Life'

[1] Émile Ajar, *Momo*. Transl. Ralph Manheim (Garden City, NY: Doubleday, 1978). On Gary's involvement in the English version, see *L'Homme que l'on croyait,* p. 273.

[2] On the presence of Victor Hugo in all the Ajar novels, see Olivier Achtouk, '*Généalogie du roman: la paternité hugolienne à l'épreuve de l'écriture ajarienne*', in *Études Romain Gary I. Signé Ajar* (La Chasse au Snark, 2004).

[3] Victor Hugo, *Les Misérables* (1862, Bibliothèque de la Pléïade, 1951, p. 1405). My translation differs slightly from that of *Les Misérables*, transl. Julie Rose (New York: The Modern Library, 2008, p. 1129).

[4] *Clair de femme*, p. 172.

[5] Ibid., pp. 85–6, 86–7.

[6] Ibid., p. 148.

[7] *L'Homme que l'on croyait*, p. 89. I've not found a trace of such comments in the press; maybe they were made in conversation, or on radio. At all events, if they were made they must have sent Gary into paroxysms of delight.

[8] *La Nuit sera calme*, p. 103.

[9] Harry Frankfurt, *The Reasons of Love*. (Princeton, NJ: Princeton University Press, 2004).

[10] Romain Gary, *Life and Death of Émile Ajar*, in *King Solomon*, p. 246.

[11] The *Encyclopédie sexuelle* by Silbermann referred to several times is an invention, and a sly homage to Jacques de Lacretelle's *Silbermann* (1922), a novel about a Jewish boy at

a Paris lycée whose teenage problems include the fear of sexual fiasco.

12 *La Nuit sera calme*, p. 45.

13 *King Solomon*, p. 203.

14 On the 'ajarisation' of Gary's writing in *The Way Out*, see Jacques Lecarme, '*Au-delà de cette limite . . . ou le nouveau ticket de Romain Gary*', in Mireille Sacotte (ed.), *Romain Gary et la pluralité des mondes*, PUF, 2002, pp. 111–28.

Chapter 30 *Hocus Bogus*, 1976

1 Anissimov, p. 758 and footnote 1 on p. 1010; Pavlowitch, p. 111.

2 Pavlowitch, p. 122.

3 *Life Before Us*, p. 38.

4 Anissimov, p. 772.

5 Pavlowitch, p. 168.

6 *Hocus Bogus*, p. 8

7 Ibid., p. 60.

8 The English translation, *Hocus Bogus*, adds flagrant anachronisms that do not correspond directly to *Pseudo*, let alone *Le Vin des morts*.

9 William Styron, *Darkness Visible* (1990, London: Vintage, 2001, p. 23).

Chapter 31 Happy Ends

1 Vina Tirgendvadum, 'Linguistic Fingerprints and Literary Fraud', *Computing in the Humanities Working Papers (CHWP)*, A.9 (1998).

2 Styron, op. cit., pp. 23–4.

3 'I've read that in New York there's a phone service that answers when you're beginning to wonder if you're there or not . . .', *Gros-Câlin*, p. 53.

4 Philippe Sollers, *Femmes* (Paris: Gallimard, 1983). As *Women*, transl. Barbara Bray (New York: Columbia University Press, 1992).

5 Fred Vargas, *L'Homme à l'envers* (Paris: Viviane Hamy, 2002). As *Seeking Whom He May Devour* transl. David Bellos (London: Harvill Press, 2004; New York: Simon & Schuster, 2006).
6 Erich Kästner, *Emil und die drei Zwillinge*, 1933, is a sequel to *Emil und die Detektive*, one possible source for the first name of Émile Ajar.
7 *Les Cerfs-volants*, p. 27.
8 From a conversation with Mike Csáky, Belsize Park, 22 March 2006.
9 *Les Cerfs-volants*, p. 363.

Chapter 32 Last Rites

1 *White Dog*, p. 114.
2 *Promise at Dawn*, p. 137.
3 It can be heard, sung in Russian by Vertinsky himself, at http://www.musicdoo.com/webshopemr/index.html?target=p_585.html&lang=fr.
4 Anissimov, p. 901.
5 Dominique Bona, *Romain Gary*, (Paris: Mercure de France, 1987, pp. 397–8).

Appendices

1 Michael Coates-Smith and Jean-François Hangouët, '*L'Œuvre publié de Romain Gary*', *L'Herne*, pp. 334–56, is the authoritative bibliography.
2 The UK edition, published simultaneously, was entitled *Nothing Important Ever Dies*.

Acknowledgements

This is not the first study of Romain Gary's life and work and I am indebted in greater or lesser degree to all my numerous predecessors, colleagues and rivals in the field. For the facts of Gary's life, Dominique Bona, Jean-Marie Catonné and especially the tireless Myriam Anissimov have provided me with much of the biographical information used in this book. For the details of Gary's publications, Jean-François Hangouët, the selfless servant of the Association Les Mille Gary, deserves special gratitude. Among the many critics who have written about Gary's work, Paul Audi deserves special recognition for his unrelenting pursuit of its deeper meanings.

Many people shared with me their personal memories of Romain Gary and his world, and others provided me with clues, information and insights of great variety. For services great and small, I would like to thank Alain Aptekman, Marie-Jeanne Aubert, Paul Audi, Galina Baranova, Christiane Baroche, Vivienne Bellos, Victor Brombert, John Brownjohn, Georgia de Chamberet, Teresa Cherfas, Mike Csáky, Brigid Dorsey, Paul Fournel, Diego Gary, Roger Grenier, Jean-François Hangouët, Fabrice Larat, Christopher MacLehose, Jeffrey Mehlman, Colin Nettlebeck, Kathryn O'Keeffe, Martine Ollion, Paul Pavlowitch, Andy Plaks, Jean-Yves Potel, Jean-Yves Pouilloux, Sir Adam Robertson, Romas Romanauskas, Jean-Pierre Salgas, Ralph Schoolcraft III, Jolanta Sell, Tom Sychterz, Marina van Zuylen, Michael Wachtel, Froma Zeitlin, and – last but not least – my wife Pascale.

I must record special thanks to my assistant, Natalia Krasicka, who ferreted out and translated for me many precious documents relating to Gary's engagement with Polish culture. All translations from Polish in this book have been done from her French versions. Jean-François Hangouët supplied many precious documents and a constant stream of good and learned advice.

The work that has led to the composition of this book would not have been possible without the generous support of Princeton University. It was first conceived during a delightful term at All Souls College, Oxford, in 2002; it would not have been undertaken without the encouragement and friendship of Christopher MacLehose, former editorial director of the Harvill Press. The meticulous attention of my editor, Briony Everroad, added clarity and precision to my first drafts. Remaining imperfections and infelicities can only be ascribed to me.

Princeton, NJ
March 2010

Index of Names

A propos de Nice (film, 1930) 43
Adamson, Joy, *Born Free* 243
Africa Adventure (film, 1954) 258
Agid, Alexandre 40
Agid, René 39–40, 71, 148, 278, 291, 299, 304, 367
Agid, Roger 299, 301, 367
Agid, Silvia 71, 145, 269, 304
Agostin, Mireille d' 187
Aix-en-Provence 1, 229
Ajaccio 300
Ajar, Émile (pseud of Romain Gary) 4, 9, 10, 44, 124, 141, 150, 161, 162, 170–2, 174, 177–8, 191, 193, 209, 213, 226, 265, 275, 281, 314, 322–3, 347, 355–65, 366–76, 377–83, 384–95, 397–8, 400–2, 411
Albania 273
Algeria 131–2, 184, 236, 294, 307
Algiers 78, 79, 114
Allied Control Commission 125, 126
Alvarez, Cecilia 300–1
Ambler, Eric 253
Amis, Kingsley 277
Angkor Wat 302
Anissimov, Myriam 6, 32, 45, 47, 52, 59, 65, 68, 70, 71, 73, 134, 139, 142, 215, 249, 274, 278, 300, 302, 338, 344, 359, 385, 392, 398, 410
Annakin, Ken 317
Ansky, S. 29
Antelme, Robert, *The Human Race* 224
Antibes 309
Antwerp 69, 70
Apollinaire, Guillaume 355
Aptekman, Alain 268
Aragon, Louis 4, 231, 364
Arizona 278
Arland, Marcel 231
Arletty 317
Arnothy, Christine 364, 368
Aron, Raymond 79, 97, 99, 100, 169, 206, 229
Arundel Castle 168
Athens 301
Auschwitz 206, 257, 340, 341, 407
Avord 67, 76, 83, 169
Aymé, Marcel 222, 227
Uranus 214

Baby, Yvonne 385
Balzac, Honoré de 52, 216, 312, 328, 331
Cousin Bette 158
Cousin Pons 158
L'Envers de l'histoire contemporaine 291

Bangui (Central Africa) 63, 168, 291
Baranova, Galina 51
Barbusse, Henri, *Le Feu* 405
Barcelona 299, 306
Barnes, Joseph 97, 187, 210, 234, 250–1, 253, 294
Barnes, Maynard 127, 128
Baroche, Christiane 358, 360
Battle of Britain (1940) 83
Beauvior, Simon de 2
The Blood of Others 212
Becker, Stephen 234
Beckett, Samuel 325
Bellow, Saul 331
Bénédictis, Odette de 187, 277, 278
Benjamin, René 230
Bergen-Belsen 202
Berne 233, 279, 280
Bertagna, Dr L. 381
Bialystok 17, 21, 405
Big Sleep, The (film, 1946) 218
Billy, André 231
Birds in Peru (film, 1968) 319–21
Blanch, Lesley
Gary's fictionalisation of his mother's name 51
comical recollection of Gary's use of bread as ear-plugs 69
and Gary's feelings for Ilona 70–1
meets and marries Gary 102–4, 124, 125
and Gary's confession concerning young girls 135
as diplomatic wife 137, 247, 277
sexual interests and liaisons 139, 148–9, 227
visit to the Simenons 151–2
on Gary's 'useless' hands 185
on Gary's need to write 187
discovers that Gary is a Jew 206
slimness of 215
constantly changes accommodation in Paris 232
Around the World in Eighty Dishes 247
The Wilder Shores of Love 247
writing career 247–8, 259, 277
remains in New York when Gary moves to London 248–9
reaction to Gary's depression 249
marriage breakdown 254–5, 277, 296, 300
Gary's childish desire to teach her a lesson 267
as character in Gary's book *Lady L* 269–70, 271
on Gary's English-language career 274
attitude to Gary's whoring 278, 296
Christmas vacation in Mexico 283
on Gary's writing of *Promise at Dawn* 294
friendship with Olga Csáky 406
scatters Gary's ashes in the Mediterranean 410
Blanchot, Maurice 231
Blanzat, Jean 231
Bloch, Marcel 169
Bolivia 173
Bonaparte, Princess Marie 65
Bondy, François 6, 39, 40, 47, 124, 150, 265, 271, 367, 380

Bonnier, Henri 188
Bordeaux 78
Bordighera 33, 41
Borgeaud, Georges 365
Bory, Jean-Louis, *Mon village à l'heure allemande* 231
Bosquet, Alain 97, 147
Bossat, Maître 364
Boulogne-Billancourt studios (Paris) 319
Bouna game reserve 244
Bourdieu, Pierre 326, 354
Bouzerand, Jacques 387
Boyd, Stephen 322
Brandon, Marjorie 300
Branicki Palace (Bialystok) 405
Breathless (film, 1959) 1, 297
Brecht, Bertolt, *Dreigroschenoper* 47
Brenot, Philippe 65
Brittany 373
Brussels Treaty (1948) 250
Buchenwald 202, 206, 407
Budapest 69, 301
Budberg, Baroness Moura 98, 99, 101, 287
Bukavu conference (1953) 237–8, 243
Bulgaria 125–8, 129, 166, 173, 209, 218, 232
Bürger, Berthold (pseud of Erich Kästner) 355
Burgess, Anthony 309, 331
  A Clockwork Orange 348
Burton, Richard 318
Butor, Michel 325
  L'Emploi du temps 260

Calcutta 302
California 173
Calmann-Lévy 104, 230
Camus, Albert 107, 131–2, 182, 227, 229–30, 260, 261, 326, 328, 331
  The Plague 182
Camus, Renaud 325
Caniac-du-Causse 363, 373, 384
Cannes 299, 300, 320
Cap Ferrat 301, 309
Carré, Martine 187, 357, 361
Carruthers, Jack 350
Casablanca 79
Catonné, Jean-Marie 317
Céline, Louis-Ferdinand 328
  Journey to the End of the Night 394
Cervantes, Miguel de 328, 329
Chaban-Delmas, Jacques 366
Chagall, Marc 20
Chancel, Jacques 74, 399, 409
Chaplin, Charlie 355
Chauvel, Jean 142, 233, 248, 279
Chellabi, Leïla 323
Chénevier, Squadron Leader 109–10
Chicago Sun-Times 320
Churchill, Winston 95, 104, 106
Cimarrón (house on Mallorca) 41, 148, 308
Clair de femme (film, 1979) 323
Clark, Bruce 318
Claudel, Paul 210
Cocteau, Jean 265
Colombia 301
Combat newspaper 107, 229, 230
Congo Vivo (film, 1961) 298–9
Conrad, Joseph 30, 64, 162, 195, 267
  Heart of Darkness 181, 239, 244, 246, 261, 286
  Lord Jim 261, 286
  Under Western Eyes 269, 286
Cooper, Gary 168–9, 281
Cooper, James Fennimore 162

The Last of the Mohicans 98
Copenhagen 385
Corneille, Pierre 52
Costa-Gavras 323
Cournot, Michel 359–60, 362, 372, 373, 374, 384, 385
Couve de Murville, Maurice 259, 294
Cresset Press 9, 101, 102, 104, 107, 265
Crimea 54
Csáky, Countess Olga 149, 406
Curtis, Tony 317

D-Day (1944) 100–1
Dakar 236
Daligot, Maurice 79
Dance of Genghis Cohn, The (TV drama, 1993) 324
Daniel, Jean 131
Darquier de Pellepoix, Louis 307
Dassin, Jules 276, 318, 319
Daudet, Léon 231
De Gaulle, Charles 79, 80, 82, 83, 84, 109–19, 125, 145, 167, 169, 206, 236, 281, 294, 303, 338, 341, 343, 344, 345, 398
De Gaulle 'Première' (documentary) 145
Death Mills (film, 1945) 202
Deighton, Len 273
Denoël (publisher) 65
Deroux, Dominique 6
Descartes, René 208, 218–19, 222
Desforges, Régine 129
Dickens, Charles 30, 162, 163, 195, 216, 325, 331
Great Expectations 261
Oliver Twist 211–12, 213–14, 215, 225, 286
Diderot, Denis 52
Dien Bien Phu (1954) 237
Dimitrov, Georgi 126
Djibouti 144
Donnini, Nathalie 324
Dorgelès, Roland 231
Dostoevsky, Fyodor 30, 42, 162, 194, 195, 225, 325, 331, 359
Bobok 65
Brothers Karamazov 194, 212, 226, 261
Crime and Punishment 213
The Double 293
The Idiot 203
Notes from the Underground 168, 212, 213, 216, 222, 286, 351–2
Double Indemnity (film, 1944) 218
Dreyfus, Alfred 21, 175
Druon, Maurice 97
Ducarne, Dr 381
Duhamel, Colette 358, 360
Durango 304
Duvalier, François 'Papa Doc' 390

Eastwood, Clint 184, 303
Ebert, Roger 320
Éboué, Félix 84
Eichmann, Karl Adolf 69
Elkabach, Jean-Pierre 184–5
Elle magazine 247
Emilfork, Daniel 322
Escarpit, Robert 360
Estouffade à la Caraïbe (film, 1966) 301, 350

Faraggi, Claude 358, 360
Fatherland Front (FF) 126
Fémina Prize 229, 230
Fermor, Patrick Leigh 316
Feuvrier, General 300
Fez (Morocco) 79
Fine Madness, A (film, 1965) 301

First Love (play, 1961) 318
Flaubert, Gustave 52, 312, 331
Éducation sentimentale 105
Fleming, Ian 273
Flint, Peter (pseud of Erich Kästner) 355
Flynn, Errol 316
Ford, John 317
Foreign Legion 75, 81, 410
Formentera 299
Forsans, Jean 79
Forsyth, Frederick 239
Foucault, Michel 301
France newspaper 87, 97
France-Soir 281, 389
Franco, General 306, 307
Frankenheimer, John 317
Frankfurt, Harry 123–4, 380
Free France 74, 79, 80, 83, 84, 109, 110, 113, 119, 129, 344, 409
Free French 7, 82, 83, 86, 110, 111, 167, 168, 169, 223, 291, 300, 326
Free French Air Force (*Les Forces aériennes de la France Libre*) (FAFL) 83, 84, 255
Free Poles 93–4
French Air Force 1, 76–7, 78
French Communist Party 231, 261, 274
French Foreign Office 125, 232, 279
Freud, Sigmund 65, 151, 286
Friedman, Bruce 315
Fuentes, Carlos 304, 305
Fuller, Sam 323

Gajewski, Stas 53
Gallimard, Claude 74, 359, 388, 400
Gallimard, Gaston 230
Gallimard, Michel 259–60
Gallimard (publishers) 42, 209, 229, 232, 252, 259, 297, 298, 326, 327, 356–9, 362, 384
Gallimard, Robert 357, 359, 360, 362, 364, 388, 389, 400
Gallimard, Simone 359, 360, 365, 372–3, 384, 385
Garvin, Louis 102
Garvin, Viola 102, 119
Gary, Alexandre-Diego (son) 142, 173, 299, 300, 303, 305, 306, 357, 369, 400, 410
Gary, Romain
overview 1–3
as invented self 3–4, 7–8, 28, 43–4, 107, 165–6, 192, 228, 289–93, 353, 356, 361
birth and childhood 5, 16, 18–20, 28, 29–34, 43–4
mother's influence on 6–7, 28, 284–6, 290–1
style of writing 9–10, 129–30, 151–4, 161–4, 177, 185–91
rediscovery of 10
as a born minoritarian 23–5
relationship with his father 26–8, 55–60
use of magic and folkore 28–9, 218–20, 227–8
thoughts of shame and suicide 30–2
description of 34, 48, 60, 308
as linguist 34, 52, 172–4
Polish and Russian influences on 34–5, 36–40, 44–50, 367
love of water 41–2
and the carnival in Nice 42–3
love of dressing up and dressing down 48, 144–5, 147, 192, 308, 373

Jewish roots and identity 50–2, 55–60, 179, 206–8, 224, 367
French cultural influence 52–3, 214–15, 223
fondness for cucumbers 55–6, 215
studies law 61–2, 66
early stories 62–6
use of pseudonyms 65, 158, 168–9, 170–2, 174–5, 226, 252–3, 347, 349, 354–65, 366–76, 378, 384–95
military service 66–7, 74–88, 90, 91–2, 100
sexual addiction and liaisons 67–73, 134–43, 148–54, 254, 277–8, 378, 398
earache due to use of bread as ear-plugs 69
awards and honours 82, 110, 124, 205, 229–32, 242, 245, 249, 253, 260–1, 268, 389
globe-trotting/jet-setting life 88, 283, 298–303, 306, 310, 373
first full-length novel 90–1, 94–6, 98, 99–108
involved with French and Polish Resistance 96–9, 107
meets and marries his first wife 102–4
Gaullist affiliations 109–19
political invention and ambiguities 120–33
diplomatic career 124–5, 169, 173, 199, 209, 232–8, 248, 250, 255, 259, 260, 266, 276–7, 278–80, 294, 296–7, 298
dislike of drink and drugs 128–9, 322
antipathy to national boundaries and ethnic discrimination 130–3
fear of venereal disease and impotence 147–8
and female frigidity 149–50
French writing phase 157–8
English writing phase 158, 265–75
second French writing phase 158
writing and re-writing of books 158–60, 163–4
thematic groupings of his stories 160–1
pseudo-Christ theme 161, 180, 204–5, 206–8
literary influences 162, 176–7, 181, 206–7, 211–15, 220–3, 225, 226–7, 239, 246, 268–9, 271, 286–8, 377
publishing career 164–5
use and invention of names 166–83, 201
as a carrier of memory 175–8, 182
as hot-tempered 184–5
ideas and beliefs of human and humane 192–6, 213–14, 223, 224–5, 227, 249, 274, 301, 335–46
novel concerning Polish identity 199–208
and 'village next door' quotation 202, 407
American influences 217–18
ecological novel 240–6
health of 249, 250, 254, 303, 380–2, 389–90, 395, 398–9
love of animals 249–50, 350–1
collapse of first marriage 254–5
lack of social graces 279

as journalist and Hollywood scriptwriter 280–2, 284
memoir of early life 283–7, 288–93, 294–5, 318–19
liaison with Jean Seberg 295–6, 297–306
film and stage work 299, 301, 302, 312–24
involvement with Spain 306–10
multiple existences of 310–11
cultural legitimacy of 325–32
Holocaust comedy 335–44
dog story 344–6
love and yearning in pet python book 347–65
comedy of race 367–76
stories concerning meaningful lives and loves 377–83
Ajar mystification story 390–5
romantic comedies 397–8, 401–8
reaction to death of Jean Seberg 399–400
writes his will and leaves instructions for his funeral 400
suicide and funeral 408, 409–11
Geneva 1, 268, 301, 306, 317, 386, 390
Georgetown, MD 299
Gesmay, Eva 69–70
Gesmay, Ilona 67–71, 72, 73, 296
Gesmay, Klara 70
Gibraltar 79
Gide, André 64
Giscard d'Estaing, Valéry 366, 367, 405
Glicksman, Edmond (*later* Edmund Glenn) 39, 40
Godard, Jean-Luc 1, 297
Gogol, Nikolai 162, 163, 286, 359
Dead Souls 227
The Inspector General 176–7
'The Overcoat' 349
Gombrowicz, Witold 6, 44, 46, 265, 293
Memoirs of a Time of Immaturity 46
Princess Ivona 46
Goncourt, Edmond de 229
Goncourt Prize 32, 111, 112, 117, 175, 187, 205, 206, 224, 229, 230–2, 242, 245, 253, 260, 262, 268, 277, 355, 384, 389, 409
Gone With the Wind (film, 1939) 218
Goodman, Jack 250
Gorce, Georges 302, 320
Gorky, Maksim 98, 191
'The Good Life' 98
The Lower Depths 29, 287–8
Mother 286–7
Grabinski, Stefan, *The Grey Room* 293
Gracq, Jacques 355
Grass, Günter 331
Graves, Robert 309
Greco, Juliette 316
Greene, Graham 222, 270, 271, 272, 309
Greenock 79
Grenier, Jean 231
Grenier, Roger 384, 386
Grimm Brothers (Jacob and Wilhelm) 29
Grisham, John 239
Gros-Câlin (film, 1979) 394
Grunwald, Anatole 252
Grunwald, Dmitri 252
Guam 302
Guardian 104

Haedens, Kléber 262, 267
Hallie, Philip, *Lest Innocent Blood Be Shed* 183
Hallier, Jean-Edern 372
Hartford Bridge airfield (now Blackbushe Airport) (Surrey) 86, 87, 88, 90, 91, 110, 291
Heifetz, Yasha 20
Henriot, Émile 231, 261
Herald Tribune 97
Hiller, Marta 245
Himes, Chester 148
Hitler, Adolf 77, 93, 126, 307
  Mein Kampf 394
Holden, William 316
Holiday magazine 48, 132, 281
Hollywood 259, 267, 276, 280, 284, 291, 319, 321
Hong Kong 298, 302
Honolulu 302
Hoog, Armand 231
Hoppenot, Hélène 28, 233
Hoppenot, Henri 28, 232–3, 234–5, 236, 259, 280
Horseman, The (film, 1971) 317
Hôtel-Pension Mermonts (Nice) 40–1, 45, 46, 68, 112, 289, 290
Howard, Elizabeth Jane 186, 259, 277
Howard, John 102
Howard, Richard 319
Howard, Trevor 316
Hoxha, Enver 273
Huelva 319
Hughes, Olwen 97
Hugo, Victor 30, 52, 195, 353
  Les Misérables 21, 162–3, 226, 261, 377
Huston, John 316
Huston, Nancy 147

Ijmuiden 88
Imbert, Claude 388
India 298
Indochina 298
Interallié Prize 229, 230
International Union for the Protection of Nature (IUPN) 237
Ionesco, Eugène 267
Israel 338

Jamal, Hakim 303–4
James, Henry 312
Japan 298
Jebb, Gladwyn 235
Jelenski, Konstantin 222
Jews 16, 16–22, 23–4, 33, 50–1, 52, 206–7, 223–4, 257, 335, 336–44, 374–5
Joan of Arc 223
Jouvet, Louis 232, 312–14
Jürgens, Curd 322

Kacew, Borukh (Gary's uncle) 26, 45, 57, 290
Kacewa, Frida (Gary's stepmother) 59, 60
Kacew, Leiba (or Arieh) (Gary's father) 18, 19–20, 22, 26–8, 40, 45, 54, 56–7, 58–60
Kacew, Pavel (Gary's half-brother) 19, 59, 60
Kacew, Roman *see* Gary, Romain
Kacewa, Valentina (Gary's half-sister) 19, 59, 60
Kacewa, Mina (née Owczynski) (Gary's mother) 17, 18, 19–20
  influence on Gary 3, 28, 29, 140, 147
  description of 6–7

Francophile 21–2
first marriage and divorce 26
second marriage and divorce 26–8, 45
as embarassment to her son 30–1
as representative of Paris couturier 32, 33
as cocotte 33–4
as manageress of boarding-house in Nice 40–1, 67
death of 41, 84, 291
and possible change of name to 'Nina' 51
health of 61–2
portrayal in *Promise at Dawn* 284–7, 289–92, 369
favourite music-hall song 410
Kacewa, Rachel (Rivka) (née Owczynski) (Gary's aunt) 26, 34, 45
Kadare, Ismail 97, 108, 398
Kafka, Franz 191, 327, 328
The Trial 166
Kanal (film, 1956) 343
Kanters, Robert 262
Karaites 54–5, 56
Kardo-Sissoeff, Sacha 39, 41, 308
Kästner, Erich 355
Emil and the Detectives 361
Emil and the Three Twins 405
Kaunas 52, 59
Kemp, Roger 231
Kennedy, John F. 299
Kessel, Joseph 97, 98
Army of the Shadows 33
The Horseman 317
L'Équipage 74
The Lion 243
Kill! Kill! Kill! (film, 1971) 322
King, Martin Luther 132, 345
King Solomon (film, 2010) 324
Kipling, Rudyard 98, 163, 223
Kites, The (TV drama, 2007) 324
Klaipeda 52
Klemens, Hetman Jan 405
Klooga 60
Koestler, Arthur 259, 277
Kolodziejczyk, Leszek 399
Kott, Jan 107, 136
Krakow 301, 318
Kreczmar Gymnasium (Warsaw) 32–3
Kreczmar, Jerzy 32
Krukowski, Lopek 46
Kundera, Milan, *The Art of the Novel* 328
Kurtz, Melchior (pseud of Erich Kästner) 355

La Dépèche du Midi newspaper 384
La Fontaine, Jean de 52, 162, 212, 223
Fables 214
La France Libre 96–7, 99, 125
La Paz (Bolivia) 173, 260
Labarthe, André 97, 99
Lacan, Jacques 286
Lacasta, Eugenia Muñoz 300, 303, 306, 369
Lady L (film, 1965) 164, 317
Lagerlöf, Selma 30, 162
Lake, Veronica 278
Langer, Arnaud 88
Laski, Marghanita 102
Laurel, Stan 355
Lausanne 299, 301
Le Chambon 182, 183
Le Figaro 281, 314
Le Havre 277
Le Monde 281, 314, 386, 387, 390
Le Nouveau Candide 281
Le Parisien libéré 314

'Le Petit Club Français' (St James, London) 97
Le Point magazine 387, 388
League of Nations 15, 16, 77
Lecoutre, Marthe 97
Lefèvre, Frédéric 231
Lemarchand, Jacques 260
Leningrad 93
Les Éditions du Pavois 231
Les Faussaires (film adaptation of *The Guilty Head*) 324
Les Misérables (film, 1958) 319
Les Misérables (musical) 195
Levinas, Emmanuel 20, 194
L'Express 338, 375
Lida 15–16
Life Before Us (aka *Madame Rosa*) (film, 1978) 322–3, 394
Life magazine 41, 115, 281, 336
Lilith (film, 1963) 299
Lima 300
Lindbergh, Charles 74
Lithuania 5, 15–22, 16, 93, 106
Locarno 68
Lockhart, Sir Robert Bruce 99
Lollobrigida, Gina 317
London 83, 96, 114, 125, 130, 148, 229, 238, 250, 279, 300
London Convention on the conservation and rational exploitation of African flora and fauna (1933) 237
Longest Day, The (film, 1962) 317–18
Looye, Romy van 277–8
Loren, Sophia 317
Lorgues (Riviera) 367
Lorraine Squadron (RAF 324 Squadron) 81, 82–3, 85, 90, 91, 99, 100–1, 110–11, 178, 181, 409, 410
Los Almendros villa (Puerto Andraitx) 300
Los Angeles 1, 137, 169, 187, 238, 255, 259, 266, 276–9, 295, 296, 300, 301, 303
Lovelace, Richard 162
Lubitsch, Ernst 342
Lumière brothers 259
Lupin, Arsène 30
Lycée de Nice 38, 39, 44, 52, 53, 61, 71, 72, 207

Madame Billy 137, 378
Madame Claude 137, 378
Madame Rosa (aka *Life Before Us*) (film, 1978) 394
Mailer, Norman 331
Maliavin, Philip 290
Malik, Charles 235
Mallorca 173, 299, 300, 301, 303, 308, 309, 317, 373
Malraux, André 64, 112–13, 114, 123, 126, 130, 148, 326, 398
L'Espoir 123
Man's Estate 112, 227, 229
Manda game reserve 238
Manheim, Ralph 377, 394
Manila 302
Marcel, Gabriel 231
Marly, Anna (Anna Betulinskaya) 97, 168
Marne, Pierre de la (pseud of Henri Vandeputte) 174
Marrakech 299
Marshalltown (Iowa) 301, 303, 305
Martin du Gard, Roger 210
Mason, James 322
Mathews, Harry 309
Matta, Raphaël 244
Maugham, William Somerset 309

Mauriac, François 206
Le Baiser au lépreux 63
May, Karl 30, 98, 162, 163
Mayne Reid, Thomas 30, 162
Mendès-France, Pierre 206, 236
Mercouri, Melina 318
Mercure de France 359, 362
Mérignac 78
Mérimée, Prosper, 'Lokis' 29
Mermoz, Jean 74
Meurice, Paul, *Fanfan La Tulipe* 200–1
Mexico 139, 283
Mexico City 69
MGM 317
Michaut, Pierre 356–7, 361, 362, 372
Michaux, Henri 191
Mickiewicz, Adam 16, 162
Pan Tadeusz 90
Miller, Lee 103
Mitosz, Czesław 20–1, 90
Mizrahi, Moshe 322, 394
Modiano, Patrick, *La Place de l'Étoile* 338
Molière 52, 355
Mollet, Guy 235
Molotov, Vyacheslav 77
Moment to Moment (film, 1964) 300
Montaigne, Michel de 52, 148, 208, 345
Montand, Yves 323
Monte Carlo 309
Montgomery, Bernard, 1st Viscount 84
Morel, Edward Dene 166, 244, 261
Moreuil, François 295, 296
Morocco 236, 299
Morosco Theater (Broadway) 318
Moszhukin, Ivan 60, 318
Muenzenberg, Willi 97
Mussolini, Benito 84

Nabokov, Vladimir 267
Glory 291
Pnin 270
Nadeau, Maurice 107, 230, 261, 262
Nancy 111
Nasser, Gamal Abdel 338
Natteau, Jacques 319
Nazis 56, 65, 80, 106, 307, 335, 341
Neff, Hildegarde 245
Neuner, Robert (pseud of Erich Kästner) 355
New Mexico 278
New York 130, 148, 234, 238, 244, 298
New York Times 281
Newman, Paul 317
Nice 1, 38, 39–41, 42–5, 50, 51, 61, 67, 112, 123, 126, 144, 145, 147, 289–90, 290, 299, 300, 301, 326, 367, 386, 397
Night and Fog (film, 1955) 257
Nkrumah, Kwame 131, 244
NKVD (Soviet secret police) 99
Nobel Prize 332
Non-Aggression Pact (1939) 77, 93
Norberg, Sigurd 39, 45, 72

Oakcrest 79
OAS (*Organisation de l'armée secrète*) 307
Oates, Joyce Carol 355
Observer 102, 104
OPEC (Organisation of Petroleum-Exporting Countries) 366

Operation Barbarossa (1941) 93
Order of the Liberation 229, 398
Östman, Charlotte 65
Ouvaliev, Petar Christoff (aka Pierre Rouve) 251–2
Owczynska, Rachel (Rivka) *see* Kacewa, Rachel (Rivka)
Owczynski, Bella (Gary's aunt) 22
Owczynski, Borukh (Boris, Boleslaw) (Gary's uncle) 20, 34, 49
Owczynski, Dinah (Gary's cousin) *see* Pavlowitch, Dinah
Owczynski, Eliasz (or Liova) (Gary's uncle) 22, 74
Owczynski, Maria (Gary's aunt) 20, 34
Owczynski, Mina *see* Kacewa, Mina

Paint Your Wagon (film, 1968) 303
Palma de Mallorca 299
Panerai (Ponary) 59
Paris 1, 50, 53, 70, 78, 122, 139, 148, 187, 216, 217–18, 228, 232, 268, 277, 295, 297, 298, 299, 300, 301, 302–3, 303, 315, 319, 326, 386
Pascal, Blaise 148, 208, 223
  Pensées 214
Paulhan, Jean 231
Paulus, Friedrich 86
Pavlowitch, Annie 373, 385, 387, 389–90
Pavlowitch, Dinah (née Owczynski) (Gary's cousin) 22, 41, 161, 300, 349
Pavlowitch, Paul
  on Gary's use of makeup 48
  as Émile Ajar 161, 357, 364, 365, 398
  on Gary's use of the name Cousin in *Gros-Câlin* 348–9
  relationship with Gary 363
  and Rio deception 364
  remodels and redecorates Gary's apartment in Paris 368
  interviewed as Hamil Raja/Émile Ajar 372–3, 384–90
  and title of Gary's second Ajar novel 373–4
  publicly identified as Émile Ajar 380
  photograph used for publicity 384–5
  and Ajar mystification book 390–5
  character traits used in *King Solomon* 402
Peace News 48
Péguy, Charles 52, 76, 162
Pendulum (film, 1968) 303
Père-Lachaise cemetery (Paris) 410
Perec, Georges 10, 22, 325
  Life: A User's Manual 328
Perier, François 314
Pétain, Philippe 78, 230
'Pete the Strangler' (python) 350–1
Petkov, Nikola 126, 127, 128
Phnom Penh 302
Piaf, Edith 355
Piatier, Jacqueline 385
Picasso, Pablo 123
Pieyre de Mandriargues, André 129
Pinay, Antoine 235

Plato 4
Playboy magazine 319
Poirot-Delpech, Bertrand 314
Poland 5, 16, 18–21, 44–50, 53, 77–8, 79, 93–5, 101, 104, 106, 194, 301, 397
Polish Air Force 79, 93
Polish Home Army 93, 106
Poniatowksi, Michel 405
Poniatowksi, Stanislaw 405
Preminger, Otto 7, 297
Prix des Critiques 231
Promise at Dawn (film, 1970) 318–19
Propintel SA 268
Proust, Marcel, *Remembrance of Things Past* 284
Prucnal, Ana 410
Prus, Boleslaw 44, 47
Pszoniak, Wojciek 53
Puerto Andraitx 173, 308, 363
Pushkin, Alexander 162
Pynchon, Thomas, *The Crying of Lot 49* 167

Queneau, Raymond 10, 107, 230, 358–9, 360, 364, 368

Rabelais, François 52
Racine, Jean 52, 208
Andromacque 214
RAF 305 Squadron ('Ziemia Wielkopolska') 92
RAF 317 Fighter Squadron ('City of Wilno') 92–3
RAF 322 Squadron 91
RAF 324 Squadron *see* Lorraine Squadron
RAF (Royal Air Force) 1, 82, 83, 93, 96, 109, 168
Rawson, Jean-Claude 394
Rayak airbase (Syria) 84
Red Army 69, 77, 86, 96, 100, 101, 118–19
Reed, Carol 222, 343
Remarque, Erich Maria, *All Quiet on the Western Front* 405
Renaudot Prize 229, 364, 391
Rendell, Ruth 355
Renoir, Jean 276
Resnais, Alain 257
Ribbentrop, Joachim von 77
Ribbons, Jack (pseud of Romain Gary) 251, 255, 354
Robbe-Grillet, Alain 24, 274, 301, 319, 325
For a New Novel 326
Romains, Jules 355
Rommel, Erwin 84
Roosevelt, Franklin Delano 104
Roots of Heaven, The (film, 1958) 316–17
Roquebrune 41–2, 187, 254, 255, 260, 308, 406, 410
Rossen, Robert 299
Roth, Madame de 233
Roth, Philip 331
Rousseau, Jean-Jacques 52
Rousset, David, *Other Kingdom* 224
Route de Corinthe (aka *Who's Got the Black Box?*) (film, 1966) 301
Rouve, Pierre (aka Petar Christoff Ouvaliev) 251–2
Ruark, Robert C. 258
Russian Empire 16, 19
Ryan, Cornelius, *The Longest Day* 317

Sagan, Françoise, *Bonjour Tristesse* 297
St Athan's airbase (South Wales) 109

Saint Aubyn, Roger 249
Saint Joan (film, 1957) 7, 297
Saint-Exupéry, Antoine
Courrier Sud 74
Vol de nuit 74
Saint-Omer 88
Saint-Paul-de-Vence (Riviera) 299
Saint-Phalle, Thérèse de 384
Salkind, Alexander 321–2
Salon-de-Provence 67, 76
Salpetrière Hospital (Paris) 381
Sana'a 144
Sarraute, Nathalie 325
The Age of Suspicion 325, 326
Fruits d'Or 379
Sarrola, Noël 300
Sarrola-Carcopino 300
Sartre, Jean-Paul 2, 3, 107, 130, 200, 227, 328, 331, 332
Anti-Semite and Jew 224
L'Enfance d'un chef 224
The Wall 218–19
What is Literature? 326
Sauvagnargues, Jean 232
Schölscher, Victor 166
Schwartz-Bart, André, *The Last of the Just* 206, 224
Scott, Walter 30
Seberg, David 142, 303
Seberg, Jean
liaison with Gary 1, 7, 73, 210, 295–6, 297, 298–300
falls under the spell of Black Power leader 7, 303–4
name as translation of Gary's teenage home 41
mental decline 73, 295–6, 304–5, 345, 399
sexual liaisons 139, 149
film career 149, 295, 297, 298–9, 300–1, 302, 303, 319, 320, 321, 322, 350, 354
marriage breakdown and divorce 158, 302, 304, 321, 335, 348
pregnancy and birth of her son Alexandre-Diego 173, 299
collapse of marriage to Gary 273, 281
concern for racial injustice 297
death of her brother 303
death of premature baby 305–6, 399–400
visits the Warsaw Historical Museum 338
aware of Gary's 'Ajar' pseudonym 357, 384–5
death of 379, 399–400
Selby, Harry 258
Sell, Jolanta 32, 338
Seven Women (film, 1966) 317
Shakespeare, William 148
Shamyl, Imam 259
Shestov, Leon 194
Sierra de Teruel (film) 123
Signoret, Simone 322, 323, 394
Simenon, Georges 151–2
Simon & Schuster 209, 210, 247
Sinibaldi, Fosco (pseud of Romain Gary) 4, 252, 255, 354
Sitges 299, 306
Six-Day War (1967) 338
Ski Bum, The (film, 1969) 318
Sliven 166
Slonimski, Antoni 44, 97
Smetona, President 93
Söderlund, Kristel 71–2, 73, 112
Sofia 103, 125, 139, 142, 166, 209, 217, 312
Sollers, Philippe 130
Women 402
Soutine, Chaim 20

Soviet Union 93, 96
Spain 299, 306–10
Spark, Muriel 270
Spitzer, Leo 163
Stalin, Joseph 96
Stalingrad 86, 101, 119
Steckel,
Frigidity in Women 148
Impotence in the Male 148
Stendhal 355
Stevenson, Robert Louis 162
The Strange Case of De Jekyll and Mr Hyde 4
The Wrong Box 177
Stockholm 65, 72, 123
Strasbourg 250
Strategic Air Command 91
Studios de la Victorine (Nice) 60, 317
Styron, William 399, 400
Sudan 84
Superman (film, 1978) 322
Sutton, John 258
Svevo, Italo, *Confessions of Zeno* 348

Switzerland 233, 290, 299, 306
Sykes, Camilla 335
Szetejnie 20
Szymonczyk, Stanislas 'Staro' 97

Tati, Jacques 252, 355
Taylor, Samuel 318
Tehran 302
Teilhard de Chardin, Pierre 244
Texas 278
Théâtre de la Michodière 205, 314
Third Man, The (film, 1949) 222, 343
Tirgendvadum, Vina 397–8
To Be or Not To Be (film, 1942) 342
Todt Organisation 60
TOE5 Bomber Squadron 83
Tolstoy, Leo 30, 328, 329, 331
War and Peace 195
Topkapi Palace (Istanbul) 149
Topolski, Feliks 97, 103
Toulouse 299, 386, 387
Tourmalet 352
Tournier, Michel 371
Trakai (Troki) 54–5, 56, 57
Travel & Leisure magazine 281
Treaty of Rome (1957) 250
Triolet, Elsa 231
Trocmé, André 182–3, 407
Truffaut, François 297
Tunisia 236
Twentieth Century Fox 316

Un Milliard dans un billard (film, 1965) 301
United Nations 130, 142, 205, 248
United Nations Security Council 233, 234–8, 240
Universal Studios 320
University of Aix-en-Provence 61
University of Warsaw 301
UNR (*Union pour la République*) 300
US Army Signals Corps 202
Ustinov, Peter 164, 309, 317

Vallin, General 111
Vandeputte, Henri 174
Varah, Chad 403
Vargas, Fred, *Seeking Whom He May Devour* 402
Venice 248, 299
Versailles Treaty (1919) 15, 16, 18, 19

Vertinsky, Aleksandr 410
Vietnam War 281
Vigo, Jean 43
Vilna *see* Wilno
Vilna University 16
Vilnius 5, 18, 19, 20, 54, 55
Vishinsky, Andrey 235
Vogue magazine 103
Voltaire, François Marie Arouet de 133
Vytautas, Grand Duke of Lithuania 41

Wajda, Andrzej 343
Wallenberg, Raoul 182
Warsaw 20, 21, 22, 32–4, 38, 44–50, 53, 123, 147, 152, 222, 266, 287, 337
Warsaw Historical Museum 338
Washington DC 142, 248
Washington Post 258
Watts riots (1968) 345
Way Out, The (film) 324
Wayne, John 317
Welles, Orson 316
Wells, H.G. 98, 287
White Dog (film, 1982) 323, 323–4
Wiadomósci Literackie (literary journal) 44
Wiesel, Elie, *Night* 206
Wilder, Billy 202
Wilhelm II 17–18, 189
Wilno (Vilna) 1, 5, 16–23, 27, 29, 38, 45, 48, 56, 59, 90, 92–3, 94–5, 100, 101, 106, 147, 175, 210, 287, 289, 290, 318, 386
Wilson, Harriette 148–9, 227
Wilson, Thomas Woodrow 15, 16, 17, 22–3, 24, 25
Winawer, Bruno 44, 46
Wizard of Oz, The (L. Frank Baum) 28
Wurmser, André 261, 262

Yad Vashem (Jerusalem) 182–3
Yale University 2
Yalta (1945) 104
Yeats, W.B. 162
Yemen 144

Zamenhof, Lejzor 17
Zanuck, Darryl 316
Ziller, René 39, 40
Zohar, the 327
Zola, Émile 21, 52
Zuylen, Gabriella van 136

Index of Titles

Adieu Gary Coooper (1969) 128, 169, 298, 421, 423
see also *Ski Bum, The*
'All's Well on the Kilimanjaro' (1945) 164–5, 180, 219, 291, 425
Anatomie du déclin (1975) 425
Au-delà de cette limite votre ticket n'est plus valable (1975) 377, 421, 423
see also *Way Out, The* (called 'Your Ticket is no Longer Valid' in USA)

'Birds in Peru' (1962) 149, 180, 300, 302, 319, 425, 426
Birds in Peru (screenplay) (1967) 319–21
'Bit of a Dreamer, a Bit of a Fool' (aka 'Birds in Peru') (1964) 426

Cet Amour que j'ai tant aimé (1974) 425
Charge d'âme (1978) 274, 421, 423
see also *Gasp, The*
Chien Blanc (1970) 421, 423, 441
see also *White Dog*
Clair de femme (1977) 136, 377, 379–80, 381, 382–3, 421, 423
see also *Womanlight*
Clair de femme (screenplay) (1979) 323
'Colonials, The' (1959) 132
Colours of the Day, The (1952 & 1953) 43, 51, 57, 129–30, 150, 152–4, 160, 174, 178, 179, 180, 185, 190–1, 216, 226, 232, 234, 247, 272, 284, 285, 288, 315–16, 320, 338, 370, 382, 419, 421, 423, 429, 431
see also *Les Clowns lyriques*; *Les Couleurs du jour*
Company of Men, The (1949 & 1950) 9, 29, 42, 44, 57–8, 125, 134, 138, 142, 150,

163, 164, 166, 174, 193, 209–20, 225–8, 232, 233, 234, 247, 283, 285, 288, 314, 338, 368, 370, 403, 404, 419, 421, 429, 431
see also *Le Grand vestiare*
Company of Men, The (theatrical version) 315
'Comrade Pigeon' (1945) 425, 426
'Courage and Farewell!' (1960) 425
'Craving for Innocence, A' (originally appeared as *JE découvre un Gauguin en vrac*) (1956) 164, 425, 427

'Dance of Genghis Cohn' (1967) 425
Dance of Genghis Cohn, The (1967 & 1968) 29, 43, 46, 48, 49, 51, 57, 61, 111–12, 115, 148, 150, 158, 160, 161, 173, 193, 195, 206, 275, 310, 314, 324, 335–44, 346, 370, 378, 419, 421, 423, 425, 430, 432
see also *La Danse de Gengis Cohn*
Dance of Genghis Cohn, The (theatrical version) 315
Dans la Nature (*later La Bonne Moitié*) (theatrical version of *The Company of Men*) 315
Day in the Life of Harry Smithowitz, A (stage play) (c1970) 315, 433
Débuts dans la vie (1960) 425
'Decadence' (1962) 425, 426
Direct Flight to Allah (1974 & 1975) 49, 141, 171, 286, 419, 421, 423, 431
see also *Les Têtes de Stéphanie*
Dix ans après (1968) 425

Éducation africaine (working title of *The Roots of Heaven*) 259
Éducation européenne (1945 & 1961) 91, 105–8, 159, 229–31, 421, 423, 430
see also *European Education, A*; *Forest of Anger*; *La forêt engloutie* ('The Drowned Forest'); *Nothing Important Ever Dies*
'Elephants' (precursor to *The Roots of Heaven*) 253
Enchanters, The (1973 & 1975) 37–8, 49, 121, 134–5, 138, 141, 145, 147, 149, 150–1, 174, 226, 266, 286, 419, 421, 432
see also *Les Enchanteurs*
Europa (1972 & 1978) 195–6, 419, 421, 423, 432

European Education, A (1945) 2, 31, 32–3, 44, 51, 57, 58, 90–1, 94–6, 100, 105, 118–19, 134, 136, 150, 160, 161, 163, 164, 165, 193, 195, 199, 201, 205, 226, 227, 270, 283, 285, 287, 312, 338, 378, 405, 419, 425
see also *Éducation européenne*; *Forest of Anger*; *La forêt engloutie* ('The Drowned Forest'); *Nothing Important Ever Dies*
European Education, A (1960) 100, 107–8, 117, 118–19, 160, 161, 265, 275, 285, 325, 421, 423, 432

'Fake, The' (1962) 425, 426
'Flamboyant Guadeloupe' (1967) 281
Forest of Anger (1944) 9, 50, 91, 98, 99–102, 103, 104–5, 174, 421, 423, 429
see also *Éducation européenne*; *European Education, A*; *La forêt engloutie* ('The Drowned Forest'); *Nothing Important Ever Dies*
Frère Océan ('Brother Ocean') cycle 160

Gasp, The (1973) 161, 164, 189, 193, 207–8, 273–4, 275, 419, 421, 423, 431, 433
see also *Charge d'âme*
Géographie humaine (1943) 178–9, 425
'Glass' (1951) 425
Gloire à nos illustres pionniers (1962) 426, 427
see also *Hissing Tales*; *New Frontier, The*
Gros-Câlin (previous title 'La Solitude du python à Paris') (1974) 150–1, 163, 174–5, 188, 207, 250, 265, 275, 347–50, 351–9, 362–5, 366, 369, 370, 372, 378, 380, 391, 393, 401, 419, 421, 423
Guilty Head, The (1968 & 1969) 138–9, 150, 160, 161, 164, 191, 208, 309, 324, 336, 419, 421, 423, 432
see also *La Tête coupable*

'Harlem' (provisional title for *Tulipe*) 199
Hissing Tales (1963 & 1964) 143, 164, 174, 319, 426, 430, 432, 439, 440
see also *Gloire à nos illustres pionniers*; 'New Frontier, The'
Hocus Bogus (1976 & 2009) 48, 51, 135–6, 151, 161,

381, 390–5, 397, 398, 419, 421, 431
see also *Pseudo*
Hope at Latitude 4°5 N (troop entertainment, 1941) 110
Horseman, The (screenplay) (1971) 317
'Humanist, A' (originally titled *Les Belles natures*) (1958) 165, 425, 426, 427

'I know a place in Paris' (1965) 281

JE mange mon soulier (1956) 425
Johnnie Coeur (theatrical version of *Tulipe* theme) (1961) 205, 299, 314, 423

Kill! Kill! Kill! (screenplay) 321–2
King Solomon (1979 & 1983) 136, 141, 193, 324, 380, 381–2, 397–8, 400–3, 407, 419, 421, 431, 433
see also *L'angoisse du roi Salomon*
King Solomon (theatrical version) 315
Kites, The (1980) 44, 45, 46, 49, 51, 58, 135, 138, 141, 151, 161, 175, 182–3, 185, 193, 195, 215, 286, 324, 397, 398, 400–1, 403–8, 419, 433
see also *Les Cerfs-volants*
La Bonne Moitié (*formerly Dans la Nature*) (theatrical version of *The Company of Men*) 315, 423
La Bourgeoisie (unpublished) 62
La Comédie américaine cycle 160
La Danse de Gengis Cohn (1967) 421, 423, 440
see also *Dance of Genghis Cohn, The*
La Forêt engloutie ('The Drowned Forest') 91, 99–100, 104–5
see also *Éducation européenne*; *European Education, A*; *Forest of Anger*; *Nothing Important Ever Dies*
La Lune (1961) 425, 427
La Lutte pour l'honneur (The Struggle for Honour) (lost or unwritten) 213
La Nuit sera calme (1974) 6, 410–11, 418, 421, 423, 441
see also *Quiet Night, A*
La Promesse de l'aube (1960 & 1980) 421, 423, 440
see also *Promise at Dawn*
'La Solitude du python à Paris' (previous title of *Gros-Câlin*) 359–62, 368
La Tendresse des pierres ('The Soft-heartedness of

Stones') (theatrical farce) (1950) 191, 314
La Tête coupable (1968 & 1980) 421, 423
see also *Guilty Head, The*
La Vie devant soi (1975) 394, 421, 423
Lady L (1958, 1963 & 1977) 150, 160, 163–4, 174, 189, 268–71, 275, 280, 285, 297–8, 317, 368, 419, 421, 423, 430, 432
L'angoisse du roi Salomon (1978) 421, 423
see also *King Solomon*
Le Blanc prophète de Harlem (1947) 425
Le Continent englouti (1944) 425
Le Grand vestiare (1949) 209–12, 221–5, 228, 421, 423
see also *Company of Men, The*
Le Radeau de la Méduse ('The Raft of *The Medusa*') (theatrical version of *Tulipe*) (1946) 313–14
Le Vin des morts ('The Wine of the Dead') (unpublished) (1934–5) 62, 64–5, 112, 180, 229, 393
Les Cerfs-volants (1980) 421, 423
see also *Kites, The*
Les Clowns lyriques (1979) 153, 160, 421, 423, 429
see also *Colours of the Day, The*; *Les Couleurs du jour*
Les Couleurs du jour (1952) 213, 421, 423, 429
see also *Colours of the Day, The*; *Les Clowns lyriques*
Les Enchanteurs (1973) 421, 423, 441
see also *Enchanters, The*
Les Mangeurs d'étoiles (1966) 298, 421, 423
see also *Talent Scout, The*
Les Oiseaux vont mourir au Pérou (1975) 426
see also 'Birds in Peru'
Les Racines du ciel (1956, 1980) 421, 423
see also *Roots of Heaven, The*
Les Têtes de Stéphanie (1974) 171, 421, 423
see also *Direct Flight to Allah*
'Letter to the Jews of France' (1970) 344
L'Évasion du professeur Ostrach (1957) 425
L'Homme à la colombe (1958 & 1984) 172, 174, 205, 250–1, 252, 283, 314, 419, 421, 423
see also *Tulipe*
Life Before Us (1975 & 1986) 10, 24–5, 29, 31, 44, 51,

135, 142–3, 159, 161, 163, 165, 170, 188, 191, 196, 213, 225, 228, 286, 314, 340, 367–76, 377, 384–90, 392, 393, 394, 402, 403, 419, 433
see also *Momo*
Life Before Us (screenplay) (1978) 322–3
Life and Death of Émile Ajar (*Vie et mort d'Émile Ajar*) (1981 & 1983) 157, 170, 266, 354–5, 365, 400, 411, 419, 421, 423, 433
'Living Statue, The' (aka 'Decadence') (1965) 426
L'Orage (The Storm) (1935, 2005) 62, 63, 425, 426
'Lute, The' (originally appeared as *Ainsi s'achève une journée de soleil*) (1954) 141–2, 248, 425, 426, 427

Man with a Dove, or The Last Adventures of Frankie and Johnnie (1955, unpublished) 251, 433
'Man Who Stayed Lonely to Save France, The' (1958) 115–16
Millions of Dollars (screenplay of *The Ski Bum*) 318, 433
Momo (1978) 421, 431, 433
see also *Life Before Us*

'Nature' (1962) 425
'New Frontier, The' (1962) 164, 193, 425
see also *Gloire à nos illustres pionniers*; *Hissing Tales*
'Night of History, The' (1945) (originally titled *Une Page d'histoire*) 425, 426–7
Noblesse et grandeur (1944) (originally titled *Grandeur nature*) 425, 426
Nothing Important Ever Dies (1960) 108–9, 430
see also *Éducation européenne*; *European Education, A*; *Forest of Anger*; *La Forêt engloutie* ('The Drowned Forest')

'Ode to the Man Who Was France' (1970) 115, 117
'Oldest Story Ever Told, The' (1962) 425
'Oriental Hotel of Bangkok, The' (1972) 281

'Penang: Tiger, tiger burning bright' (1971) 281
Pour Sganarelle (1965) 157, 160, 310, 326–32, 336, 365, 419, 421, 423
Promise at Dawn (1960) 2, 3, 5–7, 9–10, 22, 27–8, 29, 32, 33, 38, 41, 47, 51–2, 58, 61, 63, 64–6, 67, 68–70, 72, 77,

84, 124, 138, 147–8, 150, 152, 153, 154, 157, 161, 165, 172, 175–8, 179–80, 189, 216, 219, 265, 267, 270, 283–7, 288–93, 294, 295, 296, 298, 306, 310, 312, 325, 330, 366, 367, 369, 375, 376, 419, 425

Promise at Dawn (1961) 69–70, 205, 275, 318, 421, 423, 430, 432

Pseudo (1976) 390, 421, 423, 442
see also *Hocus Bogus*

Quiet Night, A (1974) 6, 47, 49, 50, 51, 70, 71, 114, 122, 124, 128, 130, 140, 157, 161, 170, 179, 184, 194, 265, 286, 367, 378, 380, 410–11, 419, 425, 433
see also *La Nuit sera calme*

Roots of Heaven, The (1956 & 1958) 51, 58–9, 111, 117–18, 130–2, 134, 135, 137, 141, 150, 166, 175, 181, 185, 186, 187–8, 190, 196, 204, 205, 216, 227, 238–46, 248, 250, 255–62, 266, 268, 270, 274, 284, 285, 286, 289, 325, 338, 419, 421, 423, 425, 429, 432
see also *Les Racines du ciel*

Roots of Heaven, The (screenplay) (1958) 316–17

'Sergent Gnama' (1946) 190, 425

Seven Women (screenplay) (1966) 317

'Singapore' (1973) 281

Ski Bum, The (1965) 49, 121, 127–8, 129, 150, 160, 166–7, 169, 191, 272–3, 275, 298, 306, 310, 314, 336, 373, 419, 421, 423, 430, 432
see also *Adieu Gary Coooper*

'Speaking of Heroism' (originally appeared as *JE rencontre un barracuda*) (1956) 425, 427

Talent Scout, The (1961) 7, 150, 160, 172, 181, 271–2, 275, 298, 304, 310, 419, 421, 423, 430, 432
see also *Les Mangeurs d'étoiles*

'To My General, with Love and Anger' (1969) 115, 116–17

Trésors de la Mer rouge ('Treasures of the Red Sea') (1970 & 1971) 115, 144, 157, 161, 419, 421, 423, 441

Tulipe (originally called 'Harlem') (1946 & 1970) 23, 27–8, 43, 49, 107, 125, 132, 160, 161, 180, 191,

193, 199–208, 209, 232, 241, 250, 268, 283–4, 297, 312, 327, 338, 368, 407, 419, 421, 423, 425, 433
see also *L'Homme à la colombe*
Tulipe (theatrical versions) 313–15

Une Page d'histoire (2002) 426
Une Petite Femme (A Brave Little Woman) (1935) 62–3, 64, 425

'Wall, The: A Christmas Tale' (1958) 425
Way Out, The (called 'Your Ticket is No Longer Valid' in USA) (1975 & 1977) 49, 151, 152, 180, 193, 286, 320, 324, 377–8, 380–3, 419, 421, 425, 431, 433
see also *Au-delà de cette limite votre ticket n'est plus valable*
White Dog (1970) 8, 10, 115, 121, 123, 132–3, 157, 161, 163, 169–70, 175, 179, 191, 250, 275, 278, 303, 310, 323, 335, 336, 344–6, 350–1, 419, 421, 423, 430–1, 432
see also *Chien Blanc*
Womanlight (1978) 49, 419
see also *Clair de femme*

Your Ticket Is No Longer Valid (1977) *see Way Out, The*